ORACLE *Oracle Press*™

Oracle Database 12c Release 2 Multitenant

ORACLE® Oracle Press™

Oracle Database 12c Release 2 Multitenant

Anton Els
Vít Špinka
Franck Pachot

McGraw Hill Education

New York   Chicago   San Francisco
Athens   London   Madrid   Mexico City
Milan   New Delhi   Singapore   Sydney   Toronto

Cataloging-in-Publication Data is on file with the Library of Congress

McGraw-Hill Education books are available at special quantity discounts to use as premiums and sales promotions, or for use in corporate training programs. To contact a representative, please visit the Contact Us pages at www.mhprofessional.com.

Oracle Database 12c Release 2 Multitenant

Copyright © 2017 by McGraw-Hill Education (Publisher). All rights reserved. Printed in the United States of America. Except as permitted under the Copyright Act of 1976, no part of this publication may be reproduced or distributed in any form or by any means, or stored in a database or retrieval system, without the prior written permission of Publisher, with the exception that the program listings may be entered, stored, and executed in a computer system, but they may not be reproduced for publication.

Oracle is a registered trademark of Oracle Corporation and/or its affiliates. All other trademarks are the property of their respective owners, and McGraw-Hill Education makes no claim of ownership by the mention of products that contain these marks.

Screen displays of copyrighted Oracle software programs have been reproduced herein with the permission of Oracle Corporation and/or its affiliates.

1 2 3 4 5 6 7 8 9 LCR 21 20 19 18 17

ISBN   978-1-25-983609-1
MHID   1-25-983609-6

Sponsoring Editor	**Technical and Language Editor**	**Composition**
Wendy Rinaldi	Mike Donovan	Cenveo® Publishing Services
Editorial Supervisor	**Copy Editor**	**Illustration**
Jody McKenzie	Lisa Theobald	Cenveo Publishing Services
Project Editor	**Proofreader**	**Art Director, Cover**
Rachel Gunn	Paul Tyler	Jeff Weeks
Acquisitions Coordinator	**Indexer**	
Claire Yee	Jerilyn Sproston	
Technical Editors	**Production Supervisor**	
Deiby Gómez, Arup Nanda	Lynn M. Messina	

Information has been obtained by Publisher from sources believed to be reliable. However, because of the possibility of human or mechanical error by our sources, Publisher, or others, Publisher does not guarantee to the accuracy, adequacy, or completeness of any information included in this work and is not responsible for any errors or omissions or the results obtained from the use of such information.

Oracle Corporation does not make any representations or warranties as to the accuracy, adequacy, or completeness of any information contained in this Work, and is not responsible for any errors or omissions.

*I would like to dedicate this to my wife, Mildie.
This would not have been possible without
your encouragement and support.
Thank you, you are the best!*

—*Anton Els*

*To my wife and kids, who have to put up with me
spending too much time investigating Oracle internals.*

—*Vít Špinka*

*I dedicate this book to the great people I've encountered during
my professional life. I was lucky to work, from the beginning,
with the kind of people who trust you and help you to improve
your skills. I wish the same to every beginner starting in IT.*

—*Franck Pachot*

About the Authors

Anton Els, **Oracle ACE**, is Vice President Engineering at Dbvisit Software Limited. Anton has more than 15 years of experience with Oracle technology, with a particular focus on the Oracle Database, backup and recovery, standby databases, Oracle Linux, virtualization, and docker. Anton is an active member of the Independent Oracle Users Group (IOUG) and vice president of the New Zealand OUG (NZOUG). He is an Oracle Certified Master (OCM) Oracle Database 11*g*; Oracle Certified Professional (OCP) Oracle Database 8*i* to 12*c*; Oracle Certified Expert (OCE) Oracle Real Application Clusters 11*g* and Grid Infrastructure Administrator; Red Hat 5 RHSA; and Oracle Solaris 10 SCSA. He regularly presents at industry and user group conferences, such as Collaborate, Oracle OpenWorld dbtech showcase Japan, NZOUG, and the Asia-Pacific and Latin America Oracle Technology Network Tour. He can be reached on Twitter @aelsnz or through his blog at www.oraclekiwi.co.nz.

Vít Špinka, **Oracle ACE Associate**, is Chief Architect at Dbvisit Software Limited. He has more than 15 years of experience with Oracle technology, with a particular focus on the Oracle Database. Vít is an active member of IOUG and a regular presenter at Oracle OpenWorld, Collaborate, UKOUG, DOAG, and NZOUG. He is an Oracle Certified Master (OCM) Oracle Database 10*g*, 11*g*, and 12*c*; Oracle Certified Professional (OCP) Oracle Database 9*i* to 12*c*; Oracle Database 10*g* Real Application Cluster Administration Expert; and LPIC-2 Linux Network Professional. He can be reached on Twitter @vitspinka or through his blog at http://vitspinka.blogspot.com/.

Franck Pachot, **Oracle ACE Director**, is Principal Consultant, trainer, and Oracle Technology Leader at dbi services (Switzerland) with more than 20 years of experience with Oracle technology. Franck is a regular presenter at Oracle OpenWorld, IOUG Collaborate, DOAG, SOUG, and UKOUG; an active member of the SOUG and DOAG user groups; and a proud member of the OraWorld Team. He is an Oracle Certified Master (OCM) Oracle Database 11*g* and 12*c*, Oracle Certified Professional (OCP) Oracle Database 8*i* to 12*c*, and Oracle Certified Expert (OCE) Oracle Database 12*c*: Performance Management and Tuning, and also holds an Oracle Exadata Database Machine 2014 Implementation Essentials certification. Franck can be reached on Twitter @franckpachot or through his blog at http://blog.pachot.net.

About the Technical Editors

Deiby Gómez was both the youngest Oracle ACE (23 years old) and ACE Director (25 years old) in the world and the first in his home country, Guatemala. He is also the youngest Oracle Certified Master 11*g* (OCM 11*g*,

February 2015) in Latin America (24 years old) and the first in Guatemala. In addition, Deiby also became the youngest Oracle Certified Master 12c in the world (26 years old, April 2016) and the first OCM 12c in Central America. He is the recent winner of *SELECT Journal* Editor's Choice Award 2016 (Las Vegas, NV) and a frequent speaker at Oracle events around the world, including Oracle Technology Network Latin American Tour 2013, 2014, 2015, and 2016; Collaborate (United States); and Oracle Open World (Brazil and United States). The first Guatemalan accepted as a beta tester by Oracle Database (version 12cR2), Deiby has had several articles published in English, Spanish, and Portuguese on Oracle's website, DELL's Toad World, and hundreds more on his blog. He appeared in *Oracle Magazine* in Nov/Dec 2014 as an outstanding expert and currently serves as the President of Oracle Users Group of Guatemala (GOUG), Director of Support Quality in Latin American Oracle Users Group Community (LAOUC), and co-founder of OraWorld Team. He also currently provides Oracle services in Latin America with his own company, NUVOLA, S.A.

Arup Nanda has been an Oracle DBA for more than 20 years, with experience spanning all aspects, from modeling to performance tuning and Exadata. He has written about 500 published articles, co-authored five books, delivered 300 sessions, blogs at arup.blogspot.com, and mentors new and seasoned DBAs. He won Oracle's DBA of the Year in 2003 and Enterprise Architect of the Year in 2012, and he is an ACE Director and a member of Oak Table Network.

About the Technical and Language Editor

Mike Donovan joined the Dbvisit team in 2007, where he has held a number of different roles, including head of the Global Support team and Digital Business Development pioneer. He has recently been appointed to the role of Chief Technology Officer (CTO). He is enthusiastic about new technologies and working with customers and partners to conceive of and build bridges between the existing RDBMS world and the new frontiers of Big Data, for businesses' benefit. He is motivated by championing smart, cost-effective approaches and alternatives. Mike has a diverse background in technology and the arts and considerable experience in technical customer support and software development. He is passionate about Oracle Database technology, having worked with it for more than a decade; spoken at numerous industry conferences including OOW, RMOUG, dbtech showcase Japan, and Collaborate; spent time as a production DBA; and gained certifications on this RDBMS platform in versions 9*i* to 12*c*.

Contents at a Glance

PART I
What Multitenant Means

1　Introduction to Multitenant 3
2　Creating the Database 35
3　Single-Tenant, Multitenant, and Application Containers 71

PART II
Multitenant Administration

4　Day-to-Day Management 87
5　Networking and Services 119
6　Security 139

PART III
Backup, Recovery, and Database Movement

7　Backup and Recovery 169
8　Flashback and Point-in-time-Recovery 199
9　Moving Data 227

PART IV
Advanced Multitenant

10	**Oracle Database Resource Manager**	259
11	**Data Guard**	289
12	**Sharing Data Across PDBs**	319
13	**Logical Replication**	345
	Index	365

Contents

Introduction xix

PART I
What Multitenant Means

1 Introduction to Multitenant 3
    History Lesson: A New Era in IT 4
        The Road to Multitenant 5
        Schema Consolidation 6
        Table Consolidation 9
        Server Consolidation 9
        Virtualization 10
        Multiple Databases Managed by One Instance 10
        Summary of Consolidation Strategies 10
    The System Dictionary and Multitenant Architecture 11
        The Past: Non-CDB 11
        Multitenant Containers 14
        Multitenant Dictionaries 16
        Working with Containers 20
    What Is Consolidated at CDB Level 27
        Data and Metadata at CDB Level 30
    Summary 33

2 Creating the Database 35
    Creating a Container Database (CDB) 36
        What About OMF? 36
        CDB Creation Options 38
    Creating a Pluggable Database 55
        Create a New PDB from PDB$SEED 56
        Create a New PDB Using the Local Clone Method 59

xi

	Create a PDB Using SQL Developer	60
	Create a PDB Using the DBCA	65
	Create a PDB Using Cloud Control	66
Using the catcon.pl Script		67
Summary		69

3 Single-Tenant, Multitenant, and Application Containers ... 71
Multitenant Architecture Is Not an Option ... 72
    Non-CDB Deprecation ... 72
    Noncompatible Features ... 73
Single-Tenant in Standard Edition ... 74
    Data Movement ... 75
    Security ... 75
    Consolidation with Standard Edition 2 ... 76
Single-Tenant in Enterprise Edition ... 77
    Flashback PDB ... 77
    Maximum Number of PDBs ... 78
Using the Multitenant Option ... 79
    Application Containers ... 80
    Consolidation with Multitenant Option ... 83
Summary ... 84

PART II
Multitenant Administration

4 Day-to-Day Management ... 87
Choosing a Container to Work With ... 88
Managing the CDB ... 89
    Create the Database ... 90
    Database Startup and Shutdown ... 90
    Drop the Database ... 90
    Modify the Entire CDB ... 91
    Modify the Root ... 92
Managing PDBs ... 92
    Create a New PDB ... 92
    Open and Close a PDB ... 93
    View the State of PDBs ... 97
    View PDB Operation History ... 97
    Run SQL on Multiple PDBs ... 97
    Modify the PDB ... 98
    Drop a PDB ... 99

	Patching and Upgrades	100
	Upgrade CDB	101
	Plugging In	111
	Patching	112
	Using CDB-Level vs. PDB-Level Parameters	113
	CDB SPFILE	114
	PDB SPFILE Equivalent	114
	SCOPE=MEMORY	116
	Alter System Reset	116
	ISPDB_MODIFIABLE	116
	Container=ALL	116
	DB_UNIQUE_NAME	117
	Summary	118
5	**Networking and Services**	**119**
	Oracle Net	120
	The Oracle Net Listener	120
	The LREG Process	121
	Networking: Multithreaded and Multitenant	123
	Service Names	125
	Default Services and Connecting to PDBs	125
	Creating Services	129
	Create a Dedicated Listener for a PDB	134
	Summary	137
6	**Security**	**139**
	Users, Roles, and Permissions	140
	Common or Local?	140
	What Is a User?	141
	CONTAINER=CURRENT	142
	CONTAINER=COMMON	144
	Local Grant	146
	Common Grant	147
	Conflicts Resolution	148
	Keep It Clear and Simple	150
	CONTAINER_DATA	151
	Roles	153
	Proxy Users	153
	Lockdown Profiles	155
	Disable Database Options	155
	Disable Alter System	156
	Disable Features	158

PDB Isolation	158
PDB_OS_CREDENTIALS	158
PATH_PREFIX	158
CREATE_FILE_DEST	159
Transparent Data Encryption	159
Setting Up TDE	159
Plug and Clone with TDE	164
TDE Summary	165
Summary	165

PART III
Backup, Recovery, and Database Movement

7 Backup and Recovery **169**
    Back to Basics 170
        Hot vs. Cold Backups 170
        RMAN: The Default Configuration 173
        RMAN Backup Redundancy 174
        The SYSBACKUP Privilege 174
    CDB and PDB Backups 175
        CDB Backups 176
        PDB Backups 180
        Do Not Forget Archive Logs! 183
    Recovery Scenarios 183
        Instance Recovery 184
        Restore and Recover a CDB 184
        Restore and Recover a PDB 187
    RMAN Optimization Considerations 189
    The Data Recovery Advisor 193
    Block Corruption 193
    Using Cloud Control for Backups 194
        Back Up to the Cloud 195
    Summary 197

8 Flashback and Point-in-time Recovery **199**
    Pluggable Database Point-in-Time 200
        Recover PDB Until Time 201
        Where Is the UNDO? 204
        Summary of 12.1 PDBPITR 205
    Local UNDO in 12.2 206
        Database Properties 207
        Create Database 207

        Changing UNDO Tablespace 208
        Changing UNDO Mode 209
        Shared or Local UNDO? 211
    PDB Point-in-Time Recovery in 12.2 211
        PDBPITR in Shared UNDO Mode 211
        PDBPITR in Local UNDO Mode 212
    Flashback PDB 213
        Flashback Logging 213
        Flashback with Local UNDO 215
        Flashback in Shared UNDO 216
        Restore Points at the CDB and PDB Levels 216
        Clean Restore Point 219
    Resetlogs 221
    Flashback and PITR 222
        When Do You Need PITR or Flashback? 222
        Impact on the Standby Database 223
        Auxiliary Instance Cleanup 225
    Summary 225

9 Moving Data **227**
    Grappling with PDB File Locations 228
    Plugging In and Unplugging 229
        Unplug and Plug In a PDB 230
        An Unplugged Database Stays in the Source 231
        What Exactly Is in the XML File? 232
        Check Compatibility for Plug-In 235
        Plug In a PDB as Clone 237
        PDB Archive File 238
    Cloning 239
        Cloning a Local PDB 240
        Cloning a Remote PDB 242
    Application Container Considerations 247
    Converting Non-CDB Database 247
        Plug In a Non-CDB 248
        Cloning a Non-CDB 250
    Moving PDBs to the Cloud 251
    Triggers on PDB Operations 252
    Full Transportable Export/Import 253
    Transportable Tablespaces 255
    Summary 256

PART IV
Advanced Multitenant

10 Oracle Database Resource Manager 259
    Resource Manager Basics 260
        Key Resource Manager Terminologies 261
        Resource Manager Requirements 263
        Resource Manager Levels 264
    The CDB Resource Plan 265
        Resource Allocation and Utilization Limits 265
        Default and Autotask Directives 267
        Creating a CDB Resource Plan 269
    The PDB Resource Plan 277
        Creating a PDB Resource Plan 278
        Enable or Disable a PDB Resource Plan 281
        Removing a PDB Resource Plan 281
    Manage PDB Memory and I/O via Initialization Parameters 281
        PDB Memory Allocations 282
        Limit PDB I/O 282
    Instance Caging 283
        Instance Caging to Resource Manager 283
    Monitoring Resource Manager 284
        Viewing the Resource Plan and Plan Directives 285
        Monitoring PDBs Managed by Resource Manager 285
    Summary 286

11 Data Guard 289
    Active Data Guard Option 291
    Creating a Physical Standby 291
        Duplicate with RMAN 292
        Create a Standby with Cloud Control 304
    Managing a Physical Standby in a Multitenant Environment 308
        Creating a New PDB on the Source 309
        Removing PDB from Source 311
        Changing the Subset 312
        Cloud Control 314
    Standby in the Cloud 315
    Summary 318

12 Sharing Data Across PDBs 319
    Database Links 320
    Sharing Common Read-Only Data 322
        Transportable Tablespaces 322
        Storage Snapshots and Copy on Write 323

	Cross-PDB Views 324
	Simple User Tables 325
	Consolidated Data 329
	Cross-Database Replication 343
	Summary 343

13 Logical Replication 345

Oracle LogMiner 347
Obsolete Features 348
    Oracle CDC 348
    Oracle Streams 348
    Oracle Advanced Replication 349
Oracle GoldenGate 349
    Multitenant Support in Oracle GoldenGate 349
    Big Data Adapters 359
Oracle XStream 361
Logical Standby 362
    Use in Upgrade 362
Other Third-Party Options 363
    Dbvisit Replicate 363
    Dell SharePlex 363
Summary 364

Index **365**

Introduction

Oracle Database 12c release 1 (12.1) introduced the new multitenant option to the world, and since this time the phrase "pluggable database" has been bandied about, often without a clear understanding of this functionality or its implications. But, simply put, multitenant is one of the most significant architectural changes to have been implemented in the Oracle Database software since its first release. It brings new features, but it also changes many of the ways in which we Oracle DBAs perform administrative tasks on a day-to-day basis. And with the second release of 12c (12.2), the features available with the multitenant option have been extended even further. What is clear is that the old architecture is deprecated and that multitenant is here to stay—and cannot be ignored.

The arrival of Oracle Database 12c Multitenant requires that DBAs adjust the way they think about and perform daily tasks. And whether you are running a single tenant or a large number of pluggable databases, there will be a substantial learning curve. So, more than covering what's new about multitenant alone, the aim of this book is to encompass how this relates to DBA tasks, from the core day-to-day operations to advanced tasks. You can read it as an Oracle Database administration guide for the 12c era, and beyond, equipping you with essential "on-the-job" knowledge about new features, syntax changes, and best practice options. This book has been written by three experienced and certified DBAs and enhanced by highly skilled reviewers, all with a passion to see Oracle Database administration done with insight and excellence.

Part I introduces multitenant functionality. Key questions include why Oracle Corporation introduced it, in what ways this mimicked other RDBMSs, and whether it is actually required by the way we design and deploy our applications nowadays. Chapter 1 addresses these questions and explains the multitenant architecture. In Chapter 2, we cover the container database (CDB) creation process and how to do it properly. Because creating a CDB is now the default option in 12c, believe it or not we actually encounter people who have created a CDB without knowing it. Before launching into detail on all the new multitenant features, Chapter 3 helps guide you toward making informed decisions between CDB or non-CDB, and it outlines the different editions and options available to you.

Part II gives you a sense of what will change in your day-to-day tasks when you use multitenant. The section starts with Chapter 4, which focuses on pluggable database (PDB) creation and administration. Upgrading to 12c is also covered, and then networking and services are detailed in Chapter 5. This is followed, in Chapter 6, by an important topic—security—in which we address isolation of PDBs, user commonality, and encryption.

Part III covers the greatly enhanced backup and duplicate operations possible at the PDB level. Chapter 7 kicks this off with a detailed look at one of the most important areas every DBA should be familiar with—backup and recovery—and how we might revert to the previous state of a database, if needed. Chapter 8 discusses how this can be achieved with flashback technology, and then follows with details on how you can perform a point-in-time recovery at the PDB level. The final chapter in this section, Chapter 9, tackles unplugging/plugging a PDB as well as cloning, transporting, and online relocation of PDBs

In Part IV you learn how to take multitenant to the next level. When consolidating multiple PDBs resource consumption, you must be aware of Resource Manager, which is the focus of Chapter 10; this often underused facility is expected to become more crucial in multitenant environments. Chapter 11 takes a look at protecting your multitenant database environment with Data Guard, because PDBs may have to interact with it, and Chapter 12 builds on this in its discussion on data sharing within a CDB. Cloud-based solutions tend to require that data be delivered in a more flexible way than physical cloning or synchronization, and this is the focus of the discussion about logical replication in Chapter 13.

PART I

What Multitenant Means

CHAPTER 1

Introduction to Multitenant

With Oracle Database 12c, Oracle introduced a major change to its database architecture. Before Oracle Database 12c, an instance could open only one database. If you had multiple databases, you would need to start multiple instances, because they were totally isolated structures, even when hosted on the same server. This differs from most other RDBMSs, where a single system can manage multiple databases.

With the release of Oracle Database 12c, one instance can open multiple *pluggable databases* or PDBs. Oracle has signaled that the new multitenant architecture is here to stay, with the deprecation of the old style. With or without the multitenant option, all future Oracle databases will run on the multitenant architecture, a fact that Oracle database administrators cannot ignore.

History Lesson: A New Era in IT

Let's start by taking a brief look at the history of database use, before introducing the architecture of the future. As you can see in Figure 1-1, we will not refer to dates, but version numbers, going back to the time when the Oracle Database became predominant.

When Oracle Database 8i and 9i were on the market, midrange computers became prevalent in data centers. We were moving from the mainframe era to a client/server era, and Oracle architecture was very well suited for that. Written in the C programming language, it was available on multiple platforms and with all user management contained within its data dictionary. It was ready for the client/server architecture, using the OS only to listen on a TCP/IP port and to store files. Furthermore, the architecture was scalable on minicomputers, thanks to the parallel server feature, which would later become RAC (Real Application Clusters).

These databases were growing along with the overall number of servers. It was common at that time to have a lot of physical servers with direct attached disks (DAS), each running one or two Oracle Database 8i or 9i instances.

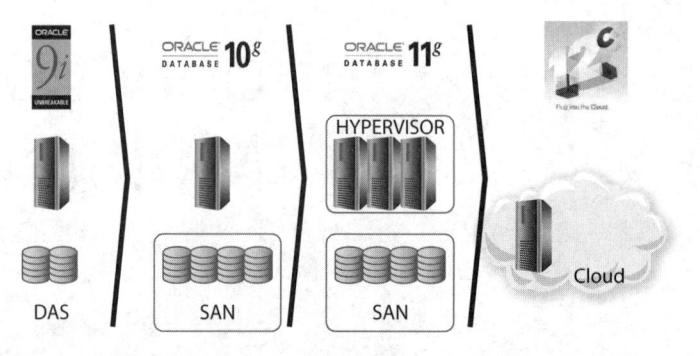

FIGURE 1-1. *From IT consolidation to the cloud*

With the number of databases increasing, it became a nightmare to maintain all those servers and disks. Having internal disks made capacity planning tremendously difficult when facing the exponential increase of data. By the time Oracle Database 10*g* was introduced, we needed to consolidate storage, so we put the database datafiles into a storage array, shared by all servers through a storage area network (SAN); that was storage consolidation.

By the time Oracle Database 11*g* rolled around, the prevailing thought was to do with servers what had been done with disks earlier. Instead of sizing and maintaining multiple servers, virtualization software brought us the possibility of putting our physical servers in a farm and provisioning virtual machines on top of them. That was the way in this previous era: application servers, SAN or network-attached storage (NAS), and virtual machines.

And now Oracle Database 12*c* accompanies a new day. Even organizations with consolidated storage and servers now realize that operating this infrastructure is not their core business, and instead, they now demand IT as a service, which is both scalable and flexible. Small companies want to provision their IT from a public cloud, and larger companies build their own private clouds. In both cases, virtualization can provide Infrastructure as a Service (IaaS). But we also *want* Application as a Service (AaaS) and *need* Database as a Service (DBaaS). This is a significant change in the technology ecosystem, similar in scale and importance to the earlier move from client/server to application servers. This new direction will not be immediate—it will take time. But it is safe to predict that over the next ten years, the hybrid mixed model (on-premise/cloud) will start strong, but be slowly supplanted by the cloud.

As is expected, a new era has different requirements, and the future of databases seems bound up with consolidation, agile development, and rapid provisioning. For Oracle, some such features came progressively from Oracle Database 9*i* to 11*g*, such as easy transport of data, cloning, and thin provisioning. But two core architectural foundations came from the previous era and were not ready to accommodate consolidation: the need to run one instance per database, and having one data dictionary per database. Oracle Database 12*c* provides the answer: multitenancy. Retaining its portability philosophy, Oracle has designed this architecture to enable you to run your application on the same database, with the same software running from small server to large cloud.

The Road to Multitenant

This new era is about consolidation. Some people can imagine it as a centralized system and centralized administration, recalling the time of mainframes. But there is another challenge that comes with it: we need more and more agility. Provisioning a database is not an easy operation today, and we cannot make it worse.

Consider an example. You are an Oracle DBA. A developer comes to your desk and asks for a new database; she is under the impression that this is a simple demand, merely requiring a few clicks of an administration interface. You look at her, wide eyed, and tell her she has to fill out a request with specifics related to storage, memory, CPU, and availability requirements. Furthermore, you explain, the request will have to be approved by management, and then it will take a few days or a week to set up. And here begins a pattern of misunderstanding between dev and ops.

The developer probably hasn't worked with Oracle databases before, so she has some notion of a database as a lightweight container for her application tables—and in many other non-Oracle RDBMSs, this is actually what is referred to as a "database."

In Oracle, however, we have lightweight containers—schemas at logical level and tablespaces at physical level—but a database is an entity that comprises much more than that. An Oracle database is a set of schemas and tablespaces, plus all the metadata required to manage them (the data dictionary), along with a significant amount of PL/SQL code to implement the features (the DBMS packages). Each database must have its own instance, including a number of background processes and shared memory. And each database also has a structure to protect the transactions, comprising undo tablespaces and redo logs.

For these reasons, provisioning a new database is not a trivial operation. To do so, you must interact with the system administrators and the storage teams, because you need server and disk resources for it. You don't want to put too many instances on the same server, but you can't have a dedicated physical server for each database. Because of this, today we often virtualize and have a dedicated virtual machine (VM) for each instance, but this is not possible for every application, for every environment, in any agile sort of way—there are just too many of them. Furthermore, you end up wasting a lot of resources when you have to allocate server, storage, and instance for each database.

Prior to Oracle Database 12c, the answer to the developer, in this scenario, probably was to create a new schema for her in an existing database. But this solution is not always possible or feasible. Let's explain why.

Schema Consolidation

Schema was exactly the objective prior to 12c. Each application had one schema owner, or a set of schemas if you wanted to separate tables and procedures. They were logically independent of each other, and security was controlled by grants.

Physically, you dedicated tablespaces to each application. This meant that, in case of a datafile loss, only one application was offline during the restore, which would also be the case if you wanted to relocate the tablespace to another filesystem. However, everything else was shared to optimize resource usage: instance processes and memory, SYSTEM and SYSAUX tablespaces, with dictionary.

The backup strategy is common, and the high availability (HA) policy is common. One DBA administers one database, and several applications run on it. This is exactly what the Oracle Database was designed for from its first versions.

Transportable Tablespaces

A large number of operations in the Oracle Database can be performed at the tablespace level. This is especially true since the inception of the transportable tablespaces feature, which enables you to physically copy your application datafiles to another database, and even to a newer version. Transportable tablespaces are significant because they were a forerunner to, and an ancestor of, multitenant. The Oracle Corporation patent for Transportable Tablespaces published in 1997 was entitled "Pluggable tablespaces for database systems." And the multitenant architecture is the foundation for pluggable databases.

In this context, *pluggable* means that you can directly plug a physical structure (datafile) into a database and have it become part of that database. The transportable tablespaces feature enabled user tablespace datafiles to be plugged into the database. Then only the metadata (dictionary entries) had to be imported so that the logical object definitions matched what was stored physically in the datafiles.

In 12c you can transport databases, which is nothing less than transporting all user tablespaces: a "FULL=Y" transportable tablespace. But metadata still has to be transferred logically, and that operation can be lengthy if you have thousands of tables, even if those tables are empty. For example, if you want to migrate a PeopleSoft database, which has 20,000+ tables, the metadata import alone can take hours to create all those empty tables.

As you will see, with the superior implementation in multitenant, the transport of pluggable databases is actually the transport of all datafiles, including SYSTEM and SYSAUX, which stores the data dictionary, and perhaps even the UNDO. This means that all metadata is also imported physically and, as such, is a relatively quick operation.

Schema Name Collision

Schema consolidation is in fact difficult to achieve in real life. You want to consolidate multiple applications into the same database, along with multiple test environments of the same application, but you are faced with a number of application constraints.

What do you do if the schema owner is hard-coded into the application and you cannot change it? We were once involved in installing a telco billing application that had to be deployed in a schema called PB, and we wanted to consolidate multiple environments into the test database, but that was forbidden. The reason was that the schema name was hard-coded into the application, and in packages, and so on. We better understood that strange schema name when we hosted a consultant from the application vendor. You may be able to guess what his initials were.

If the application design is under your control you can avoid this problem, and needless to say, you should never hard-code the schema name. You can connect with any user and then simply set ALTER SESSION SET CURRENT_SCHEMA to have all referenced objects prefixed by the application schema owner. And if you have multiple schemas? It's not a bad idea to have multiple schemas for your application.

For example, you can separate data (tables) from code (PL/SQL packages). That makes for good isolation and encapsulation of data. But even in that case, you don't need to hard-code the table schema name into the package. Just create synonyms for them into the package schema, which will reference the objects from the table schemas. You reference them from your PL/SQL code without the schema name (synonyms are in the same schema), and they are resolved to the other schema. If a name changes, you have to re-create only those synonyms. That can be done very easily and automatically.

Public Synonyms and Database Links

With the above-mentioned synonyms, we were talking about private synonyms, of course. Don't use public synonyms. They cannibalize the whole namespace. When an application creates public synonyms, you cannot consolidate anything else on it. That's a limitation for schema consolidation: objects that do not belong to a specific schema can collide with other applications and other versions or environments of the same application.

Roles, Tablespace Names, and Directories

An application can define and reference other objects, which are in the database public namespace—such is the case for roles, directories, and tablespace names. An application for which several environments can be consolidated into the same database must have parameters in the Data Definition Language (DDL) scripts so that those database objects names can be personalized for each environment. If this is not the case, schema consolidation will be difficult.

Those public objects that do not pertain to a schema also make data movement more complex. For example, when you use Data Pump to import a schema, those objects may need to have been created earlier.

Cursor Sharing

Even with an application that is designed for schema consolidation, you may encounter performance issues when consolidating everything into the same database. We once had a database with 3000 identical schemas. They were data marts: same structure, different data.

And, obviously, the application code was the same. The user connected to one data mart and ran the queries that were coded into the applications. This meant that the same queries—exactly the same SQL text—were run on different schemas. If you know how cursor sharing works in Oracle, you can immediately see the problem: one cursor has thousands of child cursors. A parent cursor is shared by all identical SQL text, and child cursors are created when the objects are different, which is the case when you are not on the same schema. Parsing has to follow a long chained list of children cursors, holding latches during that time, and that means huge library cache contention.

In multitenant, the parent cursors are shared for consolidation purposes, but enhancements may be implemented in the child cursor search to alleviate this problem.

Table Consolidation

When you want to consolidate the data for multiple environments of the same application and same version of an application, which means that the tables have exactly the same structure, you can put everything into the same table. This is usually done by adding an environment identifier (company, country, market, and so on) into each primary key. The advantage of this is that you can manage everything at once. For example, when you want to add an index, you can add it for all environments.

For performance and maintenance reasons, you can separate the data physically by partitioning those tables on the environment ID and put the partitions into different tablespaces. However, the level of isolation is very low, and that affects performance, security, and availability.

Actually most of the applications that were designed like this usually store only one environment. In most cases, the ID that is added in front of each primary key has only one value, and this is why Oracle introduced the skip scan index optimization. You can build virtual private database policy to manage access on those environments. You can manage the partitions independently, even at physical level, with exchange partitions. If you want to see an example of that, look at the RMAN repository: information for all registered databases is stored in the same tables. However, the isolation is not sufficient to store different environments (test, development, production), or to store different versions (where the data model is different).

Server Consolidation

If you want several independent databases but don't want to manage one server for each, you can consolidate several instances on the same server. If you go to Oracle's Ask Tom site (asktom.oracle.com/) for questions about the recommended number of instances per server, Tom Kyte's answer is this: "We recommend no more than ONE instance per host—a host can be a virtual machine, a real machine, we don't care—but you want ONE HOST = ONE INSTANCE." In real life, however, most database servers we have seen have several instances running on them. You can install multiple versions of Oracle (the ORACLE_HOME), and you can have a lot of instances running on one server—and you often have to do it. We have seen servers running as many as 70 instances.

There are few ways to isolate the resources between instances. As for memory, you can divide the physical memory among instances by setting the shared memory with `SGA_MAX_SIZE`, and in 12c you can even limit the process memory with `PGA_AGGREGATE_LIMIT`. You can also limit the CPU used by each instance with instance caging, setting for each instance the maximum number of processes that can run in the CPU. And with the latest license, Standard Edition 2, you don't even need Enterprise Edition to do instance caging. We will come back to this in Chapter 3.

Running a lot of instances on one server is still a problem, however. For example, when you reboot the server, you will have lot of processes to start and memory to allocate. A server outage, planned or not, will penalize a lot of applications. And you waste a lot of resources by multiplying the System Global Area (SGA) and database dictionaries.

Virtualization

Today, virtualization is a good way to run only one instance per server without having to manage a lot of physical servers. You have good isolation of environments, you can allocate CPU, memory, and I/O bandwidth, within limits. And you can even isolate them on different networks. However, even if those servers are virtual machines, you don't solve the resource wastage of multiple OSs, Oracle software, memory, and the dictionary. And you still have multiple databases to manage—to back up, to put in high-availability, in Data Guard, and so on. And you have multiple OSs to patch and monitor.

In addition to that, virtualization can be a licensing nightmare. When Oracle software is licensed by the processors where the software is installed, Oracle considers that, on some virtualization technologies, the software is installed everywhere the VM can run. The rules depend on the hypervisor vendor and on the version of this hypervisor.

Multiple Databases Managed by One Instance

The idea, then, is to find the consolidation level that fits both the isolation of the environment and the consolidation of resources. This is at a higher level than schema consolidation, but at a lower level than the instance and the database as we know it today. It means you can have several databases managed by the same instance on the same server.

This did not exist in versions of Oracle Database prior to 12c, but it is now possible with multitenant architecture. Now, one consolidation database can manage multiple pluggable databases. In addition to a new level that can be seen as an independent database, the pluggable database architecture brings agility in provisioning, moving, and upgrading.

Summary of Consolidation Strategies

Table 1-1 briefly summarizes the different consolidation alternatives prior to multitenant.

Consolidation	Pros	Cons
Table	Manage all as one	Very limited isolation Not for different environments
Schema	Share instance, dictionary, and HA	Public objects collision Limited isolation
Database	Only one server to administer	Several SGA, background processes Multiplies backup and HA configuration
Virtualization	Best isolation, separation of duties HA and vMotion features	Licensing nightmare New technology to learn Lot of hosts to run and manage

TABLE 1-1. *Consolidation Strategies Pros and Cons*

The System Dictionary and Multitenant Architecture

The major change in the multitenant architecture regards the system dictionary. Let's see how it was implemented in all previous versions and what changed in 12c.

The Past: Non-CDB

A database stores both data and metadata. For example, suppose you have the EMP table in the SCOTT schema. The description of the table—its name, columns, datatypes, and so on—are also stored within the database. This description—the metadata—is stored in a system table that is part of the dictionary.

The Dictionary

Codd's rules (created by E. F. Codd, who invented the relational model) defines that a RDBMS must represent metadata in the same way as the data: you can query both using SQL queries. As a database administrator, you do that every day. You query the dictionary views, such as DBA_TABLES, to get information about your database objects. This rule is for logical representation only, and the dictionary views provide that. But Oracle went further by deciding to store physically the metadata information in relational tables—the same kind of tables as application tables, but they are owned by SYS schema and stored in the system's tablespaces (SYSTEM and SYSAUX).

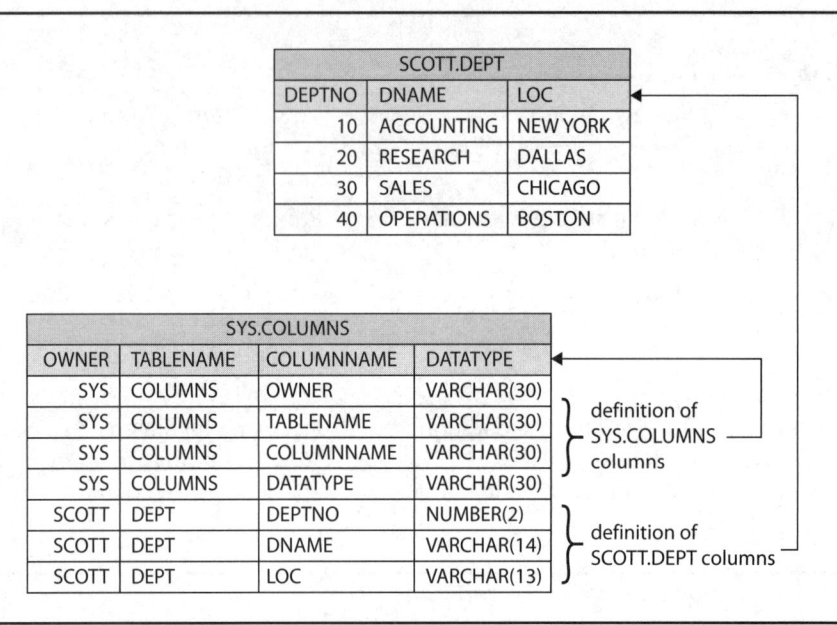

	SCOTT.DEPT	
DEPTNO	DNAME	LOC
10	ACCOUNTING	NEW YORK
20	RESEARCH	DALLAS
30	SALES	CHICAGO
40	OPERATIONS	BOSTON

SYS.COLUMNS			
OWNER	TABLENAME	COLUMNNAME	DATATYPE
SYS	COLUMNS	OWNER	VARCHAR(30)
SYS	COLUMNS	TABLENAME	VARCHAR(30)
SYS	COLUMNS	COLUMNNAME	VARCHAR(30)
SYS	COLUMNS	DATATYPE	VARCHAR(30)
SCOTT	DEPT	DEPTNO	NUMBER(2)
SCOTT	DEPT	DNAME	VARCHAR(14)
SCOTT	DEPT	LOC	VARCHAR(13)

Rows 1–4: definition of SYS.COLUMNS columns
Rows 5–7: definition of SCOTT.DEPT columns

FIGURE 1-2. *Storing metadata with data*

Without using the actual name and details of the Oracle dictionary, Figure 1-2 gives you the idea. Table SCOTT.DEPT stores user data. The definition of the table is stored in a dictionary table, SYS.COLUMNS, because it stores column information here. And because this table is itself a table, we have to store its definition in the same way.

And there are not only table definitions in the dictionary. Until version 8*i*, even the physical description of the data storage (table extents) were stored in the dictionary. That changed with Locally Managed Tablespaces, however, when tablespace became more self-contained in preparation of pluggable features. On the other hand, at each new version, a lot of new information was added to the dictionary. In the current version, a large part of the Oracle Database software is implemented as PL/SQL packages, which are stored in the dictionary.

Oracle-Maintained Objects

The implementation choice we've described is specific to the Oracle RDBMS: The dictionary is stored in the database. Each database has its own dictionary. And if you used logical export/import (EXP/IMP or Data Pump) to move a database, you probably have seen how it is difficult to distinguish the dictionary objects belonging to the system from the user objects belonging to the applications. When you import a full database (`FULL=Y` in IMPDP options, as discussed in Chapter 8) into a newly created database, you don't want to import the dictionary because it already exists in the target.

Of course, objects in the SYS schema are dictionary objects, and they are ignored by Data Pump. But if someone has created user objects, then they are lost. Grants on SYS objects are lost. And you can find system objects elsewhere, such as OUTLN, MDSYS, XDB, and so on. A lot of roles come from the system, and you can create your own role. It's difficult to distinguish them easily.

Fortunately, 12c includes a flag in DBA_OBJECTS, DBA_USERS, and DBA_ROLES to identify the Oracle-maintained objects that are created with the database and that do not belong to your application. Let's query the Oracle-maintained schemas list from a 12c database:

```
SQL> select listagg(username,',' on overflow truncate with count) within group
(order by created) from dba_users where oracle_maintained='Y';

LISTAGG(USERNAME,','ONOVERFLOWTRUNCATEWITHCOUNT)WITHINGROUP(ORDERBYCREATED)
-----------------------------------------------------------------------------
AUDSYS,SYS,SYSBACKUP,SYSDG,SYSKM,SYSRAC,SYSTEM,OUTLN,GSMADMIN_INTERNAL,GSMUSER,
DIP,XS$NULL,REMOTE_SCHEDULER_AGENT,DBSFWUSER,ORACLE_OCM,SYS$UMF,DBSNMP,APPQOSSYS,
GSMCATUSER,GGSYS,XDB,ANONYMOUS,WMSYS,OJVMSYS,CTXSYS,MDSYS,ORDDATA,ORDPLUGINS,OR
DSYS,SI_INFORMTN_SCHEMA,OLAPSYS,MDDATA,SPATIAL_WFS_ADMIN_USR,SPATIAL_CSW_ADMIN_
USR,LBACSYS,APEX_050000,APEX_PUBLIC_USER,FLOWS_FILES,DVF,DVSYS
```

This is a big improvement in 12c. You can easily determine what belongs to your application and what belongs to the system itself. The ORACLE_MAINTAINED flag is present in DBA_OBJECTS, DBA_USERS, and DBA_ROLES views and it's now easy to distinguish the objects created at database creation from those created by your application.

NOTE
Before 12c, you could try to list the objects from different views used by Oracle internally. There are the views used by the data movement, listing what they must ignore: EXU8USR for EXP/IMP, KU_NOEXP_TAB for Data Pump, and LOGSTDBY$SKIP_SUPPORT for Data Guard. There is also the DEFAULT_PWD$ table to identify some pre-created schemas. And you can also query the V$SYSAUX_OCCUPANTS or DBA_REGISTRY views.

System Metadata vs. Application Metadata

We described the metadata structures: schemas, objects, and roles. Let's go inside them, into the data. You know that table definitions are stored in dictionary tables, and in Figure 1-2 we simplified this in a SYS.COLUMN table. But the dictionary data model is more complex than that. Actually, object names are in SYS.OBJ$, table information is in SYS.TAB$, column information is in SYS.COL$, and so on.

Those are tables, and each has its own definition—the metadata—which is stored in that dictionary: SYS.TAB$, for example, has rows for your tables, but it also has rows for all dictionary tables.

SYS.TAB$ has a row to store the SYS.TAB$ definition itself. You may ask how that row is inserted at the table creation (which is database creation), because the table does not yet exist. Oracle has a special bootstrap code that is visible in the ORACLE_HOME. (It's beyond the scope of this book, but you can look at the dcore.bsq file in ORACLE_HOME/rdbms/admin directory. You can also query the BOOTSTRAP$ table to see the code that creates those tables at startup in dictionary cache, so that basic metadata is available immediately to allow access to the remaining metadata.)

All metadata is stored in those tables, but this is a problem in non-multitenant databases: system information (which belongs to the RDBMS itself) is mixed with user information (which belongs to the application). Both of their metadata is stored in the same tables, and everything is stored into the same container: the database.

This is what has changed with multitenant architecture: we have now multiple containers to separate system information from application information.

Multitenant Containers

The multitenant database's most important structure is the container. A container contains data and metadata. What is different in multitenant is that a container can itself contain several containers inside it in order to separate objects logically and physically. A container database contains several pluggable databases, and an additional one, the root, contains the common objects.

A multitenant database is a container database (CDB). The old architecture, in which a database is a single container that contains no subdivisions, is called a non-CDB. In 12c you can choose which one you want to create. You create a CDB, the multitenant one, by setting `ENABLE_PLUGGABLE=true` in the instance parameters and by adding the `ENABLE PLUGGABLE` to the `CREATE DATABASE` statement. (More details are in Chapter 2.)

This creates the CDB, which will contain other containers identified by a number, the container ID, and a name. It will contain at least a root container and a seed container, and you will be able to add your own containers, up to 252 in version 12.1, and thousands in 12.2.

Pluggable Database

The goal of multitenant is consolidation. Instead of having multiple databases on a server, we can now create only one consolidated database, the CDB, which contains multiple pluggable databases (PDBs). And each PDB will appear as a whole database to its users, with multiple schemas, public objects, system tablespaces, dictionary views, and so on.

The multitenant architecture will be used to consolidate on private or public clouds, with hundreds or thousands of pluggable databases. The goal is to provision those pluggable databases quickly and expose them as if they were a single database. By design, anyone connected to a pluggable database cannot distinguish it from a standalone database.

In addition, all commands used in previous Oracle Database versions are compatible. For example, you can run `shutdown` when you are connected to a PDB and it will close your PDB. It will not actually shut down the instance, however, because other PDBs are managed by that instance, but the user will see exactly what he would see if he shut down a standalone database.

Consider another example. We are connected to a pluggable database and we can't have undo tablespaces because they are at CDB level only (we can change this in 12.2, but you'll learn about that in Chapter 8). Let's try to create one:

```
SQL> show con_name
CON_NAME
------------------------------
PDB
SQL> create undo tablespace WHATEVER datafile '/nowhere' size 100T;
Tablespace created.
SQL> create undo tablespace WHATEVER datafile '/nowhere' size 100T;
Tablespace created.
SQL> create undo tablespace WHATEVER datafile '/nowhere' size 100T;
Tablespace created.
```

There are no errors, but the undo tablespaces are obviously not created. It's impossible to create a 100-terabyte datafile. My statements have just been ignored. The idea is that a script made to run in a database can create an undo tablespace, so the syntax must be accepted in a pluggable database. It's allowed because everything you can do in a non-CDB must be accepted in a PDB, but it is ignored because here the undo tablespace is at the CDB level only.

With multitenant, you have new commands, and all commands you know are accepted by a PDB. You can give the DBA role to a PDB user, and she will be able to do everything a DBA can do with regard to her database. And the PDB user will be isolated from the other pluggable databases and will not see what is at the CDB level.

CDB$ROOT

How big is your SYSTEM tablespace? Just after database creation, it's already a few gigabytes. By database creation, we aren't referring to the CREATE DATABASE statement, but running catalog.sql and catproc.sql. (Well, you don't call those directly in multitenant; it's catcdb.sql but it runs the same scripts.) The dictionary of an empty database holds gigabytes of dictionary structures and system packages that are part of the Oracle software—as the ORACLE_HOME binaries—but they are deployed as stored procedures and packages inside the database. And if you put 50 databases on a server, you have 50 SYSTEM tablespaces that hold the same thing (assuming that they are the same version and same patche level). If you want to consolidate hundreds or thousands of databases, as you can do with PDBs, you don't want to store the same data in each one. Instead, you can put all the common data into only one container and share it with the others. This is exactly what CDB$ROOT is: it's the only container in a CDB that is not a PDB but stores everything that is common to the PDBs.

Basically, CDB$ROOT will store all the dictionary tables, the dictionary views, the system packages (those that start with *dbms_*), and the system users (SYS, SYSTEM, and so on)—and nothing else. The user data should not go in CDB$ROOT. You can create your own users only if you need them on all PDBs. You will see more about common users in Chapter 6.

You can think of CDB$ROOT as an extension of the ORACLE_HOME. It's the part of the software that is stored in the database. It's specific to the version of the ORACLE_HOME, and it is the same in all CDBs that are in the same version. Our 12.2.0.1 CDB$ROOT is mostly the same as yours.

PDB$SEED

The goal of a multitenant database, a CDB, is to create a lot of PDBs. More than that, it should be easy and quick to create PDBs on demand. It's the architecture focused on Database as a Service (DBaaS). How do you create a database quickly with the Database Configuration Assistant (DBCA)? You create it from a template that has all datafiles. No need to re-create everything (as catalog.sql and catproc.sql do) if you can clone an empty database that already exists. This is exactly what the PDB$SEED is: it's an empty PDB that you can clone to create another PDB. You don't change it, it is read-only, and you can use it only as the source of a new PDB.

A CDB has at minimum one CDB$ROOT container and one PDB$SEED container. You can't change them; you can only use them. Their structure will change only if you upgrade or patch the CDB.

Multitenant Dictionaries

One goal of the multitenant architecture is to separate system metadata from application metadata. System metadata, common to all PDBs, is stored in the CDB$ROOT, as are all system objects. Consider, for example, the package definitions. They are stored in the dictionary table SOURCE$, which we can query through the DBA_SOURCE dictionary views. In a non-CDB, this table contains both the system packages and the packages that you create—the packages owned by SYS, as well as the packages owned by your application schema; let's call it ERP. In multitenant, the CDB$ROOT contains only system metadata, so in our previous example, that means all the SYS packages.

In our PDB dedicated to the application, let's call it PDBERP, the SOURCE$ contains only the packages of our application, the ERP ones. Let's see an example. We are in the CDB$ROOT and we count the lines in SOURCE$. We join with the DBA_OBJECT that shows which are the Oracle-maintained objects (the system objects):

```
SQL> select o.oracle_maintained,count(*)
from sys.source$ s join dba_objects o on obj#=object_id
group by o.oracle_maintained;
ORACLE_MAINTAINED   COUNT(*)
-----------------   --------
Y                     362030
```

All the lines in SOURCE$ are for Oracle-maintained objects which are system packages.

Now let's have a look in a PDB:

```
ORACLE_MAINTAINED   COUNT(*)
-----------------   --------
N                       8318
```

The lines here are not for system packages, but for our own application packages. You may have a different result, but basically this is how the dictionaries are separated in multitenant: the metadata that was stored in the same dictionary in non-CDBs is now stored in identical tables but in different containers, to keep the Oracle metadata separated from the application metadata. Note that this is not the same as partitioning; it's more like these are actually different databases for the dictionaries.

Dictionary Views

Do you know why we've queried the SOURCE$ table and not the DBA_SOURCE, which is supposed to give the same rows? Check this out:

```
SQL> select o.oracle_maintained,count(*)
from dba_source s join dba_objects o on s.owner=o.owner and s.name=o.
object_name and s.type=o.object_type
group by o.oracle_maintained;
ORACLE_MAINTAINED   COUNT(*)
-----------------   --------
Y                     362030
```

Same number of lines here in the CDB$ROOT. But when we connect to the PDB,

```
SQL> select o.oracle_maintained,count(*)
from dba_source s join dba_objects o on s.owner=o.owner and s.name=o.
object_name and s.type=o.object_type
group by o.oracle_maintained;
ORACLE_MAINTAINED   COUNT(*)
-----------------   --------
Y                     362030
N                       8318
```

We see more rows here. Actually, we see the rows from CDB$ROOT. There are two reasons for this. First, we said that what is in the CDB$ROOT is common, so it makes sense to see this from the PDB. Second, we said that a user connected to a PDB must see everything as if she were on a standalone database. And on a standalone database, a query on DBA_SOURCE shows all sources from both the system and the application. It's not the case when you query SOURCE$, but you're not expected to do that. Only the views are documented, and you're expected to query those ones.

The dictionary views in a PDB show information from the PDB and from the CDB$ROOT. It's not partitioning, and it's not a database link. We will see how Oracle does this in the next section.

When you are connected to CDB$ROOT, the DBA_SOURCE view shows only what is in your container. But new views starting with *CDB_* can show what is in all containers, as you will see later in the chapter in the section "Dictionary Views from Containers."

So, physically, the dictionaries are separated. Each container stores metadata for its user objects, and the root stores the common ones—mainly the system metadata. Logically, from the views, we see everything, because this is what we have always seen in non-CDBs, and PDBs are compatible with that.

Metadata Links

Oracle has introduced a new way to link objects from one container to another: *metadata link*. Each container has all the dictionary objects (stored in OBJ$ and visible through DBA_OBJECTS), such as the system package names in the example used earlier. But more definitions (such as the packages source text) are not stored in all of the containers, but only in the CDB$ROOT. Each container has a flag in OBJ$, visible as the SHARING column of DBA_OBJECTS, that tells Oracle to switch to the CDB$ROOT container when it needs to get the metadata for it.

Here is some information about one of those packages, which includes the same definition in all containers, from DBA_OBJECTS in the CDB$ROOT:

```
SQL> select owner,object_name,object_id,object_type,sharing,
oracle_maintained from dba_objects where object_name = 'DBMS_SYSTEM';

OWNER   OBJECT_NAME  OBJECT_ID OBJECT_TYPE   SHARING         ORACLE_MAINTAINED
------  -----------  --------- ------------  -------------   -----------------
SYS     DBMS_SYSTEM     14087  PACKAGE       METADATA LINK   Y
SYS     DBMS_SYSTEM     14088  PACKAGE BODY  METADATA LINK   Y
```

And this is from the PDB:

```
SQL> select owner,object_name,object_id,object_type,sharing,
oracle_maintained from dba_objects where object_name = 'DBMS_SYSTEM';

OWNER   OBJECT_NAME  OBJECT_ID OBJECT_TYPE   SHARING         ORACLE_MAINTAINED
------  -----------  --------- ------------  -------------   -----------------
SYS     DBMS_SYSTEM     14081  PACKAGE       METADATA LINK   Y
SYS     DBMS_SYSTEM     14082  PACKAGE BODY  METADATA LINK   Y
```

You can see the same object names and types, defined as Oracle maintained and with METADATA LINK sharing. They have different object IDs. Only the name and an internal signature is used to link them. From this, we know that those objects are system objects (Oracle maintained), and when we query one of them from a PDB, the Oracle code knows that it has to switch to the root container to get some of its information. This is the behavior of metadata links. The dictionary objects that are big are stored in only one place, the CDB$ROOT, but they can be seen from everywhere via dictionary views.

This concerns metadata. Metadata for your application is on your PDB. Metadata for Oracle-maintained objects is stored on the CDB$ROOT. The latter is static information: it's updated only by upgrades and patches. You can see that the benefit is not only a reduction in duplication, but also the acceleration of the upgrades of the PDBs, as there are only links.

Figure 1-3 shows the expanded simplified dictionary from Figure 1-2 to reveal the dictionary separation.

SCOTT.DEPT

DEPTNO	DNAME	LOC
10	ACCOUNTING	NEW YORK
20	RESEARCH	DALLAS
30	SALES	CHICAGO
40	OPERATIONS	BOSTON

SYS.COLUMNS

OWNER	TABLENAME	COLUMNNAME	DATATYPE
\multicolumn{4}{c}{LINK TO SYSTEM METADATA}
SCOTT	DEPT	DEPTNO	NUMBER(2)
SCOTT	DEPT	DNAME	VARCHAR(14)
SCOTT	DEPT	LOC	VARCHAR(13)

} definition of SYS.COLUMNS columns

} definition of SCOTT.DEPT columns

pluggable database
- -
CDB$ROOT

SYS.COLUMNS

OWNER	TABLENAME	COLUMNNAME	DATATYPE
SYS	COLUMNS	OWNER	VARCHAR(30)
SYS	COLUMNS	TABLENAME	VARCHAR(30)
SYS	COLUMNS	COLUMNNAME	VARCHAR(30)
SYS	COLUMNS	DATATYPE	VARCHAR(30)

} definition of SYS.COLUMNS columns

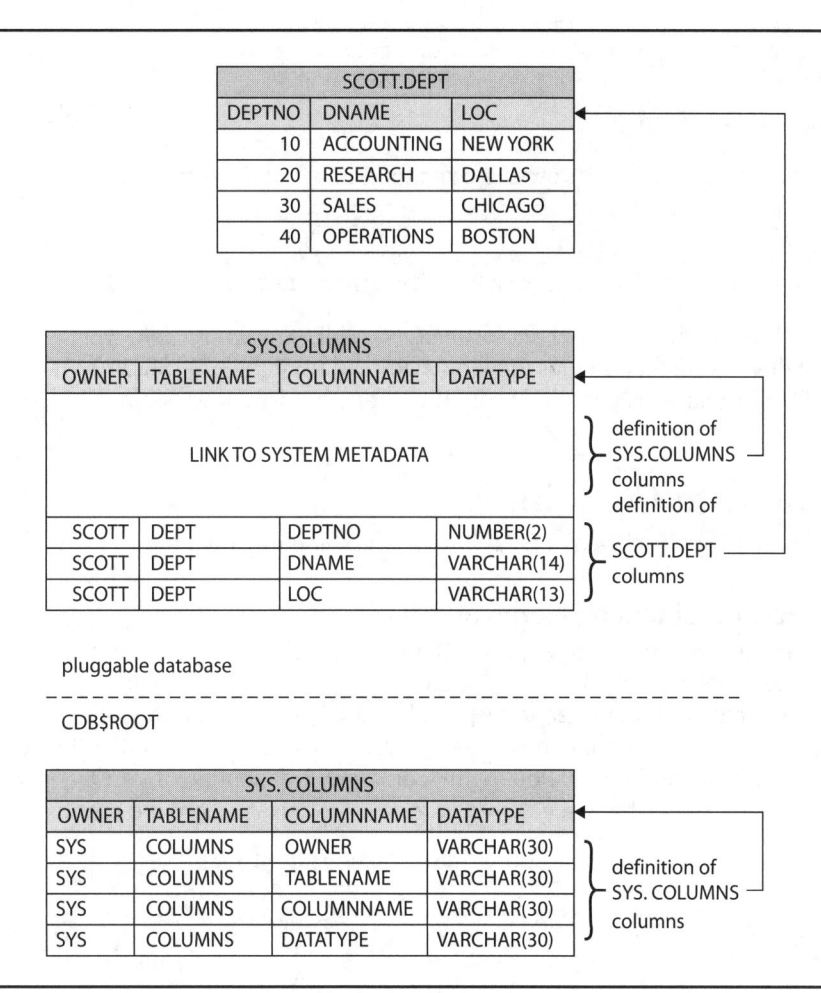

FIGURE 1-3. *Separating system and user metadata*

Data Links (called Object Links in 12.1)

There is not only metadata in the dictionary. The multitenant database also contains some data to store at the CDB level. Here's a simple example. Suppose the CDB must keep a list of its containers, which is stored in the system table CONTAINER$, which is exposed through the dictionary view DBA_PDBS. This data is updated to store the status of the containers. However, this data, which makes sense only at the CDB level, can be queried from all PDBs. Let's see how this is shared.

This is from the CDB$ROOT:

```
SQL> select owner,object_name,object_id,object_type,sharing,
oracle_maintained from dba_objects where object_name in ('CONTAINER$','DBA_PDBS');

OWNER  OBJECT_NAME OBJECT_ID OBJECT_TYPE SHARING       ORACLE_MAINTAINED
------ ----------- --------- ----------- ------------- -----------------
SYS    CONTAINER$        161 TABLE       METADATA LINK Y
SYS    DBA_PDBS         4755 VIEW        DATA LINK     Y
PUBLIC DBA_PDBS         4756 SYNONYM     METADATA LINK Y
```

And this is from the PDB:

```
OWNER  OBJECT_NAME OBJECT_ID OBJECT_TYPE SHARING       ORACLE_MAINTAINED
------ ----------- --------- ----------- ------------- -----------------
SYS    CONTAINER$        161 TABLE       METADATA LINK Y
SYS    DBA_PDBS         4753 VIEW        DATA LINK     Y
PUBLIC DBA_PDBS         4754 SYNONYM     METADATA LINK Y
```

You can see that the view that accesses CONTAINER$ is a data link, which means that the session that queries the view will read from the CDB$ROOT. Actually, the CONTAINER$ table is present in all containers, but it is always empty except in root.

Working with Containers

How do you work with so many PDBs? You begin by identifying them.

Identifying Containers by Name and ID

A consolidated CDB contains multiple containers that are identified by a name and a number, the CON_ID. All the V$ views that show what you have in an instance have an additional column in 12c to display the CON_ID to which the object is related. The CDB itself is a container, identified by container CON_ID=0. Objects that are at CDB level and not related to any container are identified by CON_ID=0.

For example, here's what we get if we query V$DATABASE from the root:

```
SQL> select dbid,name,cdb,con_id,con_dbid from v$database;
      DBID NAME      CDB     CON_ID   CON_DBID
---------- --------- ---  ---------- ----------
2013933390 CDB       YES           0 2013933390
```

And this is from the PDB:

```
SQL> select dbid,name,cdb,con_id,con_dbid from v$database;
      DBID NAME       CDB     CON_ID   CON_DBID
---------- ---------- ---  ---------- ----------
2013933390 CDB        YES           0 2621919399
```

The information may be different when viewed from different containers, but in all cases, the database information is located at the CDB level only. Information in that view comes from the control file, and you will see that it is in the common ground. So the CON_ID is 0. If you are in non-CDB, CON_ID=0 for all objects. But if you are in multitenant architecture, most of the objects pertain to a container.

The first container that you have in any CDB is the root, named CDB$ROOT and with CON_ID=1. All the other containers are PDBs.

The first PDB that is present in every CDB is the seed, named PDB$SEED, which is the second container, with CON_ID=2.

Then CON_ID>2 are your PDBs. In 12.1, you can create 252 additional PDBs. In 12.2, you can create 4,098 of them.

List of Containers

The dictionary view DBA_PDBS lists all PDBs (all containers except root) with their status:

```
SQL> select pdb_id, pdb_name, status,con_id from dba_pdbs;

    PDB_ID PDB_NAME   STATUS         CON_ID
---------- ---------- ---------- ----------
         2 PDB$SEED   NORMAL              2
         3 PDB1       NORMAL              3
         4 PDB2       NEW                 4
         5 PDB3       UNUSABLE            5
         6 PDB4       UNPLUGGED           6
```

The status is NEW when you create it and is changed to NORMAL at first open read/write, because some operations must be completed at first open. UNUSABLE is displayed when the creation failed and the only operation we can do is DROP it. UNPLUGGED is a way to transport it to another CDB, and the only operation that can be done on the source CDB is to DROP it.

Instead of NEW you can see the following in 12.1 only: NEED UPGRADE indicates it came from a different version, and CONVERTING indicates it came from a non-CDB. You'll learn about three others, the RELOCATING, REFRESHING and RELOCATED statuses, in Chapter 9.

That was the information from the database dictionary. We can list the containers known by the instance, which show the open status:

```
SQL> select con_id,name,open_mode,open_time from v$pdbs;

    CON_ID NAME       OPEN_MODE  OPEN_TIME
---------- ---------- ---------- --------------------------------
         2 PDB$SEED   READ ONLY  05-JAN-16 03.57.35.171 PM +01:00
         3 PDB1       READ WRITE 05-JAN-16 04.49.27.558 PM +01:00
         4 PDB2       MOUNTED
         5 PDB3       MOUNTED
         6 PDB4       MOUNTED
```

In non-CDB, the MOUNTED state occurs when the control file is read but the datafiles are not yet opened by the instance processes. It's the same idea here: a closed PDB does not yet open the datafiles. There is no NOMOUNT state for PDBs because the control file is common.

Note that SQL*Plus and SQL Developer have a shortcut you can use to show your PDBs or all PDBs when you are in the root container:

```
SQL> show pdbs

    CON_ID CON_NAME                       OPEN MODE  RESTRICTED
---------- ------------------------------ ---------- ----------
         2 PDB$SEED                       READ ONLY  NO
         3 PDB1                           READ WRITE NO
         4 PDB2                           MOUNTED    NO
         5 PDB3                           MOUNTED    NO
         6 PDB4                           MOUNTED    NO
```

Identify Containers by CON_UID and DBID

You have seen that in addition to its name, a container is identified by an ID, the CON_ID within the CDB. The CON_ID can change when you move the PDB. For that reason, you also have a unique identifier, the CON_UID, which is a number that identifies the PDB even after it has been moved. The CDB$ROOT that is a container but not a PDB, and does not move, has a CON_UID=1.

Because of the compatibility with databases, each container has also a DBID. CDB$ROOT is the DBID of the CDB. The DBID of PDBs is the CON_UID.

In addition, each container has a GUID, a 16-byte RAW value that is assigned at PDB creation time and never changes after that. It is used as a unique identifier of the PDB in the directory structure when using Oracle Managed Files (OMF).

All those identifiers are in V$CONTAINER, but you can also use the functions `CON_NAME_TO_ID`, `CON_DBID_TO_ID`, `CON_UID_TO_ID`, and `CON_GUID_TO_ID` to get the ID of a container. A null is returned if a container is not there. Here are some examples:

```
SQL> select CON_NAME_TO_ID('PDB$SEED'),CON_DBID_TO_ID(794366768),CON_NAME_TO_ID('XXX')
from dual;

CON_NAME_TO_ID('PDB$SEED')  CON_DBID_TO_ID(794366768)  CON_NAME_TO_ID('XXX')
--------------------------  -------------------------  ---------------------
                         2                          4
```

Connecting to Containers

We talked about multitenant as a way to overcome the schema-based consolidation limitation. So how do you switch between schemas, other than connecting directly as the schema user? You `ALTER SESSION SET CURRENT_SCHEMA`.

Of course, you can connect directly to a PDB, but we will explain that in Chapter 5 about services, because that is the right way to connect from users or application. But when, as a CDB administrator, you are already connected to the CDB, you can simply switch your session to a new container with `ALTER SESSION SET CONTAINER`.

Here, we are connected to CDB$ROOT:

```
SQL> show con_id
CON_ID
------------------------------
1
SQL> show con_name
CON_NAME
------------------------------
CDB$ROOT
```

We change our current container:

```
SQL> alter session set container=PDB;
Session altered.
```

And we are now in the PDB:

```
SQL> show con_id
CON_ID
------------------------------
3
SQL> show con_name
CON_NAME
------------------------------
PDB
```

Transactions If you have started a transaction in a container, you cannot open another transaction in another container.

```
SQL> alter session set container=PDB1;
Session altered.
SQL> insert into SCOTT.DEPT(deptno) values(50);
1 row created.
```

You can leave the transaction and change the container:

```
SQL> alter session set container=PDB2;
Session altered.
```

But you can't run DML that requires a transaction:

```
SQL> delete from SCOTT.EMP;
              *
ERROR at line 1:
ORA-65023: active transaction exists in container PDB1
```

First you must return to the previous container and finish your transaction:

```
SQL> alter session set container=PDB1;
Session altered.
SQL> commit;
Commit complete.
```

And then you can open a new transaction in another container:

```
SQL> alter session set container=PDB2;
Session altered.
SQL> insert into DEPT(deptno) values(50);
1 row created.
```

Cursors If you open a cursor in one container, you cannot fetch from it in another container. You need to go back to the cursor's container to fetch from it:

```
SQL> variable C1 refcursor;
SQL> exec open :C1 for select * from DEMO;
PL/SQL procedure successfully completed.
SQL> alter session set container=PDB2;
Session altered.
SQL> print C1
ERROR:
ORA-65108: invalid use of a cursor belonging to another container
```

Basically, it's easy to switch from one container to another, but what we do to them is isolated. Nothing is shared with the previous container state.

For example, connected to PDB1, we set `serveroutput` to on and use `dbms_output`:

```
SQL> alter session set container=PDB1;
Session altered.
SQL> set serveroutput on
SQL> exec dbms_output.put_line('==> '||sys_context('userenv','con_name'));
==> PDB1
PL/SQL procedure successfully completed.
```

The `dbms_output` line was displayed. You can see that the USERENV context shows the current container name. Now we switch to PDB2:

```
SQL> alter session set container=PDB2;
Session altered.
SQL> exec dbms_output.put_line('==> '||sys_context('userenv','con_name'));
PL/SQL procedure successfully completed.
```

Nothing is displayed here. `serveroutput` was set for PDB1, and we have to set it for PDB2:

```
SQL> set serveroutput on
SQL> exec dbms_output.put_line('==> '||sys_context('userenv','con_name'));
==> PDB2
PL/SQL procedure successfully completed.
```

Now we go back to PDB1:

```
SQL> alter session set container=PDB1;
Session altered.
SQL> exec dbms_output.put_line('==> '||sys_context('userenv','con_name'));
==> PDB1
PL/SQL procedure successfully completed.
```

No need to set `serveroutput` again. When switching back, we regained the state.

From JDBC or OCI My examples were run on SQL*Plus, but any client can do this. As long as you are connected with a user that is defined in the root (a common user) and that has been granted the SET CONTAINER system privilege on a PDB, you can switch the session to the PDB. You can do it from Java Database Connectivity (JDBC) or from the Oracle Call Interface (OCI). For example, you can have a connection pool from an application server that will switch to the required container when connections are grabbed. This is a way to have a common application server for multiple database tenants.

NOTE
If you want to use some container features that are new in 12.2, such as switching to a different character set PDB, you need to have a 12.2 client or you'll get a ORA-24964: ALTER SESSION SET CONTAINER error.

Set Container Trigger   If, for any reason, you want to run something when a session changes to another container, such as setting specific optimizer parameters, you can create a BEFORE SET CONTAINER and AFTER SET CONTAINER.

Here is how it works:

- The `BEFORE SET CONTAINER` created in PDB1 will be raised when you are in PDB1 and you execute an `ALTER SESSION SET CONTAINER`. If the trigger reads the container name, it will be PDB1.

- The `AFTER SET CONTAINER` created in PDB2 will be raised when you have executed an `ALTER SESSION SET CONTAINER=PDB2`.

This means that if both PDB1 and PDB2 have before and after triggers, changing from PDB1 to PDB2 will raise a `BEFORE SET CONTAINER` in PDB1 and an `AFTER SET CONTAINER` in PDB2.

There are two ways to work in a PDB. You can connect to it through its services, which is described in Chapter 5, and then `AFTER LOGON ON PLUGGABLE DATABASE` can be used to run some code at the beginning of the session. Or you can SET CONTAINER, and then use the `AFTER SET CONTAINER ON PLUGGABLE DATABASE`. If you want to be sure to set some sessions settings for a user working on a PDB, you will probably define both. Note that the word *PLUGGABLE* is not mandatory because of the syntax compatibility with database behavior.

Dictionary Views from Containers

A PDB includes everything that you expect from a database, which means that the queries on the dictionary views have the same behavior. You have all the DBA_/ALL_/USER_ views to show metadata for the PDB objects, or those you have access to, or those that you own. The fact that system objects are stored elsewhere is transparent: you see system objects in DBA_OBJECTS, system tables in DBA_TABLES, and instance information in the V$ views, but only the rows that are of concern in your PDB.

When you are in CDB$ROOT, you have additional CDB_ views that are like a UNION ALL of all opened containers' DBA_ views. It's a way for a CDB database administrator to view all objects. For this CDB$ROOT user, the V$ views show information about all containers.

Finally, you may want to know if you are in non-CDB or in multitenant. The CDB column in V$DATABASE provides the answer:

```
SQL> select name,cdb from v$database;

NAME        CDB
---------   ---
CDB         YES
```

What Is Consolidated at CDB Level

Sharing resources that can be common is the main goal of consolidation. Beyond the instance and the dictionary, many database structures are managed at the CDB level. We are not talking about datafiles here, because they are specific to each container, and the only commonality among them is that they must have the same character set (except when a container is transported from another CDB, but that's a topic for Chapter 9). Several other files are common to all containers in a container database.

SPFILE

The database instance is common to all containers, and the SPFILE holds the instance parameters, storing these settings for the entire CDB. The SPFILE contains the configuration elements that cannot be stored within the database or the control file, because they must be available before the database is mounted.

Some parameters can be set at the PDB level (those with ISPDB_MODIFIABLE=TRUE in V$PARAMETER). These changes can also be persisted, but even if the syntax for such an operation is SCOPE=SPFILE, this is for syntax compatibility only, as PDB level parameters are actually stored in the CDB dictionary (PDB_SPFILE$). They are not stored in the PDB itself because the parameter must be accessed before opening the PDB. We will see later that when moving pluggable databases (unplug/plug), these parameters are extracted into an XML file that you ship with the PDB datafiles.

Control Files

The control file references all other structures in the database. For example, this is the only location in which the datafile names are actually stored, and in the dictionary it is the FILE_ID alone that is used to reference them. In multitenant, the control file resides at the CDB level and holds records for all pluggable database datafiles. You will see in Chapter 9 that information relating to pluggable databases that is stored in the control file will also be exported to an XML file when a pluggable database is moved by unplug/plug.

> **NOTE**
> *When we refer to the "control file," we are actually referring to the control files (plural), because you can, and must, multiplex them to protect your database. This fundamental best practice does not change, and, if anything, the importance of database availability is even higher in multitenant, because an outage will have impact on multiple tenants.*

While on the subject of database files, there is a parameter that controls the maximum number of files opened by an instance, DB_FILES, which defaults to 200. Be aware that if you create hundreds of pluggable databases, you will very quickly reach this limit, and you will then be unable to create new tablespaces or new pluggable databases until you restart the instance. In multitenant, restarting the instance may mean an outage for a large number of applications, so you want to avoid this. So don't forget to size DB_FILES properly when you expect your container to house several pluggable databases.

UNDO

In 12.1, the first release with multitenant architecture, the UNDO tablespace, is common and implemented at the CDB level. However, in 12.2, we now also have the choice to run the CDB in local UNDO mode. If `LOCAL UNDO` is `ON`, each pluggable database has its own UNDO tablespace and all sessions writing data into PDB data blocks will place UNDO record information in this local tablespace. Only the changes performed on CDB$ROOT will put the UNDO record in the root UNDO tablespace.

In short, it is better to run in local UNDO mode if possible. UNDO contains application data, and we don't achieve pluggable database isolation if we then store this in common UNDO datafiles. One reason for this preference is that local UNDO is required for efficient flashback pluggable database and point-in-time-recovery. We will explain this in Chapter 8.

Temporary Tablespaces

Temporary tablespaces can be created at both the CDB and PDB levels. If a user is not assigned a temporary tablespace within the PDB in which the session is running, and the PDB does not have a default temporary tablespace, the session will use the CDB temporary tablespace—but this is not recommended. A quota (`MAX_SHARED_TEMP_SIZE`) can be set on pluggable database usage of the root temporary tablespace.

The CDB$ROOT temporary tablespace is normally used by sessions connected to the root container, or from a pluggable database, when a work area needs to be allocated for a recursive query on object linked views.

Once a temporary tablespace has been defined as the default, you can change it to another that you have created in that PDB, but you cannot reinstate the CDB temporary tablespace as a default after this point.

Redo Logs

The redo logs protect the instance, and because of this, they are also common. Their main objective is to record all changes made in the buffer cache and to ensure that those changes are persisted for committed transactions.

The redo stream in multitenant is similar to the stream in previous versions, except for additional information in each redo record to identify the container. Redo format is crucial for recovery operations, and, as such, Oracle changes this code very infrequently.

Having the redo thread cover all pluggable databases brings more multitenant benefits to the DBA managing the CDB. In non-CDB contexts, when you provision a new database, it takes a lot of effort and time to size the recovery area, establish the backups, and build and configure the Data Guard physical standby, when used. With multitenant, you do it only once, for your CDB, because this is where functionality related to availability runs from: your backups, your Data Guard, and your RAC configuration. Simply create a new pluggable database and it will benefit from the same already-configured availability: it is automatically backed-up with the CDB, automatically created on the physical standby (note that you need Active Data Guard for this), and automatically accessible from all RAC instances. Again, this is because the main structure used for availability, the redo stream, operates at the CDB level.

However, having only one redo stream may be a concern in terms of performance. If you have ever encountered log writer performance issues, such as long waits on "log file sync" events, then you can imagine what happens when the Log Writer (LGWR) has to write the redo from *all* pluggable databases. And the upshot is that if the LGWR cannot keep up with the redo rate, users will be forced to wait when committing.

So, for the purpose of LGWR scalability, Oracle introduced multiple LGWRs in 12*c*. LGWR is the coordinator process, and multiple slaves (LG00, LG01, and so on) are associated with this, so that the instance redo stream is written in parallel. Of course, RAC is still another means of implementing parallel threads of redo. What you must keep in mind is that tuning the LGWR and the amount of redo written is of crucial importance in multitenant. When you consolidate, pay special attention to the performance of the disks on which you put the redo logs.

Datafiles

The datafiles, which store the tablespace data blocks, belong to each container, but they are also managed by the CDB. They have a unique identifier for the CDB, which is the `FILE_ID`:

```
SQL> select file_id,con_id,tablespace_name,relative_fno,file_name
  from cdb_data_files order by 1;

FILE_ID CON_ID TABLESPACE_NAME  RELATIVE_FNO FILE_NAME
------- ------ ---------------- ------------ ---------------------------------
      1      1 SYSTEM                      1 /u02/oradata/CDB/system01.dbf
      3      1 SYSAUX                      3 /u02/oradata/CDB/sysaux01.dbf
      5      1 UNDOTBS1                    5 /u02/oradata/CDB/undotbs01.dbf
      7      1 USERS                       7 /u02/oradata/CDB/users01.dbf
      8      3 SYSTEM                      1 /u02/oradata/CDB/PDB1/system01.dbf
      9      3 SYSAUX                      4 /u02/oradata/CDB/PDB1/sysaux01.dbf
     10      3 UNDOTBS1                    6 /u02/oradata/CDB/PDB1/undotbs01.dbf
     11      3 USERS                      11 /u02/oradata/CDB/PDB1/users01.dbf
     12      4 SYSTEM                      1 /u02/oradata/CDB/PDB2/system01.dbf
     13      4 SYSAUX                      4 /u02/oradata/CDB/PDB2/sysaux01.dbf
     14      4 UNDOTBS1                    6 /u02/oradata/CDB/PDB2/undotbs01.dbf
     15      4 USERS                      11 /u02/oradata/CDB/PDB2/users01.dbf
```

The concept of a *relative file number* was introduced along with transportable tablespaces, so this aspect of the architecture of Oracle was ready long before 12c. In multitenant, within a pluggable database, the datafiles are identified by the tablespace number and the file number relative to the tablespace (RELATIVE_FNO). Furthermore, these do not have to be changed when you move, clone, or plug in the pluggable database, and it is only the absolute file number (FILE_ID) that will be renumbered to ensure that it is unique within the CDB—but that is a very quick change in the control file and datafile headers.

Data and Metadata at CDB Level

We have explained that the dictionary related to system objects, stored in the CDB$ROOT SYSTEM and SYSAUX tablespaces, is common and can be accessed by the PDBs. Beyond the basic database objects (created by catalog.sql and catproc.sql) more common information can be stored in the root.

APEX

By default, if you install APEX (in 12.2, you can choose the components), it is placed at the CDB level. The idea is that APEX, like the system dictionary, houses metadata that does not need to be installed in PDB$SEED or in all pluggable databases created. However, there is a big drawback in this approach: you have only one APEX version in your CDB and you will have problems if you want to plug a non-CDB running APEX 5.0, for example, into Oracle Cloud Services, where the CDB is installed with APEX 4.2.

> **NOTE**
> *This issue has been detailed by Mike Dietrich on his blog, blogs.oracle.com/UPGRADE/entry/apex_in_ pdb_does_not. The APEX 5.0 documentation states, "Oracle recommends removing Oracle Application Express from the root container database for the majority of use cases, except for hosting companies or installations where all pluggable databases (PDBs) utilize Oracle Application Express and they all need to run the exact same release and patch set of Oracle Application Express."*

Automatic Workload Repository

Automatic Workload Repository (AWR) collects a large amount of instance information (statistics, wait events, and so on) from the instance views, and in multitenant, this is done at the CDB level. Only one job collects all statistics for all containers, and they are stored in the CDB$ROOT. This is actually the main use case for object-link views: AWR views (those that start with DBA_HIST) can be queried from each pluggable database but actually read data that is stored in root.

There are two important consequences relating to this. The first is that if you move a pluggable database, the AWR history does not follow along with the container; instead, it remains in the original CDB. You can read the views from the original database, or export it elsewhere. But the CON_ID that is stored in AWR should be the container ID at the time the snapshot was taken, so you need to check the CON_DBID to identify a specific pluggable database. There are actually three different identifiers in each of the DBA_HIST views:

- DBID is the DBID of the CDB, same as in a non-CDB environment. This uniquely identifies the snapshot, along with the SNAP_ID and INSTANCE_NUMBER.

- CON_ID is the container ID that comes from the V$ views queried to take the snapshot. Some rows are not related to any container, and so have CON_ID=0, while others record statistics for a container object and so take the related CON_ID at the time of the snapshot.

- CON_DBID uniquely identifies a pluggable database, in the same way that DBID uniquely identifies a database.

The second consequence of having AWR collected at the CDB level is that, when you run an AWR report at PDB level, it will filter only the statistics relevant to your container, and this is exactly the same as querying V$ views from a PDB.

But you must keep in mind that you still see some statistics that are at CDB level (those that have CON_ID=0) in the same report. This means that, for example, you will see the amount of logical reads done by the instance in the instance statistics section, but the details (in SQL sections or Segment section) reveal only what is relevant to your pluggable database. Let's take a look at an example.

Before reading an AWR report details, we always check that most of the SQL statements are captured, because there is no point in continuing if we cannot go down to the statement-level detail. Here is the SQL ordered by Gets header from an AWR report:

```
SQL ordered by Gets                        DB/Inst: CDB/CDB  Snaps: 139-143
...
-> Total Buffer Gets:       24,958,807
-> Captured SQL account for    88.9% of Total
```

This shows that 89 percent of the SQL statements were captured, and we know that we will have the detail we need when we investigate the high logical reads issue. When the percentage is low, that usually means that we are analyzing a report that covers a time window that is too large, and most of the SQL statements have been aged out of the shared pool before the end snapshot. But you can see another reason for low percentages when you run the AWR report from a pluggable database:

```
SQL ordered by Gets                        DB/Inst: CDB/CDB  Snaps: 139-143
...
-> Total Buffer Gets:       24,958,807
-> Captured SQL account for    21.6% of Total
```

You don't see anything different here, except that only 21 percent of the statements have been captured. You have to check the AWR report header to see that it covers only one PDB. Actually we had two PDBs active at that time, and here is the other one:

```
SQL ordered by Gets                        DB/Inst: CDB/CDB  Snaps: 139-143
...
-> Total Buffer Gets:       24,958,807
-> Captured SQL account for    60.3% of Total
```

From one PDB, you have no way to see if all statements for that PDB have been captured. There are no statistics such as total logical reads for that pluggable database.

> **NOTE**
> *This is the behavior in 12.1, where per-PDB instance statistics are available in V$CON_SYSSTAT but not collected by AWR. In 12.2, they are collected in DBA_HIST_CON_SYSSTAT, and you have similar views from time model (DBA_HIST_CON_SYS_TIME_MODEL) and system events (DBA_HIST_CON_SYSTEM_EVENT). In 12.2 the AWR report uses them and the inconsistency above does not appear.*

Statspack If you don't have the Diagnostic Pack, you can't use AWR and you will probably install Statspack. According to the documentation (spdoc.txt), Statspack can be installed only at the PDB level. We think that it makes sense to install it at the CDB level as well, because you may want to analyze CDB$ROOT activity. Each PDB from which you want to collect snapshots will store its own statistics. Because statistics are now collected at PDB level, the behavior is different from the behavior with AWR. We've taken Statspack snapshots at the same time as the AWR snapshots in the preceding example. The session logical reads from spreport.sql show 24,956,570 logical reads when the report is run on CDB$ROOT, and 5,709,168 (22 percent) for one PDB and 17,138,586 (68 percent) for the other. Statspack collects statistics related with the CDB when run from root and with the container when run from a PDB.

Summary

In this long introduction, we have explained why multitenant was introduced by Oracle 12c in 2013. We have seen the different consolidation alternatives, and perhaps you think that you don't need to run in multitenant. However, this new architecture will eventually become the only one supported, the non-CDB being already deprecated. So even if you don't want multiple pluggable databases per instance now, you will have to run what we will call "single-tenant" in Chapter 3, and you will have to administer container databases.

In addition to consolidation, the new architecture separates the application data and metadata from the system dictionary, bringing more agility for data movement and location transparency. This will be covered in Chapter 9.

The next chapter will start from the beginning by creating a consolidated database.

CHAPTER 2

Creating the Database

In Chapter 1 we introduced the new Oracle 12c Database Multitenant option. It is interesting that we still reference this as *new*—the fact is, even though it was introduced in 2013, many DBAs and organizations have not started using this technology yet. In learning new technologies, many DBA's most effective approaches include starting simple. The acronym KISS—Keep It Simple Stupid—is still in many cases the best approach. In this chapter, we will follow such an approach to help you lay a good foundation for the world of Oracle Database 12c Multitenant, which, as you will see, scales in complexity rather quickly.

As with earlier versions, there are many ways to create an Oracle Database, and some might expect that experienced, hardcore DBA would naturally favor the command line. But you might be surprised to learn that many of them actually make use of graphical interfaces, whether it is the well-known Database Configuration Assistant (DBCA) or Oracle Database Express, and Cloud Control for the larger configurations. In this chapter, we will cover two key topics:

- Creation of the container database (CDB)
- Creation of pluggable databases (PDBs)

Creating a Container Database (CDB)

Before we dive into the CDB creation steps, we need to discuss a few crucial introductory topics that will assist you in gaining a better understanding of what happens when you create a CDB database with one or more PDBs. As detailed in Chapter 1, when you create a CDB, you end up with at least two containers: the root container (CDB$ROOT) and the seed container (PDB$SEED).

In most Oracle configurations nowadays, two main storage options are used for database files: Automatic Storage Management (ASM), which is highly recommended, or the traditional file system–based storage. In earlier versions of the Oracle Database, many system administrators were kind of scared to use ASM; because database files were not easily viewable, they felt they had no control over them. However, times have changed, and with ASM's improvements and its excellent feature set, it has now been widely adopted. In this chapter, therefore, both options will be discussed in conjunction with creating a CDB and PDBs. For more detail on the use and configuration of ASM, review the Oracle documentation.

What About OMF?

Oracle Managed Files (OMF) is an option that charges Oracle with the responsibility for database file naming, and in a multitenant environment it is highly recommended.

For those unfamiliar with OMF, this may sound dangerous, but there is no need for alarm, because it is an easy-to-use and proven option that can make a DBA's life a lot easier.

Imagine creating a tablespace. Traditionally, you would have to specify the full path and name of the datafile you are creating. But with OMF, you can simply state that you want a file of a specific size for the tablespace, and the naming of the file will be taken care of for you. An example of the file structure and naming in an OMF-enabled environment is shown in Figure 2-1.

To the uninitiated, this might take some getting used to. Note especially the subdirectory naming for the PDB. When you're working with OMF, a long hash is used as a subdirectory name for the PDB datafiles, which in this example is 2B11F0C3A0262FF6E053E902000A0D8A.

Where does this come from, and what does it mean? If you review V$CONTAINER from the CDB$ROOT, you will notice that the value used for this directory name is in fact the GUID value for the pluggable database. In short, the OMF directory structure takes the following format:

```
<DB_CREATE_FILE_DEST DiskGroup>/<db_unique_name>/<GUID>/DATAFILE/
```

Again, when using ASM, it is recommended that you use OMF. This brings us to the next step—the creation of the CDB.

```
└── oradata
    ├── CDB7
        ├── 2B11F0C3A0262FF6E053E902000A0D8A
        |   └── datafile
        |       ├── o1_mf_sysaux_ccbqhzcd_.dbf
        |       ├── o1_mf_system_ccbqhqgs_.dbf
        |       └── o1_mf_temp_ccbqj3b3_.tmp
        ├── controlfile
        |   └── o1_mf_ccbqhh2o_.ctl
        ├── datafile
        |   ├── o1_mf_sysaux_ccbqhvkv_.dbf
        |   ├── o1_mf_system_ccbqhlj1_.dbf
        ...
        ...
```

FIGURE 2-1. *Example OMF directory structure*

CDB Creation Options

A number of different methods are available for creating the CDB, but the most popular—and the recommended—method is to use the DBCA. For those interested, it is possible to create the CDB manually by running a number of SQL statements, and this option will be outlined in the next section.

The DBCA is an extremely powerful tool for creating databases, both via its GUI and with its lesser known command line (CLI) option. First, let's take a look at creating a CDB using the GUI.

Using the DBCA GUI

Over the years, the DBCA has become a much more reliable and stable tool, and it is a widely accepted and trusted method for creating new Oracle databases. A number of options are available that would require a book of their own to document, so we will focus instead on those key aspects related to the Multitenant option.

NOTE
It is recommended that you have a default listener already configured on the database server where you will be running the DBCA.

The first step is to start the DBCA by issuing the `dbca` command to invoke the executable located in the $ORACLE_HOME/bin directory. Once DBCA starts, you will see the GUI, as shown in Figure 2-2.

NOTE
A number of the DBCA options (such as Delete Database) will be available only if DBCA detects at startup that the system is already running at least one other Oracle Database.

Typical Configuration   To create a new database, select the Create A Database option, and click Next.

The next screen presents more detail (Figure 2-3) and two options: Typical Configuration or Advanced Configuration. In most cases choosing Typical Configuration is sufficient, but if you are more familiar with the Oracle Database and need to configure advanced options, such as memory allocations, choose Advanced Configuration.

The first example discussed will show the Typical Configuration steps.

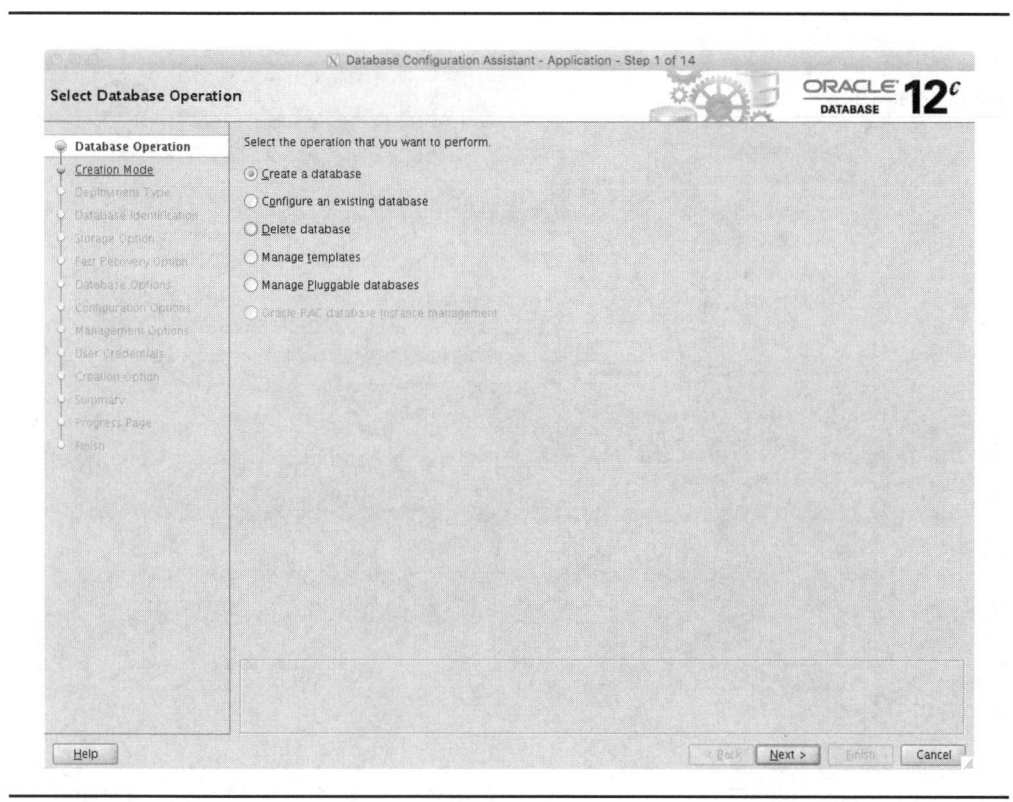

FIGURE 2-2. *DBCA step 1: Create a database*

Seven steps are highlighted in Figure 2-2:

1. Provide the default Global Database Name—in this example, CDB2.orademo.net.

2. For Storage Type, specify whether you want to use filesystem-based storage or ASM. Here, we chose ASM.

3. The default Database Files Location is ASM disk group +DATA (note that these disk groups must exist prior to running the DBCA).

4. The Fast Recovery Area (FRA) is updated to point to the +FRA disk group.

5. The Administrative Passwords in this configuration will be used for all administrative users, such as SYS, SYSTEM, and PDBADMIN (the local administrator user for the PDB).

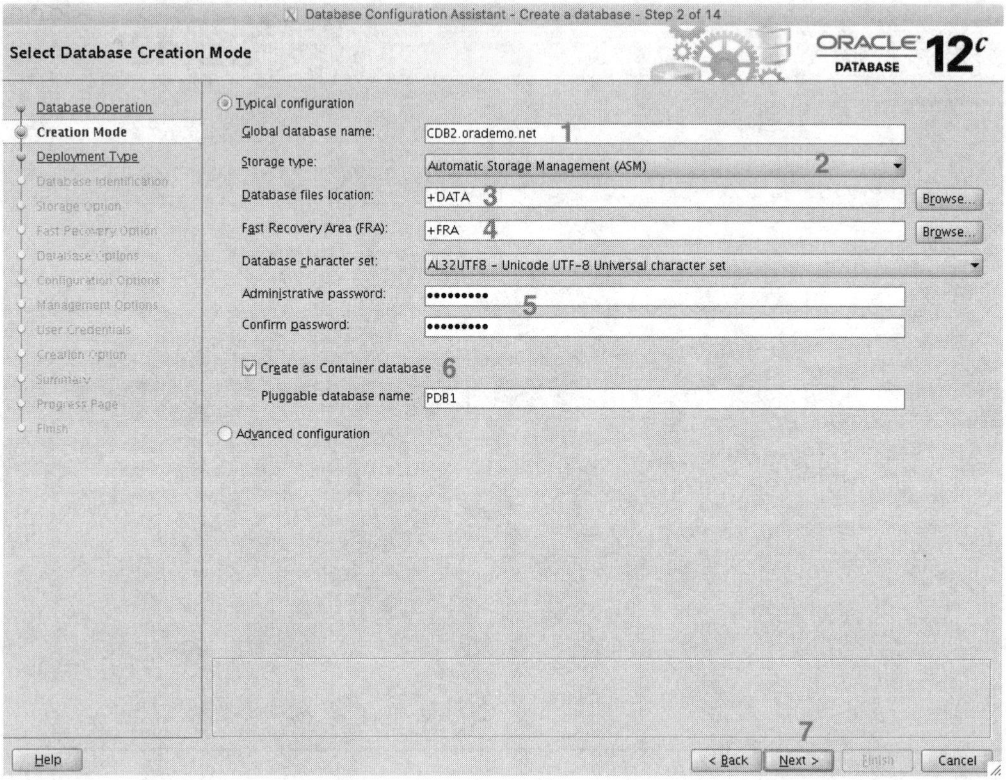

40 Oracle Database 12c Release 2 Multitenant

FIGURE 2-3. *DBCA—Typical Configuration steps*

6. For multitenancy this is an important step: select the Create As Container Database option, and provide a name for the single default PDB that will be created for you.

7. Click Next to continue.

From here, the summary screen is displayed, providing an opportunity to review the options. Click Finish to start the database creation process. You will be presented with a progress page that updates on the stages of the database creation process steps until complete.

> **NOTE**
> *You probably noticed references to the PDBADMIN user. This is the local admin user created during PDB creation. This user will be assigned the PDB_DBA role by default. The PDBADMIN user and PDB_DBA role by default have no assigned privileges.*
>
> *Later in the chapter, when we create PDBs using SQL*Plus, the ROLES clause is provided as part of the PDB creation statement. This clause is used to specify the roles you want to assign to the PDB_DBA role locally in the PDB. The PDBADMIN user does not have to be called PDBADMIN, but in most cases this is the default name. For more detail on LOCAL and COMMON users, see Chapter 6.*

Advanced Configuration   If you selected Advanced Configuration in Step 2, you'll see additional options, and the number of steps increases from 5 to 14. These are easy to follow, but we want to highlight Step 4, where you will be presented with a screen similar to that shown in Figure 2-4.

Here you can specify the Global Database Name as well as the option to create a CDB and any PDBs, as highlighted by 1 and 2. Note that you can specify the number of PDBs to be created, and a prefix will be used if more than one PDB will be created. You will also have the option from 12.2 to specify if you want to use Local UNDO tablespaces for the PDBs. This is a new feature introduced in 12.2 allowing PDBs to store their undo records in a local UNDO tablespace. For more detail please see Chapter 8.

> **NOTE**
> *In 12.1.0.x, the maximum PDBs per CDB is 253 (including the PDB$SEED). In 12.2.0.x, the limit was increased to a maximum of 4K (4096) per CDB.*

The end result is that we have a CDB called CDB1, which includes the CDB$ROOT, PDB$SEED, and two additional PDBs, PDB1 and PDB2, which will be based on the seed pluggable database.

> **NOTE**
> *The default templates used during the creation of a database are located in: $ORACLE_HOME/assistants/dbca/templates.*

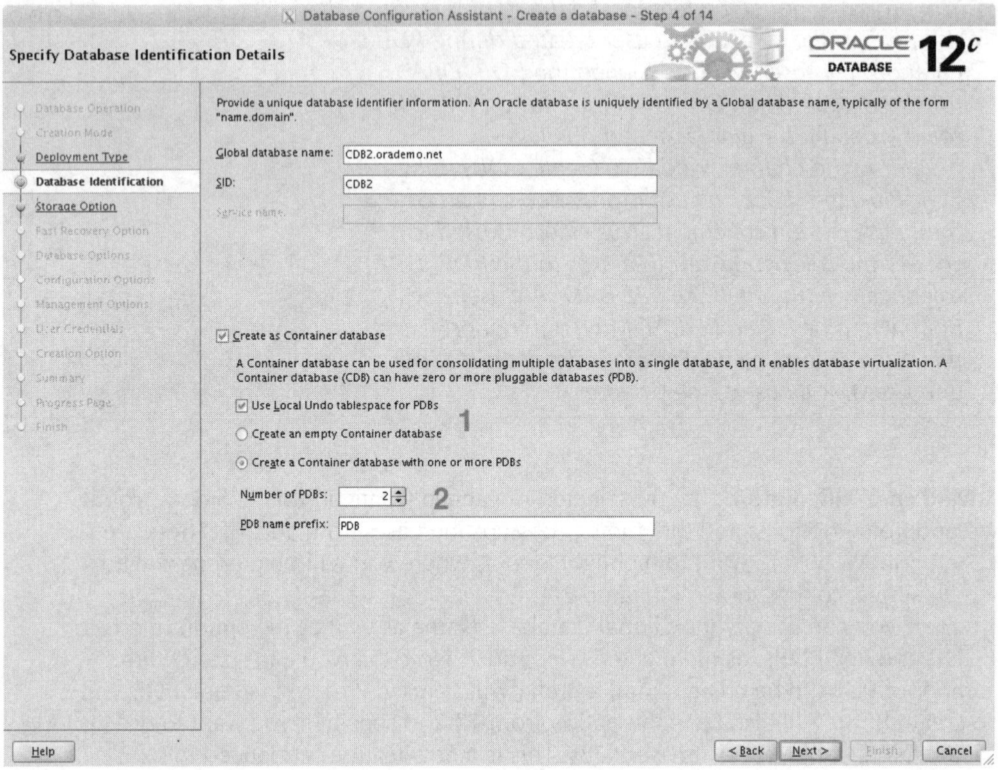

FIGURE 2-4. *DBCA—Advanced Configuration*

Using the DBCA CLI

Sometimes working with a GUI isn't possible, such as when you need to perform an installation and database creation via a remote connection and the network bandwidth is inadequate, or the connection is extremely slow. Don't be alarmed, because there are options available to you. One is to perform a silent, or unattended, installation using a response file, and a similar approach can be followed when creating a database. Another is to use the DBCA CLI and the `-silent` parameter, which invokes the same executable as the GUI via the `-silent` parameter, but presents the command line alternative. This is not a black box operation, because output is pushed to screen, and if you are interested in the details, you can interrogate the log files generated by this process.

> **NOTE**
> The default character set (AL32UTF8) should be sufficient for most database implementations, but this can be adjusted, as required.

Response File Format Change   There are some small differences between Oracle 12.1.0.x and 12.2.0.x with respect to the DBCA utility, including the use of response files. The latter actually features a new response file format, which will be a change welcomed by many.

On review of the sample response files, you will notice that the 12.1.0.x version of the response file makes use of grouping or sections, noted in square brackets—for example, [CREATEDATABASE]. These are used to identify the command being executed. This was improved in 12.2.0.x so that the response file contains only key-value pairs, and the command to be executed is passed to the dbca utility as an additional argument, such as dbca -createDatabase -responseFile.

Following is an example of a response file that can be used in 12.1.0.x. It will create a new CDB database called CDB1 with one PDB called PDB1, using the General Purpose template. The database uses ASM as the default storage type:

```
[GENERAL]
RESPONSEFILE_VERSION = "12.1.0"
OPERATION_TYPE = "createDatabase"
[CREATEDATABASE]
GDBNAME = "CDB1.orademo.net"
SID = "CDB1"
CREATEASCONTAINERDATABASE = true
NUMBEROFPDBS = 1
PDBNAME = PDB
PDBADMINPASSWORD = " Password1234"
TEMPLATENAME = "General_Purpose.dbc"
SYSPASSWORD = "Password1234"
SYSTEMPASSWORD = "Password1234"
DATAFILEDESTINATION ="+DATA"
RECOVERYAREADESTINATION="+DATA"
STORAGETYPE="ASM"
DISKGROUPNAME=DATA
AUTOMATICMEMORYMANAGEMENT = "FALSE"
TOTALMEMORY = "850"
```

If you do not specify values for at least one of the key commands (createDatabase, createTemplateFromDB, or createCloneTemplate) in the 12.1.0.x release response file (such as [CREATEDATABASE] as shown on line 4 of the preceding example), you will receive an error when running the dbca command—as per the following output, which indicates that at least one of these key commands must be configured:

```
dbca -silent -responseFile /home/oracle/responsefiles/cdb1-121.rsp
No command specified to perform. Please specify one of following commands:
createDatabase, createTemplateFromDB or createCloneTemplate
```

DBCA, Response Files, and 12.2.0.x   Using the `silent` option of the DBCA—that is, running it from the command line without starting the GUI—can be a big time-saver and is finding increased favor. And, as mentioned earlier, the CLI for the DBCA makes use of the same `dbca` executable. A substantial amount of detail is provided when executing the `dbca` command with the `-help` argument, and in 12.2.0.x the output is better structured and easier to read, compared to the initial 12.1.0.x release. You can add the `-help` flag to provide a detailed listing for the specific command you are interested in. For example, running `dbca -createDatabase -help` triggers a full and detailed listing of the available options for this command.

Using Response Files   There are two ways to use the CLI. The first is with a response file, which is similar to using a response file for the database software installation.

> **NOTE**
> *A sample response file that can be customized and used with the DBCA utility to create databases is provided as part of the database software installation at $ORACLE_HOME/assistants/dbca/ and is called dbca.rsp. Focusing on the uncommented lines is a good starting point.*

Alternatively, you can create, or save, your own response file based on the steps you perform in the DBCA interface. You may have noticed at the end of the configuration process an option to generate a response file based on all your selections and input. This is a quick-and-easy way to create one of these files to meet your requirements.

> **NOTE**
> *When using a response file, you do not have to assign values to all parameters. Most parameters have default values, which will suit most configurations and can be used without modifications.*

Let's look at two examples of using response files to create two CDB databases.

Example 1: Create CDB with two PDBs (ASM and OMF)

Here, we'll create a container database called CDB1 with two PDBs: PDB1 and PDB2. The Oracle-supplied template General_Purpose.dbc is used, and the database will be located in ASM with OMF enabled, using disk groups +DATA and +FRA. The key parameters specified in the response file are

- createAsContainerDatabase = true
- numberOfPDBs = 2
- pdbAdminPassword = Password12345
- pdbName = PDB

It is recommended that the passwords for the SYS, SYSTEM, and PDBADMIN accounts conform to Oracle standards. If you do not specify these in the response file, the user will be prompted for them on execution of the `dbca` command, because they are mandatory. The values specified in the response file are summarized as follows (in alphabetical order):

```
cdb1.rsp
automaticMemoryManagement=false
characterSet=AL32UTF8
createAsContainerDatabase=true
datafileDestination=+DATA
enableArchive=true
gdbName=CDB1.orademo.net
nationalCharacterSet=AL16UTF16
numberOfPDBs=2
pdbAdminPassword=Password12345
pdbName=PDB
recoveryAreaDestination=+FRA
recoveryAreaDestination=+FRA:
recoveryAreaSize=5120
redoLogFileSize=100
storageType=ASM
sysPassword=Password12345
systemPassword=Password12345
templateName=/u01/app/oracle/product/12.2.0/dbhome_1/assistants/dbca/templates/General_Purpose.dbc
totalMemory=850
useOMF=true
```

The command to execute the DBCA using the response file in silent mode is

```
dbca -createDatabase -responseFile <full qualified path of responsefile> -silent
```

Here's an example:

```
dbca -createDatabase -responseFile /home/oracle/responsefiles/cdb1.rsp -silent
```

Example 2: Create CDB with one PDB (FS and non-OMF)

Now let's create a container database, CDB1, with one PDB called PDB. The Oracle supplied template General_Purpose.dbc is used. The database uses normal file system–based storage, without OMF. The database files will be located in /u01/app/oracle/oradata with a FRA (recovery area destination) located at /u01/app/oracle/fast_recovery_area. The values specified in the response file are summarized as follows (in alphabetical order):

```
cdb2.rsp
automaticMemoryManagement=false
characterSet=AL32UTF8
createAsContainerDatabase=true
datafileDestination=/u01/app/oracle/oradata
enableArchive=true
gdbName=CDB2.orademo.net
nationalCharacterSet=AL16UTF16
numberOfPDBs=1
pdbAdminPassword=Password12345
pdbName=PDB
recoveryAreaDestination=/u01/app/oracle/fast_recovery_area
redoLogFileSize=100
storageType=FS
sysPassword=Password12345
systemPassword=Password12345
templateName=/u01/app/oracle/product/12.2.0/dbhome_1/assistants/dbca/templates/General_Purpose.dbc
totalMemory=850
useOMF=false
```

If the `numberOfPDBs=1`, then the `pdbName` parameter will be taken as the actual name of the PDB. So in example 2, the PDB name would be PDB. However, if the `numberOfPDBs` is greater than 1, the `pdbName` parameter is used as a prefix for the PDBs that will be created. For example, if `numberOfPDBs=3`, the end result will be PDB1, PDB2, and PDB3, which will be created from the default PDB$SEED. The command used to execute the DBCA, using the response file cdb2.rsp in silent mode is shown here:

```
dbca -createDatabase -responseFile /home/oracle/responsefiles/cdb2.rsp -silent
```

The end result of the command is a CDB database with one PDB, located on file system–based storage with archive logging enabled. For more details, you can always review the log files generated under the cfgtoollogs/dbca subdirectory located in the $ORACLE_BASE location.

NOTE
To remove a running database, such as CDB1, dbca can be used: `dbca -deleteDatabase -sourceDB CDB1 -silent`. *But be careful when invoking this command on a running instance, because it will shut it down and remove all datafiles. But the most important part: it will remove all the datafiles and it will remove any known backups. This might not be your desired outcome when executing this command.*

Using the DBCA CLI Without Response Files   Instead of using a response file, which contains all the options, you can specify the key-value pairs as arguments to the `dbca` executable. Let's take the first example from earlier to see how this works. Using the values in the response file, we can rewrite this as follows. (To make it easier to read, the format with the \ line delimiter is used.)

```
dbca -createDatabase \
-silent \
-automaticMemoryManagement false \
-characterSet AL32UTF8 \
-createAsContainerDatabase true \
-datafileDestination +DATA \
-enableArchive true \
-gdbName CDB1.orademo.net \
-nationalCharacterSet AL16UTF16 \
-numberOfPDBs 2 \
-pdbAdminPassword Password12345 \
-pdbName PDB \
-recoveryAreaDestination +FRA \
-redoLogFileSize 100 \
-storageType ASM \
-sysPassword Password12345 \
-systemPassword Password12345 \
-templateName General_Purpose.dbc \
-totalMemory 850 \
-useOMF true
```

This method of creating a CDB database works in both 12.1.0.x and 12.2.0.x; however, a small number of options such as `-enableArchive` and `-useOMF` are not available in 12.1.0.x. This method is a quick-and-easy way to establish container databases along with a number of required pluggable databases.

Using SQL*Plus
If you are looking at creating customized configurations, particularly when certain database options are not required in the database, using SQL*Plus might be a good

option. However, before doing this, you should first take note of the options provided by the DBCA—and this is where the DBCA CLI can be extremely useful. You can actually use the `-generateScripts` option to let the DBCA create scripts for you, and then review and update them before executing them manually. If we take the earlier CDB1 database creation example, you would add `-generateScripts` and `scriptDest` to the command, which will result in the database creation scripts being created in the /u01/app/oracle/admin/CDB1/scripts directory:

```
dbca -generateScripts \
-scriptDest /u01/app/oracle/admin/CDB1/scripts
-silent \
…
```

You can then review or update these settings and remove options, for example, if needed. Then simply execute the CDB1.sh master script created in the designated scripts folder to invoke the process. This is an easy way to prepare the database creations scripts, but let's review some of the manual processes at a high level.

The steps to create a CDB database using SQL*Plus may look similar to what you would have performed for non-CDB databases, but a closer look at the details reveals a number of new options—or steps—to be performed when creating a CDB. At a high level these are as follows:

- Create a password file - `orapw<SID>`.
- Create a parameter file - init<SID>.ora.
- Set the parameter enable_pluggable_database=TRUE.
- Start the new instance using the parameter file.
- Execute the CREATE DATABASE statement.
- Include the ENABLE PLUGGABLE DATABASE clause.
- Create the database catalog and options required.

The following example will take you through the high-level steps to create a CDB manually using SQL*Plus.

Example: Creating a CDB Using SQL*Plus In this example, a CDB database called CDB2 will be created using SQL*Plus. The database will be using Oracle ASM as default storage with disk group +DATA as the primary location for the database files and disk group +FRA for the recovery area.

Step 1: Prerequisite steps

If you are using role separation when installing your Oracle Database software, which means the Grid Infrastructure (GI) is installed as a different user, such as grid, and the database software is installed as the oracle user, for example, and if you have not created any databases yet, ensure that you set the correct permission on the Oracle executable inside the Oracle Database software home to allow access to ASM storage. In most cases, the ASM disks would be owned by the grid user with the default group set as asmadmin.

Oracle has made this easier for you by introducing the setasmgidwrap in 11*g*, and it is still available and used in Oracle Database 12*c*. This utility is located in the GI home and should be executed while logged in as the grid user. An example of the command to be executed is shown next:

```
/u01/app/12.2.0/bin/setasmgidwrap o=/u01/app/oracle/product/12.2.0/dbhome_1/bin/oracle
```

As part of the prerequisite steps, make sure you create the required directories, as follows:

```
cd /u01/app/oracle/admin/CDB2
mkdir adump dpdump pfile scripts
```

If you are using ASM storage create the required base directory for the database in the ASM disk groups. This can be done in a number of ways, one of which is to run these two SQL statements while connected to the ASM instance:

```
SQL> alter diskgroup DATA add directory '+DATA/CDB2';
SQL> alter diskgroup FRA add directory '+FRA/CDB2';
```

Step 2: Create a basic parameter file

Remember that some values can easily be adjusted following the creation of the CDB, and therefore in most cases it is recommended that you start with a basic parameter file. Then, once you have the database up and running, you can adjust the values as required.

Because we are creating a CDB database, it is important to ensure that the enable_pluggable_database=TRUE is specified in the parameter file. As mentioned earlier, this database will be making use of ASM. Note that the control file parameter values will be added once the database is created. The parameter file initCDB2.ora is created with the options that follow and saved in the $ORACLE_BASE/admin/CDB2/pfile/ directory.

```
log_archive_format=%t_%s_%r.arc
db_block_size=8192
open_cursors=300
db_domain=orademo.net
```

```
db_name="CDB2"
db_create_file_dest="+DATA"
db_create_online_log_dest_1=+DATA
db_create_online_log_dest_2=+FRA
db_recovery_file_dest="+FRA"
db_recovery_file_dest_size=10g
instance_name=CDB2
compatible=12.2.0.0.0
diagnostic_dest=/u01/app/oracle
nls_language="AMERICAN"
nls_territory="AMERICA"
processes=320
sga_target=1512M
audit_file_dest="/u01/app/oracle/admin/CDB2/adump"
audit_trail=db
remote_login_passwordfile=EXCLUSIVE
dispatchers="(PROTOCOL=TCP) (SERVICE=CDB2XDB)"
pga_aggregate_target=512m
undo_tablespace=UNDOTBS1
enable_pluggable_database=true
```

Step 3: Update /etc/oratab file

This step is optional, but if you are using UNIX-based systems, updating the oratab file is highly recommended. This will make it easy for you to switch between database environments, especially if you have multiple Oracle Database software installations on the same system.

On Oracle Linux, the oratab file is located at /etc/oratab. The following entry is added for the CDB2 database:

```
CDB2:/u01/app/oracle/product/12.2.0/dbhome_1:N
```

Once you have added the entry, you can make use of the oraenv utility to set the correct environment. Run the command . oraenv, and when asked to provide the ORACLE_SID, specify **CDB2**. You will notice that the required environment variables such as ORACLE_HOME will now be set. Here's an example:

```
oracle@linux3[/home/oracle]: . oraenv
ORACLE_SID = [CDB1] ? CDB2
The Oracle base remains unchanged with value /u01/app/oracle
```

Step 4: Set the correct environment for the catcon.pl script execution

This brings us to an interesting point: the catcon.pl script. This script will be discussed in more detail at the end of this chapter.

> **NOTE**
> *As of 12.2.0.x, the default Perl version that is shipped with the Oracle Database software is 5.22.*

The following commands are executed to set the correct `PATH` and `PERL5LIB` environment variable values:

```
export PERL5LIB=$ORACLE_HOME/rdbms/admin:$PERL5LIB
export PATH=$ORACLE_HOME/bin:$ORACLE_HOME/perl/bin:$PATH
```

Step 5: Create a password file

There are a few new options introduced in Oracle Database 12c, including a new password file format:

```
orapwd file=$ORACLE_HOME/dbs/orapwCDB2 force=y format=12 password=Password1234
```

Step 6: Start the Database instance in nomount state with pfile

Start the database using the parameter file created in Step 2 in a nomount state:

```
SQL> connect / as sysdba
SQL> startup nomount pfile='/u01/app/oracle/admin/CDB2/pfile/initCDB2.ora';
```

We now get to the `CREATE DATABASE` statement, and because we are using OMF, there is no need to specify datafile names and locations. The key words to notice are `ENABLE PLUGGABLE DATABASE`.

```
CREATE DATABASE "CDB2"
MAXINSTANCES 8
MAXLOGHISTORY 1
MAXLOGFILES 16
MAXLOGMEMBERS 3
MAXDATAFILES 1024
DATAFILE SIZE 700M AUTOEXTEND ON NEXT 20M MAXSIZE UNLIMITED EXTENT MANAGEMENT LOCAL
SYSAUX DATAFILE SIZE 700M AUTOEXTEND ON NEXT 20M MAXSIZE UNLIMITED
SMALLFILE DEFAULT TEMPORARY TABLESPACE TEMP TEMPFILE SIZE 1G AUTOEXTEND ON NEXT 100M
MAXSIZE 5G
SMALLFILE UNDO TABLESPACE "UNDOTBS1" DATAFILE SIZE 501M AUTOEXTEND ON NEXT  100M
MAXSIZE 5G
CHARACTER SET AL32UTF8
NATIONAL CHARACTER SET AL16UTF16
LOGFILE GROUP 1   SIZE 100M,
        GROUP 2   SIZE 100M,
        GROUP 3   SIZE 100M
USER SYS IDENTIFIED BY Password1234 USER SYSTEM IDENTIFIED BY Password1234
ENABLE PLUGGABLE DATABASE;
```

If you're using non-OMF, the `SEED FILE_NAME_CONVERT` parameter can be used to specify a location for the PDB$SEED datafiles—here's an example:

```
...
ENABLE PLUGGABLE DATABASE
SEED file_name_convert = ('/u01/app/oracle/oradata/CDB1,'/u01/app/
oracle/oradata/CDB1/SEED');
```

> **NOTE**
> *When you're creating a CDB database, always make sure you specify high enough value for `MAXDATAFILES`.*

When executing the `CREATE DATABASE` statement, you can ignore the following error: "ORA-06553: PLS-213: package STANDARD not accessible." This occurs because catalog objects have not been created yet.

Notice the control files created after the `CREATE DATABASE` statement. You will need to update the parameter file to include their location and names. Use `show parameter control_files` to obtain the created control file names. In this example, the control files were

```
'+DATA/CDB2/CONTROLFILE/current.266.903389817'
```

and

```
'+FRA/CDB2/CONTROLFILE/current.297.903389817'
```

The following can be used to add the control file names to the parameter file:

```
echo "control_files='+DATA/CDB2/CONTROLFILE/current.266.903389817', '+FRA/CDB2/
CONTROLFILE/current.297.903389817'" >> /u01/app/oracle/admin/CDB2/pfile/initCDB2.ora
```

> **NOTE**
> *The SEED pluggable database (PDB$SEED) is created as part of the `CREATE DATABASE` statement. The sql.bsq is executed, which will run dcore.bsq twice—once for the root container and once for the SEED container. This was noted when we reviewed the alert log during database creation and reviewed the dcore.bsq script.*

Step 7: Add default USERS tablespace

Here's how to add a default USERS tablespace to the CDB$ROOT:

```
CREATE SMALLFILE TABLESPACE "USERS" LOGGING
DATAFILE  SIZE 5M AUTOEXTEND ON NEXT  10M MAXSIZE UNLIMITED  EXTENT
MANAGEMENT LOCAL  SEGMENT SPACE MANAGEMENT  AUTO;
ALTER DATABASE DEFAULT TABLESPACE "USERS";
```

Step 8: Open the PDB$SEED pluggable database

We are now getting to one of the interesting parts—the SEED database. To enable you to open or close the SEED database, you have to alter the session and set _oracle_script=true;. Once this is done, you will be able to close and then open the SEED database:

```
SQL> alter session set "_oracle_script"=true;
SQL> alter pluggable database pdb$seed close;
SQL> alter pluggable database pdb$seed open;
```

Once this is done, both the ROOT and SEED containers will be open read/write, allowing you to continue creating the database catalog and loading the required options.

Step 9: Create catalog and load options—catcdb.sql

The next step is to run the catcdb.sql script located in $ORACLE_HOME/rdbms/admin. This script will make use of the catcon.pl script and will create the catalog and load the default options.

> **NOTE**
> *The catcdb.sql script was missing in the initial 12.1.0.1 release and was later added as part of the pat set updates—12.1.0.1.4 DB PSU and higher.*

The catcdb.sql script can be run as follows (using the SYS user):

```
SQL> @$ORACLE_HOME/rdbms/admin/catcdb.sql
```

This script can take a long time to run. It will ask for the SYS and SYSTEM users' passwords and run the required scripts to create the catalog and load the default options. If you do require or want to customize the CDB options loaded, you can use the catcon.pl script to create the catalog and load the required options. The bare minimum recommended (options) for a CDB environment is to run the catalog.sql, catproc.sql, and catoctk.sql scripts. An example execution of one of these scripts is shown here:

```
perl $ORACLE_HOME/rdbms/admin/catcon.pl -n 1 -l $ORACLE_BASE/admin/CDB2 -v  -b catalog -U SYS/Password1234 $ORACLE_HOME/rdbms/admin/catalog.sql
```

These are the minimum recommended options, but for most configurations, it is highly recommended that you use the catcdb.sql script and load all the default options such as Oracle JVM and Oracle Text.

> **NOTE**
> *If you want more information on loading only certain options, review MOS note 2001512.1*

Step 10: Lock/expire all unused accounts (optional)

From a security point of view, it is recommended that at this stage you lock all accounts that will not be used. This should be done in the CDB$ROOT as well as the PDB$SEED. To perform these tasks on the PDB$SEED, follow these high level steps:

```
SQL> alter session set "_oracle_script"=true;
SQL> alter pluggable database pdb$seed close;
SQL> alter pluggable database pdb$seed open;
```

Next, run the required commands to lock unused users in the CDB$ROOT, followed by locking the required users in the PDB$SEED as well. This can be done by first setting the container to PDB$SEED:

```
SQL> alter session set container=pdb$seed;
```

Once the required commands to lock unused users in the PDB$SEED were executed sucessfully, you can set the container back to CDB$ROOT:

```
SQL> alter session set container=cdb$root;
```

You can also close the PDB$SEED at this stage if required:

```
SQL> alter pluggable database pdb$seed close;
SQL> alter session set "_oracle_script"=false;
```

This gives you some insight into how you can customize the PDB$SEED pluggable database.

Step 11: Create a spfile from the pfile created in Step 2

One of the final steps is to create a server parameter file (spfile) from the parameter file you created in step 2. This is the command:

```
SQL> create spfile from pfile='/u01/app/oracle/admin/CDB2/pfile/initCDB2.ora';
```

The spfile can also be created inside ASM:

```
SQL> create spfile='+DATA' from pfile='/u01/app/oracle/admin/CDB2/pfile/initCDB2.ora';
```

In this example, the end result is a spfile being created in +DATA/CDB2/PARAMETERFILE/ spfile.268.903390805.

Step 12: Recompile all invalid objects

This is a highly recommended option and should be a well-known step to most DBAs. This script we are referring to is utrlp.sql. It is recommended that you make use of the catcon.pl script to ensure that you run this against the CDB$ROOT as well as the PDB$SEED, which at this stage is the only pluggable database in the CDB2 database.

Step 13: Optional—Add the database to Oracle Restart

This last step is optional. If GI is installed, you can make use of Oracle Restart. This enables the option to start or stop the database as part of a system restart. If offers a number of other advantages, but these are probably the most well-known reasons for using Oracle Restart.

The `srvctl` command is used to perform these tasks:

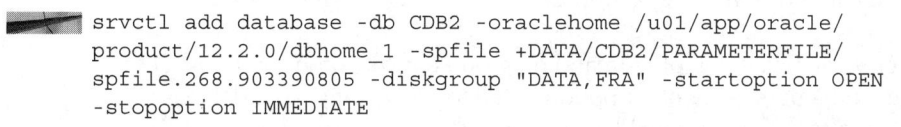

```
srvctl add database -db CDB2 -oraclehome /u01/app/oracle/
product/12.2.0/dbhome_1 -spfile +DATA/CDB2/PARAMETERFILE/
spfile.268.903390805 -diskgroup "DATA,FRA" -startoption OPEN
-stopoption IMMEDIATE
```

Step 14: Create a pluggable database

At this stage, we haven't created a CDB database, which includes the root and the SEED pluggable database. Before getting into the details in the next section, we can list the basic CREATE PLUGGABLE DATABASE statement here for completeness of the example:

```
CREATE PLUGGABLE DATABASE PDB1
    ADMIN USER PDBADMIN IDENTIFIED BY "Password1234" ROLES=(CONNECT);
```

This will create the PDB called PDB1 based on the PDB$SEED PDB. Once created, the PDB will be in a mounted state. To open it, execute the following:

```
ALTER PLUGGABLE DATABASE PDB1 OPEN;
```

The next section continues with the options for creating the PDB. Note that if you were following the DBCA options discussed earlier, you can create PDBs as part of the CDB creation. This is one reason why using the DBCA is highly recommended and used by most DBAs: it takes away most of the complexities and helps keep it simple.

Creating a Pluggable Database

Instead of jumping straight into the PDB creation process, let's take a look at the surroundings and context before diving into the details.

In a minimal Oracle PDB creation, you end up with only the CDB$ROOT and PDB$SEED PDBs. This is probably the best way to start. Why? Imagine, for example, that you are planning to create 50 PDBs and want them all to look exactly the same. You could create a simple golden image first, and then, when you need more databases, simply clone the golden image to create any new ones.

You can create new pluggable databases using a variety of tools:

- SQL*Plus
- Database Configuration Assistant (DBCA)
- SQL Developer
- Oracle Enterprise Manager Database Express
- Oracle Enterprise Manager Cloud Control

In Chapter 9, we will cover plug-in and plug-out, conversions from non-CDB to PDB, cloning, and a number of other options used to create pluggable databases. We will also discuss the new proxy PDB option introduced in release 12.2. In this chapter, the focus will be on helping you get started in creating PDBs using two basic methods:

- **Create a new PDB from the CDB SEED (PDB$SEED)**   This is used mainly for new configurations. A PDB is created based on the template SEED database called PDB$SEED, which resides inside the same CDB. This method is fast, easy, and seems almost instantaneous.

- **Clone a PDB within the same CDB (also known as the local clone method)**   This can be extremely useful in many scenarios, such as cloning an application PDB to create a secondary PDB on which you can test upgrade scripts prior to executing them the production PDB. There are a number of requirements when using this method, including that the cloned PDB name must be unique within the same CDB.

Create a New PDB from PDB$SEED

This method, as illustrated in Figure 2-5, is a quick and easy way to create a PDB based on PDB$SEED. During this process, the new PDB is generated by creating a copy of the PDB$SEEED, which should be in read-only mode.

When using OMF, the process is simplified, and a basic CREATE PLUGGABLE DATABASE command like the following can be used to create a PDB from the CDB SEED:

```
create pluggable database PDB1
admin user PDB1ADMIN identified by Password12345
ROLES = (CONNECT);
```

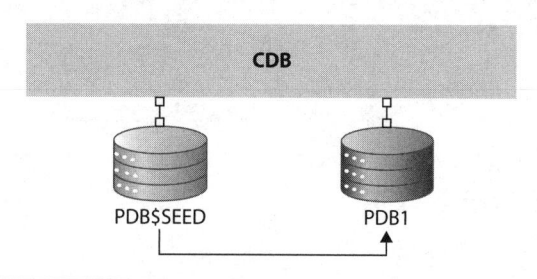

FIGURE 2-5. *Create A PDB from PDB$SEED*

The end result of this statement is the creation of PDB1, a copy of the CDB SEED—PDB$SEED. The default PDB administrator is created as PDB1ADMIN, and the default role, assigned locally to the PDB_DBA role, is CONNECT. A number of additional clauses can be used with the CREATE PLUGGABLE DATABASE statement and provide the ability to specify a number of customization options for the newly created PDB. Some of the key clauses include these:

- AS APPLICATION CONTAINER
- AS CLONE
- AS SEED
- CREATE_FILE_DEST
- DEFAULT TABLESPACE
- FILE_NAME_CONVERT
- HOST
- PORT
- NOCOPY, COPY, MOVE
- NO DATA
- PARALLEL
- ROLES
- SNAPSHOT COPY
- SOURCE_FILE_DIRECTORY

- SOURCE_FILE_NAME_CONVERT
- STANDBYS
- STORAGE
- TEMPFILE REUSE
- USER_TABLESPACES

> **NOTE**
> *Throughout this book we will reference a number of these clauses, but for full details on each, refer to the "Oracle Database SQL Language Reference" for Oracle Database 12c Releases 1 and 2.*

The CREATE_FILE_DEST clause can be specified as part of the create statement if you want to overwrite the default OMF location, which is specified by the CDB's DB_CREATE_FILE_DEST instance parameter. For example, if the requirement is to place the PDB on a different ASM disk group called +PDBDATA, the CREATE PLUGGABLE DATABASE statement can be adjusted as follows:

```
create pluggable database PDB1
admin user PDB1ADMIN identified by Password12345 ROLES = (CONNECT)
CREATE_FILE_DEST='+PDBDATA';
```

The end result will be that an OMF file structure will be created in the disk group +PDBDATA. So, for example, after the command is executed, PDB1 was created with CON_ID=4:

```
SQL> select name from v$datafile where con_id=4;
Name
--------------------------------------------------------------------------------
+PDBDATA/CDB1/2B674893CA800203E053E902000A5C20/DATAFILE/system.296.903476189
+PDBDATA /CDB1/2B674893CA800203E053E902000A5C20/DATAFILE/sysaux.293.903476189
```

If OMF is not used, the FILE_NAME_CONVERT parameter must be included when creating a new PDB from the CDB SEED. Creating a new PDB1 in a CDB, which does not make use of OMF, is illustrated next:

```
create pluggable database PDB1
admin user pdb1admin identified by Password12345 roles=(connect)
file_name_convert=('/u01/app/oracle/oradata/CDB2/pdbseed','/u01/app/oracle/oradata/CDB2/pdb1');
```

The end result here is that the new PDB is created as a copy of the PDB$SEED, and its files are located in the directory /u01/app/oracle/oradata/CDB2/pdb1.

Before moving on to the next section, let's have a look at a slightly more complex case using a number of the clauses available in the `create` statement:

```
create pluggable database PDB2
admin user PDB2ADMIN identified by Password12345 roles=(connect)
file_name_convert=('/u01/app/oracle/oradata/CDB2/pdbseed'
                  ,'/u01/app/oracle/oradata/CDB2/pdb2')
default tablespace USERS
  datafile '/u01/app/oracle/oradata/CDB2/pdb2/users01.dbf' size 10M
  autoextend on next 100M maxsize 20G
storage (maxsize 100G max_shared_temp_size 5G)
```

Breaking down the example, observe the following:

- We are creating a new PDB called PDB2.
- The PDB admin user is called PDB2ADMIN and a password is supplied.
- The CONNECT role is assigned to the local PDB_DBA role.
- The FILE_NAME_CONVERT clause is specified to ensure that the new PDB subfolder pdb2 is used.
- A new default permanent tablespace is created for the new PDB, the data file name is specified, and the size of this file is 10M with the option to grow to 20G.
- The STORAGE clause is used to limit the size of the PDB to a maximum size of 100G, and only a maximum of 5G shared temporary space can be used by this PDB.

Create a New PDB Using the Local Clone Method

The second method is creating a new PDB using the clone option (see Figure 2-6) from a local PDB located in the same CDB. This method is also referred to as creating a local clone.

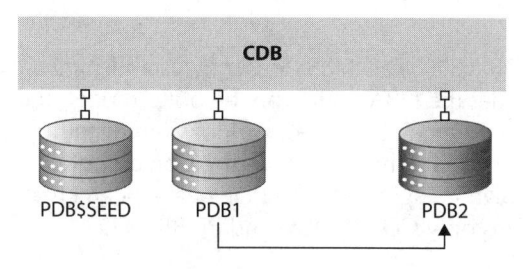

FIGURE 2-6. *Create PDB2 from PDB1 (clone PDB1)*

When using this approach, take note of the following:

- If using version 12.1.0.x, the source PDB must be in a read-only state. (As of 12.2.0.x, the source PDB can be open, as long as the CDB is in ARCHIVELOG mode with local UNDO enabled.)
- Each PDB in a CDB must be uniquely identifiable.
- Once the clone is complete, the new PDB must be opened read-write at least once to allow further operations.

When using the local cloning process, the datafiles of a source PDB (which is in a read-only state in 12.1.0.x) are read and then copied to a new uniquely identifiable PDB.

Performing a local clone in an OMF environment is easy and can be done without any additional clauses being specified. For example, to create a new PDB5 database as a clone from PDB1 in CDB1, we can execute the following two statements, cloning and then opening the new PDB in read-write mode:

```
SQL> create pluggable database PDB5 from PDB1;
SQL> alter pluggable database PDB5 open;
```

When using a non-OMF environment, the `create` statement needs to include the additional `FILE_NAME_CONVERT` clause, as follows:

```
SQL> create pluggable database PDB5 from PDB2
     file_name_convert=('/u01/app/oracle/oradata/CDB2/pdb2',
                        '/u02/oracle/oradata/CDB2/pdb5');
SQL> alter pluggable database pdb5 open;
```

Create a PDB Using SQL Developer

As mentioned in a previous section, a number of tools can be used to create PDBs. One of the utilities that is growing rapidly in popularity, and we highly recommend it if you have not tried it, is Oracle SQL Developer (Figure 2-7).

This example will use SQL Developer to create a PDB called PDB1 from the CDB1 SEED.

1. Log into the CDB (CDB1) as the SYS user by establishing a connection to the database under the DBA option on the bottom right of the main SQL Developer screen. Once connected, various administration options and areas will be listed, with the first one being Container Database. In this example, as shown in Figure 2-7, no PDBs have been created, so the CDB1 database contains only CDB$ROOT and PDB$SEED.

Chapter 2: Creating the Database **61**

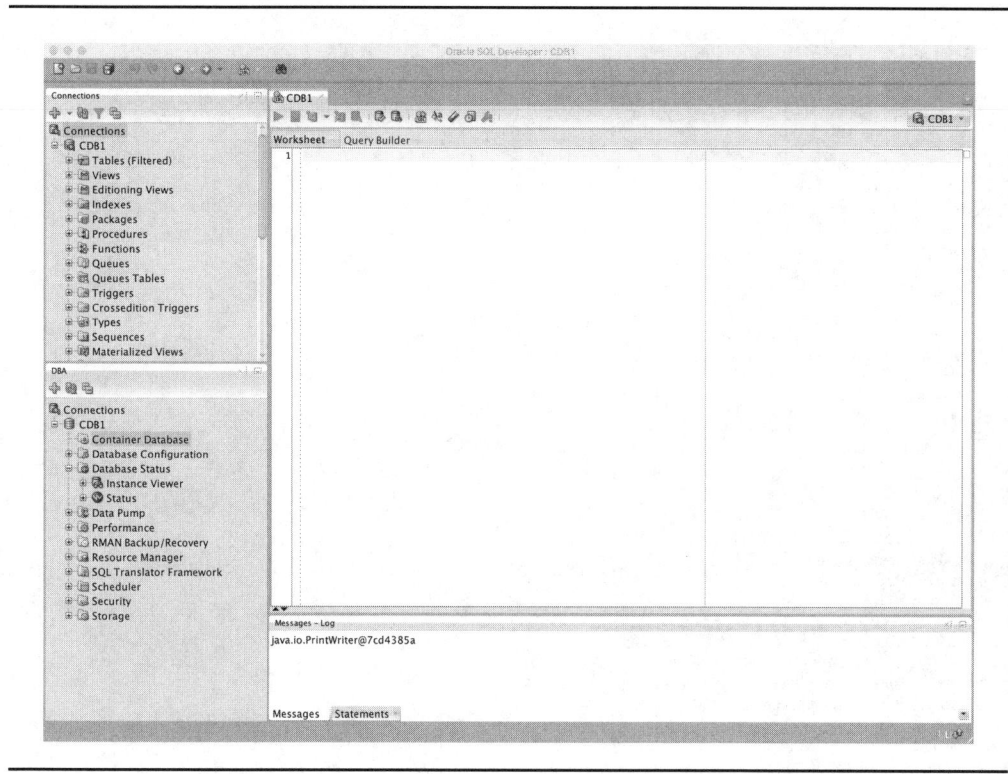

FIGURE 2-7. *Oracle SQL Developer*

2. Right-click Container Database, and you will be presented with a number of options, as shown in Figure 2-8. Select Create Pluggable Database.

3. In the next screen, add a new PDB name, Admin Name, and Password, and specify any storage requirements. As shown in Figure 2-9, a number of options are available with regard to the storage configuration. In the example, we will leave them set to the defaults, supplying only the new PDB name PDB1, and the admin username and password. As OMF is used in this configuration, the File Name Conversions are set at the default, None.

4. Optionally, review the SQL tab shown in Figure 2-10.

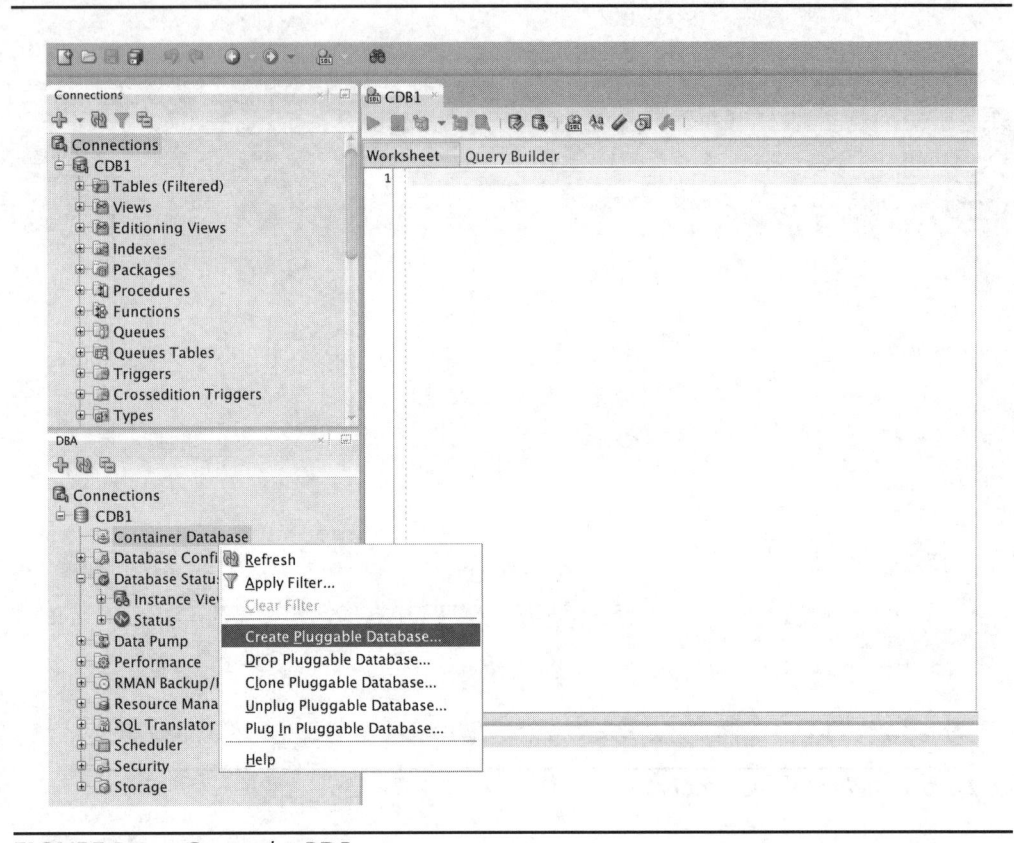

FIGURE 2-8. *Create the PDB.*

5. Click Apply and the new PDB will be created. If you now refresh the screen you will see that the new PDB1 is displayed under the Container Database folder. As shown in Figure 2-11, when you select PDB1, more information about the PDB is displayed on the right side of the screen. We can see that the PDB is currently MOUNTED and not yet open read-write.

6. Open the newly created PDB read-write by selecting and right-clicking the PDB. Choose Modify State, and a new screen will enable you to set the PDB to a specific open mode (state)—see Figure 2-12.

7. Choose the required state from the State Option drop-down list (READ WRITE, READ ONLY, RESTRICTED), and click Apply.

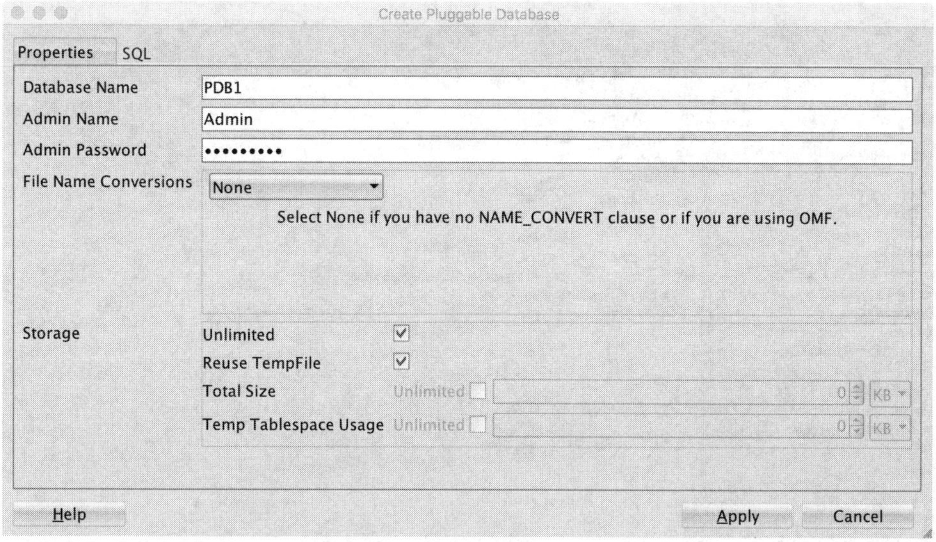
Create Pluggable Database
Properties
SQL
Database Name
PDB1
Admin Name
Admin
Admin Password
File Name Conversions
None
Select None if you have no NAME_CONVERT clause or if you are using OMF.
Storage
Unlimited
Reuse TempFile
Total Size
Temp Tablespace Usage
Help
Apply
Cancel

FIGURE 2-9. *Create PDB properties.*

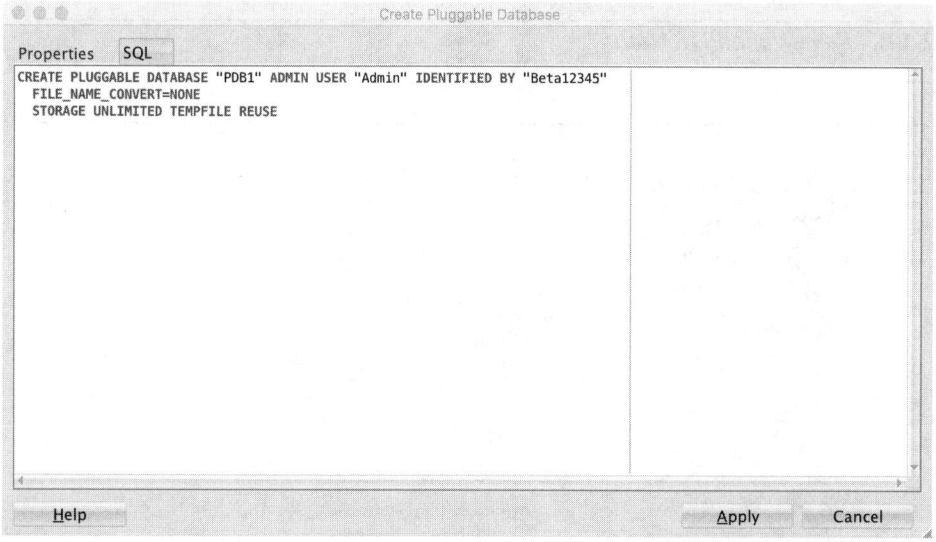
Create Pluggable Database
Properties
SQL
CREATE PLUGGABLE DATABASE "PDB1" ADMIN USER "Admin" IDENTIFIED BY "Beta12345"
FILE_NAME_CONVERT=NONE
STORAGE UNLIMITED TEMPFILE REUSE
Help
Apply
Cancel

FIGURE 2-10. *Review the SQL statement.*

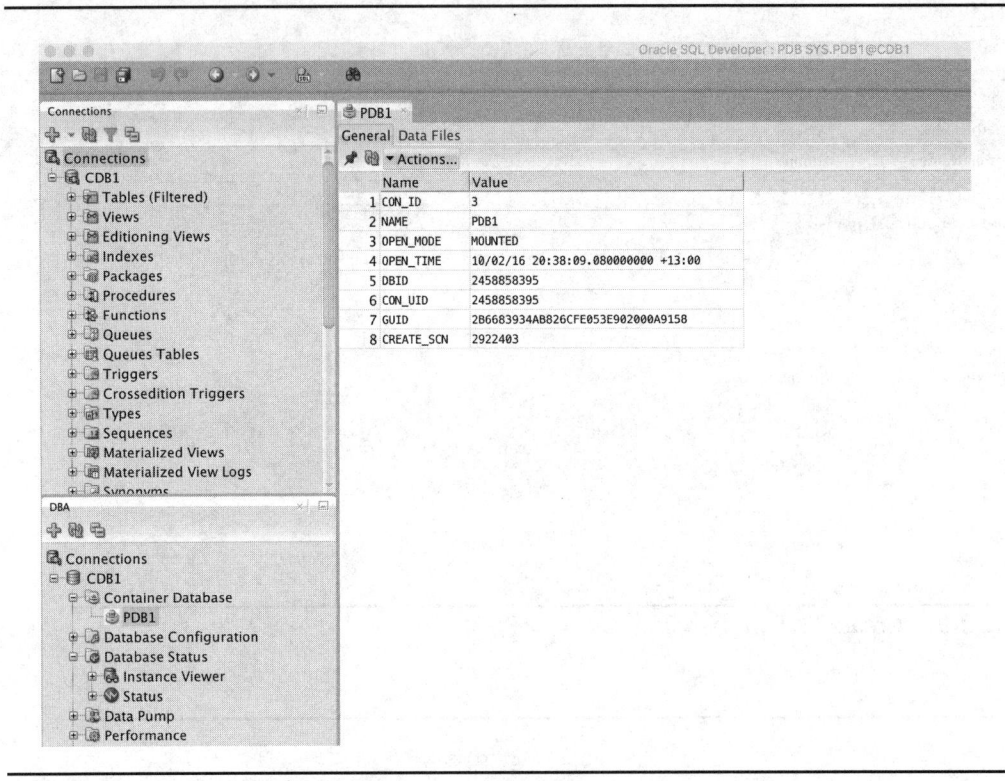

FIGURE 2-11. *Review the PDB status.*

FIGURE 2-12. *Modify the PDB state.*

Create a PDB Using the DBCA

You can also use the DBCA to create new PDBs. As with the creation of CDBs, there are two options for doing this: the GUI or the CLI.

When using the DBCA GUI, you are presented with the option of creating a PDB, along with other options. Figure 2-13 shows these options on the DBCA opening screen.

Choose Manage Pluggable Databases and you will be guided through a eight-step process to create a new PDB.

Using the DBCA is a straightforward method in which you click through a number of screens and provide basic input required to create a new PDB. But if you are looking at creating a new PDB from the CDB SEED, using SQL*Plus, SQL Developer, or the DBCA CLI (shown next) might be a much faster way to achieve this.

When using the DBCA CLI, you can use the `-createPluggableDatabase` command option. As mentioned earlier, using the `-help` keyword with this option will display all the available arguments. Following is a basic example that demonstrates

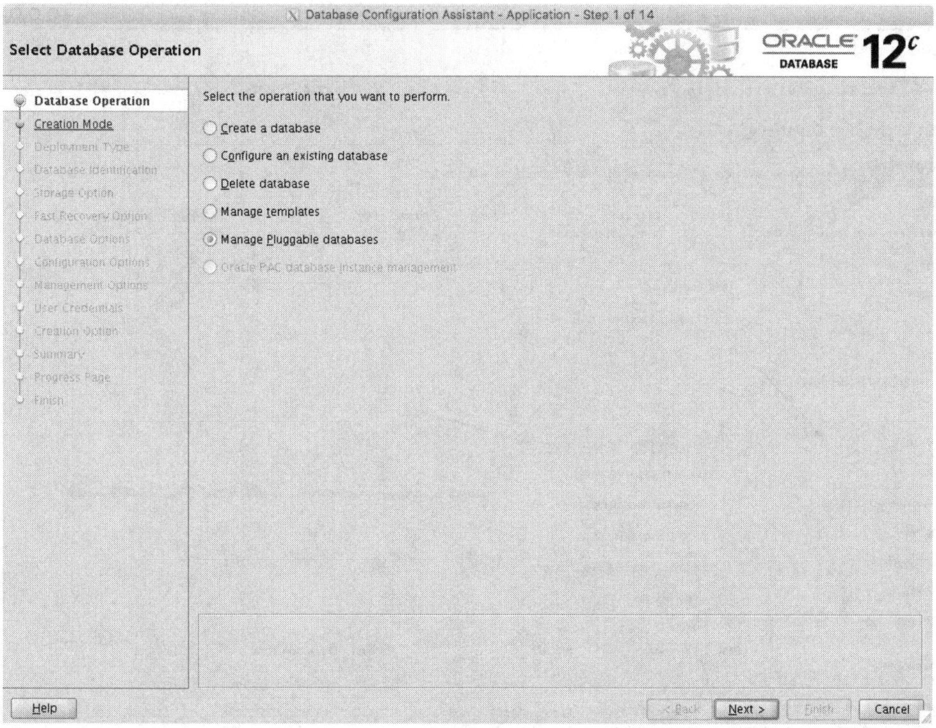

FIGURE 2-13. *DBCA—Manage Pluggable Database*

the creation of a PDB database called PDB9 in a CDB called CDB1, which uses ASM and OMF:

```
dbca -createPluggableDatabase \
-silent \
-sourceDB CDB1 \
-pdbName PDB9 \
-createPDBFrom DEFAULT \
-pdbAdminUsername PDB9ADMIN \
-pdbAdminPassword Password12345
```

Create a PDB Using Cloud Control

Another option for creating ODBs is Enterprise Manager Cloud Control. Using this method is straightforward, because the tool will guide you through the process. From the Oracle Database drop-down menu path, navigate to Provisioning, and then select the Provision Pluggable Databases option. This will start the process of creating a PDB. Figures 2-14 and 2-15 show the start of the wizard-driven process that assists in creating a PDB.

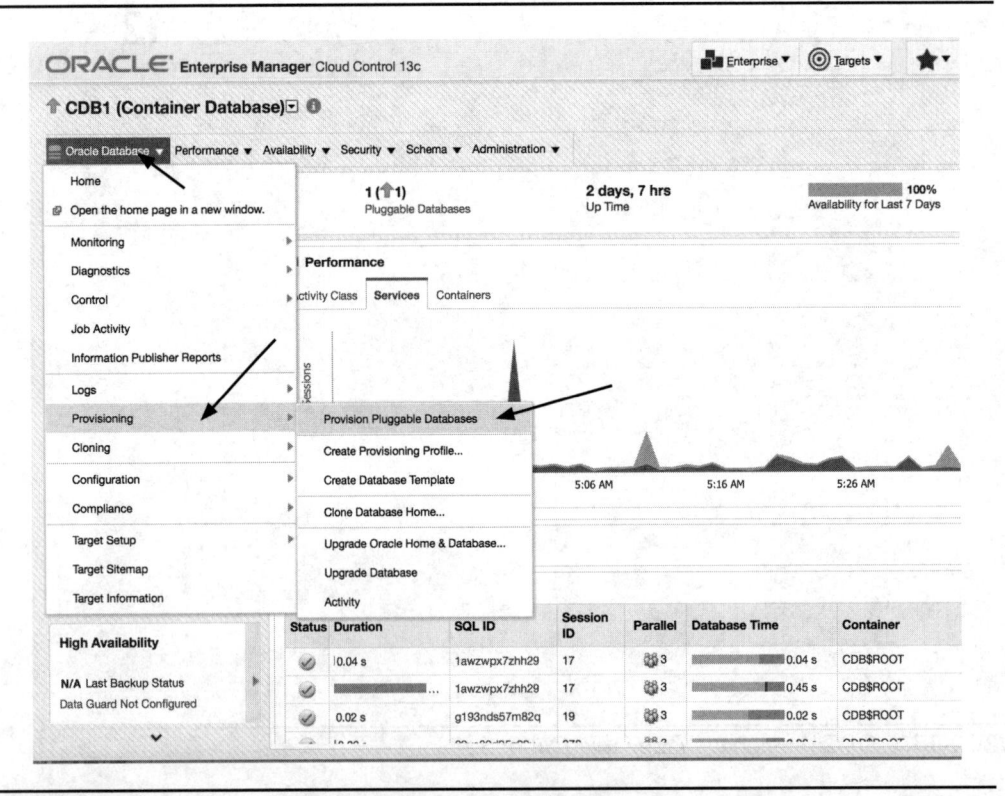

FIGURE 2-14. *Choose Provision Pluggable Databases*

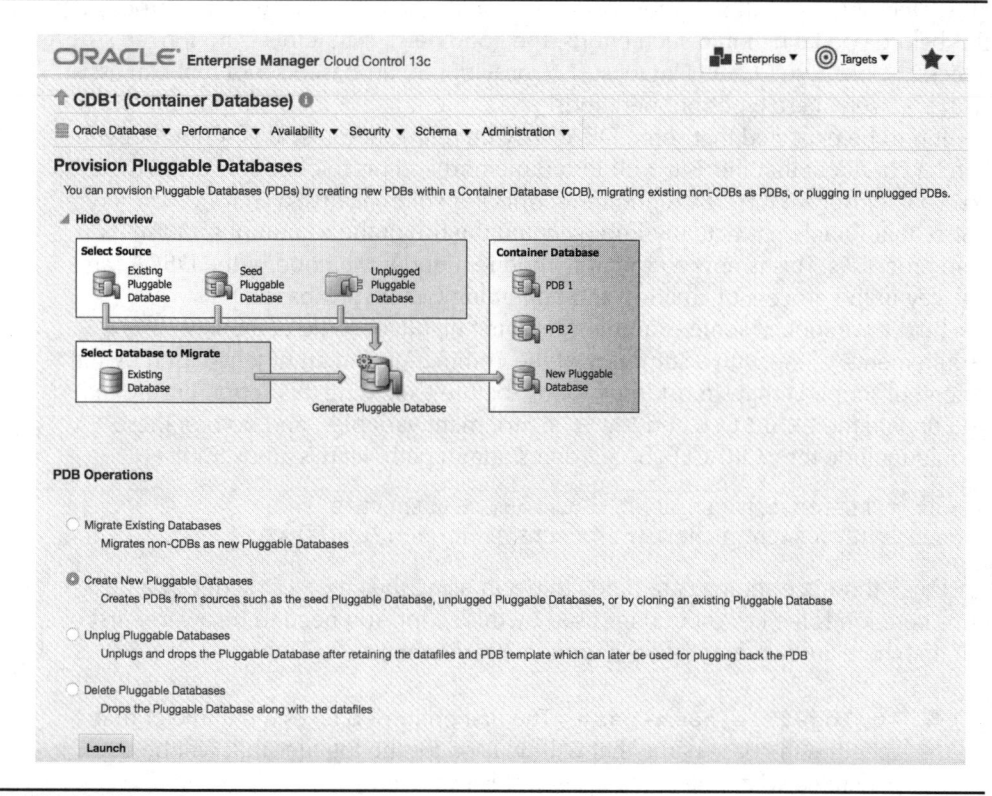

FIGURE 2-15. *Creating a new PDB*

For more information on using Cloud Control, refer to the online documentation for EM Cloud Control 13*c*.

Using the catcon.pl Script

Imagine that you have a CDB with 100 PDBs, and each database is used for the same application, but by 100 different customers, so that each has its own copy of the data. These might be production customers, or perhaps the end customer is 100 developers, again each with his or her own copy of the application database (PDB). The application vendor issues an update script to be executed against every PDB to upgrade to the latest application version.

This entails running a single script, which could be either basic or complex, on each of these PDBs. Needless to say, this can be a time-consuming job, perhaps alleviated only by writing some clever additional scripts to assist with the process. But before you launch into such efforts, the good news is that this is no longer necessary, because Oracle Database 12c provides a Perl-based script that can assist with precisely these types of operations!

It is to be expected that some DBAs may be reluctant to use this script, but you can be confident that this is a well-tested method and piece of code. Furthermore, if you look closely at the DBCA and the scripts it invokes against a CDB, you will notice that Oracle has actually implemented the use of the catcon.pl script in its own processes. This is now a critical component under the hood of the DBCA, and it is key in the process of creating and upgrading Oracle databases.

Before we look at some examples, let's first highlight some of the key requirements, along with a summary of the commands and arguments, used by the catcon.pl script. Perhaps most importantly, before executing this script, ensure that you update the `PERL5LIB` and `PATH` environment variables, and both of these should include the $ORACLE_BASE/rdbms/admin path. Here's an example:

```
export PERL5LIB=$ORACLE_HOME/rdbms/admin:$PERL5LIB
export PATH=$ORACLE_HOME/bin:$ORACLE_HOME/perl/bin:$PATH
```

Once these are set, you are ready to begin using the catcon.pl script. The next consideration is the key input flags used by this script. You need to be aware, first of all, that there are two mandatory argument requirements:

- **`-b log-file-name-base`** The first option -b takes a parameter that specifies the base name that will be used for the log files that will be generated when the catcon.pl script is executed.

- **`--<sqlplus-script>`** The second option is the name of a SQL*Plus script that should be executed.

Or

- **`--x<sql-statement>`** The second option can be a standalone SQL statement.

Other key arguments for the catcon.pl script include these:

- **`-d`** Directory where script to be executed is located
- **`-l`** Directory to be used for spool files
- **`-c`** Container(s) in which scripts/SQL are to be executed
- **`-C`** Container(s) in which scripts/SQL are *not* to be executed

- **-u** Username/password (optional) to run user-supplied scripts (defaults to / as sysdba)

- **-w** Environment variable that will hold the user password for user specified with -u

- **-U** Username/password (optional) to run internal tasks (defaults to / as sysdba)

- **-W** Environment variable that will hold the user password for user specified with -U

- **-e** Sets echo on while running SQL*Plus scripts

For more detail on the options available, execute the catcon.pl script without any options specified to generate a full usage listing and description of each.

So, for example, to run a script called xyz.sql in all PDBs except CDB$ROOT and PDB$SEED, you would enter the following:

```
export PERL5LIB=$ORACLE_HOME/rdbms/admin:$PERL5LIB
export PATH=$ORACLE_HOME/bin:$ORACLE_HOME/perl/bin:$PATH
cd $ORACLE_HOME/rdbms/admin
perl catcon.pl -e -C 'CDB$ROOT PDB$SEED' -l /home/oracle/logs -b xyz-out -d /home/oracle/sql xyz.sql
```

Summary

This chapter covered the basics to get you started with Oracle Database 12c Multitenant. It detailed the creation of the CDB as well as one or several PDBs. However, there is a lot more to multitenant. What is clear is that some of the benefits and advantages of using multitenant are becoming apparent—especially the ability to create a PDB in a few seconds and the flexibility it can bring to provisioning.

But at this stage you probably have more questions. Should you stay with the old architecture, or move to multitenant? You may not be sure that you can even move to multitenant, but, if possible, how is it done? And what if you are using Standard Edition (SE, SE1 or SE2)—is multitenant even an option? Or perhaps you are using Enterprise Edition and cannot wait to get your hands on the new technology—did you know it is an additional licensed option? The next chapter will assist you in answering these questions, and much more.

CHAPTER 3

Single-Tenant, Multitenant, and Application Containers

In the previous chapter we detailed how to create a container database, an indispensable foundation of the multitenant architecture. However, at this point you may be wondering whether multitenant is for you. Perhaps you have heard the term "multitenant option," which suggests that additional licensing is required, or you exclude yourself because you are running Oracle Database Standard Edition. On the other hand, you are also aware that the old architecture, known as non-CDB (non–container database), is now deprecated. So what should you do?

These are important questions and concerns that we will consider before going on to describe the multitenant features in detail. Of course, to describe what is available with the different editions and options, we will make mention of specific features—but don't worry, because we will return to address the features thoroughly in later chapters.

Multitenant Architecture Is Not an Option

Let's make it clear from the get-go: the multitenant architecture is available in 12c for all editions, with no additional licensing option required. The main characteristic of multitenant is the separation of dictionaries: system metadata and system data are in CDB$ROOT, whereas user data and metadata are in a pluggable database (PDB). This new architecture is defined at the database creation stage with `ENABLE PLUGGABLE DATABASE`. It is available at no additional cost for the Enterprise Edition or Standard Edition. At the time of writing, there is no XE edition for 12c, but we expect that when it is released, it will be multitenant as well.

You need to be aware of one limitation regarding multitenant: You cannot create more than one PDB per CDB unless you have purchased a multitenant option license. This means that without purchasing the option, your multitenant database has at maximum one tenant—it is a *single-tenant configuration*. Although the multitenant architecture was obviously introduced with the multitenant option in view (hence its name), it is also available and usable without this.

If you don't intend to purchase the multitenant option, or if you are using Standard Edition, you may think that you don't need to delve into this new architecture and acquire new skills for its administration. But you need to rethink this approach. In this chapter we will explain the advantages of using a single-tenant database, but before we get to this, there is one fundamental reason to move ahead with it.

Non-CDB Deprecation

Chapter 1 introduced multitenant as a major change in the Oracle Database. There are likely scores of places in the Oracle Database code where the developers had to introduce additional operations for the multitenant context, but the existing code for non-CDB is still there. Obviously, as the software evolves in the future, new features will be implemented on the new architecture as a priority. The old architecture is still supported, so you can create non-CDB databases in 12c and obtain support and fixes, but if you want to benefit from all the latest features (and innovation of development focus), then it is recommended that you move to the multitenant architecture. This is exactly what deprecation means, as it relates to the non-CDB architecture, and the "Oracle Database Upgrade Guide" is clear that "deprecated features are features that are no longer being enhanced but are still supported for the full life of the release."

Is it bad to use deprecated features? Absolutely not! But it's a bad idea to completely ignore new features that are introduced to replace the deprecated ones. For example, when you start work on a brand-new project, the usual recommendation is to avoid using deprecated features, because you want to benefit from all the latest features available, and because deprecated features may become desupported in the foreseeable future. However, if you are upgrading a current application that will likely exist for only a few more years, you probably just want to keep it as it is, without major changes.

For multitenant, the same principle holds, and you probably won't move all your existing production databases to multitenant architecture when upgrading to 12c; instead, you'll retain some of them as non-CDB. Still, it is a good idea that you begin to learn about and create CDB databases, perhaps for a test environment to begin with, so that you build your familiarity with multitenant. With this approach, you have time to learn and adapt your scripts to this new architecture, not because you need it immediately, but because it's sure to be in your future.

Our message about the non-CDB deprecation is this: Don't worry; the non-CDB that you know will still be around for years, and you can stay with it as long as you are not comfortable with multitenant. It is still supported in 12c and will probably continue to be for several future releases. But that should not prevent you from learning and trying out multitenant on noncritical databases.

Noncompatible Features

Another reason to keep the non-CDB architecture for your database is to make use of one of the few features that is not yet supported in multitenant. There are two possible reasons for such a scenario:

- The feature/functionality itself was already deprecated when multitenant arrived, so it has not been enhanced to work in a CDB. This is the case, for example, with Oracle Streams. Oracle has deprecated this and recommends using an additional alternative product, Golden Gate. Oracle Streams is still supported in 12c, but only with the non-CDB architecture. Note that alternatives will be covered in Chapter 13.

- Some new features have been developed independently of multitenant and may not be immediately available in CDB. That was the case with Information Lifecycle Management features (Heat Map and Automatic Data optimization), which arrived in 12.1, but only for non-CDB. This limitation has now been removed with the release of 12.2. Another example is *sharding*, a new feature in 12.2, which is not compatible with multitenant at the time of writing. Even features that are available in multitenant may be available only at the CDB level. This is the case with Real Application Testing in 12.1, for example, which cannot be used at the PDB level, although this limitation has been overcome with the release of 12.2.

NOTE
At the time of writing, features such as Change Notification, Continuous Query Notification, and Client Side Result Cache are not yet available for a CDB in release 12.2.

Single-Tenant in Standard Edition

In the Standard Edition, you don't have access to the multitenant option that allows for more than one user PDB; this is an inherent limitation of this edition. Furthermore, in the Standard Edition, features that are not available are disabled at installation time. For example, the following shows a container database with one pluggable database, PDB, in addition to the seed:

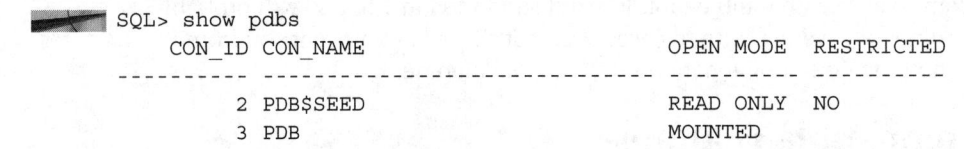

```
SQL> show pdbs
    CON_ID CON_NAME                       OPEN MODE  RESTRICTED
---------- ------------------------------ ---------- ----------
         2 PDB$SEED                       READ ONLY  NO
         3 PDB                            MOUNTED
```

Creating more pluggable databases is explicitly disallowed:

```
SQL> create pluggable database NEWPDB admin user admin identified by oracle
file_name_convert=('pdbseed','newpdb');
create pluggable database NEWPDB admin user admin identified by oracle
ile_name_convert=('pdbseed','newpdb')
                *
ERROR at line 1:
ORA-65010: maximum number of pluggable databases created
```

The maximum number of PDBs in a Standard Edition CDB is two: one PDB$SEED (that you are not allowed to change except for modifying the undo tablespace) and one user PDB.

Data Movement

Given the limited features available in the Standard Edition, you may ask if it's better to have a single-tenant CDB rather than a non-CDB. When you create a CDB, you immediately see the overhead: three containers for only one database, which means more datafiles to store the CDB$ROOT and the PDB$SEED. Multitenant is designed for consolidation, but here we see the opposite, because each database uses more space. But you must remember that multitenant is also beneficial for agility in data movement, and this is a great feature even for single-tenant.

There are three ways in which to transport data. The first is a very flexible, but very slow, method: logical transport through Data Pump. Data is extracted by Data Manipulation Language (DML), target tables are created by Data Definition Language (DDL), rows are inserted by DML, and then indexes are rebuilt. When you want something faster than this, you can use transportable tablespaces, where data is shipped physically with the datafiles and only metadata is created logically. This is generally quick, except when you have thousands of tables, as many enterprise resource planners (ERPs) do, and it still takes considerable time to create those tables, even though most are empty. Note, however, that the transportable tablespaces' import functionality is not available in Standard Edition.

In multitenant architecture, the user metadata is stored separately from the system metadata. Each PDB has its own SYSTEM tablespace that contains this user metadata only, meaning that it can be transported physically. This is a key feature that PDBs provide: the ability to transport by unplug/plug. This mechanism is even superior to transportable tablespaces, which is why Oracle product manager Bryn Llewellyn calls it the "third generation of Data Pump" in his Oracle multitenant white paper. The really good news is that plug/unplug operations are allowed in the Standard Edition and in remote cloning, so you can clone a PDB into a new CDB with a simple command.

Thanks to the agility of PDBs, the small overhead of the CDB structure pales against the ease and efficiency of database movement and cloning operations across servers and versions. This more than makes up for the missing transportable tablespaces functionality in the Standard Edition.

Security

Multitenant has been developed to cater to large numbers of PDBs, such as in cloud environments, and for this reason, many new security and isolation features have been introduced. We will cover those features in Chapter 6, but some of them also are very interesting from the single-tenant perspective, and perhaps the best example is the ALTER SYSTEM lockdown. In a developer database, you may be tempted to give ALTER SYSTEM privileges to the developers in case they want to test new settings, kill their own sessions, and the like. But this privilege is definitely too broad and powerful, as with ALTER SYSTEM you can basically do whatever you like on the system. With the new PDB lockdown profiles you can, alternatively, grant ALTER SYSTEM and enable or disable exactly those operations and access to parameters you deem appropriate.

Lockdown profiles and OS credentials are also very interesting for those applications in which the application owner must be granted powerful privileges. In multitenant, you can give the CREATE DIRECTORY privilege and constrain the absolute path where the PDB users (even the DBA) can create a directory. Multitenant architecture brings a separation of roles between root and the PDB, and you will appreciate this even in the Standard Edition.

Consolidation with Standard Edition 2

Because you can have only one PDB per CDB, you will probably have a number of CDBs on a server. Even among different CDBs, each PDB must have a unique name because, as you will see in Chapter 5, its name will be a service registered to the listener, and you may not want one listener per CDB in this context. Take care when naming CDBs, because you may be tempted to differentiate them with a trailing number, but it is recommended that you ensure that the ORACLE_SID remains unique for each server even when ignoring trailing numerics. Figure 3-1 shows the warning displayed in the Database Configuration Assistant (DBCA).

This advice probably results from Real Application Clusters (RAC) considerations, where the database name includes an instance number suffix. And remember that in Standard Edition 2, you can have high availability, because RAC is still available on a two-socket total cluster.

Because several CDBs are on the same server, you don't want one instance to use all the CPU available. Standard Edition 2 limits each database to run, at maximum, 16 user processes on CPU, but you can lower this by decreasing the `CPU_COUNT` parameter. This *instance caging* was not available in the Standard Edition before 12.1.0.2, but it is now. It's a side effect of the new SE2 limitation that we can turn to our advantage to ensure that critical databases have enough resources.

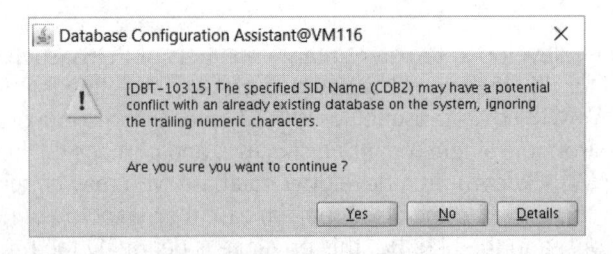

FIGURE 3-1. *Warning when only suffix numbers differ in ORACLE_SID*

Another consideration with several single-tenant CDBs is the overhead of having one PDB$SEED for each CDB. Because PDB$SEED is needed only to create new PDBs, you might surmise that it is not needed after you have created your PDB. Although you may be tempted to drop it, you must remember that dropping this is not a supported operation. However, there is something you can do to avoid to backing up PDB$SEED every day, and that is to configure `BACKUP OPTIMIZATION ON`, so that it will be skipped as any read-only tablespace. Just be careful that you don't have an external expiration policy set that is shorter than the RMAN one if you do this.

We hope that we have convinced you that multitenant is also important in the future of Standard Edition. And even if it seems like a paradox at the outset, you can also consider consolidation with Standard Edition 2 alongside single-tenant agility.

Single-Tenant in Enterprise Edition

If you are using the Enterprise Edition without the multitenant option, you can, and should, run single-tenant container databases. If you haven't read the preceding section about the Standard Edition, you should do so now, because all that has been said there is relevant for Enterprise Edition, and we will only detail here what is possible specifically in Enterprise Edition.

As a sample, here is an operation that can be done in multitenant that you cannot do in a non-CDB:

```
SQL> shutdown;
SQL> alter database open;
```

In non-CDB, or in a CDB at root level, when you close the database, you have to shut down the instance. Here, the statements have been run within a PDB and the shutdown closes only the PDB, but the instance, which is common, is still up. Then it is possible to open the PDB again. You can open and close a PDB as many times as you want without restarting the instance. This may sound inconsequential, but when you think about operations that require mount mode and a closed database, you soon realize its value.

Flashback PDB

The flashback database feature in the Enterprise Edition can revert the state of the database to a previous point in time; this was available only at the CDB level in 12.1. But with the release of 12.2, you can flashback a PDB—this will be covered in Chapter 8.

For now, let's consider a test database in which the developers perform continuous integration tests. They often need to revert to the initial data before each run, but a restore or Data Pump import can take a long time to complete. The quickest way to resume the same set of data is to create a guaranteed restore point for the initial state and execute flashback database between each run. This is a fast operation except when you have to restart the instance. But in multitenant, as outlined in the previous section, this is not required, and you can now close, flashback, and open the database in mere seconds, which makes the operation possible to run hundreds or thousands of times.

Maximum Number of PDBs

With the Enterprise Edition, you must be careful when you create a PDB, because creating more than one PDB will activate the usage of the multitenant option. If you haven't licensed this option, you must prevent this from happening. There are no easy ways to achieve this in 12.1, but 12.2 introduced the "max_pdbs" parameter which, when set on CDB$ROOT, is the maximum number of user PDBs allowed. It defaults to 4098 in Enterprise Edition but should be set to 1 when the option has not been purchased.

In the Enterprise Edition you must monitor the usage of features to be sure that only licensed options are used. The feature name of CDB is "Oracle Multitenant" (or "Oracle Pluggable Databases" in 12.1.0.2 because of Bug 20718081).

Figure 3-2 shows the Enterprise Manager Database Express interface, which indicates that multitenant is used. This means that the database is a CDB. It does not

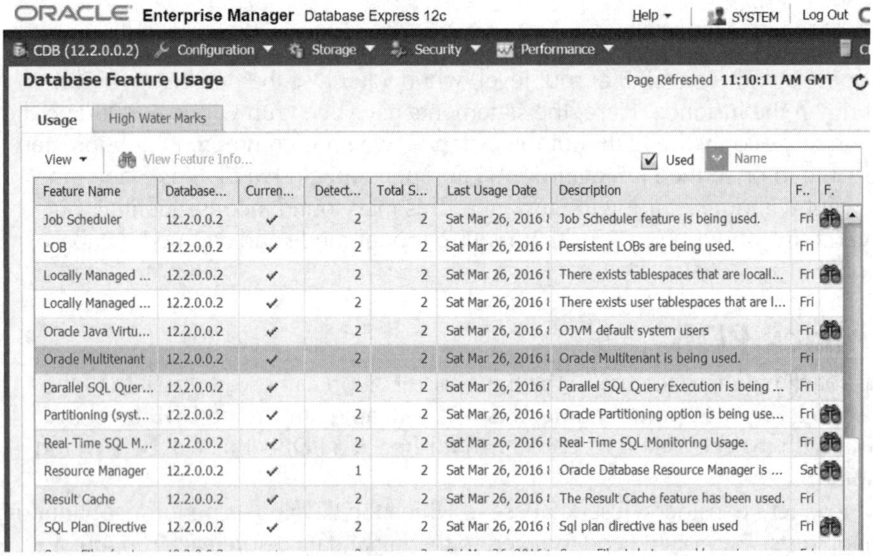

FIGURE 3-2. *Multitenant feature usage from the Enterprise Manager Express*

provide further indication of the usage of the option beyond this, because a single-tenant is still counted as a multitenant database.

More detail is available from the DBA_FEATURE_USAGE_STATISTICS view, where the AUX_COUNT column shows the total number of user PDBs (not including PDB$SEED).

```
SQL> select name, version, detected_usages, currently_used, aux_count, feature_info
from dba_feature_usage_statistics where name = 'Oracle Multitenant';
NAME                  VERSION      DETECTED_USAGES CURRE AUX_COUNT FEATURE_IN
-------------------- ------------ --------------- ----- --------- ----------
Oracle Multitenant   12.2.0.0.2                 2 TRUE          2
```

This example comes from a CDB in which two PDBs have been created. Basically, AUX_COUNT is calculated as the number of PDBs that have CON_ID > 2, so that PDB_SEED is excluded. If AUX_COUNT is 1, you don't need the option. In the preceding example, you must either license the option or drop (move it to a new CDB) one PDB.

What should you do if you have created more than one PDB by mistake? Don't worry, because AUX_COUNT is only the latest value with no history for past values. You can just move the additional PDB to another CDB that you create for it, and then drop the additional PDB to restore the configuration to single-tenant.

The next run of the feature usage sampling will bring back the AUX_COUNT = 1, and you can even run the sampling manually if you want:

```
SQL> exec sys.dbms_feature_usage_internal.exec_db_usage_sampling(sysdate); commit;
PL/SQL procedure successfully completed.
```

At this point, we have listed some interesting features that multitenant architecture brings to single-tenant. Nonetheless, the full advantage of multitenant becomes clear only when you consolidate several PDBs in a container database.

Using the Multitenant Option

When you use the multitenant option, you can create hundreds, or even thousands, of PDBs. You can do this in a test CDB to provide a database to each developer, or in a cloud service to provide on-demand databases with Database as a Service (DBaaS). The additional cost of the option can be balanced by the benefit of consolidation, because it enables you to share expensive compute resources at a high level (disk, memory, and background processes). The multitenant option also brings the agility of lightweight PDBs within a consolidated CDB, and you can administer (backup, upgrade, and so on) as one.

Of course, you will likely not put all your databases into the same CDB, for a number of reasons. First, a CDB is a specific version, so when a new patch set is released, you will probably create a new CDB running in that new version, and then move your PDBs to it. This is the first reason to have several CDBs, and you can think of multiple PDBs in the same way as having different Oracle Homes. A second reason is that you don't want to mix environments (for example, production CDBs will not hold test PDBs). Third, you may also have different availability requirements: one CDB protected in Data Guard and/or in RAC. Changing the availability features for one PDB is as easy as moving it to the appropriate CDB. What is clear is that you cannot consolidate everything and will probably have multiple CDBs to manage.

On the other hand, this does not mean that your CDBs will have only a few PDBs. First, you will probably create different PDBs for the schemas that were consolidated into the same database, aware that multitenant offers better isolation than schema consolidation. Furthermore, the amazing cloning capabilities covered in Chapter 9 will cause you to think differently about managing development databases. You can offer many more environments for development, without increasing the complexity of the CDBs you manage.

Of course, multitenant is new, and our recommendation is to learn it slowly. Take your time, and do not attempt to manage hundreds of PDBs immediately.

Application Containers

You may have a case where your CDB will contain multiple PDBs that run the same application—for example, you may provide your application as a service to multiple customers. In this scenario, you can provision one PDB for each customer, and each will have its own data, but with the same data model. You might immediately think about what Oracle did with the metadata and object links, where the common metadata and objects are stored once in the root only, and ask whether the same can be done for your application. Well, the good news is that in 12.2 with the multitenant option, you can do that with *application containers*. You create one PDB that will behave as the root for your application, and then create another PDB for each "application tenant" that links to that application root.

We will not go into the details of application containers here, because probably very few readers of this book are SaaS providers (Software as a Service). However, a quick example will demonstrate this feature and serve as an occasion to strengthen what we said in Chapter 1 about metadata and object links. Note that with the introduction of application containers in 12.2, "object links" are now called "data links" and "common data" is called "extended data."

First, we create the application root, which is itself a PDB, with the `AS APPLICATION CONTAINER` clause:

```
SQL> connect sys/oracle@//localhost/CDB as sysdba
Connected.
SQL> create pluggable database MYAPP_ROOT as application container admin user MYAPP_
ADMIN identified by oracle roles=(DBA);
Pluggable database created.
SQL> alter pluggable database MYAPP_ROOT open;
Pluggable database altered.
```

Then we connect to it and declare that we are starting installation of the application:

```
SQL> connect sys/oracle@//localhost/MYAPP_ROOT as sysdba
Connected.
SQL> alter pluggable database application MYAPP begin install '1.0';
Pluggable database altered.
```

Next we can create the required tablespaces and users:

```
SQL> create tablespace MYAPP_DATA datafile size 100M autoextend on maxsize 500M;
Tablespace created.
SQL> create user MYAPP_OWNER identified by oracle default tablespace MYAPP_DATA
container=ALL;
User created.
SQL> grant create session, create table to MYAPP_OWNER;
Grant succeeded.
SQL> alter user MYAPP_OWNER quota unlimited on MYAPP_DATA;
User altered.
```

Now that we have the application owner, we can create the application schemas. In this example, we will create one common metadata table (same structure but different data for each application tenant) and a common data table (same data for all tenants), to show the new syntax.

```
SQL> alter session set current_schema=MYAPP_OWNER;
Session altered.
SQL> create table MYAPP_TABLE sharing=metadata (n number primary key);
Table created.
SQL> create table MYAPP_STATIC sharing=data (n number primary key, s varchar2(20));
Table created.
SQL> insert into MYAPP_STATIC values(1,'One');
1 row created.
SQL> insert into MYAPP_STATIC values(2,'Two');
1 row created.
```

When this is done, we declare the end of application installation:

```
SQL> alter pluggable database application MYAPP end install '1.0';
Pluggable database altered.
```

You can see that, in this example, we have provided an application name and version. This is for the initial install, but similar syntax is available to manage patches and upgrades during the application lifecycle.

Now we create a PDB for each application tenant; we must be connected to the application root for this:

```
SQL> connect sys/oracle@//localhost/MYAPP_ROOT as sysdba
Connected.
SQL> create pluggable database MYAPP_ONE admin user MYAPP_ONE_ADMIN identified by
oracle;
Pluggable database created.
SQL> alter pluggable database MYAPP_ONE open;
Pluggable database altered.
```

For the moment, the PDB belongs to the application root, but it is completely empty. The linkage to the application root common metadata and data is achieved by syncing this, as follows:

```
SQL> connect sys/oracle@//localhost/MYAPP_ONE as sysdba
Connected.
SQL> alter pluggable database application MYAPP sync;
Pluggable database altered.
```

At this point everything is now ready; our users and tables are there, as you can see:

```
SQL> connect MYAPP_OWNER/oracle@//localhost/MYAPP_ONE
Connected.

SQL> desc MYAPP_TABLE;
 Name                    Null?    Type
 ----------------------- -------- --------------------------------------
 N                       NOT NULL NUMBER

SQL> select * from MYAPP_STATIC;
         N S
---------- --------------------
         1 One
         2 Two
```

Finally, let's connect back to CDB$ROOT and check the information about our containers:

```
SQL> select con_id, name, application_root, application_pdb, application_root_con_id
from v$containers;

    CON_ID NAME       APPLICATION_ROOT APPLICATION_PDB APPLICATION_ROOT_CON_ID
---------- ---------- ---------------- --------------- -----------------------
         1 CDB$ROOT   NO               NO
         2 PDB$SEED   NO               NO
         3 PDB        NO               NO
         4 MYAPP_ROOT YES              NO
         5 MYAPP_ONE  NO               YES                                   4
```

The application containers are identified by and have the CON_ID of their application root. Now our application will have its lifecycle. As we did `begin install` we can `begin upgrade` and `begin patch`.

Application containers can go even further: you can automatically partition your application into several PDBs thanks to the container map that we will cover in Chapter 12.

Consolidation with Multitenant Option

The multitenant option brings two new levels to database consolidation on a server. PDBs can belong to an application root, which belongs to the CDB. Figure 3-3 depicts some example use cases. Without the multitenant option, only single-tenant is possible; thus PDB1 and PDB2 in the example stand alone in their CDB01 and CDB02 container databases. With the multitenant option, you can have several PDBs per CDB, as illustrated by PDB3 to PDB5. Finally, you have the possibility of managing common metadata and data in one place for PDBs that belong to the same application (APP1 to APP4).

In addition, of course, the schema level provides logical separation in each PDB, and tablespaces provide physical separation.

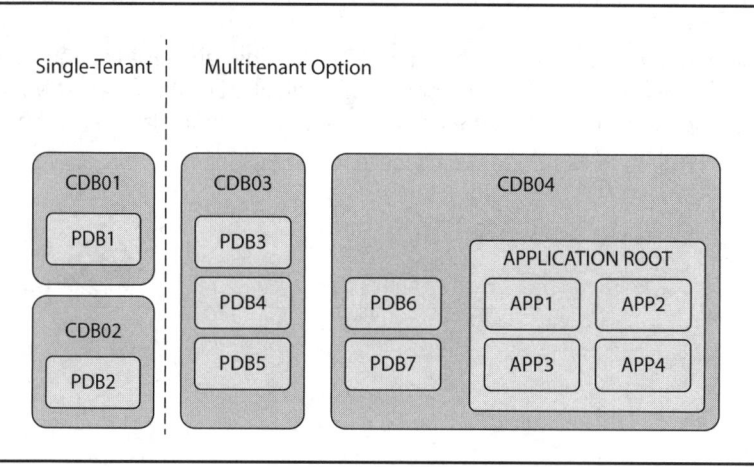

FIGURE 3-3. *Different levels of consolidation on a server*

Summary

This chapter ends Part I, which introduced multitenant and its constituent concepts and components. We explained why Oracle Corporation developed this new architecture. As a database professional, you appreciate the Oracle Database because of its reliability, and a major architecture change can raise concerns that this would be compromised. However, as we outlined in Chapter 1, multitenant is not so much a revolution as a logical extension to the transportable tablespaces functionality that has been in place, and working very well, for a number of years. We endeavored to explain that the metadata and object links (data links) are new features and simply provide internal flags to indicate that the code has to switch to the root container to obtain information.

In Chapter 2, we detailed the different ways of creating a CDB, which is new in part, but shares much in common with the approach used for databases and instances you have known for years. Finally, after reading Chapter 3, we hope that you now realize and appreciate that multitenant is not just for big shops or cloud providers. It is clear that multitenant is the wave of the future for the Oracle Database, and although it brings many changes, it includes a raft of benefits, even for Standard Edition users.

We have named a few features, such as fast provisioning, availability, and cloning, and we hope that this has awakened your curiosity. Let's turn our attention next to daily practicalities and a consideration of database administration in the context of multitenant.

PART II

Multitenant Administration

CHAPTER 4

Day-to-Day Management

In the first part of the book, you became familiar with the concepts and promises this new multitenant world brings to the table. Now it's time to get your head out of the clouds, plant your feet firmly on the ground, and begin using it in earnest.

In this chapter, we will focus on a number of common tasks that DBAs perform, concentrating specifically on those that are transformed in the move away from old-fashioned noncontainer databases (non-CDBs).

Choosing a Container to Work With

In a non-CDB, an object is identified by schema name and object name—for example, SCOTT.EMP. These two component labels, plus the object type (which is a table in this example), are sufficient to identify the object uniquely in the database.

> **NOTE**
> *Specifying the schema name is not always required, because it is implied in the user session itself. Within a session, the* current schema *is most often the user we connected as, but this can be changed by running the* `ALTER SESSION SET CURRENT_SCHEMA` *command within a connected session.*

In a pluggable database (PDB) environment, three pieces of information are required to identify an object: PDB, schema, and object name. However, unlike with schema selection, there is no way to specify the PDB explicitly, because it is always derived from the session. This means that a session always has a PDB container set and, similar to schema, this is implicitly set when the session is initiated. It can also be changed later in an existing session with proper privileges.

We will discuss this in Chapter 5, but let's look at a simple description of the process here. Each PDB offers a service and we connect to the database specifying `SERVICE_NAME`. This implies the container we connect to: the CDB root or a PDB.

If the user account for a connection is a common one and has the appropriate privileges (see Chapter 6), we can change the current container simply with

```
SQL> alter session set container=PDB1;

Session altered.
```

To query the container currently selected, we can either use these SQL*Plus commands,

```
SQL> show con_id

CON_ID
------------------------------
     4

SQL> show con_name

CON_NAME
------------------------------
PDB2
```

Or, should we need to get this information in a query or program, we can use the following:

```
SQL> select sys_context('USERENV', 'CON_ID') con_id,
         sys_context ('USERENV', 'CON_NAME') con_name from dual;

CON_ID     CON_NAME
---------- ----------
4          PDB2
```

Data Manipulation Language (DML) operations, that is those that actually access data, are limited to the current container only, unless we apply some of the special options (as outlined in Chapter 12) and the objects accessed are resolved using the implied container, as just described. And although we can change the current container on the fly, a transaction can modify a single container only. You will see, however, that some DDL commands can work on more than one container at a time, while others allow us to specify the PDB explicitly.

Managing the CDB

From the DBA's point of view, a CDB as a whole is very similar to a non-CDB. If we want to use it, we must start an instance; if there is no running instance, it is unavailable to users. Apart from the datafiles, all the files associated with the database are owned by the CDB—this means the SPFILE, control files, password file, alert log, trace files, wallet, and other files.

One major difference, however, is that you cannot connect to a CDB per se, because a connection is always to a container. So, for example, if we want to connect to the CDB, we connect to the root container; this makes the root container a very special type of container, which represents both the database as a whole and the root container itself. This can create confusion, as some of the commands issued in this context affect the database as a whole, while others affect the root CDB$ROOT container only—and, with enough permissions, they can also affect other PDBs.

> **NOTE**
> *This implies that many tasks are performed in similar ways in the root and in PDBs; it is the context that is different.*

Create the Database

Creating the database, either with the `CREATE DATABASE` command or with the Database Configuration Assistant (DBCA), generates a CDB with the root container and the SEED PDB. The database does not have any PDBs when created, although DBCA offers the option to create some immediately. The CDB$ROOT root container, however, is mandatory because it contains information for the entire database, along with PDB$SEED, which serves as the template on which new PDBs will be based.

Creating a CDB versus a non-CDB involves a single click, which we described in detail in Chapter 2.

Database Startup and Shutdown

Starting up a CDB is no different from starting any other database:

```
SQL> startup
ORACLE instance started.
Total System Global Area  419430400 bytes
Fixed Size                  2925120 bytes
Variable Size             264244672 bytes
Database Buffers          146800640 bytes
Redo Buffers                5459968 bytes
Database mounted.
Database opened.
```

And a shutdown stops the database:

```
SQL> shutdown immediate;
Database closed.
Database dismounted.
ORACLE instance shut down.
```

These operations also look the same in the Enterprise Manager Cloud Control, as shown in Figure 4-1.

Drop the Database

Version 10g introduced the `DROP DATABASE` command, which completely deletes the database. This command has no notion of PDBs, so it deletes all datafiles and all PDBs. To delete a PDB, use the `DROP PLUGGABLE DATABASE` command.

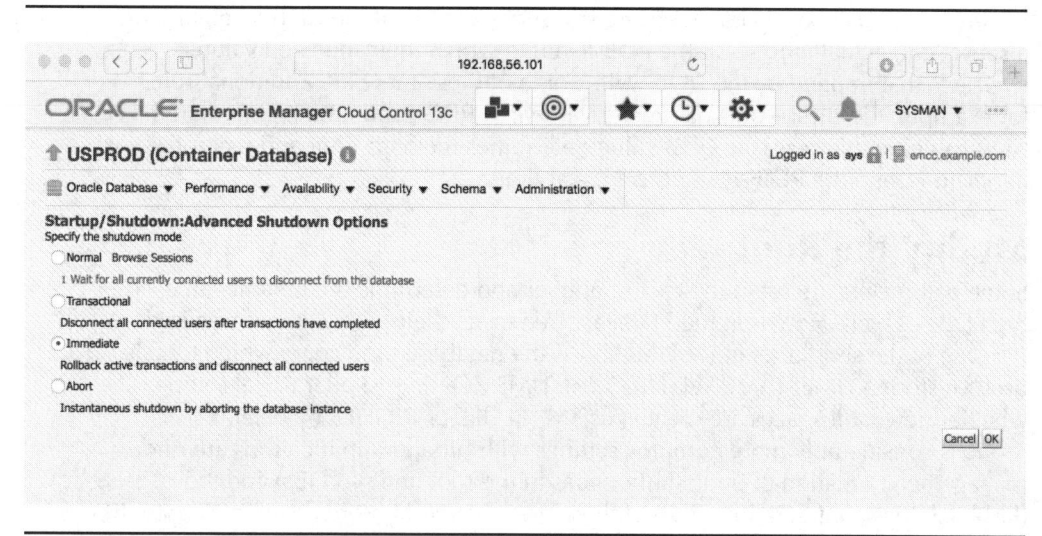

FIGURE 4-1. *Startup/shutdown in Enterprise Manager Cloud Control*

Modify the Entire CDB

Objects and functionality shared by all the containers, including CDB$ROOT, are managed at the CDB level. And although we are connected to the root for this, we are in reality changing the configuration for the whole database, including every PDB.

First of all, the redo logs are global and they contain changes made by all PDBs. Essentially there is no difference between managing redo logs of a CDB and those of a non-CDB, except that with a CDB, we have to size the logs according to the combined load of all the PDBs plugged into the database.

Consequently, the archivelog or noarchivelog mode is set for the entire CDB, as well as parameters such as archived log destinations, Recovery Manager (RMAN) retention policies, standby databases, and so on. We discuss backups in more detail in Chapter 7 and Data Guard in Chapter 11.

Another database-global file type is the control file. The control files describe the complete structure of the database—that is, all database files and all PDBs. Their content is thus updated by many DDL commands, issued when connected to the root and when connected to a PDB. Commands that work with the control file directly need to be issued at the root container; these include creating standby control files as well backing these up to a file or to trace.

Several important parameters have similar database-wide scope, and a couple of the key ones include global database name (and thus default domain for PDBs) and block change tracking for RMAN incremental backups.

In fact, all database parameters are still set by default at the CDB level, and only a subset can actually be set at the PDB level, in which their specified value overrides that implied by the CDB. With some of these there are additional rules—for example, the SESSIONS parameter value in a PDB cannot be higher than the CDB value. In this case, the CDB value determines the hard limit and memory allocations, and the PDB sets only a logical limit.

Modify the Root

Some parameters are set in the root container and determine the default values for the PDBs as well. However, the PDBs are free to set their own value, if required.

One of the simple settings of this sort is the database time zone, which Oracle uses for storing TIMESTAMP WITH LOCAL TIME ZONE. A similar trivial setting is whether new tablespaces are created as SMALLFILE or BIGFILE by default.

Two considerably more complex settings with broader ramifications are undo management (creation of undo tablespaces in the root and/or PDBs) and the flashback logs configuration. Both of these are covered in more detail in Chapter 8.

Temporary Tablespaces

Every Oracle database can have multiple temporary tablespaces, and 10g introduced temporary tablespace groups to assist in their administration. In short, we can use a default temporary tablespace (group) for the database, and we can assign every user a different tablespace.

This is logically expanded in a multitenant database. There is a default set for the whole CDB (set at the root container), and every PDB can override it to use a temporary tablespace created in that PDB; an ALTER USER command can override both to set it at the user level.

Managing PDBs

At the broad operational level, the whole CDB resembles a non-CDB for a DBA, and the PDB looks almost indistinguishable from a non-CDB for the ordinary user or the local PDB administrator. But this leaves an administrative gap: management of the PDB by the DBA. It is in this area that we find a number of new tasks and associated commands to invoke them.

Create a New PDB

A PDB first has to be created (see Chapter 1) or copied from another (see Chapter 9). Both approaches are faster and simpler than creating an entire CDB and, after all, this agility is one of the key selling points of the multitenant architecture. With Oracle 12c, it is now easy to provision one or more databases, whether it is for testing, development, or production, or because a user has requested a new database in his or her Oracle Public Cloud dashboard.

Open and Close a PDB

Starting a CDB does not imply that all of its member PDBs are opened automatically, as Oracle actually leaves the decision to us. A PDB can be in one of four states, as listed next; notice that there is no NOMOUNT state. Only the CDB as a whole can be started in NOMOUNT state, and in that case there is no control file opened, so the instance does not know which PDBs are in the database.

- **MOUNTED**   Data is not accessible, and only an administrator can modify the structure, including files, tablespaces, and so on
- **MIGRATE**   Used during various Oracle maintenance operations (such as running scripts for patching)
- **READ ONLY**   Accessible to users, in read only
- **READ WRITE**   Fully accessible to users for both read and write operations

All three open states can be further constrained to enable only those users with the RESTRICTED SESSION privilege access.

Alter Pluggable Database Statement

The most obvious way to change the open state is by using ALTER PLUGGABLE DATABASE statement. The syntax is very similar to ALTER DATABASE for the CDB as a whole:

```
alter pluggable database open;
alter pluggable database open read only;
alter pluggable database open upgrade restricted;
alter pluggable database close;
alter pluggable database close immediate;
```

In this basic form, it affects only the currently selected container. It would be a lot of typing to switch to a container, open it, and to repeat this for each and every one. Instead, we can directly specify which container to modify.

So, for example, when in the root we can execute this:

```
alter pluggable database PDB1 open;
alter pluggable database ALL open;
alter pluggable database ALL EXCEPT PDB2 open;
```

This syntax is permitted even if the current container is a PDB; however, the specified PDB must be the current container, or we get an error:

```
SQL> alter pluggable database PDB2 open;
 alter pluggable database PDB2 open
 *
 ERROR at line 1:
 ORA-65118: operation affecting a pluggable database cannot be
performed from another pluggable database
```

Startup Pluggable Database Statement

For those DBAs who like the SQL*Plus STARTUP command, this has been enhanced in 12c and now also supports PDBs. This is not an SQL command, per se, which constrains it to the SQL*Plus console, and the list of supported options is also limited.

When the current container is the root, you will also notice that the command is often longer than its ALTER counterpart:

```
startup pluggable database PDB2;
startup pluggable database PDB2 open;
startup pluggable database PDB2 open read only restrict;
```

The FORCE keyword is also available in this context; it closes the database first, before opening it again:

```
startup pluggable database PDB2 force;
```

When the current container is a PDB, and working within that PDB, the startup and shutdown commands imitate the syntax of a non-CDB. This is part of Oracle's pledge to have "all things work like before" with the move to 12c's multitenant architecture. So the PDB admin can simply connect to the database and issue the old, trusted, and proven startup/shutdown commands and receive the expected results.

```
SQL> startup

Pluggable Database opened.

SQL> shutdown;

Pluggable Database closed.
```

Note that even the shutdown abort and transactional keywords are accepted in these commands, but, functionally speaking, they are ignored.

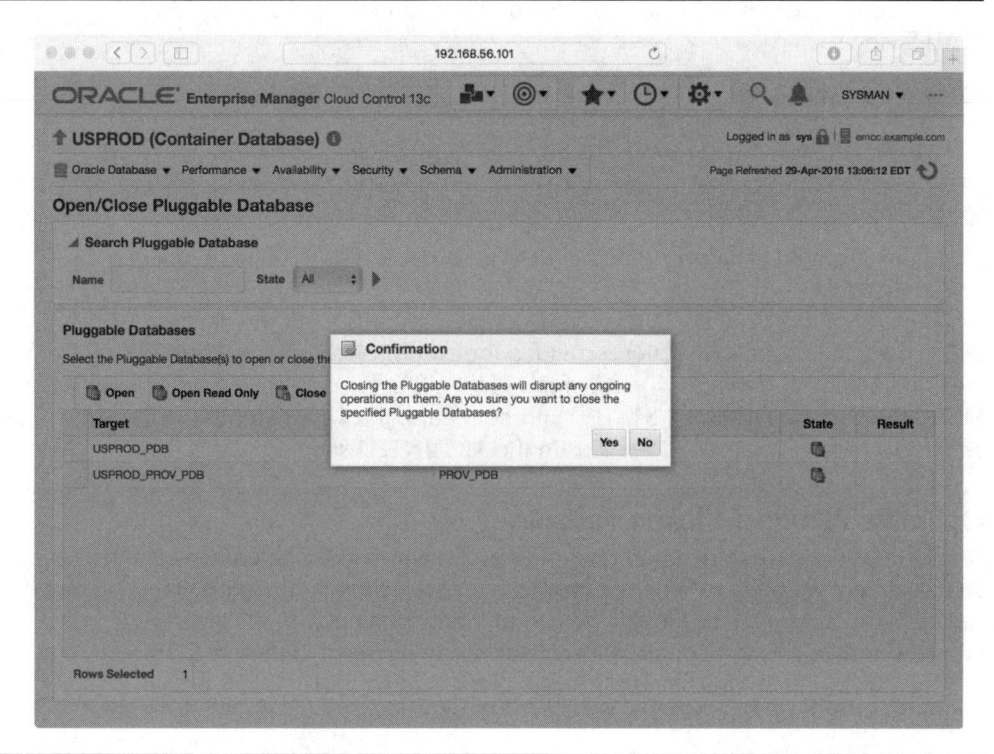

FIGURE 4-2. *Close a pluggable database*

Use Enterprise Manager
With Enterprise Manager Cloud Control it is also possible to open and close PDBs, as shown in Figure 4-2.

Save the PDB Open State
When 12.1.0.1 was first released, starting up a CDB left all PDBs mounted and inaccessible, and the DBA had to open them manually or write system triggers to do it automatically. However, since 12.1.0.2, there is now a provision to have Oracle do this for us automatically, every time the CDB is started and opened again. We can set the desired state using the SAVE STATE command.

We need to put the PDB into the desired state, and then set this as the requested after-restart mode using this command:

```
SQL> alter pluggable database PDB2 save state;

Pluggable database altered.
```

The command stores the current state of the PDB in the DBA_PDB_SAVED_STATES view:

```
SQL> select con_name, state from DBA_PDB_SAVED_STATES;

CON_NAME    STATE
----------  --------------
PDB2        OPEN READ ONLY
```

In this example, whatever state the PDB is in, upon restart it will be opened read-only again.

The DBA_PDB_SAVED_STATES view contains records in all the databases for which we have issued save states, provided the current state is not MOUNTED. To clear this setting and remove the row for a PDB, either execute save state when it is MOUNTED or use DISCARD STATE. With no record, the PDB will not be opened after CDB restart, and instead remains in the MOUNTED state.

Open the PDB in a Cluster Database

A PDB does not have to be open on all instances, and we can actually pick and choose where we open it. Where it has been opened, though, the mode must be the same among all instances, though we can mix only one open mode and the mounted mode. This is, after all, the same as for an entire CDB or non-CDB.

The ALTER PLUGGABLE DATABASE OPEN and ALTER PLUGGABLE DATABASE CLOSE commands can specify which instances to affect:

```
alter pluggable database open instances = ('DB1', 'DB2');
alter pluggable database open instances = all;
alter pluggable database open instances = all except ('DB3', 'DB4');
```

One interesting option in this context is the RELOCATE command. This is shorthand syntax for "close here, open somewhere else." The CLOSE statement closes the PDB on the current instance (specifying relocation is mutually exclusive with listing instances to affect) and the RELOCATE keyword instructs Oracle to open the PDB on an instance either specified by us or chosen by Oracle:

```
alter pluggable database close relocate to DB4;
alter pluggable database close relocate;
```

Saving the state is also a per-instance operation, so we must issue the ALTER PLUGGABLE DATABASE SAVE STATE on each of the instances. However, this may not be needed if we use grid infrastructure to manage database services—for example, in a RAC environment. Starting a service on an instance automatically opens that PDB (see Chapter 5).

View the State of PDBs

We can query the current state of all PDBs easily with the V$PDBS view:

```
SQL> select name, open_mode, restricted from v$pdbs;

NAME            OPEN_MODE   RES
--------------- ----------  ---
PDB$SEED        READ ONLY   NO
PDB1            READ WRITE  NO
PDB2            READ ONLY   NO
```

View PDB Operation History

The simplest journey of events over the lifetime of a PDB would see it starting and ending with its creation. However, as you will see in Chapter 9, things can get decidedly more complicated than this. The CDB_PDB_HISTORY view provides a way of reviewing this, and even for a simple PDB, it's a handy way to see its inception date:

```
SQL> select pdb_name, op_timestamp, operation from cdb_pdb_history
order by 2;

PDB_NAME    OP_TIMEST  OPERATION
----------  ---------  ----------------
PDB$SEED    07-JUL-14  UNPLUG
PDB$SEED    07-JUL-14  UNPLUG
PDB$SEED    23-FEB-16  PLUG
PDB$SEED    23-FEB-16  PLUG
PDB1        23-FEB-16  CREATE
PDB2        28-FEB-16  CREATE
```

You might wonder where the first four records come from. These refer to when the DBCA template was created and then when DBCA created the database from that template.

Run SQL on Multiple PDBs

There are some restrictions to keep in view when an SQL statement, which is usually intended for a single PDB, needs to be run on more than one PDB. First, user management and privilege grants behave differently for a PDB than for a non-CDB, as you will see later in this chapter. Second, Chapter 12 shows some examples of PDBs working together in tandem, sharing the data structures and data.

Aside from these options, it is possible to implement a simple workaround. If we log in to the root, we can change the current container on the fly, privileges permitting. So it follows that we can execute the desired SQL in various containers, one by one, by selecting the container in the session, running the SQL, and repeating. This can be done by using an SQL script or with dynamic SQL; execute `immediate` or `DBMS_SQL`.

We don't even have to code the container switch ourselves, because `DBMS_SQL.PARSE` has a new parameter, `CONTAINER`, that allows us to specify where the statement should be run.

Note that the rule that a transaction cannot span multiple containers is still in effect, so we have to commit the changes before running SQL in a different container.

```
DECLARE
  cur INTEGER;
  rc INTEGER;
  cmd VARCHAR2(32767) :=
    'BEGIN update SCOTT.EMP set SAL=SAL*1.1 where EMPNO=1; COMMIT; END;';
BEGIN
  cur := DBMS_SQL.OPEN_CURSOR;
  DBMS_SQL.PARSE (c => cur, statement => cmd,
       language_flag => DBMS_SQL.NATIVE, container => 'PDB1');
  rc := DBMS_SQL.EXECUTE(c => cur);
  DBMS_SQL.PARSE (c => cur, statement => cmd,
       language_flag => DBMS_SQL.NATIVE, container => 'PDB2');
  rc := DBMS_SQL.EXECUTE(c => cur);
END;
/
```

Modify the PDB

The datafiles are owned by the PDBs and the usual SQL statements still apply, so there is no change in creating tablespaces, adding datafiles, or taking them online or offline.

As discussed, in the PDB we can override some of the default parameters set at the CDB level: database time zone, default temporary tablespace, and the choice of BIGFILE/SMALLFILE datafile default, for example.

What is set only at the PDB level is the default tablespace. Because permanent tablespaces are private to PDBs, there is no CDB-level setting. Similarly, the default PL/SQL edition is also set at the PDB level only.

All of these features are present in a non-CDB so, for SQL compatibility, they can also be issued using the `ALTER DATABASE` command when connected to a PDB. Again, this means that the PDB administrator can use the existing trusted and proven commands, which are useful especially if the admin has built up a library of favorite SQL scripts over time.

A unique feature for multitenant PDBs is storage limit. This parameter enables us to determine the maximum allowed size of all tablespaces as well as the maximum space occupied in a CDB-level temporary tablespace:

```
SQL> alter pluggable database storage (maxsize 2G max_shared_temp_size 100m);
Pluggable database altered.
```

It is also possible to specify `FORCE LOGGING` mode in a PDB. Normally this is done at the CDB level to ensure that any `NOLOGGING` operations are actually logged, and thus the integrity and completeness of a standby database, for one, is ensured. But in some cases, we may want to change this setting at the PDB level, possibly disabling the `FORCE LOGGING` mode for that particular PDB (it's a temporary testing database or is not included in any standby, for example). Alternatively, we can set a specific PDB to force logging, while keeping CDB level force logging disabled. (Note that the usual options for setting `FORCE LOGGING` at tablespace level and `NOLOGGING` at table level still apply. In other words, it is possible to create a messy, multilayered setup, although we would advise against this and recommend keeping things simple instead.)

The database must be in restricted mode to run these commands, and then we can invoke the desired setting:

```
SQL> startup restrict

Pluggable Database opened.

SQL> alter pluggable database enable force logging;

Pluggable database altered.

SQL> alter pluggable database disable force logging;

Pluggable database altered.

SQL> alter pluggable database enable force nologging;

Pluggable database altered.
```

Note that there is also a `LOGGING` and `NOLOGGING` clause for a PDB, and this establishes the default mode for any new tablespace created in it. As these clauses set only the default setting for tablespaces created in the future, they do not have an immediate effect on the database, unlike the `FORCE LOGGING` clauses.

```
SQL> alter pluggable database nologging;

Pluggable database altered.

SQL> alter pluggable database logging;

Pluggable database altered.
```

Drop a PDB

The life of a PDB ends with a drop operation. It requires a SYSDBA connection, but it is one of the simplest operations to enact. The syntax suggests that the only additional input we have in this decision is whether to keep the datafiles on disk or not. In reality, however, only an unplugged database can keep its datafiles, while others have to drop them. (See Chapter 9 for a detailed description on unplugging a PDB.)

To effect this operation, the PDB has to be closed (or unplugged), and this must be performed from the root container.

The default option is to keep the datafiles, and Oracle apparently assumes that moving a database by virtue of unplugging and plugging is a more frequent operation than outright dropping.

```
SQL> drop pluggable database PDB1;

Pluggable database dropped.
```

Patching and Upgrades

Each Oracle software major version (such as 12c) has a number of additional releases (for example, the 12c first release is 12.1, and the second release, 12.2, is also called 12cR2). Between these releases, patch sets are released. For example, the 11gR2 final patchset is 11.2.0.4. The patch sets, despite the name, are actually distributed as full, standalone software installations. All these levels of software distribution (edition, release, patch set) provide new features and bug fixes. Additionally, on top of patch sets, you can (and should) apply the Patch Set Updates (PSUs, or bundle patches in Windows, which include the patch sets).

NOTE
Upgrading and patching are inherently dynamic processes, but to understand the features available for their administration, you should refer to the Oracle documentation. Information about upgrades is constantly evolving as bugs and issues are encountered, so, for this reason, the standard documentation is not always sufficient, and you must also review the My Oracle Support (MOS) notes about them. For a friendly and helpful read in light of this, we recommend you bookmark and regularly monitor the excellent upgrade blog from Mike Dietrich, the Master Product Manager for Upgrades and Migrations at Oracle: https://blogs.oracle.com/UPGRADE/.

You can upgrade to 12.2 directly from 11.2.0.3, 11.2.0.4, 12.1.0.1, and 12.1.0.2. If you are using a previous version of the Oracle Database, you can upgrade in several steps, or choose a logical migration approach with a utility such as Data Pump. In this chapter, we discuss physical upgrades, in which data in the actual datafiles remains unchanged.

Upgrade CDB

In the same way that you can upgrade a database, you can upgrade a CDB. This is the simplest way to upgrade all PDBs at the same time, provided you have a maintenance window in which you can stop all their services at the same time.

To upgrade all PDBs, they must first be opened:

```
SQL> alter pluggable database all open;
Pluggable database altered.
```

If you want one or more PDBs to remain closed to postpone their upgrade, they will need to be explicitly excluded within the catcon.pl and catctl.pl utility commands, using the -C argument.

Pre-Upgrade

In Oracle Database 11gR2 you used the utlu112i.sql script to check the database you wanted to upgrade. Oracle Database 12*c* comes with a new pre-upgrade script that installs a package and runs it, detailing suggestions for manual or automatic actions to perform before and after the upgrade. The script is preupgrd.sql, and it calls utluppkg.sql, which installs the package.

There are two important points to note about this script. First, it is shipped in the rdbms/admin directory of the ORACLE_HOME of the new version of the Oracle software, but remember that it will be run in the database that you want to upgrade, with its older ORACLE_HOME. If both ORACLE_HOME directories are located on the same server, you can call the scripts from the new directory. But you can also copy the preupgrd.sql and utluppkg.sql files.

NOTE
The upgrade files shipped in an ORACLE_HOME are actually useless for the databases running from this ORACLE_HOME. Those files are to be used for a database from a previous version ORACLE_HOME.

The second important point is that the shipped upgrade files come from the release of the patch set, but those scripts may evolve over time. You can, and should, always download the latest version from My Oracle Support MOS ID 884522.1 at support.oracle.com/epmos/faces/DocContentDisplay?id=884522.1.

When you run preupgrd.sql, it installs the dbms_preup package and generates a log file and fixup scripts in the following directory: $ORACLE_BASE/cfgtoollogs/<db_unique_name>/preupgrade/.

> **NOTE**
> *If ORACLE_BASE is not set, it will be replaced by ORACLE_HOME.*

Remember that you are in a multitenant environment, so running the script from SQL*Plus will execute it only on CDB$ROOT. You must use the catcon.pl utility introduced in Chapter 2 to enact this at the PDB level. Here is an example in which we run the preupgrd.sql from the future ORACLE_HOME:

```
cd $ORACLE_BASE/product/12202EE
```

First we create the log directory that we will specify with the -l argument:

```
mkdir $ORACLE_BASE/admin/$ORACLE_SID/preupgrd
```

Then we run the preupgrd.sql script located in rdbms/admin of the future ORACLE_HOME, specified with the -d argument with an absolute path to the current directory:

```
$ORACLE_HOME/perl/bin/perl $ORACLE_HOME/rdbms/admin/catcon.pl \
  -d ./rdbms/admin \
  -l $ORACLE_BASE/admin/$ORACLE_SID/preupgrd -b $(date +%Y%m%d%H%M%S) \
  preupgrd.sql
```

The output of catcon.pl goes into the directory and files defined with -l and -b, but the pre-upgrade package still writes its output in $ORACLE_BASE/cfgtoollogs. Here is an example of the files generated from a two PDB, CDB upgrade:

```
cd $ORACLE_BASE/cfgtoollogs/CDB/preupgrade ; tree
.
├── pdbfiles
│   ├── postupgrade_fixups_pdb1.sql
│   ├── postupgrade_fixups_pdb2.sql
│   ├── postupgrade_fixups_pdb_seed.sql
│   ├── preupgrade_fixups_pdb1.sql
│   ├── preupgrade_fixups_pdb2.sql
│   ├── preupgrade_fixups_pdb_seed.sql
│   ├── preupgrade_pdb1.log
│   ├── preupgrade_pdb2.log
│   └── preupgrade_pdb_seed.log
├── postupgrade_fixups.sql
├── preupgrade_fixups.sql
└── preupgrade.log
```

You have a set of logs, pre-upgrade fixes, and post-upgrade fixes for the CDB, and in the pdbfiles subdirectory, one for each PDB.

Note that preupgrade_fixups.sql and postupgrade_fixups.sql contain the code for all containers (CDB$ROOT and all those in the pdbfiles subdirectory), so you can run those scripts with catcon.pl on all containers.

preupgrade.jar   In 12.2, the pre-upgrade process received a further enhancement, being bundled into a Java utility, and the previous versions were deprecated. Making use of the same environment as before, where ORACLE_HOME is set to the current environment and the new one is installed in the 12202EE at the same level, we can run this:

```
cd $ORACLE_HOME/../12202EE
./jdk/bin/java -jar ./rdbms/admin/preupgrade.jar FILE TEXT
```

> **NOTE**
> *Use the -help flag to show the options for changing the output directories.*

At the time of writing, the Java solution does not automatically generate a master script to run with catcon.pl, but you can achieve this by concatenating the per-container scripts:

```
cd $ORACLE_BASE/cfgtoollogs/CDB/preupgrade
cat preupgrade_fixups_*.sql > preupgrade_fixups.sql
cat postupgrade_fixups_*.sql > postupgrade_fixups.sql
```

Then, as with the previous method, you end up with one file with "if con_name" conditions that you can run for each container.

Backup or Restore Point

Invoking an upgrade process is a simple operation and is fully automated when you use the Database Upgrade Assistant (DBUA). But problems may occur at any time during the upgrade process. Imagine, for example, that you plan one hour of downtime to upgrade a 10TB database, and there's no problem with that because the time to upgrade does not depend on the size of the database per se. But what do you do if the upgrade fails in the middle—perhaps due to a bug, server crash, remote connection unexpectedly closed, and so on? Did you count the fallback scenario within the one-hour outage? How long will it take to restore 10TB and recover all the redo generated since the time of this backup?

What is critical is that, before starting an upgrade, you must plan out the fallback scenario. The easiest method for doing this, if you are using Enterprise Edition, is to create a guaranteed restore point:

```
SQL> create restore point BEFORE_UPGRADE guarantee flashback database;
```

Then, in case of failure, you can flashback the database quickly to revert to this pre-upgrade point:

```
SQL> shutdown immediate
SQL> startup mount
SQL> flashback database to restore point BEFORE_UPGRADE;
SQL> alter database open resetlogs;
```

Of course, this assumes that your database is in archivelog mode and that you have enough space allocated for the flashback logs. Helpfully, the required size for the fast recovery area (FRA) is one of the precheck activities performed by the preupgrd.sql script.

You may choose other means by which to back up the database, such as taking a storage snapshot when the database is closed. If your database is in noarchivelog mode, and you want to do a cold backup before the upgrade, keep in mind that the upgrade will not update anything in your user data. Then you can put your user tablespaces in read-only mode and don't need to back them up. Only the system tablespaces remain open (SYSTEM, SYSAUX, UNDO, and all those that have system components objects) and so require backup. This means that you don't need to back up the user tablespaces, which reduces the time to restore if you do need to perform a point-in-time recovery before the upgrade. This can also be automatically achieved with the upgrade utilities: the `-T` option of `catctl.pl` or `-changeUserTablespacesReadOnly` of the DBUA.

Pre-Upgrade Script

The pre-upgrade scripts generated by preupgrd.sql in the cfgtoollogs/<db_unique_name>/preupgrade directory can be run on each container with catcon.pl, as follows:

```
mkdir $ORACLE_BASE/admin/$ORACLE_SID/preupgrade_fixups
$ORACLE_HOME/perl/bin/perl $ORACLE_HOME/rdbms/admin/catcon.pl \
   -d $ORACLE_BASE/cfgtoollogs/CDB/preupgrade \
   -l $ORACLE_BASE/admin/$ORACLE_SID/preupgrade_fixups -b $(date
+%Y%m%d%H%M%S) \
   preupgrade_fixups.sql
```

You also have to fix any manual recommendations, but don't hesitate to invoke the pre-upgrade script again to check and confirm that the recommended actions have been completed.

Here is a quick check of the manual tasks that were recommended in one test example we ran:

```
$ grep -E "Executing in container|MANUAL" *
201602261856320.log:Executing in container:  CDB$ROOT
201602261856320.log:Previously failed CHECK pga_aggregate_target is still presently
failing.  It must be resolved MANUALLY by the DBA.
201602261856320.log:Executing in container:  PDB$SEED
201602261856320.log:Previously failed CHECK pga_aggregate_target is still presently
failing.  It must be resolved MANUALLY by the DBA.
201602261856321.log:Executing in container:  PDB1
201602261856321.log:Previously failed CHECK pga_aggregate_target is still presently
failing.  It must be resolved MANUALLY by the DBA.
201602261856322.log:Executing in container:  PDB2
201602261856322.log:Previously failed CHECK pga_aggregate_target is still presently
failing.  It must be resolved MANUALLY by the DBA.
```

These fixes required manual intervention. In this example, we had to increase `PGA_AGGREGATE_TARGET`. Note that we did it manually, and only at CDB level, because the CDB value is the default for the PDB. More detail about parameters will follow later in this chapter in the section "CDB SPFILE."

Upgrade with catupgrd.sql

Now, to upgrade, you must shut down the CDB. The downtime begins. Prior to this, check to ensure that the `COMPATIBLE` parameter is set. You can set this parameter to the current value in case you need to downgrade later. If you have created a restore point, this is actually mandatory; otherwise you will get an ORA-38880 error when mounting from the new ORACLE_HOME.

From here, you can copy the SPFILE to the new ORACLE_HOME, and then change the /etc/oratab file. Then you can start the database from the new ORACLE_HOME in upgrade mode, ensuring that all PDBs are in the required upgrade mode:

```
SQL> shutdown immediate
```

Change /etc/oratab to

```
CDB:/u01/app/oracle/product/12202EE
```

And set the environment like so:

```
. oraenv <<< CDB
```

Then you are ready to startup upgrade:

```
SQL> startup upgrade
SQL> alter pluggable database all close;
SQL> alter pluggable database all open upgrade;
```

Note that the OPEN_MODE displayed by `show pdbs` is MIGRATE here:.

```
SQL> show pdbs
    CON_ID CON_NAME                       OPEN MODE  RESTRICTED
---------- ------------------------------ ---------- ----------
         2 PDB$SEED                       MIGRATE    YES
         3 PDB1                           MIGRATE    YES
```

Time to run the upgrade. The utility to run the catupgrd.sql script is not SQL*Plus but catctl.pl, the parallel upgrade utility optimized to minimize the time the process takes by parallelizing and reducing the number of restarts. In 12.2, running catupgrd.sql directly is not supported.

```
mkdir $ORACLE_BASE/admin/$ORACLE_SID/upgrade
cd $ORACLE_HOME/rdbms/admin
$ORACLE_HOME/perl/bin/perl $ORACLE_HOME/rdbms/admin/catctl.pl \
  -n 4 -N 2 -M \
  -d $ORACLE_HOME/rdbms/admin \
  -l $ORACLE_BASE/admin/$ORACLE_SID/upgrade \
  catupgrd.sql
```

In this example we have added the -n 4 to parallelize with four processes in total, and -N 2 to use two processes per container, which means that the upgrade of PDBs will take place on two PDBs at a time. One additional point worth noting: Parallel operations are usually unavailable in the Standard Edition (SE), but this is not the case with upgrades. They work the same in SE as in Enterprise Edition (EE), meaning that you can perform parallel upgrades in SE.

You will also see that we have added another parameter, -M. By default, once the CDB$ROOT has been upgraded, the instance that was in upgrade mode is restarted to normal mode before the PDBs are upgraded. This is good if you need to open PDBs as soon as they are upgraded, without waiting for the others to complete. Here, with the –M flag, the CDB$ROOT stays in upgrade mode until the end. It's faster, but we will have to wait until all of the PDB upgrades finish for them to be open and accessible.

You may choose to have the PDBs open as soon as they are upgraded, and in 12.2 you can even prioritize the way they are processed by using the -L argument.

The main log file for the upgrade process is upg_summary.log, which details the elapsed time of the upgrade per container and per component. You can also review the results again like this:

```
sqlplus / as sysdba @ ?/rdbms/admin/catresults.sql
```

At the time of writing, the PDBs upgrade process takes the same time as the CDB$ROOT upgrade process, or even longer, but this will be improved in the future. Actually, thanks to metadata links, a large part of the upgrade DDL does not need to be run on PDBs, but this optimization is implemented only partially now.

Let's review an example of time taken by an upgrade. The following is the CDSB$ROOT part of the upg_summary.log from 12.1 to 12.2. You can see that the Oracle Server section is only 21 minutes within an overall elapsed period of 92 minutes:

```
Oracle Database 12.2 Post-Upgrade Status Tool      03-07-2016 16:07:02
                        [CDB$ROOT]

Component                              Current        Version      Elapsed Time
Name                                   Status         Number       HH:MM:SS

Oracle Server                          VALID          12.2.0.0.2   00:21:31
JServer JAVA Virtual Machine           VALID          12.2.0.0.2   00:07:37
Oracle Real Application Clusters       OPTION OFF     12.2.0.0.2   00:00:01
Oracle Workspace Manager               VALID          12.2.0.0.2   00:02:11
OLAP Analytic Workspace                VALID          12.2.0.0.2   00:00:42
Oracle OLAP API                        VALID          12.2.0.0.2   00:00:24
Oracle Label Security                  VALID          12.2.0.0.2   00:00:17
Oracle XDK                             VALID          12.2.0.0.2   00:02:11
Oracle Text                            VALID          12.2.0.0.2   00:01:00
Oracle XML Database                    VALID          12.2.0.0.2   00:02:42
Oracle Database Java Packages          VALID          12.2.0.0.2   00:00:26
Oracle Multimedia                      VALID          12.2.0.0.2   00:02:41
Spatial                                VALID          12.2.0.0.2   00:10:51
Oracle Application Express             VALID          5.0.3.00.02  00:14:44
Oracle Database Vault                  VALID          12.2.0.0.2   00:00:32
Final Actions                                                      00:03:49
Post Upgrade                                                       00:01:41
Post Compile                                                       00:13:46

Total Upgrade Time: 01:32:39 [CDB$ROOT]

Database time zone version is 25. It meets current release needs.

Summary Report File = /u01/app/oracle/cfgtoollogs/dbua/upgrade2016-03-06_06-20-12-PM/
CDB/upg_summary.log
```

Our recommendation, in view of this, is not to install any components that you don't need. With the multitenant option, you will likely create lots of PDBs, so perhaps you will choose to install all components in case you need them in the future. But that will make upgrades take longer. Note that without the multitenant option, in single-tenant, it's always better to choose only what is actually needed.

Taking our previous example as a test case, you may choose to upgrade Oracle Application Express (APEX) in advance. Or even better, remove it from CDB$ROOT completely with $ORACLE_HOME/apex/apxremov_con.sql, because it's not a good idea to have APEX in the root container or the APEX version will be tied to the database version.

Open Normally

At the end of the upgrade process, when everything has completed successfully, we can open the CDB and the PDBs:

```
SQL> shutdown immediate
SQL> startup;
SQL> alter pluggable database all open;
```

Upgrade Resume

In 12.2, if the upgrade fails, look at the PHASE_TIME number. Then, if you are able to fix the problem, you can continue the upgrade with the -p option. You can also use the -c option to choose (and prioritize) the containers.

For example, let's imagine our upgrade has been interrupted. The catresult.sql shows that the post-upgrade step has not been performed. The log for PDB phases PDBSOracle_Server.log shows nothing after Phase 105 for PDB:

```
Serial     Phase #:102    [PDB$SEED] Files:1     Time: 2s
******************    Migration    ******************
Serial     Phase #:102    [PDB] Files:1     Time: 223s
Serial     Phase #:103    [PDB$SEED] Files:1     Time: 19s
Serial     Phase #:104    [PDB$SEED] Files:1     Time: 245s
Serial     Phase #:103    [PDB] Files:1     Time: 9s
Serial     Phase #:104    [PDB] Files:1     Time: 167s
****************    Post Upgrade    ****************
Serial     Phase #:105    [PDB$SEED] Files:1     Time: 239s
****************    Post Upgrade    ****************
Serial     Phase #:105    [PDB] Files:1     Time: 181s
***************    Summary report    ****************
Serial     Phase #:106    [PDB$SEED] Files:1     Time: 3s
Serial     Phase #:107    [PDB$SEED] Files:1     Time: 7s
Serial     Phase #:108    [PDB$SEED] Files:1     Time: 0s
```

And the log file for PDB shows that it started the PHASE_TIME number 106 but didn't finish:

```
grep -H PHASE_TIME catupgrdpdb0.log | tail -2
catupgrdpdb0.log:PHASE_TIME___END 105 16-03-06 10:35:06
catupgrdpdb0.log:PHASE_TIME___START 106 16-03-06 10:35:08
```

To resume, we can run it again from this specific phase—that is, only for the PDB container and starting at PHASE_TIME 105:

```
cd $ORACLE_HOME/rdbms/admin
$ORACLE_HOME/perl/bin/perl $ORACLE_HOME/rdbms/admin/catctl.pl \
   -n 4 -N 2 -M \
   -d $ORACLE_HOME/rdbms/admin \
   -l $ORACLE_BASE/admin/$ORACLE_SID/upgrade \
   -c PDB -p 105 \
catupgrd.sql
```

Without the `-P` flag, which specifies an end phase, it will run all the remaining phases until the end—and in our example the output shows that this will be Phase 108:

```
------------------------------------------------------
Phases [105-108]          Start Time:[2016_03_07 16:18:21]
Container Lists Inclusion:[PDB] Exclusion:[NONE]
------------------------------------------------------
    Time: 8s
****************   Post Upgrade    *****************
Serial   Phase #:105  [PDB] Files:1   Time: 17s
****************   Summary report  *****************
Serial   Phase #:106  [PDB] Files:1   Time: 1s
Serial   Phase #:107  [PDB] Files:1   Time: 1s
Serial   Phase #:108  [PDB] Files:1   Time: 0s
------------------------------------------------------
Phases [105-108]          End Time:[2016_03_07 16:18:46]
Container Lists Inclusion:[PDB] Exclusion:[NONE]
------------------------------------------------------
```

If you encounter an issue with this process, you can obtain a detailed debug trace with the `-Z` option, but that is beyond the scope of this book.

Post-upgrade Script

The post-upgrade scripts that have been generated by the preupgrd.sql in the cfgtoollogs/<db_unique_name>/preupgrade directory can be run with catcon.pl:

```
$ORACLE_HOME/perl/bin/perl $ORACLE_HOME/rdbms/admin/catcon.pl \
  -d $ORACLE_BASE/cfgtoollogs/CDBPRD01/preupgrade \
  -l $ORACLE_BASE/admin/$ORACLE_SID -b postupgrade_fixups$(date +%Y%m%d%H%M%S) \
  -- postupgrade_fixups.sql
```

And then you can recompile all invalid objects with utlrp:

```
$ORACLE_HOME/perl/bin/perl $ORACLE_HOME/rdbms/admin/catcon.pl \
  -d $ORACLE_home/RDBMS/ADMIN \
  -l $ORACLE_BASE/admin/$ORACLE_SID -b utlrp$(date +%Y%m%d%H%M%S) \
  utlrp.sql
```

Test and Open the Service

From here you can test the application(s) and open the service. Don't forget to drop any guaranteed restore points, if any were used.

> **How Long Does an Upgrade Take?**
> Because upgrading is an operation that you perform when an application is offline, you need to estimate the time it will take. Upgrading a CDB takes longer than upgrading a non-CDB because you have multiple containers. However, the upgrade of PDBs is optimized. As the CDB$ROOT is upgraded first, upgrading the metadata and object links should be faster than upgrading a standalone database. Thanks to this, upgrading a multitenant with N PDBs should theoretically be faster than upgrading N standalone databases. This is, at least, one goal of multitenant architecture from the get-go, but this optimization has not yet been fully implemented. If you are in the single-tenant configuration, upgrading the CDB takes longer than upgrading a non-CDB because three containers are involved: CDB$ROOT, PDB$SEED, and your PDB.
>
> Note that the size of the database, per se, does not determine the time to upgrade, because it is only the data dictionary that is affected. Obviously, a huge number of objects can increase the time to upgrade, but the major cause for extended upgrade duration is the number of components installed.

Database Upgrade Assistant

We have described the manual procedure, which hopefully helps you understand the phases of the upgrade process. However, as in previous versions, the procedure outlined is fully automated with the DBUA, available from the Oracle Home of the new version. There, you can choose the database to upgrade, along with the different upgrade options.

If you don't have the graphical environment set up, or you want to script the upgrade, you can also run DBUA in silent mode. There is no response file, but all options are available from the command line. You can also run the pre-upgrade step only from the new Oracle Home, as per the following:

```
./bin/dbua -silent -executePreReqs -sid CDB -sysDBAUsername sys -sysDBAPassword …
```

The output directory created under $ORACLE_BASE/cfgtoollogs/dbua is displayed and you will find all log, pre-upgrade, and fixup scripts directed there.

For the upgrade, you can see all options from the inline help:

```
./bin/dbua -silent -help
```

An example of a useful additional option is to create a restore point automatically with the `-createGRP` argument.

We will not offer any preference here to the manual or DBUA upgrade, because this depends on a number of factors, such as your experience, the requirements, and the complexity of the database. In short, you can have more control with the manual procedure, but everything is possible with DBUA, graphically or in a scripted way.

Plugging In

Upgrading the CDB is fastest when you have a large maintenance window to upgrade all the PDBs at the same time. But in real life, you probably don't want to upgrade all at the same time because PDBs are for multiple applications or "tenants." And here the multitenant architecture can help. Several ways to move PDBs across containers will be covered in Chapter 9, and those movements do not require that you work in the same version. In addition, a very interesting way to upgrade a PDB is to move it to a CDB that is in a higher version. This is an option with plug-in and remote cloning, and it is even possible without the multitenant option, where you have only one PDB per CDB.

The data movement process is described in Chapter 9, but it's important to note that once you've plugged in or cloned from a previous version, you need to bring your PDBs to the new version. Remember that most of the PDB dictionary objects are links to the CDB$ROOT, so they are usable only when those metadata and object links are upgraded to the CDB version. The same catupgrd.sql script performs this action, and it is run in a specific container with the catctl.pl script, using the -c option.

NOTE
If you choose to unplug/plug in, remember that you always need to have the PDB protected by a backup. Drop it from the source only when it is upgraded and backed up in the target.

Basically, upgrading a plugged PDB is the same as upgrading a PDB in a CDB. You specify the container with the -c option of the catctl.pl script. Verification of the need to upgrade can be checked from PDB_PLUG_IN_VIOLATIONS:

```
SQL> select name,cause,type,status,action from pdb_plug_in_violations;

NAME   CAUSE           TYPE  STATUS
-----  -------------   ----- -------
ACTION
-----------------------------------------------------------
MESSAGE
-----------------------------------------------------------
MYPDB  VSN not match  ERROR PENDING
Either upgrade the PDB or reload the components in the PDB.
PDB's version does not match CDB's version: PDB's version 12.1.0.2.0. CDB's version
12.2.0.0.1.
```

Remote Clone from Previous Version

Remote cloning uses the remote file server (RFS) process, which may return an error if the client uses a higher version:

```
ORA-17628: Oracle error 17630 returned by remote Oracle server
ORA-17630: Mismatch in the remote file protocol version client server
```

For example, when cloning into 12.2 from a remote 12.1.0.2 database, you receive the following error, with the remote alert.log showing:

```
ORA-17630: Mismatch in the remote file protocol version client 3 server 2
```

The solution is to apply patch18633374: COPYING ACROSS REMOTE SERVERS on the source (https://updates.oracle.com/download/18633374.html) to allow file transfers to a higher version.

The cloning procedure will be described in Chapter 9, and the dictionary upgrade is performed by running catupgrd.sql on the container.

Patching

Upgrades to new releases (such as from 11.2.0.4 [11gR2 Patch set 3] to 12.1.0.1 [12cR1]) or to a new patch set (such as 12.1.0.1 [12cR1] to 12.1.0.2 [12cR1 Patch set 1]) are provided by installing a new Oracle Home and then, from that new Oracle Home, executing `startup upgrade` and catuprgd, as shown earlier. New versions, releases, and even patch sets provide large numbers of bug fixes and new features, and thus change significant amounts of dictionary structure and data.

Between these Oracle releases, partial patches are released, which contain only important fixes and changes in a few libraries in the Oracle Home. These have minimal impact on the dictionary:

- **Security Patch Update (SPU)**   Previously referred to as CPU (Critical Patch Update), these updates provide the quarterly cumulative security fixes.

- **Patch Set Update (PSU)**   Provides SPU and additional important fixes. Their goal is to stabilize—that is, to fix critical issues without the risk of regressions.

- **Bundle Patch Update (BPU)**   Contains a bunch of patches related to a particular component. For example, CBO patches are not in PSU but can be provided in the Proactive Bundle Patch.

Those include only the libraries or files that are changed and are applied by the OPatch utility. In 12c, the changes to the dictionary are done through the datapatch utility provided in the OPatch. Datapatch checks all containers to know which ones have to be patched. However, only open PDBs are verified, so those that are closed will be in restricted mode when they are opened, and datapatch will need to be run again for them.

Here is an example in which we have plugged the PDB2 PDB to a CDB that has a patch set additional to the CDB of origin:

```
$ORACLE_HOME/OPatch/datapatch -verbose
......
Currently installed SQL Patches:
  PDB CDB$ROOT: 17027533
  PDB PDB$SEED: 17027533
  PDB PDB2:
......
For the following PDBs: PDB2
  Nothing to roll back
  The following patches will be applied: 17027533
......
Patch 17027533 apply (pdb PDB2): SUCCESS
```

Only the PDB2 has to be patched.

In this example, the multitenant architecture brings significant benefit even when you have only one PDB (the single-tenant that you can use without the multitenant option). If you want to upgrade or patch the entire CDB, it will take longer, because there are three container dictionaries to update. But if you create a new CDB with a new version, you can simply unplug/plug in. There is no file movement needed, because it is on the same server; then run catupgrd or datapatch. This is faster because there are only relatively few metadata links to check and update.

Using CDB-Level vs. PDB-Level Parameters

Initialization parameters control the instance behavior. Their first utilization is at instance startup, which is why they are called "initialization parameters." These parameters are also used later, however, and can control the session behavior. Note that each session actually inherits settings from the instance, and some of these can be changed by the session. It's also possible to use different parameters at the statement level, with the OPT_PARAM hint.

The parameters are not stored within the database itself, because a large number of them are needed before opening the database. In older versions of Oracle Database, they were stored in a text file, which Oracle calls the PFILE (the parameter file), and that many DBAs referred to as the init.ora. This file was read by the session running the startup command, but in current versions of Oracle, the parameters are stored in a server parameter file (SPFILE), which is managed by the instance. We can change parameters in the SPFILE with the ALTER SYSTEM command, or we can re-create the SPFILE from a PFILE if we are unable to start the instance.

This does not change in multitenant, except that we have a new level between the instance and the session: the PDB.

CDB SPFILE

The CDB SPFILE is the same as the SPFILE you are familiar with in the non-CDB context. It stores all parameters that are set by ALTER SYSTEM SET ... SCOPE=SPFILE when this command is run at CDB$ROOT level. Those parameters are read when the instance is started, are used by CDB$ROOT, are the defaults for sessions in CDB$ROOT, and also serve as the default for the PDBs when they do not have their own setting.

PDB SPFILE Equivalent

PDBs offer the same Oracle Database functionality, so you are able to set your initialization parameters with the ALTER SYSTEM statement. As an example, when connected to PDB1 we set the following:

```
SQL> alter system set optimizer_dynamic_sampling=8 scope=spfile;
System altered.
```

And we can query it with SHOW SPPARAMETER:

```
SQL> show spparameter optimizer_dynamic_sampling

SID      NAME                              TYPE        VALUE
-------- --------------------------------- ----------- -----
*        optimizer_dynamic_sampling        integer     8
```

This is similar to what we know in non-CDBs, but here the settings are not stored in the instance SPFILE. In multitenant, we have the CDB$ROOT to store information about the containers, and this resides in the PDB_SPFILE$ system table:

```
SQL> show con_name
CON_NAME
------------------------------
CDB$ROOT
SQL> select db_uniq_name,pdb_uid,sid,name,value$ from pdb_spfile$;
DB_UNIQ    PDB_UID    SID NAME                              VALUE$
-------    ----------  --- --------------------------------  ----------
CDB_GVA    1342292939  *   db_securefile                     'PREFERRED'
CDB_GVA    4064530355  *   db_securefile                     'PREFERRED'
CDB_GVA    1532325936  *   db_securefile                     'PREFERRED'
CDB_GVA    4064530355  *   optimizer_dynamic_sampling        8
```

You don't see the CON_ID here, but only the PDB_UID, which we can use to match to our PDB name with V$PDBS:

```
SQL> select con_id,con_uid,name from v$pdbs;
    CON_ID    CON_UID NAME
---------- ---------- ----------
         2 1342292939 PDB$SEED
         4 4064530355 PDB1
         5 1532325936 PDB2
```

In this example, our SPFILE parameter for optimizer_dynamic_sampling in PDB1 is actually stored in the root.

When you are connected to a PDB, you can query the SPFILE parameters with `show spparameter` or with a query on V$SPPARAMETER. You can also dump all parameters defined into a text file, because the CREATE PFILE syntax is supported:

```
SQL> create pfile='/tmp/init.ora' from spfile;
File created.

SQL> host cat /tmp/init.ora
*.db_securefile='PREFERRED'
*.optimizer_dynamic_sampling=8
```

Keep in mind, however, that this text file cannot be used to start the instance, and the name PFILE is there only for syntax compatibility. This is because we are connected to a PDB, and an instance is not at that level.

Another possibility is to generate the describe file, the same XML file that is used by the unplug/plug in operations we will cover in Chapter 9, because it houses information (parameters) about the container that are not stored within the container itself.

```
SQL> exec dbms_pdb.describe('/tmp/pdb1.xml','PDB1');
PL/SQL procedure successfully completed.
SQL> host grep "<spfile>" /tmp/pdb1.xml
     <spfile>*.db_securefile='PREFERRED'</spfile>
     <spfile>*.optimizer_dynamic_sampling=8</spfile>
```

These are persisted across operations such as PDB close, instance startup, unplug/plug in, and cloning. The PDB_SPFILE$ in PDBs is usually empty, except when the PDB is unplugged, in which case it serves as a backup for the XML file.

Both the CDB SPFILE file and the PDB SPFILE table can store a comment. It is highly recommended to add the COMMENT clause to any parameter changed permanently; you have 255 characters to document the date and the reason for the change.

SCOPE=MEMORY

Setting a parameter with `SCOPE=SPFILE` changes the persistent setting, the value that is displayed by `show spparameter`, for future startup only. The `SCOPE=MEMORY` clause, on the other hand, changes the current value of the parameter until the next startup. Without the `SCOPE` clause the parameter is set both in MEMORY and in the SPFILE. This behavior is the same in root and in PDBs, except that shutdown/startup means close/open in the PDB context.

Alter System Reset

You can use `ALTER SYSTEM RESET` to remove the persistent setting for a parameter, which means that when the database is next opened it will take the CDB memory value as the default. Unfortunately there is no reset with the `SCOPE=MEMORY` option, so either you set the value or you reset it in the SPFILE and close/open the PDB.

ISPDB_MODIFIABLE

The `V$PARAMETER` shows all parameters with their names, descriptions, and the current values for your session. There are flags that identify the parameters that can be changed only by restarting the CDB instance (`ISSYS_MODIFIABLE=FALSE`), that can be changed for the instance without restart for future sessions (`ISSYS_MODIFIABLE=IMMEDIATE`), and that can be changed for current sessions as well (`ISSYS_MODIFIABLE=DEFERRED`). In 12.2, there is also a flag to identify the parameters that can be changed in a PDB without close/open (`ISPDB_MODIFIABLE=YES`), and these are a subset of the `ISSYS_MODIFIABLE` group.

In short, parameters relating to the instance itself, such as all memory sizing options, are not PDB-modifiable. However, a large number of parameters can be set by the session, and they are PDB-modifiable, with this value adopted as the default for new sessions. In addition, some parameters require an instance restart, which necessitates closing all PDBs.

Container=ALL

By default, a parameter is set for your current container (`CONTAINER=CURRENT`). However, when you are in the CDB$ROOT, you can change a parameter for all PDBs by adding the `CONTAINER=ALL` clause. The goal is not to enact a parameter change, one by one, in every PDB. Instead, when you want to use the same parameter for all containers, you can set it in CDB$ROOT and let it unset within the PDBs. This command can be used to change the value for all containers immediately, without restarting them, as well as to modify the CDB$ROOT SPFILE for future startup. Note that when the command is combined with `SCOPE=SPFILE`, this makes the parameter's value the default for the whole instance. For example, from CDB$ROOT, we set the temporary undo to true:

```
SQL> alter session set container=cdb$root;
Session altered.
SQL> alter system set temp_undo_enabled=true container=all scope=both;
System altered.
```

Because of the `scope=both`, it is changed in memory and also in the SPFILE:

```
SQL> show spparameter temp_undo_enabled
SID       NAME                         TYPE         VALUE
--------  ---------------------------  -----------  ------------------------
*         temp_undo_enabled            boolean      TRUE

SQL> show parameter temp_undo_enabled
NAME                                   TYPE         VALUE
-------------------------------------  -----------  ------------------------
temp_undo_enabled                      boolean      TRUE
```

Then in all PDBs, it is changed in memory, but not actually stored in PDB_SPFILE$:

```
SQL> alter session set container=pdb1;
Session altered.
SQL> show spparameter temp_undo_enabled
SID       NAME                         TYPE         VALUE
--------  ---------------------------  -----------  ------------------------
*         temp_undo_enabled            Boolean

SQL> show parameter temp_undo_enabled
NAME                                   TYPE         VALUE
-------------------------------------  -----------  ------------------------
temp_undo_enabled                      boolean      TRUE
```

On reflection, this actually makes sense, because there is no need to store a parameter for all containers when the default inherited from the CDB is correct.

DB_UNIQUE_NAME

In our query on PDB_SPFILE$, we saw a DB_UNIQUE_NAME column with value CDB_GVA, which is the database unique name for our CDB. The parameters that are set in a PDB with SCOPE=SPFILE are valid only for one CDB database unique name. We will cover Data Guard in Chapter 11, but you should already know that the DB_UNIQUE_NAME is the correct way to distinguish a primary from its standby database(s). Having the parameter identified by the CDB unique name means that a parameter changed for a PDB in the primary will not be used on the standby database. This makes sense, especially in the context of Active Data Guard, where the standby can be used for reporting, and you may also want to define different optimizer parameters for the online transaction processing (OLTP) on the primary, and the reporting on the standby. In our preceding example, we set the dynamic sampling to 8, but now we want the default value on the primary CDB_GVA (so we reset it) and the level 8 on the standby CDB_BSL. This can be achieved with the DB_UNIQUE_NAME clause:

```
SQL> alter session set container=pdb1;
Session altered.
SQL> alter system reset optimizer_dynamic_sampling;
System altered.
SQL> alter system set optimizer_dynamic_sampling=8 db_unique_name='CDB_BSL' scope=spfile;
System altered.
```

At the time of writing, there are some limitations with this feature. For example, we cannot reset a parameter with the DB_UNIQUE_NAME clause. A workaround for now is probably to remove the row from pdb_spfile$. Another point is that the DB_UNIQUE_NAME provided is case-sensitive, though we have opened enhancement requests for this.

CAUTION
The SPFILE parameters are related to a site and not to a service. In case of switchover or failover, some services will run on another site. For example, the OLTP will failover to the site where the optimizer parameter is defined for reporting. In view of this, particularly when it comes to maintaining different optimizer parameters, it's probably a good idea to set these from a logon trigger that depends on the service name, rather than to a per-site setting.

Summary

In this chapter we covered the basic administration of PDBs after you have a CDB. You can create PDBs, patch them, upgrade them, parameterize them, and drop them. Most of these operations are the same ones that every DBA performs daily, but they are adapted to incorporate two levels in multitenant: CDB and PDB. You will see that a number of new operations are made possible with the multitenant architecture, mostly in Part III, where we delve into recovery and data movement. You need to know and understand the basic operations, and all administration procedures and scripts that are adapted, to function in the new multitenant paradigm.

This chapter focused primarily on the DBA who operates at the CDB level, who is often connected to root, and who invokes SET CONTAINER when needed. In the next chapter, you will see how to make use of those PDBs, which provide a service to which you can connect directly.

CHAPTER 5

Networking and Services

Before we dive into Oracle networking, related specifically to the Oracle Database *12c* multitenant option, we need to take a look again at some of the core concepts. We will not go into detail here on Oracle networking features and functionality, because that is a book on its own; for more in-depth information, we recommend you review the "Oracle Net Services Administrator Guide." In this chapter we will cover the new listener registration (LREG) background process, including brief mention of the new Oracle Database 12*c* multithreaded option, before diving into the details of services and Oracle Database 12*c* Multitenant.

Oracle Net

Oracle Net is the software component that provides the network layer for communication between the client and the Oracle database instances. It forms a communication channel between the client and database instance once a connection has been established.

Oracle Net Services consists of a number of components, such as Oracle Net, that facilitate connectivity between distributed environments. It also includes the Oracle Net Listener, the Connection Manager (CMAN), and two key configuration utilities: Oracle Net Configuration Assistant (NETCA) and Oracle Net Manager (netmgr).

The Oracle Net Listener

The listener is one of the most important components to consider when establishing a new Oracle Database environment, yet many DBAs treat it lightly, paying it only minimal attention. Perhaps this is because, in many cases, once the listener is configured you can forget about it. But in Oracle Database 12*c*, with the introduction of multitenant, there is more to the listener than meets the eye.

Let's begin with a recap of the basics of a database connection in the traditional model. When a database starts it will, by default, register with the listener, providing it with one or more service names. But here is where it can get confusing:

- A service might identify more than one instance (in the case of Oracle Real Application Clusters [RAC]).

- A single instance can be registered by more than one listener.

- The database may register more than one service with the listener.

When looking at the process of a client connecting to a database, we can see there are three high-level steps performed, as shown in Figure 5-1. First, the client

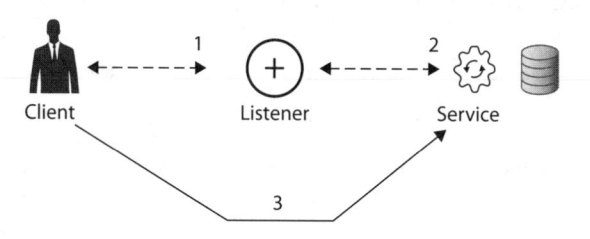

FIGURE 5-1. *Basic connection overview*

initiates communication by requesting a connection from the listener to a particular service. Then the listener identifies the appropriate service and passes the details to the client, after which it will make a direct connection to it. Once the connection is established, it is important to note that the listener is not involved in any way in the communication going forward.

This brings us to an interesting change in Oracle Database12c: the new listener registration (LREG) background process.

The LREG Process

Instance registration with the listener in Oracle 12c behaves a bit differently from that of previous versions. In 12c, the LREG is a new background process that will register the database instance with the listener, which was a task performed in earlier versions by the Process Monitor PMON) process. On UNIX, this process is easily identified at the OS level, because "lreg" is included in the visible process name. This can be seen in the following code block:

```
# ps -ef|grep lreg|grep -v grep
oracle    6865    1   0 Feb14 ?    00:00:14 asm_lreg_+ASM
oracle    6996    1   0 Feb14 ?    00:00:20 ora_lreg_CDB1
```

The format of the process is ora_lreg_*SID*.

Note that this background process is classified as critical for the database instance, and, if it is terminated, the Oracle Database instance will actually abort. The code blocks that follow show the output of the alert log when this background process is killed:

```
# ps -ef|grep lreg|grep -v grep
oracle    6865    1   0 Feb14 ?    00:00:14 asm_lreg_+ASM
oracle    6996    1   0 Feb14 ?    00:00:20 ora_lreg_CDB1
oracle@linux3[/home/oracle]: kill -9 6996
```

From the alert log, notice the following messages when the LREG is terminated:

```
...
Instance Critical Process (pid: 25, ospid: 6996, LREG) died unexpectedly
PMON (ospid: 6938): terminating the instance due to error 500
System state dump requested by (instance=1, osid=6938 (PMON)), summary=[abnormal
instance termination].
System State dumped to trace file /u01/app/oracle/diag/rdbms/cdb1/CDB1/trace/CDB1_
diag_6962_20160220204645.trc
...
Instance terminated by PMON, pid = 6938
USER (ospid: 7185): terminating the instance
Instance terminated by USER, pid = 7185
...
```

The LREG background process also writes out information regarding service updates in the listener log. These include service_update, service_register, and service_died messages; here's an example:

```
20-FEB-2016 20:57:07 * service_update * CDB1 * 0
2016-02-20 20:57:35.907000 +13:00
```

NOTE
When we used the strace utility to view additional detail on the LREG process (though it is not recommended that you use this utility on background processes in production systems), we observed a review of the load average (/proc/loadavg) approximately every 33 seconds.

When running in the new multithreaded mode, LREG does not run as a process on its own, but is run as a thread. Following is an excerpt from a Linux system that shows the LREG process running as a thread (thread ID 4696) under the process ID 4658:

```
SQL> select pid, spid, stid, pname, username, program from v$process where
pname='LREG';

   PID SPID   STID  PNAME USERNAME     PROGRAM
------ ------ ----- ----- ------------ --------------------------------
    29 4658   4696  LREG  oracle       oracle@linux2.orademo.net (LREG)
```

From the preceding example, we now have the operating system process ID 4658. If we review the process listing for the database CDB2, we can easily identify this process:

```
oracle@linux2[/home/oracle]: ps -ef|grep CDB2
oracle    4656     1  0 22:06 ?        00:00:00 ora_pmon_CDB2
oracle    4658     1  0 22:06 ?        00:00:01 ora_u002_CDB2
oracle    4662     1  0 22:06 ?        00:00:00 ora_psp0_CDB2
```

```
oracle     4664      1  2 22:06 ?        00:00:21 ora_vktm_CDB2
oracle     4671      1 12 22:06 ?        00:02:03 ora_u005_CDB2
oracle     4675      1  0 22:06 ?        00:00:00 ora_ofsd_CDB2
oracle     4684      1  0 22:06 ?        00:00:00 ora_dbw0_CDB2
oracle     4686      1  0 22:06 ?        00:00:02 ora_lgwr_CDB2
oracle     13247 12521 0 22:23 pts/1     00:00:00 grep CDB2
```

Taking process 4658, we can again use the `ps` command to list the threads associated with this:

```
oracle@linux2[/home/oracle]: ps -eLo "pid tid comm args" |grep 4658
 4658   4658 ora_scmn_cdb2    ora_u002_CDB2
 4658   4659 oracle           ora_u002_CDB2
 4658   4660 ora_clmn_cdb2    ora_u002_CDB2
 4658   4667 ora_gen0_cdb2    ora_u002_CDB2
 4658   4668 ora_mman_cdb2    ora_u002_CDB2
 4658   4678 ora_dbrm_cdb2    ora_u002_CDB2
 4658   4681 ora_pman_cdb2    ora_u002_CDB2
 4658   4689 ora_ckpt_cdb2    ora_u002_CDB2
 4658   4691 ora_smon_cdb2    ora_u002_CDB2
 4658   4696 ora_lreg_cdb2    ora_u002_CDB2
12539  12539 grep             grep 4658
```

By reviewing the output of the `ps` command, we can identify the LREG thread.

NOTE
The new multithreaded option for UNIX-based systems was introduced in 12.1.0.1. To enable the multithreaded mode, the database parameter THREADED_EXECUTION must be set to TRUE and the database restarted. The multithreaded model enables Oracle Database processes to execute as operating system threads in separate address spaces. Some background processes run as processes containing only a single thread, but the other Oracle processes run as threads within processes. Multithreaded brings some interesting new options and changes.

Networking: Multithreaded and Multitenant

One of the key advantages of multitenant is consolidation: multiple database (non-CDB) environments can be configured to run as pluggable databases (PDBs) in a single consolidated container database. This enables you to get the most out of your valuable resources by not having to allocate unnecessary resources. For example, instead of running ten databases on one server, each with its own System Global Area (SGA) and background processes, you could consolidate into a single container database with PDBs, which would mean one SGA and one set of background processes. And the multithreaded mode takes this one step further by reducing the amount of processes on the system, with the possibility of improved performance and scalability.

When you're configuring the multithreaded option (by setting THREADED_EXECUTION=TRUE and restarting the CDB), consider that you will also need to make a change in the listener to allow threads, rather than processes, to be spawned. To enable this, set the parameter DEDICATED_THROUGH_BROKER_<listener_name>=ON in the listener.ora configuration file, and then restart the listener so that the changes take effect. As a result, when the listener receives a client connection request, it will pass this onto a connection broker (Nnnn), which will then verify the authentication, and a new thread will be spawned in an existing process.

The total number and type of connection brokers can be set using the CONNECTION_BROKERS database parameter. By default, two brokers are configured—one of type DEDICATED and one of type EMON. To view the status of the connection brokers (which are also spawned threads), you can review the status of the services using the listener control (lsnrctl) command, as follows:

```
# lsnrctl service listener_pdb
LSNRCTL for Linux: Version 12.2.0.0.2 - Beta on 27-FEB-2016 15:37:19
Copyright (c) 1991, 2015, Oracle.  All rights reserved.

Connecting to (DESCRIPTION=(ADDRESS=(PROTOCOL=TCP)(HOST=linux2.orademo.net)
(PORT=1531)))
Services Summary...
…
Service "dpdb1.orademo.net" has 1 instance(s).
  Instance "CDB2", status READY, has 12 handler(s) for this service...
    Handler(s):
      "D000" established:0 refused:0 current:0 max:1022 state:ready
         DISPATCHER <machine: linux2.orademo.net, pid: 4634_4664>
         (ADDRESS=(PROTOCOL=tcp)(HOST=linux2.orademo.net)(PORT=23595))
      "N000" established:280 refused:0 state:ready
         CMON <machine: linux2.orademo.net, pid: 4634_4666>
         (ADDRESS=(PROTOCOL=tcp)(HOST=127.0.0.1)(PORT=46921))
      "DEDICATED" established:0 refused:0 state:ready
         LOCAL SERVER
      "N001" established:234 refused:0 state:ready
         CMON <machine: linux2.orademo.net, pid: 4634_15873>
         (ADDRESS=(PROTOCOL=tcp)(HOST=127.0.0.1)(PORT=57571))
…
The command completed successfully…
```

A quick way to see the thread and process details is to use the `ps` command:

```
# ps -eLo "pid tid comm args" |grep 4634 |egrep '4666|15873'
 4634  4666 ora_n000_cdb2    ora_u005_CDB2
 4634 15873 ora_n001_cdb2    ora_u005_CDB2
```

And looking further at V$PROCESS, we see the following:

```
SQL> select spid, stid, pname, execution_type from v$process where spid=4634 and stid
in (4666,15873);

SPID   STID   PNAME EXECUTION_TYPE
-----  -----  ----- -----------------
4634   4666   N000  THREAD
4634   15873  N001  THREAD
```

NOTE
Do not attempt to kill thread processes via the command line (using the `kill` command) because you might end up killing a number of other thread connections as well. Instead, consider using ALTER SYSTEM KILL SESSION by passing in the correct SID and SERIAL# values. Make sure you are working with the correct session by first looking at V$SESSION and V$PROCESS.

If you want to configure certain clients to use the threaded option and others to use processes, you will need to configure two listeners, each one using different ports. It is also possible to create a dedicated listener for a specific PDB, but you'll learn more about this a bit later in this chapter.

Service Names

When using a multitenant configuration, you will need to be aware of the changes introduced with services. In this section we will cover the important changes you should be aware of when creating and maintaining Oracle Database 12c Multitenant environments.

Default Services and Connecting to PDBs

When creating a new PDB, a new default service is automatically generated for it, with the same name as the PDB. The service will be registered with the listener and client connections, and connections to the PDB can begin to make use of the new service once the PDB is opened. The automatic registration might take a few seconds, although you can run `alter system register` to force the registration to occur immediately.

So, for example, if a new PDB called PDB1 is created, a new default service of the same name will also be created. The new service details can be viewed by looking at v$services or cdb_services:

```
SQL> select service_id, name, network_name, PDB from v$services
        where network_name is not null order by 1;

SERVICE_ID NAME                          NETWORK NAME                  PDB
---------- ----------------------------  ----------------------------  ----------
         5 CDB2XDB                       CDB2XDB                       CDB$ROOT
         6 CDB2.orademo.net              CDB2.orademo.net              CDB$ROOT
         7 pdb1.orademo.net              pdb1.orademo.net              PDB1
```

Reviewing the listener status and services will indicate whether the new service name is registered:

```
# lsnrctl status listener
LSNRCTL for Linux: Version 12.2.0.0.2 - Beta on 27-FEB-2016 20:19:33
Copyright (c) 1991, 2015, Oracle.  All rights reserved.
Connecting to (DESCRIPTION=(ADDRESS=(PROTOCOL=TCP)(HOST=linux2.orademo.net)(PORT=1521)))
…
Services Summary...
…
Service "CDB2.orademo.net" has 1 instance(s).
  Instance "CDB2", status READY, has 1 handler(s) for this service...
Service "pdb1.orademo.net" has 1 instance(s).
  Instance "CDB2", status READY, has 1 handler(s) for this service...
The command completed successfully
# lsnrctl service listener
LSNRCTL for Linux: Version 12.2.0.0.2 - Beta on 27-FEB-2016 20:28:00
Copyright (c) 1991, 2015, Oracle.  All rights reserved.
Connecting to (DESCRIPTION=(ADDRESS=(PROTOCOL=TCP)(HOST=linux2.orademo.net)(PORT=1521)))
Services Summary...
…
Service "CDB2.orademo.net" has 1 instance(s).
  Instance "CDB2", status READY, has 1 handler(s) for this service...
    Handler(s):
      "DEDICATED" established:14 refused:0 state:ready
         LOCAL SERVER
Service "pdb1.orademo.net" has 1 instance(s).
  Instance "CDB2", status READY, has 1 handler(s) for this service...
    Handler(s):
      "DEDICATED" established:14 refused:0 state:ready
         LOCAL SERVER
The command completed successfully
```

The end user/application can now connect to this PDB using the new service name via a number of methods, such as via the Oracle Net Services name using the tnsnames.ora file or an easy connect string. The basic easy connect string takes the format @[//*Host*[:*Port*]/<*service_name*>], and when this method is used, no entry is required in the tnsnames.ora file.

Here's an example of using the easy connect method to connect to the newly created PDB1:

```
SQL> connect aels/aelspassword@//linux2.orademo.net/pdb1.orademo.net
```

You can also add and use an Oracle Net Services name entry in the tnsnames.ora file:

```
PDB1 =
  (DESCRIPTION =
    (ADDRESS = (PROTOCOL = TCP)(HOST = linux2.orademo.net)(PORT = 1521))
    (CONNECT_DATA =
      (SERVER = DEDICATED)
      (SERVICE_NAME = PDB1.orademo.net)
    )
  )
```

Once the entry is added to the tnsnames.ora file, it can be used to connect to the PDB:

```
SQL> connect aels/aelspassword@PDB1
Connected.
SQL> show con_name
CON_NAME
------------------------------
PDB1
```

Figure 5-2 illustrates two basic concepts. When each PDB is created, each will have a service name created that matches the PDB name; the service is automatically registered with the default listener. When a client connection is requested to the listener for a specific service name for a PDB, the listener prompts a server process to be spawned and the connection between the client and the PDB will be established, with the listener no longer involved.

NOTE
When running more than one CDB on a single system with PDBs using the same service names, it is recommended that you use separate listeners for each CDB. If only one listener is used, you will end up with both CDB databases having service names for the PDBs registered with the same listener. The end result could be that an incorrect connection may be established, which may lead to undesirable results. In view of this, it is recommended that all service names on a system should be unique to avoid such collisions or, alternatively, separate listeners configured for each CDB.

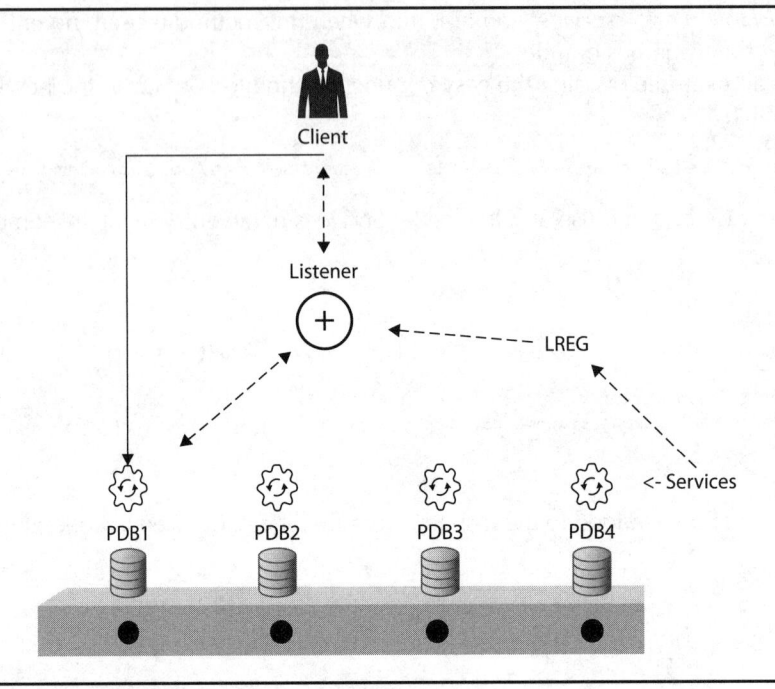

FIGURE 5-2. *Service name registration (LREG) and client connection*

Before moving on to the next section it is worth mentioning that you can also use the local environment variable TWO_TASK (on UNIX) or LOCAL (on Windows) to specify a default connect identifier (connect string). When you set this variable, the user will be able to connect to a database without explicitly specifying the connect string. Here's an example:

```
# export TWO_TASK=pdb1
# sqlplus aels/aelspassword

SQL*Plus: Release 12.2.0.0.2 Beta on Sun Feb 28 12:37:07 2016
Copyright (c) 1982, 2015, Oracle.  All rights reserved.
Last Successful login time: Sun Feb 28 2016 05:52:55 +13:00
Connected to:
Oracle Database 12c Enterprise Edition Release 12.2.0.0.2 - 64bit Beta
With the Partitioning, OLAP, Advanced Analytics and Real Application Testing options

SQL> show con_name
CON_NAME
------------------------------
PDB1
```

This method might be required by various applications. Also note that the easy connect string can be used as well; this removes the dependency of having a required entry in the tnsnames.ora file (example: `export TWO_TASK=//linux3.orademo.net/PDB1.orademo.net`).

Creating Services

By default, a service is generated for each PDB on creation. In many cases, the requirement will be to create additional services and associate them with the particular PDB. This can be especially useful in Oracle RAC configurations, where you might want a specific application to connect to its PDB only from one of the instances. Creating a service and setting up the rules to run on only one particular node in the cluster can be an extremely useful capability to have.

When creating a new service, you can set an optional PDB property at creation time, which can be modified at any time after. The PDB property is important because it associates the service to a particular PDB.

If a user connects to a service that does not have a value specified for the PDB property, the user name would be resolved in the context of the root container. However, if the value is specified for the PDB property, the user name will be resolved in the context of the specified PDB.

Note the following regarding service creation:

- Services become active (listed in v$active_services and registered with the listener) only when the PDB is opened.

- Service names must be unique within the CDB, but they must also be unique between all databases using a specific listener.

- When using Oracle Restart or Oracle Clusterware, you can use either the SRVCTL utility or the DBMS_SERVICE package to add, modify, and manage new services. Using the SRVCTL utility in this case is recommended.

- The PDB property must be set using `-pdb <PDB>` when you're using SRVCTL. If you're using the DBMS_SERVICE package, the PDB property will automatically be set to the current connected container, so make sure you connect to the correct PDB before creating the service using DBMS_SERVICE.

- The PDB property cannot be changed with the DBMS_SERVICE package. The service will need to be re-created from within the correct PDB.

- If you are not using Oracle Restart or Oracle Clusterware, the DBMS_SERVICE package is used to add, modify, or remove new services.

- Stopping a service using the SRVCTL utility does not change the status of the PDB it is associated with. The SRVCTL `stop` command will affect only the service, not the PDB.

- When you unplug a PDB, the service will not be removed, so this should be managed manually. The same applies when a PDB is dropped. If the service is no longer required, it should be removed manually.

Creating a Service with SRVCTL

Creating services with the SRVCTL command line utility is very easy, and you can quickly understand why you should be using this with Oracle Restart or Oracle Clusterware.

In the next two examples, two new services will be created: the first uses a single-instance configuration, and the second uses a two-node Oracle RAC cluster.

Adding a Service for a PDB in a Single-Instance Database The CDB database CDB1 consists of PDB1 and PDB2. It is a single-instance database in which Oracle Restart is used. Each of the PDBs already has the default service created and registered with the default listener. In addition, the following services are required:

- PDB1 will use service CRMDEV.
- PDB2 will use service HRDEV.

As the Oracle database software owner, which in this installation is the user name *oracle* for the UNIX environment, set the environment to the correct Oracle Home and use the `srvctl` command to add the two services. Then review their status and start these two services. See the code blocks that follow for more detail on these steps.

1. Create the services.
    ```
    #  srvctl add service -db CDB1 -pdb PDB1 -service CRMDEV
    #  srvctl add service -db CDB1 -pdb PDB2 -service HRDEV
    ```
2. Review the service status.
    ```
    #  srvctl status service -db CDB1
    Service CRMDEV is not running.
    Service HRDEV is not running.
    ```
3. Start the services.
    ```
    # srvctl start service -db CDB1 -service CRMDEV
    # srvctl start service -db CDB1 -service HRDEV
    ```
4. Show the status of the services following the startup.
    ```
    # srvctl status service -db CDB1
    Service CRMDEV is running
    Service HRDEV is running
    ```

Now that the services are created, review what the listener knows. Notice that these newly added services are also registered with the listener, as per the extracts from these listener status commands. Here's the first one:

```
# lsnrctl status listener
LSNRCTL for Linux: Version 12.2.0.0.2 - Beta on 28-FEB-2016 07:44:14
Copyright (c) 1991, 2015, Oracle.  All rights reserved.

Connecting to (ADDRESS=(PROTOCOL=tcp)(HOST=)(PORT=1521))
…
Service "crmdev.orademo.net" has 1 instance(s).
  Instance "CDB1", status READY, has 1 handler(s) for this service...
Service "hrdev.orademo.net" has 1 instance(s).
  Instance "CDB1", status READY, has 1 handler(s) for this service...
…
The command completed successfully
```

And here's the second one:

```
# lsnrctl service listener
LSNRCTL for Linux: Version 12.2.0.0.2 - Beta on 28-FEB-2016 07:44:48
Copyright (c) 1991, 2015, Oracle.  All rights reserved.

Connecting to (ADDRESS=(PROTOCOL=tcp)(HOST=)(PORT=1521))
Services Summary...
…
Service "crmdev.orademo.net" has 1 instance(s).
  Instance "CDB1", status READY, has 1 handler(s) for this service...
    Handler(s):
      "DEDICATED" established:1688 refused:0 state:ready
         LOCAL SERVER
Service "hrdev.orademo.net" has 1 instance(s).
  Instance "CDB1", status READY, has 1 handler(s) for this service...
    Handler(s):
      "DEDICATED" established:1688 refused:0 state:ready
         LOCAL SERVER
…
The command completed successfully
```

Reviewing V$SERVICES, you can also see the newly created services:

```
SQL> select con_id, service_id, name, network_name, pdb
     from v$services
     where pdb in ('PDB1','PDB2') order by 1,2;

CON_ID SERVICE_ID NAME              NETWORK NAME       PDB
------ ---------- ----------------- ------------------ ------
     3          1 CRMDEV            CRMDEV             PDB1
     3          7 pdb1.orademo.net  pdb1.orademo.net   PDB1
     4          1 HRDEV             HRDEV              PDB2
     4          9 pdb2.orademo.net  pdb2.orademo.net   PDB2
```

You can now use these new services to connect to the respective PDBs—here's an example:

```
SQL> connect aels/aelspassword@//linux3/CRMDEV.orademo.net
Connected.
SQL> show con_name
CON_NAME
------------------------------
PDB1
```

Adding a Service for an Oracle RAC PDB   The steps for adding a new service for a PDB under Oracle RAC are almost identical to those used in the preceding example for a single-instance database: the SRVCTL utility is invoked to add the service. In this case, however, you need to keep in mind one particular question: Do you want the service to be enabled on all the instances, or just one?

In the next example, the Oracle RAC database, RCDB, consists of two nodes running two PDB databases: RPDB1 and RPDB2. The requirement is that RPDB1 be accessible only via node 1 (instance 1, RCDB1) and that RPDB2 be accessible from both nodes. By creating two services, this can easily be achieved.

To create the service for RPDB1 to run from only instance 1, we use the following commands, executed as the Oracle Database software owner, which is the *oracle* UNIX user in this case.

1. Create new service CRMPRT to run on one instance only.

   ```
   # srvctl add service -db RCDB -service CRMRPT -preferred "RCDB1"
   -available "RCDB2" -pdb RPDB1
   ```

2. Create new service CRMPRD to run on both instances.

   ```
   # srvctl add service -db RCDB -service CRMPRD -preferred
   "RCDB1,RCDB2" -pdb RPDB2
   ```

3. Review the status of the service.

   ```
   # srvctl status service -db RCDB
   Service CRMPRD is not running.
   Service CRMRPT is not running.
   ```

4. Start both services.

   ```
   # srvctl start service -db RCDB -service CRMRPT
   # srvctl start service -db RCDB -service CRMRPD
   ```

5. Review statuses following service startup:

   ```
   # srvctl status service -db RCDB
   Service CRMPRD is running on instance(s) RCDB1,RCDB2
   Service CRMRPT is running on instance(s) RCDB1
   ```

The status output shows that the service CRMPRD is now running and available on both instances in the Oracle RAC cluster, whereas the service CRMRPT runs only on the preferred instance, RCDB1. Users or clients will be able to start using them for connections—here's an example:

```
SQL> connect reportadmin/reportadmin@//rac12-scan/CRMRPT.orademo.net
Connected.
SQL> show con_name
CON_NAME
------------------------------
RPDB1

SQL> select instance_name from v$instance;
INSTANCE_NAME
---------
RCDB1
```

To modify or remove services, you can use the `modify service` or `remove service` option provided by the `srvctl` command:

```
# srvctl modify service -db RCDB -service CRMRPT -pdb RPDB2
# srvctl stop service -db RCDB -service CRMRPT
# srvctl remove service -db RCDB -service CRMRP
```

NOTE
For more information on using the SRVCTL utility, use the `srvctl -h` command to obtain detailed help options. If you specify `srvctl add service -h`, you can also obtain help specific to the addition of new services. Substitute with the `modify` or `remove` keyword to list information on the respective help option.

Creating a Service with DBMS_SERVICE

When using environments in which Oracle Restart or Oracle Clusterware is not installed, you need to use the DBMS_SERVICE package to create and manage new services. As mentioned, when creating new services for a specific PDB, you need to ensure that you are connected to that PDB when performing this operation. Otherwise, the service will be created in the context of the PDB you are connected to at the time, as the PDB property is set to the connected PDB.

1. Switch to the PDB and create the new service.

   ```
   SQL> alter session set container=PDB1;
   SQL> begin
         dbms_service.create_service (service_name => 'CRMPROD'
                                    , network_name=> 'CRMPROD.orademo.net');
        end;
   /
   PL/SQL procedure successfully completed.
   ```

2. Review the services.

   ```
   SQL> select service_id, name, network_name, creation_date, pdb from dba_services;

   SERVICE_ID NAME              NETWORK NAME           CREATION_DATE         PDB
   ---------- ----------------  --------------------   ------------------    -------
            7 pdb1.orademo.net  pdb1.orademo.net       7/02/2016:18:31:40    PDB1
            1 CRMPROD           CRMPROD.orademo.net    28/02/2016:04:01:50   PDB1
   ```

3. List all the active services.

   ```
   SQL> select service_id, name, network_name from v$active_services;

   SERVICE_ID NAME              NETWORK NAME
   ---------- ----------------  --------------------------------------
            7 pdb1.orademo.net  pdb1.orademo.net
   ```

4. Start the service and review active services.

   ```
   SQL> exec dbms_service.start_service ('CRMPROD');
   PL/SQL procedure successfully completed.

   SQL> select service_id, name, network_name from v$active_services;

   SERVICE_ID NAME              NETWORK NAME
   ---------- ----------------  --------------------------------------
            7 pdb1.orademo.net  pdb1.orademo.net
            1 CRMPROD           CRMPROD.orademo.net
   ```

In this section we have demonstrated how easy it is to create new services for a PDB, using either the SRVCTL utility or the DBMS_SERVICE package.

Create a Dedicated Listener for a PDB

In some cases, you may need to use a specific dedicated listener port for one or more PDBs. This will require that you create a new listener and then ensure that the PDB is registered with it. In this section, we will show you how this can be done.

In a consolidated database environment with a large number of PDBs within a CDB, you may need to segment some PDBs off or, from a security point of view, maintain both encrypted and unencrypted connections. To do this, you first create a new listener.

In the following example, we will call the listener LISTENER_PDB and have it listen on port 1531. The following entry is added to the listener.ora file to introduce the new listener:

```
LISTENER_PDB =
   (DESCRIPTION_LIST =
     (DESCRIPTION =
       (ADDRESS = (PROTOCOL = TCP)(HOST = linux2.orademo.net)(PORT = 1531))
     )
   )
```

Once the new listener entry has been added, we can start it with the `lsnrctl start listener_pdb` command. When the listener is started, we can then add a net alias to the tnsnames.ora file:

```
LISTENER_PDB =
   (ADDRESS = (PROTOCOL = TCP)(HOST = linux2.orademo.net)(PORT = 1531)
```

We are now ready to configure our PDB, which happens to be PDB1 in this case, to use this listener. We update the `LISTENER_NETWORKS` parameter specific to the PDB:

```
SQL> alter session set container=PDB1;
SQL> alter system set listener_networks='((NAME=PDB_NETWORK1)(LOCAL_LISTENER=LISTENER_PDB))' scope=both;
```

The syntax for the `LISTENER_NETWORKS` parameter is as follows:

```
LISTENER_NETWORKS =
  '((NAME=network_name)(LOCAL_LISTENER=["]listener_address[,...]["])
  [(REMOTE_LISTENER=["]listener_address[,...]["])])'  [,...]
```

NOTE
The `listener_address` string is an address (or address list) that resolves to a specific listener. An alias can be used, which is the case in the example used here, although it requires that you add an address entry into the tnsnames.ora file prior, as shown in the code block `Add net alias to tnsnames.ora file`.

If we now review the listener, we will notice that the PDB1 services are registered automatically by the LREG process, following the execution of the preceding commands.

```
# lsnrctl status listener_pdb
LSNRCTL for Linux: Version 12.2.0.0.2 - Beta on 28-FEB-2016 05:45:36
Copyright (c) 1991, 2015, Oracle.  All rights reserved.

Connecting to (DESCRIPTION=(ADDRESS=(PROTOCOL=TCP)(HOST=linux2.orademo.net)
(PORT=1531)))
STATUS of the LISTENER
------------------------
Alias                     listener_pdb
Version                   TNSLSNR for Linux: Version 12.2.0.0.2 - Beta
Start Date                28-FEB-2016 05:34:25
Uptime                    0 days 0 hr. 11 min. 11 sec
Trace Level               off
Security                  ON: Local OS Authentication
SNMP                      OFF
Listener Parameter File   /u01/app/oracle/product/12.2.0/dbhome_1/network/admin/
listener.ora
Listener Log File         /u01/app/oracle/diag/tnslsnr/linux2/listener_pdb/alert/log.
xml
Listening Endpoints Summary...
  (DESCRIPTION=(ADDRESS=(PROTOCOL=tcp)(HOST=linux2.orademo.net)(PORT=1531)))
Services Summary...
Service "2cbaba1bf0dc4817e0538428a8c0ec8a.orademo.net" has 1 instance(s).
  Instance "CDB2", status READY, has 2 handler(s) for this service...
Service "pdb1.orademo.net" has 1 instance(s).
  Instance "CDB2", status READY, has 2 handler(s) for this service...
The command completed successfully

# lsnrctl service listener_pdb
LSNRCTL for Linux: Version 12.2.0.0.2 - Beta on 28-FEB-2016 05:45:38
Copyright (c) 1991, 2015, Oracle.  All rights reserved.

Connecting to (DESCRIPTION=(ADDRESS=(PROTOCOL=TCP)(HOST=linux2.orademo.net)
(PORT=1531)))
Services Summary...
Service "2cbaba1bf0dc4817e0538428a8c0ec8a.orademo.net" has 1 instance(s).
  Instance "CDB2", status READY, has 2 handler(s) for this service...
    Handler(s):
      "D000" established:0 refused:0 current:0 max:1022 state:ready
         DISPATCHER <machine: linux2.orademo.net, pid: 15376>
         (ADDRESS=(PROTOCOL=tcp)(HOST=linux2.orademo.net)(PORT=36434))
      "DEDICATED" established:0 refused:0 state:ready
         LOCAL SERVER
Service "pdb1.orademo.net" has 1 instance(s).
  Instance "CDB2", status READY, has 2 handler(s) for this service...
    Handler(s):
      "D000" established:0 refused:0 current:0 max:1022 state:ready
         DISPATCHER <machine: linux2.orademo.net, pid: 15376>
         (ADDRESS=(PROTOCOL=tcp)(HOST=linux2.orademo.net)(PORT=36434))
      "DEDICATED" established:0 refused:0 state:ready
         LOCAL SERVER
The command completed successfully
```

Now that the PDB is registered with the listener, we can connect to it using the new listener that is running on port 1531, as follows:

```
SQL> connect aels/aelspassword@//linux2:1531/pdb1.orademo.net
Connected.
SQL> show con_name
CON_NAME
------------------------------
PDB1
```

If you are not using the easy connect string connection method, but are instead using a Net Service name using the tnsnames.ora file entries, you need to make sure to add the following entry to the tnsnames.ora file to reflect the new port change for this PDB:

```
PDB1=
  (DESCRIPTION =
    (ADDRESS = (PROTOCOL = TCP)(HOST = linux2.orademo.net)(PORT = 1531))
    (CONNECT_DATA =
      (SERVER = DEDICATED)
      (SERVICE_NAME = PDB1.orademo.net)
    )
  )
```

Summary

In this chapter, we covered only the tip of the iceberg of information available regarding Oracle networking to highlight key features and functionalities you should be aware of when using the Oracle Database 12c Multitenant option. Creating and managing services in a multitenant configuration turns out to be less complex than you might have thought, even when using Oracle RAC. Using the SRVCTL utility or the DBMS_SERVICE package can help you achieve the required results quickly.

Now that you know how to connect, the next logical topic to address is security. For many DBAs, this is a daunting and intimidating topic, but in the next chapter, we will systematically walk you through its key aspects, including explaining the difference between different types of users, roles, and permissions, along with discussions about encryption, isolation, and the lockdown of profiles.

CHAPTER 6

Security

So far in Part II we have described a number of operations you can perform on pluggable databases (PDBs) and the many different ways to connect to them. At this point we also need to factor security considerations into the mix, as the most prevalent attack vector is an abuse of database privileges. Rather than granting administrator rights too widely, we should instead apply the principle of minimal privileges. In 12c, with the Enterprise Edition and the Advanced Security option, the privilege analysis functionality offered can be a great help in this area.

With respect to multitenant, your effective user security administration starts by thinking about which users should have access only to specific PDBs, as users and roles can be created common or locally. Privileges can also be granted common or locally, and beyond this, multitenant (including single-tenant) brings additional fine-grained control via powerful commands, courtesy of lockdown profiles. Of course, when you issue powerful privileges locally to a PDB, you need to prevent any side effects on the container database (CDB), and 12.2 introduced a number of PDB isolation features to mitigate this.

In terms of data security, Oracle Virtual Private Database is still an option to limit access at row level, as is the Oracle Database Vault to protect against rogue database administrators (but we will not detail them here, because they're not specific to multitenant). Another type of possible attack is network sniffing—that is, reading data directly off the network—and network encryption is available in all Oracle 12c editions without options. Bulk data sets that leave the confines of the company premises, such as backups stored off site or in the cloud, are also potentially vulnerable. We will cover backup encryption in Chapter 7.

Finally, we may want to protect against unauthorized access at disk level, and this is highly recommended in a multitenant database, where data from different sources will be consolidated on the same CDB. This protection becomes mandatory when we put our data on a public cloud, and for these reasons we will cover Transparent Data Encryption at the end of this chapter.

Users, Roles, and Permissions

At a high level, when you connect to an Oracle Database, you do so with a database user that is declared within the database, in the dictionary, along with the user's privilege definition. We have not yet defined which container this user information is stored in, and they can actually be common and thereby stored in CDB$ROOT or local and stored in a PDB.

Common or Local?

A common user's information is stored in CDB$ROOT and exists in every single PDB. You create common users for the CDB administrators or for users that have the same identity in all tenants. In both cases, they must connect to CDB$ROOT to change their passwords. In contrast, a local user is stored in a single PDB and exists only in that PDB.

For users, roles, profiles, and privileges, we have to work with the key words *common* and *local*. But before we go any further, let's ensure that we are all on the same page in terms of our definitions of a user and a role in the Oracle Database, because this is not an obvious given.

What Is a User?

In Oracle, a *user* and a *schema* are synonymous—or at least that was the case before the introduction of multitenant. When you create a user, you implicitly create a schema for the user objects, and when you have a schema, its owner is a user. Because this chapter is about security and not database objects, we will use the term "user" here. However, keep in mind that the one-to-one relationship between users and schemas has changed with multitenant, and one common user is now a different schema in each PDB.

A *user* is just a name that is employed when you connect to the database, and a session is always associated with a user. No matter which way you connect to the database, you will have a username, and this user is the vehicle that enables a session to perform operations on the database. You grant privileges to the user, and the connected user can enact whatever is permitted by those privileges.

Because it is highly likely that you will have several users with the same allotted privileges, or users with requirements for the same groups of privileges, you can define roles. In this way, you grant specific privileges to a role, and then grant the role to the users. Roles are also useful to enable the switching of users from one group of privileges to another. For example, the same user may have a read-only role when connecting with SQL Developer and a read/write role when connected through the application, because the application can encapsulate some form of access control.

User and role definitions are actually stored in the same data dictionary table, USER$, where the TYPE# defines whether it is a user (1) or a role (0):

```
SQL> select user,name,type# from user$ order by 1;

USER                      NAME                             TYPE#
------------------------  ------------------------------   ------
SYS                       SYS                                  1
SYS                       PUBLIC                               0
SYS                       CONNECT                              0
SYS                       RESOURCE                             0
SYS                       DBA                                  0
SYS                       AUDIT_ADMIN                          0
SYS                       AUDIT_VIEWER                         0
SYS                       AUDSYS                               1
SYS                       SYSTEM                               1
SYS                       SELECT_CATALOG_ROLE                  0
...
```

You might think that when you have no database, you would have no user definitions, because there is no dictionary yet; however, as it turns out, some users are actually hard-coded. Here we connect to an "idle instance" as we would do when wanting to create a database:

```
$ ORACLE_SID=DUMMY sqlplus / as sysdba
SQL*Plus: Release 12.1.0.2.0 Production on Tue Mar 8 16:00:45 2016
Copyright (c) 1982, 2014, Oracle.  All rights reserved.
Connected to an idle instance.
SQL> show user
USER is "SYS"
SQL> connect / as sysoper
Connected to an idle instance.
SQL> show user
USER is "PUBLIC"
```

SYSDBA privilege is mapped to the SYS user and SYSOPER privilege is mapped to the PUBLIC role. The authentication is handled through OS groups or via a password file, because there is no dictionary at this stage.

A number of users and roles are generated when you create the database, and these are maintained by Oracle. Starting in 12c, multitenant or not, there is an easy way to identify system users, because they have the ORACLE_MAINTAINED column set to TRUE in DBA_USERS. The creation of new users and roles is handled with the CREATE USER and CREATE ROLE statements. Both statements have a new optional clause in 12c multitenant, CONTAINER=CURRENT or CONTAINER=ALL, to define whether they are to be created for the current container or are to be common to all of them.

CONTAINER=CURRENT

When connecting to a PDB, we can connect to the root and ALTER SYSTEM SET CONTAINER, but, as we saw in the previous chapter, connecting via the listener to a service switches the session directly to the service's container:

```
SQL> connect sys/oracle@//localhost/PDB as sysdba
Connected.
```

Once connected, we can then create a user:

```
SQL> create user PDBUSER1 identified by oracle container=current;
User created.
```

In fact, when connected to a PDB, we can create only local users, so the container clause is not mandatory and defaults to local:

```
SQL> create user PDBUSER2 identified by oracle;
User created.
```

If we try something else, we get an error:

```
SQL> create user PDBUSER3 identified by oracle container=all;
create user PDBUSER3 identified by oracle container=all
                                                      *
ERROR at line 1:
ORA-65050: Common DDLs only allowed in CDB$ROOT
```

So basically nothing changes here when working in a PDB; we simply create users in the way we are used to, and we can add the `container=current` just to be explicit.

When we want to create a user with Oracle Enterprise Manager, connected to a PDB, we don't have the choice. We receive a message, "Note: Created user will be a local user since you are in PDB container," as shown in Figure 6-1.

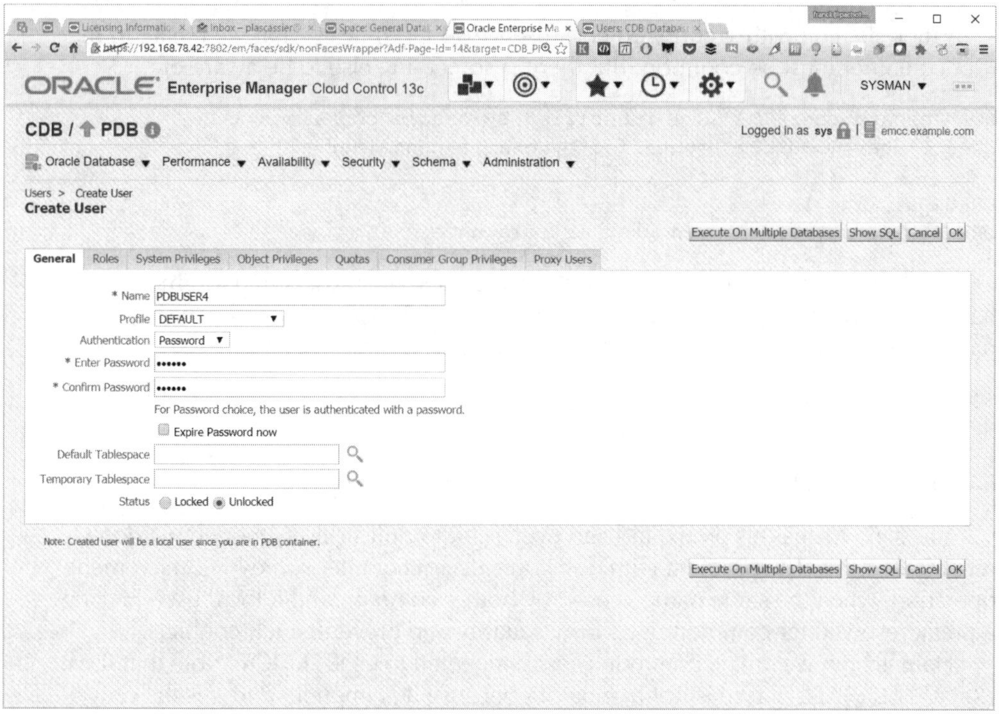

FIGURE 6-1. *Creating a local user in OEM 13c*

CONTAINER=COMMON

Now let's see what we can do from CDB$ROOT:

```
SQL> connect sys/oracle@//localhost/CDB as sysdba
Connected.
SQL> show con_name

CON_NAME
------------------------------
CDB$ROOT
```

First of all, trying to create a local user fails:

```
SQL> create user CDBUSER1 identified by oracle container=current;
create user CDBUSER1 identified by oracle container=current
                                                  *
ERROR at line 1:
ORA-65049: creation of local user or role is not allowed in CDB$ROOT
```

When dealing with security objects (users, roles, profiles), what we create in the root container must be common. But there is something else to be aware of:

```
SQL> create user CDBUSER1 identified by oracle container=all;
create user CDBUSER1 identified by oracle container=all
            *
ERROR at line 1:
ORA-65096: invalid common user or role name
```

The best practice is to avoid mixing common and local users in the same namespace by setting a prefix for all common users. The prefix is set by the parameter COMMON_USER_PREFIX which defaults to C##:

```
SQL> show parameter common
NAME                                 TYPE        VALUE
------------------------------------ ----------- ------------
common_user_prefix                   string      C##
```

You can change this prefix and can even set it to null string, although we don't recommend this. The problem with doing this can occur after some PDB movement operation, when the same name is used by both a common and a local user. Having a prefix reserved for common users brings clarity and prevents such conflicts.

Here is how we create common users connected to CDB$ROOT. Note that the CONTAINER=ALL clause is not mandatory because it is implicit, and it is the only valid value in this context:

```
SQL> create user C##USER1 identified by oracle container=all;
User created.
SQL> create user C##USER2 identified by oracle;
User created.
```

Figure 6-2 shows this user creation within OEM, clearly displaying the information, "Common user name must begin with 'C##'"; it is a common user because it is created from root. Note that this message is static and does not take into account changes made to `COMMON_USER_PREFIX`.

We can check the users from CDB$ROOT:

```
SQL> select username, common from dba_users where oracle_maintained='N';

USERNAME     COM
----------   ---
C##USER1     YES
C##USER2     YES
C##USER3     YES
```

In this example, we query only for users we have created recently. Note that the Oracle-maintained users (such as SYS, SYSTEM, and so on) are common users even if they don't have the common prefix.

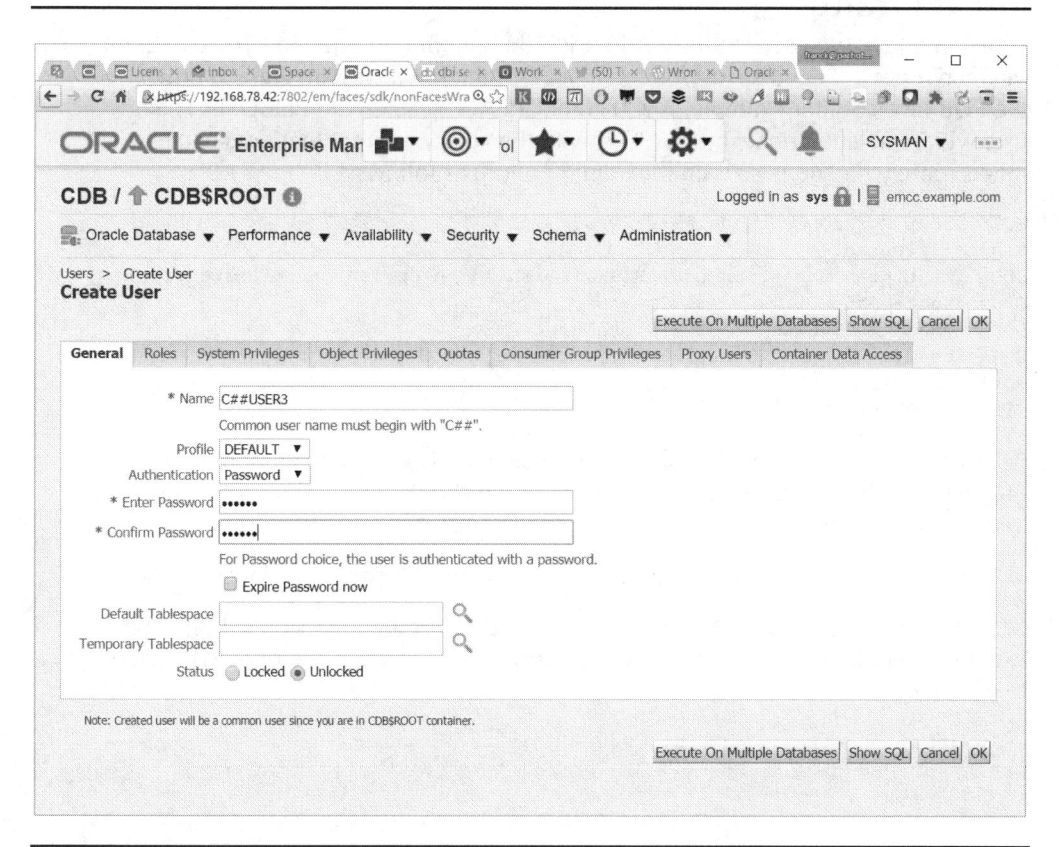

FIGURE 6-2. *Creating a common user in OEM 13c*

And here's the same query from our PDB:

```
SQL> alter session set container=PDB;
SQL> select username,common from cdb_users where oracle_maintained='N';

USERNAME    COM
----------  ---
C##USER1    YES
C##USER2    YES
C##USER3    YES
PDBUSER1    NO
PDBUSER2    NO
PDBUSER4    NO
```

In the PDB, we inherit the common users along with those defined locally. Once again, we have not displayed the Oracle-maintained users or the admin user that is generated when the PDB is created.

Local Grant

When in a PDB, you see local users in addition to common ones and you can grant them privileges. Of course, as you are in a PDB, the privileges are granted only at the PDB level. So, for example, if you grant CREATE SESSION to PDBUSER1, this user will be able to connect to its PDB, with the ability to grant that privilege to others, only when done so with the admin option, as follows:

```
SQL> alter session set container=PDB;
Session altered.
SQL> grant create session to PDBUSER1 with admin option container=current;
Grant succeeded.
SQL> connect PDBUSER1/oracle@//localhost/PDB
Connected.
SQL> show user
USER is "PDBUSER1"
```

This is, in fact, the only possibility, because in a PDB you can grant privileges only locally. The `CONTAINER=CURRENT` clause is the default, so it is not mandatory, and if you try something else you get this:

```
ORA-65029: a Local User may not grant or revoke a Common Privilege or Role
```

You can grant to a common user, but this will be for the local context only. For example, here in a PDB we grant the common user C##USER1 the right to connect to our PDB:

```
SQL> grant create session to C##USER1;
Grant succeeded.
```

The default, and only possibility, is `CONTAINER=CURRENT`, which we have omitted. We can see that the grant is there in PDB with `COMMON=NO`:

```
SQL> connect C##USER1/oracle@//localhost/PDB
Connected.
SQL> select * from user_sys_privs;
USERNAME        PRIVILEGE               ADM COMMON
------------    ---------------------   --- ------
C##USER1        CREATE SESSION          YES NO
```

However, the C##USER1 is known to all containers but does not have the CREATE SESSION privilege set for these:

```
SQL> alter session set container=CDB$ROOT;
ERROR:
ORA-01031: insufficient privileges
```

In a PDB, you can create users and roles and grant privileges to them locally. In addition, you inherit common users and roles and can also grant privileges to them locally. It is entirely possible for a common user to have different privileges specified in every PDB; the user is the same, because it is common, but it has different behaviors and privileges in each PDB.

Common Grant

In addition to local grants, we can also grant *common* privileges from CDB$ROOT. For the moment, our three users have no such privileges defined, so let's look at an example. As we did in our PDB, we can grant CREATE SESSION to the C##USER1 when in CDB$ROOT:

```
SQL> connect / as sysdba
Connected.
SQL> grant create session to C##USER1 container=current;
Grant succeeded.
```

This means that C##USER1 now has the right to connect to CDB$ROOT, in addition to the right to connect to PDB, which was just granted. We can also equip C##USER1 with the ability to connect to any PDB, whether currently existing or to be created later (which we show for theoretical rather than practical purposes) in the CDB:

```
SQL> grant create session to C##USER1 container=all;
Grant succeeded.
```

So let's see the current grants from CDB$ROOT:

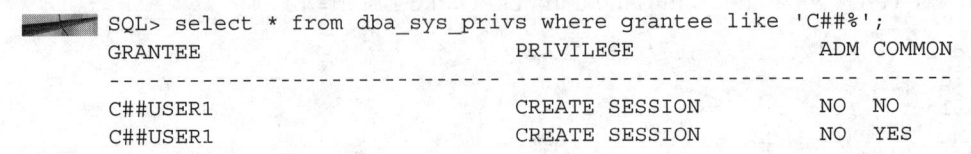

```
SQL> select * from dba_sys_privs where grantee like 'C##%';
GRANTEE                         PRIVILEGE                ADM COMMON
------------------------------- ------------------------ --- ------
C##USER1                        CREATE SESSION           NO  NO
C##USER1                        CREATE SESSION           NO  YES
```

Both grants are there, even if the local ones are redundant, as long as the common ones exist.

> **NOTE**
> *Be careful with the default value for CONTAINER in a grant statement. The default is CURRENT, even when in CDB$ROOT, which means the privilege will be granted only locally. This is different from the CREATE USER default. Our recommendation is always to specify the* `CONTAINER` *clause.*

Let's use the CDB_SYS_PRIVS that shows the result from each container's DBA_SYS_PRIVS (Chapter 9 will detail these cross-PDB views):

```
SQL> select * from cdb_sys_privs where grantee like 'C##%';

GRANTEE                    PRIVILEGE              ADM COMMON   CON_ID
-------------------------- ---------------------- --- ------ --------
C##USER1                   CREATE SESSION         NO  NO          1
C##USER1                   CREATE SESSION         NO  YES         1
C##USER1                   CREATE SESSION         NO  NO          3
C##USER1                   CREATE SESSION         NO  YES         3
C##USER1                   CREATE SESSION         NO  YES         4
C##USER1                   CREATE SESSION         NO  YES         5
```

These results mirror the output from our previous examples, in that we see a local grant for CDB$ROOT (CON_ID=1) and PDB (CON_ID=3), and common grants made from CDB$ROOT, which are visible in all containers. From an administration perspective, this lack of clarity does not make sense, and it is better not to mix common and local privileges for the same users.

Conflicts Resolution

Data movement and database plug-in will be addressed in Chapter 9, but you are already aware that multitenant and PDBs bring agility in data movement and cloning. However, you can only imagine the kinds of conflicts you may encounter when plugging in a PDB with a local user that shares the same name as a common one, or vice versa. Oracle will attempt to merge them, but you may have to resort to resolving conflicts manually.

Let's take an example here with the C##USER1. We unplug the PDB and drop the C##USER1:

```
SQL> alter pluggable database PDB close immediate;
Pluggable database altered.
SQL> alter pluggable database PDB unplug into '/tmp/PDB.xml';
Pluggable database altered.
SQL> drop pluggable database PDB;
Pluggable database dropped.
SQL> drop user C##USER1;
User dropped.
```

Then we plug it back in—that is, a PDB that had a common user then plugged into a PDB without one:

```
SQL> create pluggable database PDB using '/tmp/PDB.xml' nocopy;
Pluggable database created.
SQL> alter pluggable database PDB open;
Pluggable database altered.
SQL> select * from cdb_sys_privs where grantee like 'C##%';
GRANTEE                        PRIVILEGE             ADM COMMON  CON_ID
------------------------------ --------------------- --- ------ ----------C##USER1
CREATE SESSION          NO  NO              3
C##USER1                       CREATE SESSION        NO  YES            3
```

This shows a common user in the PDB, although it is actually unknown from the CDB$ROOT:

```
SQL> select username,common,con_id from cdb_users where username like 'C##%';
USERNAME      COMMON   CON_ID
------------ ------ ----------
C##USER1      YES            3
```

Here you see the process of *inheritance* that we have described as working differently. Common users are not shared; instead, they are propagated to containers. In our example, we dropped the common user but it remained in the unplugged database, with local and common grants all intact.

But no user at CDB$ROOT means we cannot connect:

```
SQL> connect C##USER1/oracle@//localhost/CDB
ERROR:
ORA-01017: invalid username/password; logon denied
```

So are we able to connect to the PDB, because the user is there, with the CREATE SESSION privilege?

```
SQL> connect C##USER1/oracle@//localhost/PDB
ERROR:
ORA-28000: the account is locked
```

In fact, because Oracle was not able to merge the common user automatically with CDB$ROOT, as that user did not exist in CDB$ROOT, the user has been locked until we resolve this issue manually.

If we want to keep this user as the common user, we have to create it from CDB$ROOT:

```
SQL> connect / as sysdba
Connected.
SQL> create user C##USER1 identified by oracle;
create user C##USER1 identified by oracle
                    *
ERROR at line 1:
ORA-65048: error encountered when processing the current DDL statement in
pluggable database PDB
ORA-01920: user name 'C##USER1' conflicts with another user or role name
```

To avoid such conflicts, we need to close the PDB first:

```
SQL> alter pluggable database PDB close;
Pluggable database altered.
SQL> create user C##USER1 identified by oracle;
User created.
```

All conflicts are then resolved at open, because the common user now matches in both containers:

```
SQL> alter pluggable database PDB open;
Pluggable database altered.
SQL> select username,common,con_id from cdb_users where username like 'C##USER1';
USERNAME        COMMON  CON_ID
------------    ------  ----------
C##USER1        YES             3
C##USER1        YES             1
```

There is no need to unlock the account—everything is OK, and we can successfully connect to the PDB:

```
SQL> connect C##USER1/oracle@//localhost/PDB
Connected.
```

Of course, if we want to connect to CDB$ROOT with this user, we need to grant CREATE SESSION from the root, so it's best to grant it with CONTAINER=ALL and revoke the CREATE SESSION privilege that was granted locally.

Keep It Clear and Simple

Be assured that there is nothing to be afraid of here, because it is all very logical if you understand that, physically speaking, the commonality is neither a link nor a logical inheritance, but only the propagation of privileges when DDL is issued.

Second, any conflicts that may appear when plugging in a PDB coming from another CDB are resolved when the PDB is opened. And don't forget to check PDB_PLUG_IN_VIOLATIONS for more detail.

We can't include all the conflicts that may appear, but let's imagine a common user with a local function to validate the password. You must ensure that the function exists in all PDBs. Our recommendation is to keep it simple, and use the prefix, which enforces a name convention to make it clear about what is common or local. In general terms, common users are mainly for administrators, while local users are for application schemas. Note that if you want to use external authentication with common users, you can match COMMON_USER_PREFIX with OS_AUTHENT_PREFIX.

With regard to the common user prefix, you should be aware of two additional points. First, the comparison of the prefix is case-insensitive, and second, even if you change it from its default, the C## is still forbidden for local users, so you will have two prefixes that can lead to ORA-65094: invalid local user or role name.

Note that in 12.2 it is possible to have your own root for your application, which is called an *application container*, where you can manage application user commonality in the same way. There is the APPLICATION_USER_PREFIX for this, which is empty by default, and it cannot be set to C##.

CONTAINER_DATA

Common users can see information from the whole CDB, so they can query the V$ views because they show information about the instance, and the instance is common. They can also query the CDB_ views, which collate information from the DBA_ views, from each of the containers. However, the CONTAINER_DATA parameter option is a means of implementing fine-grained control, and it enables the administrator to restrict common user access to a subset of containers. Here is an example in which we allow C##USER1 to see V$SESSION common data only from CDB (CON_ID=0), CDB$ROOT (CON_ID=1), and PDB1 (CON_ID=4):

```
SQL> show con_name
CON_NAME
------------------------------
CDB$ROOT
SQL> show user
USER is "SYSTEM"
```

The ALTER USER statement to authorize container access from a query on V$SESSION at root level is as follows:

```
SQL> alter user C##USER1 set container_data=(CDB$ROOT,PDB1) for
v$session container=current;
User altered.
```

We can then check what is now permitted, from the DBA_CONTAINER_DATA dictionary view:

```
SQL> select * from dba_container_data where username='C##USER1';
USERNAME    DEFAULT_AT OWNER        OBJECT_NAM ALL_CONTAI CONTAINER_
----------  ---------- ------------ ---------- ---------- ----------
C##USER1    N          SYS          V_$SESSION N          CDB$ROOT
C##USER1    N          SYS          V_$SESSION N          PDB1
```

Note that the object to which the restrictions apply is V_$SESSION here, which is the dictionary view on the V$SESSION fixed view. However, the V$SESSION in our statement is actually the public synonym that has been resolved to that view. This is interesting to know, because if you attempt to do the same as SYS you will get an error (ORA-02030: can only select from fixed tables/views): from SYS the V$SESSION is the fixed view itself. So if you want to do something similar from SYS, you have to name the dictionary view directly:

```
SQL> alter user C##USER1 set container_data=(CDB$ROOT,PDB1) for
v_$session container=current;
```

In the following, we are connected as SYSTEM and can, therefore, count sessions from all containers:

```
SQL> select con_id,type,count(*) from v$session group by con_id,type;

    CON_ID TYPE        COUNT(*)
---------- ----------- ----------
         4 USER                 1
         1 USER                 2
         0 BACKGROUND          51
         5 USER                 1
```

But if we attempt the same with the C##USER1 user, we don't see information from PDB2 (CON_ID=5), because it was not included in the authorization list:

```
SQL> connect C##USER1/oracle@//localhost/CDB
Connected.

SQL> show con_name

CON_NAME
------------------------------
CDB$ROOT

SQL> show user
USER is "C##USER1"
```

```
SQL> select con_id,type,count(*) from v$session group by con_id,type;

    CON_ID TYPE         COUNT(*)
---------- ---------- ----------
         4 USER                1
         1 USER                2
         0 BACKGROUND         51
```

Remember that this restriction is only for queries executed from CDB$ROOT. And, as we have granted the SET CONTAINER to C##USER1 on container PDB2, this user can always switch to it and view the sessions there:

```
SQL> alter session set container=PDB2;
Session altered.

SQL> select con_id,type,count(*) from v$session group by con_id,type;

    CON_ID TYPE         COUNT(*)
---------- ---------- ----------
         0 BACKGROUND         52
         5 USER                2
```

The same result is also possible by connecting directly to PDB2 as C##USER1, which has the CREATE SESSION privilege there. So don't forget to restrict access from all possible avenues: CONNECT_DATA for query from CDB$ROOT, and GRANT/REVOKE within the PDB itself.

Roles

As with users, you can create roles that are either local or common. However, keep in mind that a big advantage of the multitenant architecture is the ability to separate user metadata from system metadata, so don't mix system roles with user roles. If you want to create roles with a subset of the DBA privileges for your administrators, you can create them common, and perhaps grant them to individual local users in PDBs. But as far as user roles go, these should pertain to a specific PDB.

Proxy Users

Proxy users enable you to connect to a user without knowing the user password. This is useful for a DBA who needs to create an object, which can be created only by its owner, such as a database link. It is also a good way to audit who logs in by name and still behaves as if logged in by the schema user. This option is still possible in multitenant, which means that local users can actually proxy through a common user. For example, in PDB1, the DBA enables the common user C##USER1 to be a proxy user for the local user APPOWNER:

```
SQL> alter user APPOWNER grant connect through C##USER1;
User altered.
```

The C##USER1 can then connect to APPOWNER by providing his own password:

```
SQL> connect C##USER1[APPOWNER]/oracle@//localhost/PDB1
Connected.
SQL> show user
USER is "APPOWNER"
```

And from then on, everything functions as if connected with APPOWNER directly.

It's a good practice to disallow direct logon so that you are sure to audit who was connected by their actual usernames. You cannot lock the account, because proxy connections will be blocked as well, but you can set a password that nobody knows. There's also a better option, but this was not yet documented at the time of writing:

```
SQL> alter user APPOWNER proxy only connect;
User altered.
SQL> connect APPOWNER/oracle@//localhost/PDB1
ERROR:
ORA-28058: login is allowed only through a proxy
```

With this clause, the connection can be performed via a proxy user. This behavior can be canceled with the following:

```
SQL> alter user APPOWNER cancel proxy only connect;
User altered.
```

This `proxy only connect` option is interesting, but our recommendation is to wait until it is officially documented before using it.

One final note about proxy users—for security reasons, if you connect as a common user through a local proxy user, you are locked in the container of the proxy user. Here is an example in which we allowed the common user C##USER1 in PDB1 to connect through the local user ADMIN:

```
alter user C##USER1 grant connect through ADMIN;
```

When the common user connects directly to the PDB, the user can change to another container later, as long as the user has the SET CONTAINER privilege:

```
SQL> connect C##USER1/oracle@//localhost/PDB1
Connected.
alter session set container=CDB$ROOT;
Session altered.
```

However, this operation is not allowed when connected through a local proxy user:

```
SQL> connect ADMIN[C##USER1]/oracle@//localhost/PDB1
Connected.
SQL> alter session set container=CDB$ROOT;
ERROR:
ORA-01031: insufficient privileges
```

This is a security lockdown hard-coded since 12.1, and 12.2 has brought more possibilities to control this through lockdown profiles.

Lockdown Profiles

PDBs bring a new separation of database administrator roles. The DBA administers the CDB but can delegate the administration of individual PDBs. Let's take an example of a CDB that is a dedicated development environment. The fast and thin provisioning features we will see with snapshot clones make it possible to give a PDB to each developer. Because it is their database, the CDB administrator can grant developers the DBA role for the PDB, so that developers can do whatever they want there, as long as their privileges are limited to this PDB.

In 12.1, this strategy is almost impossible to implement. Even if the DBA role is granted locally only to a local PDB user, this privilege enables the user to do things that can potentially break the CDB or the server. For example, a local DBA can create files wherever he wishes, can execute any program on the host (which will run as the oracle user), and can generate massive trace files. If we want to limit what a local DBA can do, we need better control over these privileges, and this is why 12.2 introduced lockdown profiles.

Here, connected to CDB$ROOT, we create a profile for our application DBAs:

```
SQL> create lockdown profile APP_DBA_PROFILE;
Lockdown Profile created.

SQL> select * from DBA_LOCKDOWN_PROFILES;
PROFILE_NAME   RULE_TYPE RULE           CLAUSE CLAUSE_OPT OPTION_VAL STATUS
-------------  --------- -------------- ------ ---------- ---------- ------
APPDBA_PROF                                                          DISABLE
```

Disable Database Options

With profiles, we can disable access to some features available only with licensed options. For example, if we don't have the partitioning option, we must be sure that nobody will create a partitioned table, so let's disable it from our application DBA profile:

```
SQL> alter lockdown profile APPDBA_PROF disable option = ('Partitioning');
Lockdown Profile altered.

SQL> select * from DBA_LOCKDOWN_PROFILES;
PROFILE_NAME   RULE_TYPE RULE           CLAUSE CLAUSE_OPT OPTION_VAL STATUS
-------------  --------- -------------- ------ ---------- ---------- ------
APPDBA_PROF    OPTION    PARTITIONING                                DISABLE
```

We can now apply the lockdown profile to PDB1 simply by setting the `pdb_lockdown` parameter for that container:

```
SQL> alter session set container=PDB1;
Session altered.
SQL> alter system set pdb_lockdown=APPDBA_PROF;
System altered.
```

So now let's try to create a partitioned table in that PDB1:

```
SQL> connect admin/oracle@//localhost/PDB1
Connected.
SQL> create table DEMO(id number) partition by hash(id) partitions 4;
create table DEMO(id number) partition by hash(id) partitions 4
              *
ERROR at line 1:
ORA-00439: feature not enabled: Partitioning
```

As you can see, this is impossible because the feature has been disabled.

The ENABLE and DISABLE clauses of ALTER LOCKDOWN PROFILE can also be specified with an ALL option:

```
SQL> alter lockdown profile APPDBA_PROF disable option all;
SQL> alter lockdown profile APPDBA_PROF disable option all except = ('Oracle Data Guard');
```

Disable ALTER SYSTEM

The ALTER SYSTEM privilege is very powerful, but with the GRANT syntax you can only allow or disallow it. However, with lockdown profiles you have fine-grained control, because you can enable or disable specific clauses of the statement. Let's say, for example, that you want to allow your developers to kill sessions in their PDB, but no other ALTER SYSTEM activities. From CDB$ROOT you can add the following rule:

```
SQL> alter lockdown profile APPDBA_PROF disable statement = ('ALTER SYSTEM')
clause all except = ('KILL SESSION');
SQL> select * from DBA_LOCKDOWN_PROFILES;
PROFILE_NAME   RULE_TYPE  RULE           CLAUSE              CLAUSE_OPT OPTION_VAL STATUS
-------------- ---------- -------------- ------------------- ---------- ---------- -------
APPDBA_PROF    OPTION     PARTITIONING                                             DISABLE
APPDBA_PROF    STATEMENT  ALTER SYSTEM   KILL SESSION                              ENABLE
```

With this, a user in the PDB who has the lockdown profile assigned will get an "ORA-01031: insufficient privileges" message for any ALTER SYSTEM command, except an ALTER SYSTEM KILL SESSION.

The scope of control can be defined further with the `ALTER SYSTEM SET` command, because you can even control which parameters are allowed. For example, the following will allow only some parameters to be set at the PDB level:

```
SQL> alter lockdown profile APPDBA_PROF disable statement = ('ALTER SYSTEM')
clause = ('SET');
Lockdown Profile altered.
SQL> alter lockdown profile APPDBA_PROF  enable statement = ('ALTER SYSTEM')
clause = ('SET') option = ('undo_retention', 'temp_undo_enabled', 'resumable_
timeout', 'cursor_sharing', 'session_cached_cursors', 'heat_map', 'resource_
manager_plan', 'optimizer_dynamic_sampling');
Lockdown Profile altered.
```

We can query the dictionary to see these defined:

```
SQL> select * from DBA_LOCKDOWN_PROFILES where profile_name='APPDBA_PROF';
PROFILE_NAME    RULE_TYPE  RULE            CLAUSE  CLAUSE_OPTION              STATUS
------------    ---------  ----            ------  -------------              ------
APPDBA_PROF     STATEMENT  ALTER SYSTEM    SET                                DISABLE
APPDBA_PROF     STATEMENT  ALTER SYSTEM    SET     CURSOR_SHARING             ENABLE
APPDBA_PROF     STATEMENT  ALTER SYSTEM    SET     HEAT_MAP                   ENABLE
APPDBA_PROF     STATEMENT  ALTER SYSTEM    SET     OPTIMIZER_DYNAMIC_SAMPLING ENABLE
APPDBA_PROF     STATEMENT  ALTER SYSTEM    SET     RESOURCE_MANAGER_PLAN      ENABLE
APPDBA_PROF     STATEMENT  ALTER SYSTEM    SET     RESUMABLE_TIMEOUT          ENABLE
APPDBA_PROF     STATEMENT  ALTER SYSTEM    SET     SESSION_CACHED_CURSORS     ENABLE
APPDBA_PROF     STATEMENT  ALTER SYSTEM    SET     TEMP_UNDO_ENABLED          ENABLE
APPDBA_PROF     STATEMENT  ALTER SYSTEM    SET     UNDO_RETENTION             ENABLE
```

From a PDB where this lockdown profile is set, we can set one of these allowed parameters:

```
SQL> alter system set optimizer_dynamic_sampling=4;
System altered.
```

But we will receive a privilege error when trying to set one that is not in the permitted list:

```
SQL> alter system set optimizer_index_cost_adj=1;
alter system set optimizer_index_cost_adj=1
*
ERROR at line 1:
ORA-01031: insufficient privileges
```

When disabling the change of a parameter, we can also define a value to be set at the same time, when the `PDB_LOCKDOWN` parameter is set:

```
alter lockdown profile APPDBA_PROF disable statement=('ALTER SYSTEM')
clause=('SET') option=('cursor_sharing') value=('EXACT');
```

This is an effective means of creating a lockdown profile with several parameters set to values that cannot be changed later.

Disable Features

We will not go into detail on disable features here, but in the same way that you can disable database options, you can also disable features. For example, the following command disables the specified PL/SQL package usage:

```
SQL> alter lockdown profile APPDBA_PROF disable feature = ('UTL_
HTTP','UTL_SMTP','UTL_TCP');
```

> **NOTE**
> *You can disable all networking packages with the `NETWORK_ACCESS` feature name.*

PDB Isolation

In 12.2, in addition to the `PDB_LOCKDOWN` parameter that can be used to set a lockdown profile to limit network access, you can also limit the interaction with the OS file system and processes.

PDB_OS_CREDENTIALS

From a dbms_scheduler job, or through an external procedure, it is possible to run a program on the host server. But, more than likely, you will probably not want to let the PDB administrator run anything with the oracle user privileges. In this case, you can create a credential, from the root, defining the OS user and password, and also including a domain if you are on Windows:

```
exec dbms_credential.create_credential( credential_name=>'PDB1_OS_
USER', username=>'limitedUser', password=>'secret');
```

You can limit a PDB to this user when running jobs or external procedures:

```
alter session set container=PDB1;
alter system set pdb_os_credential=CDB_PDB_OS_USER scope=spfile;
```

PATH_PREFIX

In a similar vein, a PDB administrator can create a directory and write files anywhere on the system. This was not a problem before multitenant, because the DBA controls both the database and the host, but in multitenant you can delegate some administration tasks to the PDB administrator and then need more control on how the PDB admin can interact with the host. Since 12.1, it has been possible to define a `PATH_PREFIX` as the root of all directories created in a PDB, which is then defined with a relative path from there. Note that you cannot change the `PATH_PREFIX` after creation.

CREATE_FILE_DEST

Another way to write files onto a server is to create tablespaces and add datafiles, and this is also an operation the CDB administrator needs to restrict. Starting with 12.1.0.2, you can now set the `CREATE_FILE_DEST` to a directory specific for the PDB, so that datafiles are written there. However, a user with CREATE or ALTER TABLESPACE privileges can still specify a fully qualified filename, and then write everywhere the oracle user can write. OS credentials are not used here.

> **NOTE**
> We have opened an enhancement request regarding this gap, and we hope to have the option to lockdown a PDB administrator to use OMF only, without specifying an absolute file path or a disk group, in the near future.

Transparent Data Encryption

Encrypting data on disk is a key part of a sound security strategy; however, authorized users can still access the data unencrypted. This means that the database has the decryption key onboard, and such encryption does not prevent an attack that accesses the data through the database software.

There are still other paths to compromise the system, such as getting access at OS level or directly accessing the disks, and data encryption does protect against this.

There are essentially two ways to implement a sound security strategy: programming access procedures and encrypting data ourselves, or using Transparent Data Encryption (TDE).

In the first case, it's the application that does the encryption and decryption—that is, the database stores and presents the encrypted data, oblivious to the fact that it is encrypted. The disadvantages of this method are that it is more difficult to implement, and we have to be very careful to implement key management correctly; it's no use encrypting the data if an attacker can compromise the keys himself.

Second, Oracle Database provides, as part of the Advanced Security Option, another solution: TDE. This is part of the Oracle Database, and it's a trusted, proven, and supported solution that is well documented; many DBAs are familiar with it. If we are really serious about security, TDE also supports hardware security modules, which are dedicated pieces of hardware that securely store encryption keys.

Setting Up TDE

Each encrypted database has a master key that is used to generate all additional keys, whether for separate tables or tablespaces. This master key is the only one stored outside of the database itself, and it's the only one that the database needs to open.

There are several reasons why the Oracle Database uses multiple keys internally, and not just the master. First of all, encrypting data with the master key directly can be slow and expensive, especially hardware-stored keys, which have very limited throughput and can be licensed by capacity. In addition, we can change the master key when we decide to do so—for example, if the key is compromised, or simply to alter master keys on a schedule. Changing the master key re-encrypts the subordinate (table) keys, but not the data in the database itself.

Let's go through an example of setting up TDE for a multitenant database. In this example we will use a software keystore, not a hardware one.

Setting Up the Keystore Location

A *software keystore* is essentially a file in a specified directory. Oracle Database also supports wallets for storing secure information, which enables scripts, for example, to log in without hard-coding passwords. Conceptually, wallets are very similar, and the way to administer them is also similar to the TDE keystore. In fact, in 11*g*, both were called "wallets," and some syntax and documentation still refer to both by this name; even the location for each can default to the same value. Nevertheless, we recommend keeping these separate, as they do contain different data with different purposes.

The location of the keystore is defined in sqlnet.ora. It is important that you know that each CDB or non-CDB has its own keystore, so if we have multiple databases running on the same host, we must configure a path that is different for each database.

We could create multiple sqlnet.ora files and make sure each database is started with the correct one, but the easiest method—and the least error-prone—is to include the ORACLE_SID in the path.

Sqlnet.ora is in the TNS_ADMIN path, which is $ORACLE_HOME/network/admin by default. The entry for database encryption can be set as follows:

```
ENCRYPTION_WALLET_LOCATION=
  (SOURCE=
    (METHOD=FILE)
    (METHOD_DATA=
      (DIRECTORY=$ORACLE_BASE/WALLET/$ORACLE_SID)))
```

Creating the Keystore

Creating the keystore involves one simple command in the root container. All the commands that work with the keystore need SYSKM or ADMINISTER KEY MANAGEMENT privilege.

```
SQL> administer key management create keystore '/u01/app/oracle/WALLET/CDBSRC' identified by "AVeryLongPassword";

keystore altered.
```

> **NOTE**
> *This command requires a full path to the directory where the keystore will be created. This must be the same as we specified (or will specify) in sqlnet.ora, and be aware that the command does not check that these two paths match. This command is new in Oracle Database 12c, replacing* `alter system set encryption` *commands from earlier versions.*

A keystore created in this way will require the same password to open. Oracle Database also supports autologin wallets, which alleviate the need to specify the password. (Refer to the documentation for more details.)

Setting Up Using Cloud Control

Most of these operations can also be performed using Enterprise Manager Cloud Control. Figure 6-3 shows the TDE home screen, from which we can set up the keystore and manage the keys.

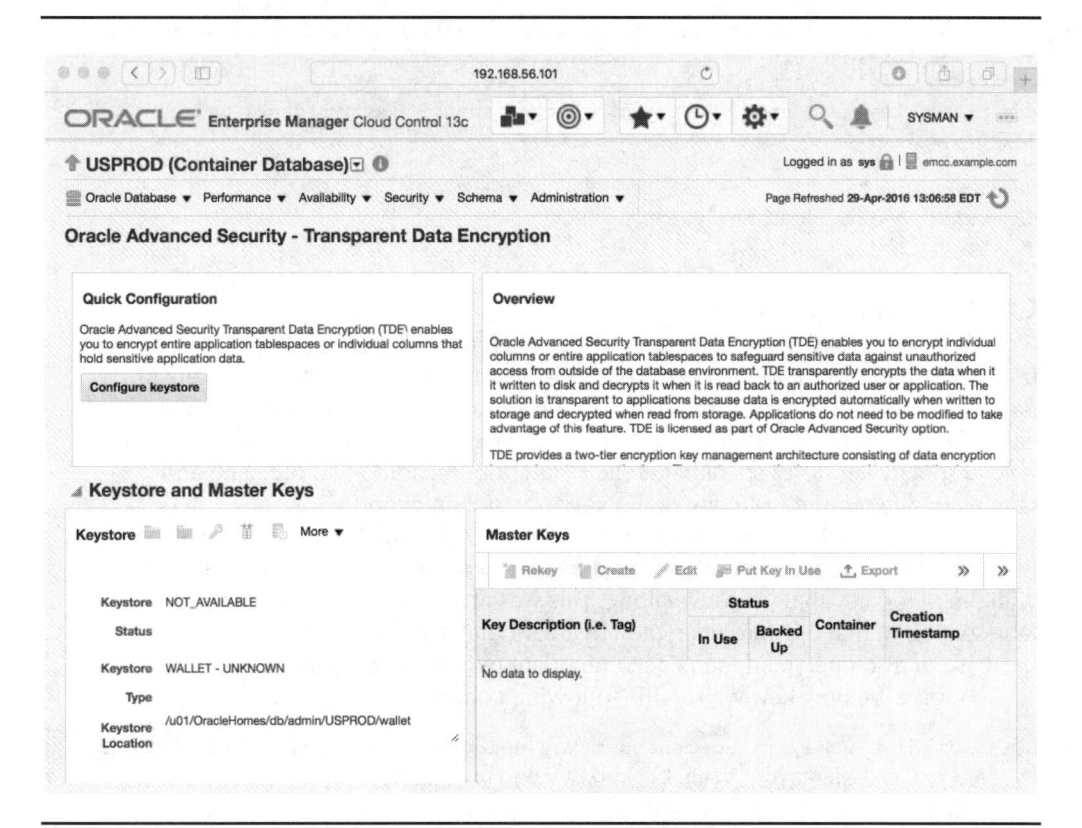

FIGURE 6-3. *TDE in Enterprise Manager Cloud Control*

Opening the Keystore

Before anyone can use the keystore, we must open it in the root container and then in the PDBs. Only then we can set up the master key and read or modify the encrypted data.

```
SQL> administer key management set keystore open identified by
"AVeryLongPassword";

keystore altered.
```

We can also use the `CONTAINER` clause syntax introduced by multitenant, and then in the root container, open the keystore in all PDBs:

```
SQL> administer key management set keystore open identified by
"AVeryLongPassword" container=all;

keystore altered.
```

It is in this step that we will find out whether the configuration of the wallet location has been done correctly—if not, we will receive an error like this:

```
SQL> administer key management set keystore open identified by identified
by  "AVeryLongPassword";
ENCRYPTION_WALLET_LOCATION=
administer key management set keystore open identified by identified by
"AVeryLongPassword"
*
ERROR at line 1:
ORA-28367: wallet does not exist
```

Creating the Master Key

Now that we created an *empty* keystore, the obvious next step is to generate a master key and store it in the keystore; this is where things differ for a multitenant database. As noted earlier, each CDB has one keystore; however, in that keystore, each PDB has its own master key. In Oracle Database 12c Release 2, we should be able to specify keystores specific for each PDB, too, meaning that plugging and cloning would require just copy of the keystore, not an export.

This means a bit more work is required during the setup, but it also means that PDBs can be unplugged and cloned and moved into another CDB (see Chapter 9), with their own key that we move along. This was always an issue with transportable tablespaces, in that they are encrypted by their database key, and the target database, if also encrypted, can't accommodate two different master keys.

To create the new key, we run the following command:

```
SQL> administer key management set key using tag 'our key 1' identified
by "AVeryLongPassword" with backup using 'backup1';

keystore altered.
```

This can be run in the container for which we want to create the key—either CDB$ROOT or a PDB. And, again, we can add the `CONTAINER=ALL` clause when running the command in CDB$ROOT to create keys in all PDBs. However, this also sets the same descriptive comment (the tag) for all keys, which may not be desired.

It is also mandatory to specify a backup of the wallet, so that, should the operation go wrong, we would still have the previous copy and would not lose the keys. So, after adding the first key, we now have two files in the wallet directory, as in the following example:

```
-rw-r--r-- oracle oinstall 4022 Mar  3 19:26 ewallet.p12
-rw-r--r-- oracle oinstall 2400 Mar  3 19:26 ewallet_2016030319264839_
backup1.p12
```

Verifying the Created Keys

We can now simply check which keys have been created so far:

```
SQL> select key_id, tag, user, con_id from V$ENCRYPTION_KEYS;

KEY_ID                                              TAG         USER        CON_ID
--------------------------------------------------  ----------  ----------  -------
ATuQBA32eU+bv5beU2m0vNwAAAAAAAAAAAAAAAAAAAAAAAAAA    PDB1 key    SYS              3
AX1CULHXvU/2v83pq36VH7UAAAAAAAAAAAAAAAAAAAAAAAAA    our key 1   SYS              1
```

As you can see, the key ID is a long, generated base64 encoded value, while the tag value is a human-readable comment.

Encrypting the Data

Encryption of the data is defined at the PDB level, using the same syntax and rules as in a non-CDB database.

TDE can encrypt column(s) in a table, which we can request by simply adding the `ENCRYPT` keyword:

```
create table scott.emp_enc(
  empno number(4) primary key,
  ename varchar2(10),
  job varchar2(9),
  mgr number(4),
  hiredate date,
  sal number(7,2) ENCRYPT,
  comm number(7,2) ENCRYPT,
  deptno number(2));

Table created.
```

The second way TDE can work is at the tablespace level, encrypting all data in this entity:

```
SQL> create tablespace tbsenc
  datafile '/u01/app/oracle/data/CDBSRC/PDB1/tbsenc01.dbf'
  size 100m
  encryption using 'AES256'
  default storage (ENCRYPT);

Tablespace created.
```

We can see a list of all TDE-encrypted columns in DBA_ENCRYPTED_COLUMNS:

```
SQL> select * from dba_encrypted_columns;

OWNER      TABLE_NAME COLUMN_NAM ENCRYPTION_ALG                SAL INTEGRITY_AL
---------- ---------- ---------- ----------------------------- --- ------------
SCOTT      EMP_ENC    SAL        AES 192 bits key              YES SHA-1
SCOTT      EMP_ENC    COMM       AES 192 bits key              YES SHA-1
```

And the list of encrypted tablespaces is displayed in v$encrypted_tablespaces:

```
SQL> select ts#, encryptionalg, encryptedts, status from  v$encrypted_tablespaces;

       TS# ENCRYPT ENC STATUS
---------- ------- --- ----------
         5 AES256  YES NORMAL
```

Plug and Clone with TDE

When a PDB is copied/moved to a new CDB, the target CDB needs to know its encryption key. If the operation is a clone, Oracle will do this for us automatically. But if we plug in/unplug a PDB, we must ship the master key along with the XML file and the datafiles. This is achieved by exporting the key on the source into a password-protected file:

```
SQL> administer key management export encryption keys with secret
"exportPassword" to '/home/oracle/exportPDB1.p12' identified by
"AVeryLongPassword";

keystore altered.
```

We then proceed with the plug-in as per normal (see Chapter 9). The PDB will refuse to open and will instead remain open in restricted mode. But now that the target database knows about the PDB, we can connect or switch to it and import the keystore export file, as follows:

```
SQL> administer key management import encryption keys with secret "exportPassword"
from '/home/oracle/exportPDB1.p12' identified by oracle with backup;

keystore altered.
```

From here we can close and then open the PDB again, and access the encrypted data.

TDE Summary

TDE is a feature that is, on paper at least, easy to use, but it comes with its own limitations, and it is a key management process that is complicated at times.

It's important that we build a thorough understanding as to how this feature works if we are going to use it. After all, this is data security we are talking about—an area where it is often difficult to assess whether we have done something wrong, until it's too late.

TDE is a topic that warrants a book on its own, and we have only lightly scratched the surface here. The message is clear, however: TDE still functions the same as before, with the only change in multitenant being one key for each PDB, and thus multiple keys in a single CDB.

Summary

In a multitenant environment, particularly in the cloud, all the features covered in this chapter are must knows—and must use. Some of these can be distilled into simple directives, such as: don't have all your database administrators connecting as sysdba, and the system administrators should have their common usernames to administer the CDB. It is probable that all other users will be local to PDBs, so their actions are appropriately isolated. Moving beyond this type of access protection, encryption is a powerful means of preventing illegitimate access to data, although this is not sufficient protection alone. Even with the best security policy, an error may occur that results in some data being lost or corrupted. This brings us to the most important facets of data protection, backup and recovery, which are covered in the next chapter.

PART
III

Backup, Recovery, and Database Movement

CHAPTER 7

Backup and Recovery

Backup and recovery is an exciting topic. Creating backups is straightforward, but many DBAs do not spend much time digging into this area until an actual restore and recovery is required. Then all the books and notes are dusted off in search of the correct commands or processes to follow. Although this might not be optimal, it does highlight something of utmost importance when talking about backup and recovery: documentation. And this brings us to the goal of this chapter—to document the key concepts and areas relative to backup and recovery when using the Oracle Database 12*c* Multitenant option.

In this chapter we will first review the basics to highlight a number of key aspects that will help you quickly establish effective backup and recovery procedures in your multitenant environment. What you will notice as we progress is that, in many cases, it does not make a difference whether you are using a container database (CDB) or a non-CDB; overall, the principles are similar, if not identical, for both.

Back to Basics

Our encouragement is this: Do not be afraid of backup and recovery. In fact, the more time you spend on planning and testing your backups, the easier the second part—restore and recovery—will become. But before we dive into the detail, let's consider two key areas:

- Hot versus cold backups
- ARCHIVELOG mode versus NOARCHIVELOG mode

NOTE
In this chapter a number of examples will make use of the RMAN `TAG` option. Strictly speaking, this is not necessary, but it is a recommended option in certain scenarios because it makes it easier for you to identify specific backups. For more detail on the use of the `TAG` option, refer to the Oracle online documentation.

Hot vs. Cold Backups

Nowadays, there are few references to cold backups. So what is this and why would you use it? In short, cold backups (also called consistent backups) are created when a database is not open for transactions—that is, it has been shut down with the `IMMEDIATE`, `TRANSACTIONAL`, or `NORMAL` option. The effect of one of these clean shutdowns is that when the database is restored following this type of backup, no additional recovery is required to bring it to a consistent state, because it was in this state when the backup was performed.

In this day and age, most companies simply cannot afford downtime on their primary systems, so the cold backup is not the ideal backup method, because it requires an outage (planned downtime) on your primary database. You may ask, why have downtime when creating backups at all, if this is not required? The answer depends on an organization's requirements, but a cold backup is still an option for the modern DBA, even when using the multitenant option.

Performing a cold backup is simple: the database is closed when backups are being performed. If RMAN *is not* used to perform cold backups, the database must be completely shut down. When RMAN *is* used, the database must be in a *mounted* state. Here's an example of creating a cold backup of a CDB:

```
RMAN> connect target /
RMAN> shutdown immediate;
RMAN> startup force dba;
RMAN> shutdown immediate;
RMAN> startup mount;
RMAN> backup format '/backups/%U' database;
RMAN> backup format '/backups/cfc-%U' current controlfile;
RMAN> alter database open;
RMAN> alter pluggable database all open;
```

In this example, a consistent backup of the CDB is performed and the backup is stored on disk in the /backups folder. By default, RMAN backup sets are used with the backup command. If required, you can also perform a cold backup using image copies; to do so, you would replace the fifth line in the preceding code with this:

```
RMAN> backup as copy format '/backups/%U' database;
```

As you can see, creating consistent cold backups is easy. The database can be in NOARCHIVELOG mode when you performing them. But the downtime required that renders these types of backups is not acceptable for most.

This brings us to hot, or online/inconsistent, backups. In contrast, when creating these backups, the database may be online—open read/write. However, there is one key requirement when you are performing hot backups: the database must be in ARCHIVELOG mode. For most DBAs, this is likely to be the default option when creating a new database in any case. Enabling ARCHIVELOG mode is easy and brings with it the advantage of enabling you to perform backups while the database is in full use. Yes, backups created in this fashion are considered inconsistent, but by using the archive logs that are generated during the process, the backup can be restored and recovered to a consistent state so that the database can be opened again.

Archive logs assist in resolving Oracle split blocks, which may occur during hot backups. Oracle data blocks, the smallest units of data used by a database (which is made up of multiple operating system blocks), include identifying start and end markers. The start and end markers of blocks are compared during recovery, and if they do not match, the block is considered inconsistent and the redo copy of the block is required to recover (reconstruct) the block to a consistent state.

> **NOTE**
> *For more detail on split blocks, refer to Oracle Support Note 1048310.6 and the Oracle Database 12c documentation regarding the `LOG_BLOCKS_DURING_BACKUP` initialization parameter.*

Enabling ARCHIVELOG mode in a CDB is no different from doing it in a non-CDB configuration:

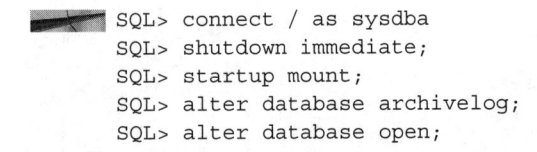

```
SQL> connect / as sysdba
SQL> shutdown immediate;
SQL> startup mount;
SQL> alter database archivelog;
SQL> alter database open;
```

You can use the SQL command `archive log list` to confirm whether a database has ARCHIVELOG mode enabled, or by reviewing the `V$DATABASE.LOG_MODE` value.

> **NOTE**
> *When you enable ARCHIVELOG mode in a CDB, an outage is required, because the database needs to be restarted in a mount state. Also note that ARCHIVELOG mode can be set only at the CDB level.*

To perform a basic backup on a CDB database that is open and has ARCHIVELOG mode enabled, run the following commands:

```
RMAN> connect target /
RMAN> backup format '/backups/db-%U' database;
RMAN> backup format '/backups/arc-%U' archivelog all;
RMAN> backup format '/backups/cfc-%U' current controlfile;
```

With the fundamentals of hot and cold backups now covered, let's review some of the default RMAN configuration options before we get into the details of backup and recovery concepts in a container database environment.

RMAN: The Default Configuration

By default, to back up a database using RMAN, the simplest command is `backup database`. It doesn't get any easier than that! For most purposes, however, this simple command is not really adequate; to get the most from your backups and to provide more options, you have to go a bit further than this. But before we launch into this, we need to discuss the default RMAN configuration options.

When you run the `backup database` command, a number of default options are invoked behind the scenes. Many of them are perfectly acceptable and may never need changing, but by adjusting a key few, you can make backup and recovery of your Oracle 12c database even easier.

Use NLS_DATE_FORMAT

The `NLS_DATE_FORMAT` environment variable is highly recommended. In case you hadn't noticed, when running RMAN commands, the default date format is limited to displaying only the day, month, and year:

```
BS Key  Type LV Size       Device Type Elapsed Time Completion Time
------- ---- -- ---------- ----------- ------------ ---------------
10      Full    1.32G      DISK        00:00:08     07-MAR-16
```

Notice that there is no time option in the output. For many, this might not be an issue, but having additional date/time output in the log files and on the screen when running RMAN commands is extremely useful:

```
BS Key  Type LV Size       Device Type Elapsed Time Completion Time
------- ---- -- ---------- ----------- ------------ -------------------
10      Full    1.32G      DISK        00:00:08     07/03/2016:22:38:02
```

To enable better display of date and time when using RMAN, simply set the `NLS_DATE_FORMAT` environment variable prior to starting your RMAN session:

```
oracle@linux3[/home/oracle]: export NLS_DATE_FORMAT=dd/mm/yyyy:hh24:mi:ss
```

List and Adjust Default Configuration

The default RMAN configuration can be reviewed in two ways: you can use the RMAN `show all` command, or you can review the details in `V$RMAN_CONFIGURATION`.

> **NOTE**
> *V$RMAN_CONFIGURATION will show only the nondefault values. If you have not changed the default configuration, no rows will be returned.*

For example, to adjust the default configuration to allow the autobackup of the control file (a recommended setting) to a specified location, including the enabling of compressed backup sets for the disk type backups, you can execute the following at the RMAN prompt:

```
RMAN> configure controlfile autobackup on;
RMAN> configure controlfile autobackup format for device type disk to '/backups/cfa-%F';
RMAN> configure channel device type disk format '/backups/%U';
RMAN> configure device type disk backup type to compressed backupset;
```

Once this has been executed, you can review the settings with the following:

```
RMAN> show all;
```

In this state, you can run the `backup database` command and RMAN will take your default settings into account.

RMAN Backup Redundancy

Backups are important, and to help you protect this resource, RMAN enables you to duplicate your backups—up to four of them in fact. You can take this additional measure to ensure that your backups are protected from media failure or human error. The COPIES clause can be used with the `backup` command to specify how many backup copies should be created, or, if you prefer, you can update the default configuration and specify the COPIES clause as part of your default configuration. The command that follows demonstrates how this can be done with the RMAN backup command:

```
RMAN> backup copies 2 pluggable database XPDB1
      format '/backups/CDB1-%U', '/backups2/CDB1-%U';
```

In this example, while connected to CDB$ROOT, the pluggable database (PDB) XPDB1 is backed up to /backups, and the backup is then duplicated to /backups2 as well. To enable the duplicate option in the default configuration, using two copies for both the datafile and archive log backups, for example, you can use the following commands while connected to the CDB$ROOT:

```
RMAN> configure channel device type disk
      format '/backups/CDB1-%U', '/backups2/CDB1-%U';
RMAN> configure datafile backup copies for device type disk to 2;
RMAN> configure archivelog backup copies for device type disk to 2;
```

The SYSBACKUP Privilege

In Oracle Database 12c, separation of administration duties has been extended from the few basic options in earlier versions. One of the new system privileges introduced is SYSBACKUP, which can be granted to users who need to perform backup and recovery operations. A user with the SYSBACKUP privilege will be restricted to allow only backup and recovery operations. This permission can also be granted to a local user account in a PDB, equipping the user with backup and recovery permissions on a specific PDB. Let's review the different connection options available with this role.

Connecting as the SYS user with SYSDBA permission:

```
RMAN> connect target /
```

Connecting as a common user with SYSBACKUP permission:

```
SQL> connect c##backup as sysbackup;
```

Using RMAN to connect to the CDB root:

```
RMAN> connect target '"c##backup@cdb1 as sysbackup"';
```

Using a local PDB account with SYSBACKUP permission:

```
RMAN> connect target 'localadmin@pdb1 as sysbackup'
```

For more detail on the new administrative privileges and user security when using Oracle Database 12c Multitenant, see Chapter 6.

CDB and PDB Backups

There are two key aspects to backups in an Oracle Database 12c Multitenant environment: backups at the CDB level, and then those at the PDB level. You can connect to a PDB and perform backup and recovery operations, albeit with a few restrictions, which we will get to later in this chapter. You can use RMAN to perform backups on a CDB or PDB, and later we will cover two additional options: Oracle Cloud Control and Oracle SQL Developer. But first let's focus on using RMAN via the command line interface.

Before jumping in, note an important change introduced in Oracle Database 12c. When connected to CDB$ROOT, if we specify only the key word DATABASE in our `backup`, `restore`, or `recover` command, it applies to the whole database (CDB root and all its PDBs). Here's an example:

```
RMAN> backup database;
```

However, if you are connected to a PDB, the commands apply specifically to the PDB you are connected to. In Oracle Database 12c, Oracle introduced a new RMAN clause, PLUGGABLE DATABASE, which enables you to perform tasks on specific PDBs, as follows, while connected to the CDB$ROOT:

```
RMAN> backup pluggable database PDB1;
```

In the next sections, we will outline additional syntax changes that have been introduced.

CDB Backups

In most cases you will find that backups will be scheduled and performed at the CDB level, so that CDB$ROOT and PDB$SEED, as well as all the other PDBs associated with a CDB, will be backed up. But this does not mean you cannot be more specific, and in this section we will show you, by way of example, how easy it is to perform backups while connected to the CDB root as target.

Full CDB Backups

When you perform a full (whole) CDB backup, the following files should be included:

- The control file
- All datafiles (CDB$ROOT, PDB$SEED, and all PDBs)
- All archived logs

Backing up the SPFILE is recommended, but in most cases it can easily be rebuilt, so this is not mandatory. If you do have autobackup of the control file enabled (which is highly recommended), the SPFILE will automatically be backed up together with the control file when any structural changes are made in the database.

Multiple options are available to you when backing up the whole CDB database. Backup sets are common and the default, but using image copies can be useful, and if kept locally—in the fast recovery area (FRA), for example—they can be switched rapidly for fast recovery. This is especially the case if the image copies are kept up-to-date with incremental backups applied regularly. Backing up the entire CDB is perhaps the most common method and is demonstrated in the following examples, which assume that the RMAN environment is configured with the settings outlined earlier, and the autobackup of the control file is enabled.

This first example uses the most basic form for backing up the whole CDB. The command is executed while connected to CDB$ROOT:

```
RMAN> backup database plus archivelog;
```

In the next example, while connected to CDB$ROOT, we take this a little further and explicitly specify the use of compressed backup set output, along with the location for this output, specified in the FORMAT option. In addition, we include a TAG, which can be extremely useful to identify particular backups:

```
RMAN> run {
   backup as compressed backupset
       format '/backups/%U' database tag='FULLCDB';
```

```
      backup as compressed backupset
              format '/backups/a-%U' archivelog all tag='FULLCDB';
      backup format '/backups/c-%U' current controlfile tag='FULLCDB';
}
```

Next, we make use of image copies. Here we assume that sufficient redundant storage is available, and a disk group called +DBBACKUP exists, which will be used to store the image copies. Archived logs not yet backed up will be written to the /backups folder on the file system. The database can then be backed up as follows (while connected to the root container):

```
RMAN> run {
      backup as copy
              format '+DBBACKUP ' database tag='CDBIMGCOPY';
      backup as compressed backupset
              format '/backups/a-%U' archivelog all not backed up;
}
```

The end result is that a backup copy of the CDB database, including all PDBs, can be located in the +DBBACKUP disk group. If something were to happen to any of the primary files in this example on the +DATA disk group, we could switch to an image copy quickly, followed by recovery of the image copy, which in some cases can be much faster than restoring from a backup set. This method of backup can be extremely useful, but note that sufficient storage is required to keep the copy of the database. It is also possible to adjust the FORMAT specification and write the image copies to a file system location.

TIP
To identify your RMAN backup sessions easily in V$SESSION, you can use the RMAN command to set the command ID for the session: `RMAN> set command id to "FULLCDBBKP";`. *In the end, you will be able to use the* `CLIENT_INFO` *and look for the value* `id=FULLCDBBKP`.

At this stage, you can use the LIST command to view the backup details, including listing the image copies that have been created; by using the PLUGGABLE DATABASE flag, you can specify a specific PDB to provide listings for. So to detail the image copies for PDB1, created in the third example in the preceding examples, use the LIST COPY command as follows:

```
RMAN> list copy of pluggable database PDB1 tag='CDBIMGCOPY';
List of Datafile Copies
=======================
```

```
Key     File S Completion Time       Ckp SCN    Ckp Time            Sparse
------- ---- - -------------------- ---------- -------------------- ------
22      8    A 08/03/2016:21:46:59  4719331    08/03/2016:21:46:57  NO
        Name: +DBBACKUP/CDB1/2D5B1DE419B57F1CE053E902000A271D/DATAFILE/
system.278.905982417
        Tag: IMGCOPY
        Container ID: 3, PDB Name: PDB1

19      9    A 08/03/2016:21:46:39  4719275    08/03/2016:21:46:36  NO
        Name: +DBBACKUP/CDB1/2D5B1DE419B57F1CE053E902000A271D/DATAFILE/
sysaux.270.905982397
        Tag: IMGCOPY
        Container ID: 3, PDB Name: PDB1

27      10   A 08/03/2016:21:47:11  4719345    08/03/2016:21:47:11  NO
        Name: +DBBACKUP/CDB1/2D5B1DE419B57F1CE053E902000A271D/DATAFILE/
users.299.905982431
        Tag: IMGCOPY
        Container ID: 3, PDB Name: PDB1
```

These examples demonstrate how easy it can be to back up an entire CDB.

Partial CDB Backups

In some cases, you might not want to back up the full CDB, but only a subset. This is where the `PLUGGABLE DATABASE` keywords are invoked to get the task done. The examples in this section are executed while connected to the root container. In this first example, we will back up only CDB$ROOT, PDB$SEED, and PDB1:

```
RMAN> backup pluggable database "CDB$ROOT","PDB$SEED", PDB1;
```

As illustrated, you can selectively specify the PDBs to include in the backup. Note that when performing a partial CDB backup, CDB$ROOT should be included.

In the second example, only the CDB root is backed up. Both possible command options for this are listed:

```
RMAN> backup pluggable database "CDB$ROOT";
```

or

```
RMAN> backup database root;
```

It is also possible to take a more fine-grained approach and back up only a specific tablespace. In this example the command will back up the USERS tablespace located in PDB1; it is executed while RMAN is connected to CDB root:

```
RMAN> backup tablespace PDB1:USERS;
```

Note that the USERS tablespace needs to be prefixed with its PDB name of origin; if the name is omitted, RMAN will attempt to back up this tablespace from CDB$ROOT since we are connected to CDB$ROOT.

The final example demonstrates how we can back up the USERS tablespaces in CDB$ROOT, as well as in PDB1:

```
RMAN> backup tablespace USERS, PDB1:USERS;
```

CDB Reporting Using RMAN

When connected to the CDB as target, the `report schema` command will list details for the CDB$ROOT, PDB$SEED, and all the PDBs associated with this CDB. The next example shows the RMAN `report schema` command output on a CDB using Automatic Storage Management (ASM) and Oracle Managed Files (OMF), with one PDB called PDB1. A closer look at the Tablespace column also reveals that the CDB$ROOT tablespaces do not have a prefix, whereas all other PDBs, including those in PDB$SEED's tablespaces, have this defined.

```
RMAN> report schema;
using target database control file instead of recovery catalog
Report of database schema for database with db_unique_name CDB1
List of Permanent Datafiles
===========================
File Size(MB) Tablespace           RB segs Datafile Name
---- -------- -------------------- ------- ------------------------
1    900      SYSTEM               YES     +DATA/CDB1/DATAFILE/system.278.905794969
3    770      SYSAUX               NO      +DATA/CDB1/DATAFILE/sysaux.276.905795015
4    175      UNDOTBS1             YES     +DATA/CDB1/DATAFILE/undotbs1.270.905795049
5    270      PDB$SEED:SYSTEM      NO      +DATA/CDB1/28E530CCFE9C1B52E0534940E40A
7A88/DATAFILE/system.266.905795111
6    5        USERS                NO      +DATA/CDB1/DATAFILE/users.268.905795051
7    510      PDB$SEED:SYSAUX      NO      +DATA/CDB1/28E530CCFE9C1B52E0534940E40A
7A88/DATAFILE/sysaux.277.905795111
8    280      PDB1:SYSTEM          NO      +DATA/CDB1/2D5B1DE419B57F1CE053E902000A27
1D/DATAFILE/system.273.905795557
9    610      PDB1:SYSAUX          NO      +DATA/CDB1/2D5B1DE419B57F1CE053E902000A27
1D/DATAFILE/sysaux.285.905795557
10   5        PDB1:USERS           NO      +DATA/CDB1/2D5B1DE419B57F1CE053E902000A27
1D/DATAFILE/users.265.905795573

List of Temporary Files
=======================
File Size(MB) Tablespace           Maxsize(MB) Tempfile Name
---- -------- -------------------- ----------- --------------------
1    137      TEMP                 32767       +DATA/CDB1/TEMPFILE/temp.274.905795107
2    58       PDB$SEED:TEMP        32767       +DATA/CDB1/28E530CCFE9C1B52E0534940E40A
7A88/DATAFILE/temp012016-03-06_17-45-40-432-pm.dbf
3    20       PDB1:TEMP            32767       +DATA/CDB1/2D5B1DE419B57F1CE053E902000A
271D/TEMPFILE/temp.297.905795561
```

To display additional details of backups and image copies that have been created, you can run the `LIST` command. It is easy to use and can help you quickly identify backup sets and image copies. The commands detailed next are a small subset of those that you may find helpful:

```
RMAN> list backup;
RMAN> list backup tag=FULLCDB;
RMAN> list backup of datafile 1;
RMAN> list backup of pluggable database PDB1;
RMAN> list copy of database;
RMAN> list copy of datafile 1;
RMAN> list copy of pluggable database PDB1;
```

PDB Backups

Now that you have seen how you can back up an entire CDB, let's focus on PDBs, which can be backed up while connected to the CDB root as the target in RMAN, or you can connect directly to a PDB to perform a full or partial backup. In this section we will review both of these methods.

Full PDB Backups

You can perform full backups of a PDB in a number of ways. You can back up the PDB while connected to the CDB$ROOT as target, as shown in the following example. First, the entire PDB, PDB1, is backed up with a single command:

```
RMAN> backup pluggable database PDB1;
```

If you are looking at using image copies, you can also specify this as follows:

```
RMAN> backup as copy pluggable database PDB1;
```

This command can be extended to include more than just one PDB in the backup. Simply specify the PDBs in a comma-delimited list, provided that you are connected to the CDB root as the target. Here's an example:

```
RMAN> backup as copy pluggable database PDB1, PDB2, PDB5;
```

The next option is to connect directly to a specific PDB as the target, and perform a full backup of the connected PDB. Here's an example:

```
RMAN> connect target sys@pdb1
target database Password:
connected to target database: CDB2:PDB1 (DBID=1739880102)
```

Or, here's an example using a local account with SYSBACKUP permission:

```
RMAN> connect target 'localadmin@pdb1 as sysbackup';
target database Password:
connected to target database: CDB1:PDB1 (DBID=1543305986)
```

Once you are connected to the specified PDB, you can execute the `backup database` commands without the `PLUGGABLE` keyword, because all `backup` commands in this context will apply only to the specified PDB. If you try to use the `PLUGGABLE DATABASE` syntax instead of only `DATABASE`, the following error will be generated:

```
RMAN-07538: Pluggable Database qualifier not allowed when connected to
a Pluggable Database
```

Several key options are available when creating a backup of a specific PDB while connected directly to it, as shown with PDB1 here:

```
RMAN> backup database;
RMAN> backup database tag='PDB1';
RMAN> backup as copy database tag='PDB1_IMCOPY';
RMAN> backup as compressed backupset format '/backups/%U' database TAG='PDB1';
```

When connected to a PDB as a target, you can use the `LIST` or `REPORT` command to display information specific to this PDB. In terms of the archived logs, you can show them with the `LIST` command, but other operations, such as backup, restore, or delete, are not permitted while connected to the PDB as a target.

Partial PDB Backups

While connected to a specific PDB as a target, you are allowed to perform only operations that are specific to that PDB—so you cannot, for example, perform backups of other PDBs in this context.

Once connected to a PDB, you can perform backups of datafiles or tablespaces as per normal:

```
RMAN> connect target sys@pdb1
target database Password:
connected to target database: CDB1:PDB1 (DBID=1543305986)
RMAN> backup tablespace users tag='PDB1_USERSTS';
```

If you then connect to the CDB root and list the backups with TAG=PDB1_USERSTS, you will see the following output, noting the highlighted line showing the container ID and PDB name.

```
RMAN> list backup tag='PDB1_USERSTS';
using target database control file instead of recovery catalog
List of Backup Sets
===================
BS Key  Type LV Size       Device Type Elapsed Time Completion Time
------- ---- -- ---------- ----------- ------------ -------------------
78      Full    1.02M      DISK        00:00:00     09/03/2016:11:40:08
        BP Key: 78   Status: AVAILABLE  Compressed: YES  Tag: PDB1_USERSTS
        Piece Name: /backups/3lr01t8o_1_1
  List of Datafiles in backup set 78
  Container ID: 3, PDB Name: PDB1
```

```
File LV Type Ckp SCN    Ckp Time              Abs Fuz SCN Sparse Name
---- -- ---- ---------- ------------------- ----------- ------ ----
  10    Full 5020501    09/03/2016:11:40:08                 NO  +DATA/CDB1/2D5B1DE419
B57F1CE053E902000A271D/DATAFILE/users.265.905795573
```

It is possible to perform partial PDB backups from the CDB root. This enables you to back up specific PDBs or specific tablespaces from them. Following are two such examples, run while connected to the CDB root as target. In the first, we back up the USERS tablespace in the CDB$ROOT, as well as the USERS tablespace from PDB1 and PDB2:

```
RMAN> backup tablespace USERS, PDB1:USERS, PDB2:USERS tag='ALL_USERSTS';
```

NOTE
The datafile number within a CDB is unique.

The second example illustrates backing up specific datafiles from various PDBs. Note that you do not have to specify the PDB names, but you must know its datafile number within the CDB.

```
RMAN> backup datafile 6,10 tag='USERDF';
…
RMAN> list backup tag='USERDF';
List of Backup Sets
===================
BS Key  Type LV Size       Device Type Elapsed Time Completion Time
------- ---- -- ---------- ----------- ------------ -------------------
86      Full    1.02M      DISK        00:00:00     09/03/2016:11:49:57
        BP Key: 86   Status: AVAILABLE  Compressed: YES  Tag: USERDF
        Piece Name: /backups/3tr01tr5_1_1
  List of Datafiles in backup set 86
  File LV Type Ckp SCN    Ckp Time              Abs Fuz SCN Sparse Name
  ---- -- ---- ---------- ------------------- ----------- ------ ----
    6     Full 5021431    09/03/2016:11:49:57                 NO  +DATA/CDB1/DATAFILE/
users.268.905795051

BS Key  Type LV Size       Device Type Elapsed Time Completion Time
------- ---- -- ---------- ----------- ------------ -------------------
87      Full    1.02M      DISK        00:00:00     09/03/2016:11:49:58
        BP Key: 87   Status: AVAILABLE  Compressed: YES  Tag: USERDF
        Piece Name: /backups/3ur01tr6_1_1
  List of Datafiles in backup set 87
  Container ID: 3, PDB Name: PDB1
  File LV Type Ckp SCN    Ckp Time              Abs Fuz SCN Sparse Name
  ---- -- ---- ---------- ------------------- ----------- ------ ----
   10     Full 5021432    09/03/2016:11:49:58                 NO  +DATA/CDB1/2D5B1DE419
B57F1CE053E902000A271D/DATAFILE/users.265.905795573
```

PDB Reporting

As noted earlier, when connected to a PDB as the target, you can view only details relating to that particular PDB—for example, using the `report schema` command.

Restrictions

When you are connected to a PDB as your target, some restrictions are placed on backups, including the following:

- You are not permitted to back up, restore, or delete archived logs while connected to a PDB as target. Tasks related to archive logs must be managed from the CDB$ROOT. Note that during the recovery process (if connected to a PDB as target), if required, RMAN will restore any archived logs needed.

- You cannot update the default RMAN configuration using the `CONFIGURE` command, because this is managed from the CDB level.

Do Not Forget Archive Logs!

As a rule, when performing backups, you should always be sure to include the archive logs in the backup schedule. In Oracle Database 12c, you back up the archive logs from CDB$ROOT. Following are a number of basic variations that can be used for this.

Here's how to back up all available archive logs:

```
RMAN> backup archivelog all;
```

Adding an additional step, you can purge the archive logs once they are backed up:

```
RMAN> backup archivelog all delete input;
```

Here's how to back up all archived logs not backed up at least twice:

```
RMAN> backup archivelog all not backed up 2 times;
```

It is also possible to update the archive log deletion policy for the default RMAN configuration. For more detail on managing archive logs with RMAN, see the Oracle Database 12c online documentation.

Recovery Scenarios

Several levels of recovery are possible in a CDB environment. For example, media recovery can be performed for the entire CDB, or for just one or multiple PDBs. As with non-CDB configurations, you can perform media recovery on database files, tablespaces, and even at the block level.

Instance Recovery

Instance recovery is specific to a CDB as a whole. There is only one instance for the entire CDB, rather than instances allocated on a per-PDB basis. This means that there is a single redo stream, and during crash recovery the redo information is used to recover the instance when the CDB root is opened. This process requires that the datafiles be consistent with the control file, so the redo information is used to roll back any uncommitted transactions at the time of the instance failure. And once the CDB root is opened, all PDBs will be in a mount state.

When reviewing the alert log during system startup, you will notice messages similar to the following, indicating instance crash recovery:

```
Beginning crash recovery of 1 threads
 parallel recovery started with 3 processes
...
 read 168075 KB redo, 9027 data blocks need recovery
2016-03-09T17:05:23.221280+13:00
Started redo application at
 Thread 1: logseq 58, block 88657, offset 0
2016-03-09T17:05:23.232114+13:00
Recovery of Online Redo Log: Thread 1 Group 1 Seq 58 Reading mem 0
  Mem# 0: +DATA/CDB1/ONLINELOG/group_1.279.905795099
  Mem# 1: +DATA/CDB1/ONLINELOG/group_1.282.905795101
2016-03-09T17:05:23.391522+13:00
...
Completed redo application of 15.28MB
2016-03-09T17:05:24.589190+13:00
Completed crash recovery at
 Thread 1: RBA 60.68923.16, nab 68923, scn 0x0000000000518eb5
 9027 data blocks read, 8527 data blocks written, 168075 redo k-bytes read
...
Thread 1 advanced to log sequence 61 (thread open)
Thread 1 opened at log sequence 61
   Current log# 1 seq# 61 mem# 0: +DATA/CDB1/ONLINELOG/group_1.279.905795099
   Current log# 1 seq# 61 mem# 1: +DATA/CDB1/ONLINELOG/group_1.282.905795101
Successful open of redo thread 1
..
Completed: alter database open
```

The next section will focus on restore and recovery of an entire (whole) CDB, and will also explore the full restore of a PDB. Point-in-time recovery (PITR), including the use of Flashback Database, will be covered in more detail in Chapter 8.

Restore and Recover a CDB

The restore and recovery of the CDB database includes all contained PDBs, assuming that you followed the steps outlined in the previous section to perform the backups. If backups are performed correctly, executing restore and recovery procedures becomes a much easier task.

Restore a CDB Using a Cold Backup

As mentioned, you can back up a full CDB using a cold backup, in which it is possible for the database to run in NOARCHIVELOG mode.

The following steps can be used to perform a full restore. In this example, the autobackup of the control file is used (in this case the file was called cfc-CDB3-c-603345334-20160309-01') to restore the SPFILE and control file. However, if you already have the SPFILE, you can skip the step of restoring the SPFILE and continue with the next:

```
RMAN> startup nomount;
RMAN> restore spfile from '/backups/cfc-CDB3-c-603345334-20160309-01';
RMAN> shutdown immediate;
RMAN> startup nomount;
RMAN> restore controlfile from '/backups/cfc-CDB3-c-603345334-20160309-01';
RMAN> alter database mount;
RMAN> restore database;
RMAN> alter database open resetlogs;
RMAN> alter pluggable database all open;
```

Perform a Complete Recovery of a CDB

Performing a full restore and complete recovery of a CDB is almost as easy as performing a full backup. Again, the assumption is that you have followed the steps from earlier in this chapter to perform the full backup of the CDB, and that these backups are available. In this scenario, note that all required archive logs are available to perform the recovery. The archive logs may still be available on disk, or perhaps they are part of the backup as well.

The RMAN connection is initiated to the CDB$ROOT as target:

```
RMAN> startup mount;
RMAN> restore database;
RMAN> recover database;
RMAN> alter database open;
RMAN> alter pluggable database all open;
```

Perform a Complete Recovery of CDB$ROOT

The process required to restore the CDB$ROOT container alone, when all other PDBs are intact without any issues, is similar to the previous steps:

```
RMAN> startup mount;
RMAN> restore database "CDB$ROOT";
RMAN> recover database "CDB$ROOT";
RMAN> alter database open;
RMAN> alter pluggable database all open;
```

Recover from a Lost CDB$ROOT Tablespace

The steps required to perform a full restore and recovery of a CDB$ROOT tablespace should be executed while connected to the CDB$ROOT as target. It is not necessary to have the CDB in a mounted state, or even to have the PDBs closed, as long as the tablespace in question is not the CDB$ROOT SYSTEM or UNDO tablespace. The tablespace must be offline when the restore is performed.

The steps to follow to restore and recover the USERS tablespace in this context are shown here:

```
RMAN> alter tablespace USERS offline;
RMAN> restore tablespace USERS;
RMAN> recover tablespace USERS;
RMAN> alter tablspace USERS online;
```

If a restore or recovery is required for the SYSTEM or UNDO tablespace, the CDB root must be in a mounted state before the `restore` and `recover` commands are executed.

Recover from a Lost CDB$ROOT Datafile

Recovery from a lost datafile in the root container can be accomplished without restarting the CDB in a mounted state, as long as the datafiles do not belong to a SYSTEM or UNDO tablespace (which otherwise would necessitate a restart into a mounted state, prior to executing restore or recovery). The following commands demonstrate restore and recovery of a lost datafile from the USERS tablespace (datafile 6 in this case) located in the CDB$ROOT. The connection here is with the CDB root as the target:

```
RMAN> alter database datafile 6 offline;
RMAN> restore datafile 6;
RMAN> recover datafile 6;
RMAN> alter database datafile 6 online;
```

Recover from Loss of Tempfiles

If you have lost a tempfile due to media failure, you have two possible options to resolve this. The first is simply to add a new tempfile to the temporary tablespace and drop the old file. The second option will take effect on the next restart of the CDB. The tempfile will be re-created on the next restart of the CDB root, and if it belongs to a PDB, on the next open of the PDB the tempfile will be created. Following is an extract from the alert log showing this:

```
...
Errors in file /u01/app/oracle/diag/rdbms/cdb3/CDB3/trace/CDB3_dbw0_28682.trc:
ORA-01186: file 201 failed verification tests
ORA-01157: cannot identify/lock data file 201 - see DBWR trace file
```

```
ORA-01110: data file 201: '/u01/app/oracle/oradata/CDB3/temp01.dbf'
2016-03-09T10:55:17.459152+13:00
File 201 not verified due to error ORA-01157
2016-03-09T10:55:17.465595+13:00
Re-creating tempfile /u01/app/oracle/oradata/CDB3/temp01.dbf
...
```

Restore and Recover a PDB

In this section we will cover the recovery steps with specific focus at the PDB level, and the key scenarios will be addressed.

Restore and Recover a PDB

If a PDB is lost, you can restore and recover it without having the root container in a mounted state, although the restore and recovery process is managed via the root container as the target connection. If the PDB is still open, you must close it before executing the restore and recovery commands:

```
RMAN> alter pluggable database PDB1 close;
RMAN> restore pluggable database PDB1;
RMAN> recover pluggable database PDB1;
RMAN> alter pluggable database PDB1 open;
```

What if your backups included image copies of the PDB? Using image copies may be very effective in reducing any downtime, rather than waiting for a restore of the full PDB from backup. When performing restore and recovery operations, time is of the essence, and the faster a database can be restored and brought back online for users the better. So if image copies are available for a PDB, why not use them? You can switch to use the image copies, create a new backup of the PDB as an image copy in the original location, and then schedule a switch back during a quiet period.

Here are the steps to follow:

```
RMAN> alter pluggable database PDB1 close;
RMAN> list copy of pluggable database PDB1;
RMAN> switch pluggable database PDB1 to copy;
RMAN> recover pluggable database;
RMAN> alter pluggable database PDB1 open;
```

Recover a Lost PDB System Datafile

If a datafile from a PDB's SYSTEM or UNDO tablespace (when using local undo) is lost, the recovery process must be performed from the root container. The root container, including all other PDBs, can be open read-write, but the affected PDB must be in a mounted state.

The steps to perform a restore of datafile 8, which is the SYSTEM datafile for PDB1 in this particular example, can be restored from the CDB$ROOT as follows:

```
RMAN> alter pluggable database PDB1 close;
RMAN> restore datafile 8;
RMAN> recover datafile 8;
RMAN> alter pluggable database PDB1 open;
```

Recover a Lost PDB Nonsystem Datafile

If the lost datafile in a PDB is not part of the SYSTEM or UNDO (if using local undo) tablespace, the restore and recovery process can occur from either the CDB$ROOT or the PDB. The PDB does not have to be in a mounted state, but the datafile must be taken offline, if it's not already down, prior to performing the restore and recovery.

In the following example, the restore and recovery is performed while connected to the PDB. The `report schema` command is used to confirm the datafile number, which, in this case, is datafile 10 (one of the USERS tablespace datafiles):

```
RMAN> connect target sys@pdb1
RMAN> report schema;
RMAN> alter database datafile 10 offline;
RMAN> restore datafile 10;
RMAN> recover datafile 10;
RMAN> alter database datafile 10 online;
```

As with our earlier example, if image copies are available, the option also exists to switch to using this. Note that if you do so, the location of the image copy will most likely differ from the current file location. You can replace the `restore datafile 10` command with the following if a copy is available (use the `list copy` command to identify datafile copies):

```
RMAN> switch datafile 10 to copy;
```

Recover a Lost PDB Tablespace

If a tablespace needs to be restored and recovered in a PDB, two options are available. This can be done within the PDB (as long as this is not a SYSTEM or UNDO tablespace), or it can be done from the CDB$ROOT. The tablespace must be taken offline prior to starting the restore, and this should be done from within the PDB:

```
RMAN> connect target sys@pdb1
RMAN> alter tablespace users offline;
```

Then you can restore the tablespace from within the PDB with the following commands:

```
RMAN> restore tablespace USERS;
RMAN> recover tablespace USERS;
RMAN> alter tablespace USERS online;
```

Alternatively, you can perform the restore and recover commands from the CDB$ROOT:

```
RMAN> restore tablespace PDB1:USERS;
RMAN> recover tablespace PDB1:USERS;
```

We've covered a number of the key areas you should be familiar with when performing complete recovery operations in an Oracle Database 12c Multitenant environment. In the next chapter we will look at using PITR and the Flashback Database options.

RMAN Optimization Considerations

Working with large databases is a prevalent trend today, and it is less common to find the need to purge old data. Data is retained for longer periods, and often it will never be removed. This increase in overall database sizes affects backup and recovery, and optimizing backup and recovery operations is becoming more and more important. Furthermore, backup windows are shrinking, while additional load on production systems needs to be kept to a minimum. To assist with this issue, Oracle introduced a number of options, including the following:

- Incremental backups
- Block change tracking
- Multiple channel backups (parallel backup and recovery)
- Multisection backups
- RMAN backup optimization

In this section we will review the first four of these five options, which are highly recommended when using multitenant.

Incremental Backups

Two key options are available for incremental backups: differential and cumulative backups. By default, the differential option is selected, and when using this method all database blocks changed since the previous backup will be included. Table 7-1 illustrates a schedule that employs differential backups; first an incremental level 0—a full backup—is performed on Monday, followed by a differential backup each day thereafter.

If you need to perform a restore on Thursday, the full backup from Monday, as well as the incremental backups from Tuesday and Wednesday, will be required. One of the potential risks when relying on incremental differential backups is that if

Mon	Tue	Wed	Thu	Fri
FULL				
	|----->			
		|----->		
			|----->	
				|----->

TABLE 7-1. *Differential Incremental Backup*

you were to lose one of the incremental backups, you might not be able to restore and recover to the required point in time. This risk can be reduced by ensuring that archive logs are backed up at least twice, so that if one day's worth of backups is lost, it may still be possible to use archive logs to recover past this point. For example, to back up PDB1 using differential incremental backups, we'd follow these steps.

1. Create the base incremental level 0 backup:

   ```
   RMAN> backup incremental level 0 pluggable database PDB1;
   ```

2. Create the differential incremental level 1 backup:

   ```
   RMAN> backup incremental level 1 pluggable database PDB1;
   ```

With the cumulative incremental backup, as with the differential incremental backup, only changed blocks are backed up; in this instance, however, the backup includes the data since the last base incremental level 0 backup. Table 7-2 illustrates this.

Mon	Tue	Wed	Thu	Fri
FULL				
--------	|----->			
--------	--------	|----->		
--------	--------	--------	|----->	
--------	--------	--------	--------	|----->

TABLE 7-2. *Cumulative Incremental Backup*

First an incremental level 0 backup is created, and every cumulative incremental backup following this will back up all the changed blocks since the last full level 0 backup. This method does extra work in backing up blocks more than once and requires additional storage, but the overall risk is less. When using this approach, the keyword CUMULATIVE must be used—so, for example, if we want to back up PDB1 using this method, the following commands can be run.

1. Create the base incremental level 0 backup:

    ```
    RMAN> backup incremental level 0 pluggable database PDB1;
    ```

2. Create the differential incremental level 1 backup:

    ```
    RMAN> backup incremental level 1 cumulative pluggable database PDB1;
    ```

Incremental backups can be extremely useful, especially in large database environments. But this brings us to our next point, which is that during an incremental backup, the datafile blocks are scanned to identify changed blocks in need of backup. This process can take time, perhaps even as long as a full backup itself. To make this faster, Oracle introduced block change tracking.

Block Change Tracking

When you're working with incremental backups, the use of block change tracking is highly recommended. Note, however, that this is an Enterprise Edition feature and cannot be used in Standard Edition. This feature cannot be enabled within a PDB, but instead should be enabled while connected to the CDB$ROOT. If you do attempt to enable block change tracking while connected to a PDB, an ORA-65040 error will be generated, as shown in the following example:

```
ORA-65040: operation not allowed from within a pluggable database
```

Enabling or disabling this option is easy, especially when using OMF. The block change-tracking file is created and will grow in 10MB chunks as needed; the default location when using OMF is DB_CREATE_FILE_DEST. If you are not using OMF, the filename and location should be specified manually. The file will track all the changed blocks in the database and can be enabled with the following command:

```
SQL> alter database enable block change tracking;   --- if using OMF
SQL> alter database enable block change tracking using file '/u01/oracle/oradata/DEV/bc-track.dbf';   --- if not using OMF
```

Block change tracking can be disabled with the following command:

```
SQL> alter database disable block change tracking;
```

Using this option together with incremental backups is recommended for multitenant environments, especially for larger configurations, because it will assist in creating faster backups and reducing resource consumption.

Multiple Channel Backup

Using multiple channels may also lead to faster backup and recovery times. However, having sufficient CPU and I/O capability to accommodate this is equally important; otherwise, you may slow down operations when using multiple channels. If you want to use this option by default, you can update the default configuration and specify the parallelism parameter as shown here:

```
RMAN> configure device type disk parallelism 4;
```

You may also allocate multiple channels as part of your backup and recovery commands:

```
RMAN> run {
 allocate channel ch1 type disk;
 allocate channel ch2 type disk;
 backup database plus archivelog;
 }
```

Multisection Backups

Combining incremental backups with multiple channels can help speed backup and recovery operations. Prior to 12c, with large files, this did not always provide significant benefit, but since 12c, parallel incremental backups can be taken one step further. As of Oracle Database 12c Release 1 (12.1), RMAN now also supports multisection incremental backups, as well as the use of multisection with image copy backups. The COMPATIBLE parameter must be set to 12.0.0 or higher to allow for this. Note that using this option forces the FILESPERSET option to be set to 1 for backup sets. The following syntax can be used to back up a PDB database called XPDB2 with large datafiles using multisection backups, and the command is executed from the CDB$ROOT:

```
RMAN> configure device type disk parallelism 4;
RMAN> backup incremental level 1 section size 200M pluggable database XPDB2;
```

As mentioned, the use of multisection can now also be used with image copy backups. In the following example, an image copy backup is taken of the XPDB PDB with the SECTION SIZE clause specified as follows:

```
RMAN> configure device type disk parallelism 4;
RMAN> backup as copy section size 200M pluggable database XPDB2;
```

NOTE
If the section size specified is larger than the file to be backed up, multisection backups will be ignored for the file and not be used.

The Data Recovery Advisor

Backup and recovery can become incredibly complex, especially when diagnosing and deciding on the correct repair options. To assist with this, Oracle introduced the Data Recovery Advisor in 11g, and it has been extended and improved in Oracle Database 12c. The Data Recovery Advisor can help list potential corrective actions, and, if you want, even perform these tasks for you. You can use either RMAN or Oracle Enterprise Manager Cloud Control to obtain information provided by the Data Recovery Advisor and execute the required tasks.

At the time of writing, the Data Recovery Advisor could be used in a non-CDB as well as in a single-instance (non-Oracle RAC) CDB. The Data Recovery Advisor is not supported in Oracle RAC configurations. It may be run only from the CDB$ROOT, not from within a PDB, and if this is attempted an RMAN-07536 error will be displayed.

The standard Data Recovery Advisor commands to be invoked from within the CDB$ROOT include these:

```
RMAN> list failure;
RMAN> advise failure;
RMAN> repair failure;
RMAN> change failure;
```

Block Corruption

Block corruption is a nightmare for DBAs, and only the most fortunate avoid coming across it in their careers. Fortunately, Oracle provides tools that can be used to ensure your databases are valid and that block corruption is not hiding under the covers. Running these health checks on a regular basis is, therefore, highly recommended.

The `VALIDATE` command is very easy to use to perform these checks. When the command is run from RMAN, a detected problem will trigger a failure assessment. This will then be recorded in the Automatic Diagnostic Repository (ADR), where it can be accessed by the previously discussed Data Recovery Advisor.

The `VALIDATE` command can be executed against a running database (CDB, non-CDB, and PDBs) and also on backups, including RMAN backup sets and image copies.

The following is a short listing of some of the options available with the `VALIDATE` command; for more detail see the Oracle 12c Database documentation.

```
RMAN> validate database;
RMAN> validate pluggable database PDB1;
RMAN> validate backupset 13;
RMAN> validate copy of pluggable database PDB1;
RMAN> backup validate pluggable database PDB1;
RMAN> restore pluggable database PDB1 validate;
```

Using Cloud Control for Backups

Backup and recovery operations can also be performed from within Oracle Enterprise Manager Cloud Control. Figure 7-1 and Figure 7-2 illustrate some of the options available.

For example, if Availability | Backup & Recovery (Figure 7-1) is selected, you will see a number of options to help guide you through creating and scheduling backups, along with performing restores and recoveries. Selecting the Schedule Backup option presents the options shown in Figure 7-2, including the ability to back up a specific PDB.

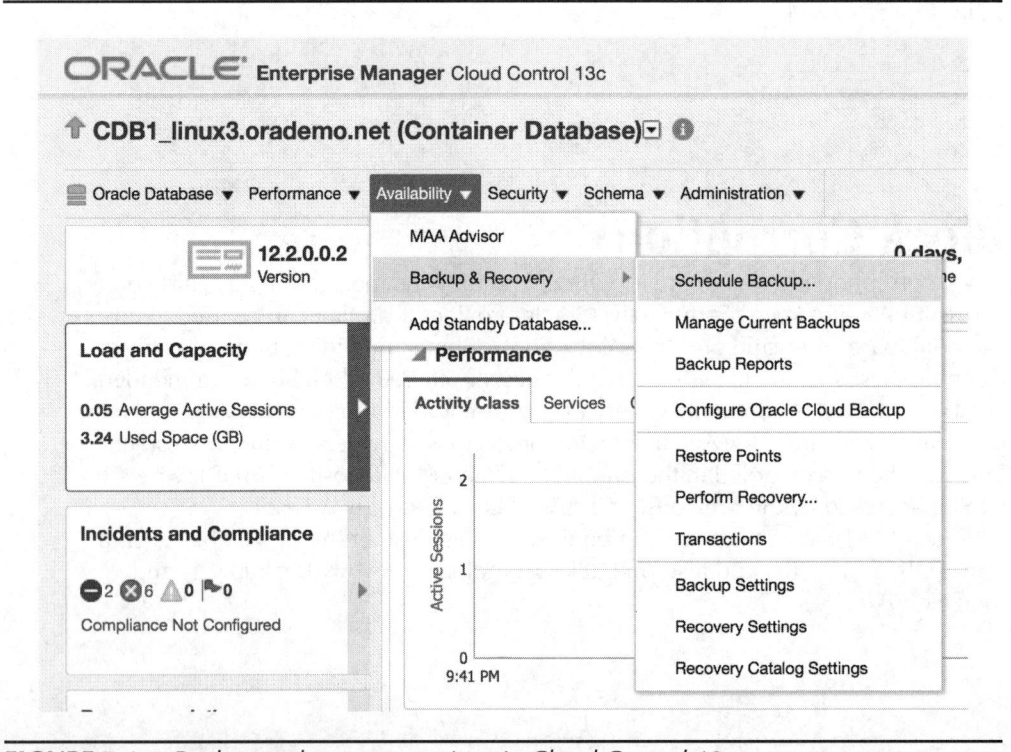

FIGURE 7-1. *Backup and recovery options in Cloud Control 13c*

FIGURE 7-2. *Backup options in Cloud Control 13c*

Back Up to the Cloud

With the growing interest in using cloud-based solutions, a number of options are available for backing up Oracle Databases to the cloud. Two key players present such offerings: Amazon Web Services (AWS) and the Oracle Cloud Services.

NOTE
If you sign up for Oracle Cloud Services to perform RMAN backups to the Oracle Cloud, you can use the required RMAN encryption free of charge. This is even the case when using Oracle Standard Edition, although a specific patch will need to be applied to a Standard Edition environment to allow this.

To configure the Oracle Database Backup Service, you first need to create an Oracle Cloud account, and then sign up for both the Backup Service and the Oracle Storage Cloud Service. Here is a summary, at a high level, of the steps required to back up to the Oracle Cloud:

1. Create an Oracle Cloud account and sign up for the backup and storage services.

2. Download the Oracle Database Backup Cloud Module.

3. Install the module. See readme.txt file for parameter details (run as oracle software owner):

   ```
   # java -jar opc_install.jar -serviceName Storage \
   -identityDomain yourDomain -opcId 'your-account@example.com' \
   -opcPass '<yourpassword>' -walletDir /u01/app/oracle/cloud/wallet \
   -configFile /u01/app/oracle/cloud/conf/ocb.ora -libDir /u01/app/oracle/cloud/lib
   ```

   Once the module is configured, three files are created: the wallet with your cloud account details loaded, a parameter file, and the module library.

4. When allocating the SBT_TAPE channel, options need to be supplied to indicate the use of the library and your configuration:

   ```
   allocate channel ch1 type SBT_TAPE PARMS 'SBT_LIBRARY=/u01/app/oracle/cloud/lib/libopc.so, ENV=(OPC_PFILE=/u01/app/oracle/cloud/conf/ocb.ora)';
   ```

5. You must use encryption when using the Oracle Database Backup Service with the cloud module configured here. The backup encryption can be enabled using three possible options: password encryption, Transparent Data Encryption (TDE), or a combination of both. The quick and easy method is to use the password option, which is enabled by running the following command:

   ```
   RMAN> SET ENCRYPTION ON IDENTIFIED BY 'YourPasswordHere' only;
   ```

6. Run your RMAN backup commands:

   ```
   RMAN> SET ENCRYPTION ON IDENTIFIED BY 'YourPasswordHere' only;
   RMAN> run {
     allocate channel ch1
     type SBT_TAPE PARMS  'SBT_LIBRARY=/u01/app/oracle/cloud/lib/libopc.so,
     ENV=(OPC_PFILE=/u01/app/oracle/cloud/conf/ocb.conf)';
     backup as compressed backupset database plus archivelog;
     backup current controlfile;
   }
   ```

For more detail on using the Oracle Cloud, and how to work with advanced configurations in the Cloud backup module, see the Oracle Database Backup Service documentation.

Summary

Oracle Database backup and recovery can be one of those areas that busy DBAs may not spend a lot of time on yet, but, as we have shown, it is one of the most critical areas in managing a multitenant environment. The emergence of this new multitenant paradigm (CDBs and PDBs) has generated a number of explanatory analogies, and one that seems apt is having all your eggs in one basket. It is clear that you need to look after this basket, because if something goes wrong, you could end up with a difficult cleanup situation.

The same can be said of using Oracle Database 12*c* Multitenant: you are creating a container that houses multiple PDBs, and if you do not have adequate backups (both at the container and pluggable database levels), you may end up with a very difficult scenario should disaster strike.

This chapter demonstrated that performing backup and recovery in a multitenant environment is not particularly complex or onerous, and getting a handle on the basics means you can perform complete recovery with just a few easy commands. The next chapter will take this one step further to discuss point-in-time recovery and Flashback Database.

CHAPTER 8

Flashback and Point-in-time Recovery

In previous chapters you have learned that most of the backup and recovery tasks are performed at the container database (CDB) level, and this is perfect in terms of protecting all your pluggable databases (PDBs) from media failure. Simply create a new PDB in the CDB, and the PDB will be automatically protected in the same way.

However, a PDB administrator may have different requirements. Rarely in production, but frequently in test environments, we may need to do point-in-time recovery (PITR), so we appreciate a smart alternative: Flashback Database. Release 12.1 brought us multitenant, and although Flashback Database was not available in this release, in 12.2 this has changed thanks to the introduction of the local UNDO mode.

Pluggable Database Point-in-Time

Recall that we said that the ancestor of PDBs was the transportable tablespace. Here (whether you are using PDBs or not), we'll take a look at how you restore a tablespace to a previous state.

A tablespace has its own datafiles, so the first step is easy: Restore the datafiles from the previous backup. Then you have to apply REDO to bring the files forward, up to the desired point-in-time you are working to; but that's not enough. Datafiles by themselves are just a bunch of bits without the metadata that details what is stored within. This information is contained in the dictionary, so this is why you cannot do a tablespace point-in-time recovery (TSPITR) in place. Instead, you must also recover the SYSTEM and SYSAUX tablespaces to the same point-in-time, which has to be done into an auxiliary database.

With PDBs, you don't expect to encounter the same problem, because they have their own SYSTEM and SYSAUX tablespaces that can be recovered to the same point-in-time. This means that you can bring your PDB to a specific point-in-time. But that's not enough, because you still can't open it in this state. As a refresher, look back at the section "Accessing Database Files at the CDB Level" in Chapter 1 and you will see what is missing.

When you recover a database, the final step is to roll back all the ongoing transactions that did not complete at that point-in-time. This is the "A" from the ACID property: atomicity of transactions. The principle holds that you need to apply the UNDO for the transactions that were there at that time, which is why you require a PITR of the UNDO tablespace as well.

In Figure 8-1, you can see the restore, roll-forward, and rollback phases of recovery illustrated. All files are brought up to the required point-in-time state by applying REDO to them. Uncommitted transactions are cleaned out by applying UNDO to roll them back.

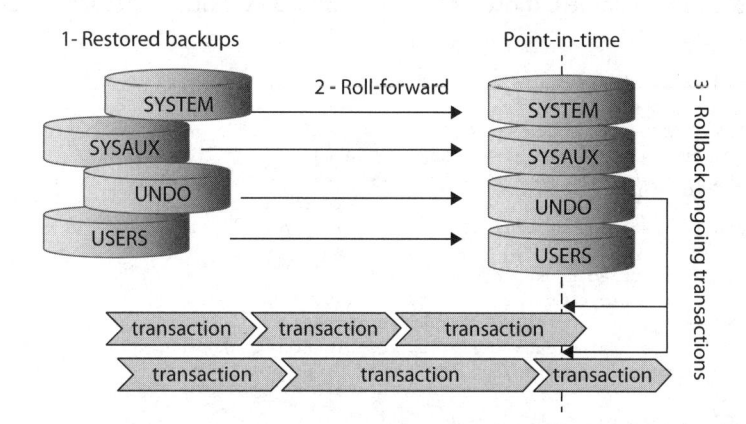

FIGURE 8-1. *The roll-forward and rollback phases of recovery over the transaction timeline*

Let's see how it works in 12.1 Multitenant. With PDBs, you don't need to restore *everything* into an auxiliary instance as you do for tablespace PITR. It is now possible to restore the complete PDB tablespaces in place because they contain their system tablespaces. However, you still need to restore UNDO, and for this you need an auxiliary instance. You cannot overwrite the common UNDO which is also used by the current transactions running on the other containers.

Recover PDB Until Time

Here is an example of the Recovery Manager (RMAN) commands you can run to restore and recover a PDB, specifying the point-in-time with a system change number, as of SCN 1610254, and using /var/tmp for the auxiliary instance:

```
alter pluggable database PDB close;
run {
 set until SCN = 1610254 ;
 restore pluggable database PDB;
 recover pluggable database PDB auxiliary destination='/var/tmp';
 alter pluggable database PDB open resetlogs;
}
```

In the RMAN output you can see the operations that it is performing. RMAN is verbose here, so we only show those sections of output that help you understand how it works.

First, all the PDB datafiles, those of SYSTEM, SYSAUX, and USERS tablespaces, are restored in place:

```
Starting restore at 29-JAN-16
allocated channel: ORA_DISK_1
channel ORA_DISK_1: SID=136 device type=DISK
channel ORA_DISK_1: starting datafile backup set restore
channel ORA_DISK_1: specifying datafile(s) to restore from backup set
channel ORA_DISK_1: restoring datafile 00143 to /u02/app/oracle/oradata/PDB/system01.dbf
channel ORA_DISK_1: restoring datafile 00144 to /u02/app/oracle/oradata/PDB/sysaux01.dbf
…
channel ORA_DISK_1: restored backup piece 1
channel ORA_DISK_1: restore complete, elapsed time: 00:00:03
channel ORA_DISK_1: starting datafile backup set restore
channel ORA_DISK_1: specifying datafile(s) to restore from backup set
channel ORA_DISK_1: restoring datafile 00146 to /u02/app/oracle/oradata/PDB/usertbs01.dbf
…
channel ORA_DISK_1: restored backup piece 1
channel ORA_DISK_1: restore complete, elapsed time: 00:00:01
Finished restore at 29-JAN-16
```

Then recovery must start, and RMAN needs to determine the tablespaces that may contain UNDO:

```
Starting recover at 29-JAN-16
current log archived
using channel ORA_DISK_1
RMAN-05026: WARNING: presuming following set of tablespaces applies to specified
Point-in-time
List of tablespaces expected to have UNDO segments
Tablespace SYSTEM
Tablespace UNDOTBS1
```

Notice the warning, which we will explain later. Here RMAN is making a reasonable guess that those tablespaces that contain UNDO currently are the same as those that contained UNDO at the point-in-time you want to recover to, and RMAN lists them out.

Those tablespaces that contain UNDO cannot be restored in place, because they would override the CDB tablespaces that are used by the other containers, so for this purpose we need an auxiliary instance:

```
Creating automatic instance, with SID='ggzB'
initialization parameters used for automatic instance:
db_name=CDB
db_unique_name=ggzB_pitr_pdb_CDB
compatible=12.0.0
db_block_size=8192
db_files=200
diagnostic_dest=/u01/app/oracle
_system_trig_enabled=FALSE
```

```
sga_target=1024M
processes=150
db_create_file_dest=/var/tmp
log_archive_dest_1='location=/var/tmp'
enable_pluggable_database=true
_clone_one_pdb_recovery=true

starting up automatic instance CDB
…
Automatic instance created
```

As you can see, RMAN takes responsibility for creating an instance, using Oracle Managed Files (OMF) file naming with destination set to /var/tmp, which we defined earlier as an auxiliary destination. So let's review the parameters that are used. It is possible to define additional options, but the following are mandatory:

- `db_name` and `compatible` must be the same.
- `SID` and `db_unique_name` must be unique.
- `_clone_one_pdb_recovery` specifies that only CDB$ROOT and one PDB will be recovered.
- `_system_trig_enabled` disables the system triggers to be sure that the auxiliary instance does not have any unintended impact outside of itself.

Then this instance must use the files from the PDB that have been restored in place:

```
# switch to valid datafilecopies
switch clone datafile   143 to datafilecopy
 "/u02/app/oracle/oradata/PDB/system01.dbf";
switch clone datafile   144 to datafilecopy
 "/u02/app/oracle/oradata/PDB/sysaux01.dbf";
switch clone datafile   146 to datafilecopy
 "/u02/app/oracle/oradata/PDB/usertbs01.dbf";
```

And the CDB datafiles for SYSTEM, SYSAUX, and UNDO will be restored to the OMF destination:

```
# set destinations for recovery set and auxiliary set datafiles
set newname for clone datafile  1 to new;
set newname for clone datafile  5 to new;
set newname for clone datafile  3 to new;
# restore the tablespaces in the recovery set and the auxiliary set
restore clone datafile  1, 5, 3;
…
```

```
channel ORA_AUX_DISK_1: restoring datafile 00001 to /var/tmp/CDB/
datafile/o1_mf_system_%u_.dbf
channel ORA_AUX_DISK_1: restoring datafile 00005 to /var/tmp/CDB/
datafile/o1_mf_undotbs1_%u_.dbf
channel ORA_AUX_DISK_1: restoring datafile 00003 to /var/tmp/CDB/
datafile/o1_mf_sysaux_%u_.dbf
```

At this point, we have an auxiliary instance with access to all the necessary CDB$ROOT and PDB files, which have been restored to the specific point-in-time of interest. Next, it's time to recover them:

```
# recover pdb
recover clone database tablespace  "SYSTEM", "UNDOTBS1", "SYSAUX"
pluggable database 'PDB'  delete archivelog;
sql clone 'alter database open read only';
```

The rollback phase of the recovery, which rolls back the transactions that were opened at the system change number (SCN) 1610254, reads the temporarily restored UNDO, but it actually updates the datafiles that were restored in place. At the end, the auxiliary instance and temporarily restored datafiles are automatically removed.

Where Is the UNDO?

In the previous example, the following warning was generated:

```
RMAN-05026: WARNING: presuming following set of tablespaces applies to
specified Point-in-time
List of tablespaces expected to have UNDO segments
Tablespace SYSTEM
Tablespace UNDOTBS1
```

RMAN needs to restore all tablespaces that may contain UNDO segments or the recovery will fail, so it lists the current tablespaces which contain UNDO. But we need the UNDO from the point-in-time we want to recover. And this may differ if we have changed the UNDO tablespace in the meantime.

In the following example, we alter the UNDO tablespace to UNDO2, dropping UNDO1, which existed as the prior default. The "recover PDB to a point-in-time" process then presents the following warning:

```
RMAN-05026: warning: presuming following set of tablespaces applies to
specified point-in-time
List of tablespaces expected to have UNDO segments
Tablespace SYSTEM
Tablespace UNDO2
```

And finally it fails, because that tablespace did not exist at the point-in-time we want to recover to:

```
RMAN-00571: ===========================================================
RMAN-00569: =============== ERROR MESSAGE STACK FOLLOWS ===============
RMAN-00571: ===========================================================
RMAN-03002: failure of recover command at 02/07/2016 16:18:58
RMAN-03015: error occurred in stored script Memory Script
RMAN-06026: some targets not found - aborting restore
RMAN-06023: no backup or copy of datafile 17 found to restore
```

Datafile 17 was from the UNDO2 tablespace, but we can't restore it, and we don't need it in any case; but we do need the datafile from UNDO1.

Here the syntax of the RECOVER command is useful because it allows us to specify the specific tablespaces to restore when we know which one holds UNDO:

```
recover pluggable database PDB auxiliary destination='/var/tmp'
    undo tablespace 'UNDO1';
```

We have seen cases in which RMAN does not know how to restore these datafiles, but it's probably not a good idea to rely solely on the fact that you know the name of the tablespace that was present at a previous point-in-time either.

But no need to worry, because the solution is to have the PDBPITR operation automatically restore the correct UNDO tablespace using an RMAN catalog. Then there will be no warnings or errors, and RMAN will restore the correct UNDO tablespace itself.

Summary of 12.1 PDBPITR

From what we have discussed so far, two recommendations follow: First, to be fully automated, even in those instances when the UNDO tablespace has changed, you need an RMAN catalog. If you anticipate running PITR, you should have an RMAN catalog to facilitate a large retention period. In fact, there are no irrefutable reasons not to use an RMAN catalog! Remember that you can put this anywhere, even on a virtual machine, because you don't have to license it separately. Second, even if the auxiliary instance is supposed to be removed automatically by RMAN, if a failure occurs, you may have to clean it up manually. You can find its ORACLE_SID in the RMAN log and use this to connect and shutdown abort if needed.

Figure 8-2 shows the CDB that is at the current SCN, where PDB2 has been restored to a point-in-time SCN, and an auxiliary instance is able to undo the uncommitted transactions because it has restored the CDB level UNDO at that SCN.

The creation and cleaning of the auxiliary instance is automated by RMAN, but this still takes time. You need to restore and recover all tablespaces that may contain UNDO, even though you may need only a few UNDO records—specifically those that cover the open transactions for your PDB. Perhaps there is a better way, so let's imagine that UNDO was stored at the PDB level.

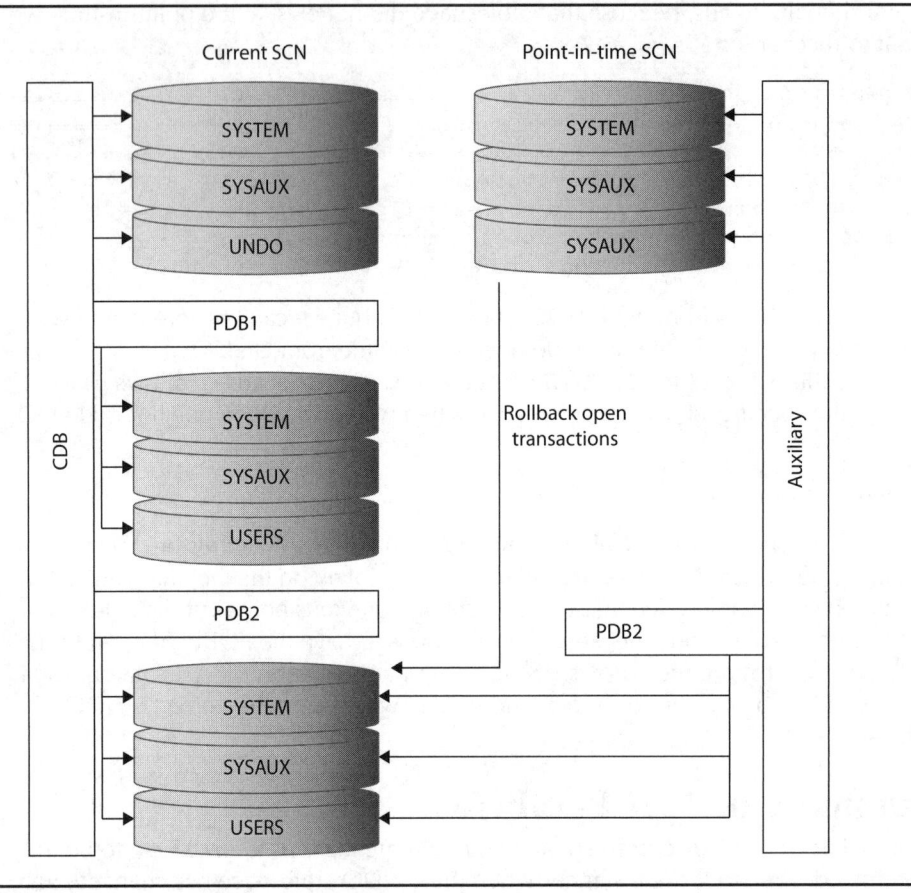

FIGURE 8-2. *Point-in-time recovery using auxiliary instance*

Local UNDO in 12.2

In 12.1 the UNDO tablespace is common, meaning that it is shared among the entire CDB, to store information about all transactions. Furthermore, only the CDB administrator can create the UNDO tablespace. So in working with a PDB, the statement to create the UNDO tablespace is simply ignored.

The problem with shared UNDO is that it stores data from all other containers. As mentioned, UNDO contains information relating to transactions, which is necessary to clean up any uncommitted transactions as required. This means that PDBs on a shared UNDO CDB are essentially not self-contained, except for a closed PDB that has been shut down cleanly.

This is why it was impossible to flashback a PDB in 12.1. And in older versions, the only way to affect a PITR of part of the database was to use TSPITR, which could not be done in place. It was, in fact, necessary to restore the SYSTEM, SYSAUX, and UNDO tablespaces, in addition to the tablespace that you specifically wanted to restore, because the metadata from the system tablespace is required, along with UNDO record information, to roll back the transactions.

When 12c was introduced, each PDB had its own system tablespaces but UNDO was shared, which again meant that PDBs were not isolated enough for particular types of operations, such as those that shift tablespaces to another time or location.

However, beginning with 12.2, you can define the UNDO mode to local, which means that each PDB stores its own UNDO records in a local UNDO tablespace pertaining solely to that PDB. This enables many operations on an open PDB that were previously impossible, such as relocating, plugging, and flashback of a PDB. Furthermore, it improves the PITR of PDBs because the need for an auxiliary instance has been removed.

In 12.2, you can still use the shared UNDO mode if you prefer, as in 12.1, but certain operations will not be available or will require the PDB to be cleanly closed so that there are no active transactions, and no need for any UNDO records.

In short, having the UNDO local to the tablespace improves the efficiency of unplugging and PITR of PDBs, and it is mandatory for online relocate or clone. (Note: in shared mode these operations require the source to be open read-only to ensure that there are no ongoing, open transactions.) Local UNDO is also mandatory for the referenced PDB when creating a proxy database.

Database Properties

If you have a CDB already created, you can check the UNDO mode from the database properties:

```
SQL> select * from database_properties where property_name like '%UNDO%';
PROPERTY_NAME          PROPERTY_VALUE        DESCRIPTION
---------------------  --------------------  -----------------------------------
LOCAL_UNDO_ENABLED     TRUE                  true if local undo is enabled
```

The `LOCAL_UNDO_ENABLED` property is set to TRUE when you are in local UNDO mode, and it is set to FALSE in shared UNDO mode. Be careful if you don't see anything, because this means that the database was created with shared UNDO, either when UNDO mode was not specified in the `CREATE DATABASE` statement or if it was upgraded from 12.1

Create Database

You choose the local UNDO mode when you create the database. You can check the option on the Database Configuration Assistant (DBCA), or add `LOCAL UNDO ON` to the `ENABLE PLUGGABLE DATABASE` clause of the `CREATE DATABASE` statement.

When you create the database in local UNDO mode, in addition to the UNDO tablespace of the CDB$ROOT container, you have an UNDO tablespace in PDB$SEED and in *any* PDB that you create. Here is an example, noting again that in the `report` schema the tablespace names are prefixed with the PDB name:

```
RMAN> report schema;
Report of database schema for database with db_unique_name CDB
List of Permanent Datafiles
===========================
File Size(MB) Tablespace             RB segs Datafile Name
---- -------- --------------------   ------- --------------------
1    700      SYSTEM                 YES     /u02/oradata/CDB/system01.dbf
2    210      PDB$SEED:SYSTEM        NO      /u02/oradata/CDB/pdbseed/system01.dbf
3    550      SYSAUX                 NO      /u02/oradata/CDB/sysaux01.dbf
4    165      PDB$SEED:SYSAUX        NO      /u02/oradata/CDB/pdbseed/sysaux01.dbf
5    270      UNDOTBS1               YES     /u02/oradata/CDB/undotbs01.dbf
6    225      PDB$SEED:UNDOTBS1      NO      /u02/oradata/CDB/pdbseed/undotbs01.dbf
7    5        USERS                  NO      /u02/oradata/CDB/users01.dbf
8    210      PDB:SYSTEM             NO      /u02/oradata/CDB/pdb/system01.dbf
9    185      PDB:SYSAUX             NO      /u02/oradata/CDB/pdb/sysaux01.dbf
10   225      PDB:UNDOTBS1           NO      /u02/oradata/CDB/pdb/undotbs01.dbf
11   5        PDB:USERS              NO      /u02/oradata/CDB/pdb/users01.dbf
List of Temporary Files
=======================
File Size(MB) Tablespace             Maxsize(MB) Tempfile Name
---- -------- --------------------   ----------- --------------------
1    20       TEMP                   32767       /u02/oradata/CDB/temp01.dbf
2    20       PDB$SEED:TEMP          32767       /u02/oradata/CDB/pdbseed/temp01.dbf
3    20       PDB:TEMP               32767       /u02/oradata/CDB/pdb/temp01.dbf
```

Changing UNDO Tablespace

The default UNDO tablespace that is created with a PDB may not suit your needs. It is generated based on PDB$SEED, or from the CDB$ROOT if PDB$SEED has no UNDO tablespace. If you want to change the UNDO tablespace, you can drop it and re-create as you want. Let's look at an example:

```
SQL> alter session set container=PDB;
Session altered.
SQL> select tablespace_name,contents from dba_tablespaces;

TABLESPACE_NAME                CONTENTS
------------------------------ --------------------
SYSTEM                         PERMANENT
SYSAUX                         PERMANENT
UNDOTBS1                       UNDO
TEMP                           TEMPORARY
USERS                          PERMANENT
```

We have the UNDOTBS1 UNDO tablespace that has been created with our PDB. As we are in local UNDO mode, we can't drop it:

```
SQL> drop tablespace UNDOTBS1 including contents and datafiles;
drop tablespace UNDOTBS1 including contents and datafiles
*
ERROR at line 1:
ORA-30013: undo tablespace 'UNDOTBS1' is currently in use
```

This tablespace is the one defined for our PDB:

```
SQL> show parameter undo
NAME                                 TYPE        VALUE
------------------------------------ ----------- ------------------------------
temp_undo_enabled                    boolean     FALSE
undo_management                      string      AUTO
undo_retention                       integer     900
undo_tablespace                      string      UNDOTBS1
```

So, first, we have to create a new UNDO tablespace, then switch to it, and then drop the old one when there are no transactions in it. As an example, we want to define an UNDO tablespace as a bigfile tablespace, with guaranteed retention.

```
SQL> create bigfile undo tablespace UNDOTBS2 datafile '/u02/oradata/
CDB/pdb/undotbs02.dbf' size 100M autoextend on next 100M maxsize 5G
retention guarantee;
Tablespace created.
```

Once the UNDO tablespace is created, we can then switch to it:

```
SQL> alter system set undo_tablespace='UNDOTBS2';
System altered.
```

And then we can drop the old one:

```
SQL> drop tablespace UNDOTBS1 including contents and datafiles;
Tablespace dropped.
```

Of course, you may want to wait for the UNDO retention time to elapse before dropping the old tablespace; otherwise, you may risk having some queries fail with the infamous ORA-1555 error.

Changing UNDO Mode

If you have created the database in shared UNDO mode, you can change it later, but this requires downtime on the CDB because you need to be in upgrade mode to do so.

In the following example, we have no rows in our database properties relating to UNDO mode, which means that `LOCAL_UNDO_ENABLED` is set to off.

```
SQL> select * from database_properties where property_name like '%UNDO%';
no rows selected
```

If you try to change this property you get the following error:

```
SQL> alter database local undo on;
alter database local undo on
*
ERROR at line 1:
ORA-65192: database must be in UPGRADE mode for this operation
```

However, once you have a maintenance window, you can work this through with the following commands:

```
SQL> shutdown immediate
SQL> startup upgrade
SQL> alter database local undo on;
SQL> shutdown immediate
SQL> startup
```

And we now see this change reflected in the UNDO mode property setting:

```
SQL> select * from database_properties where property_name like '%UNDO%';
PROPERTY_NAME          PROPERTY_VALUE         DESCRIPTION
---------------------- ---------------------- ----------------------------------
LOCAL_UNDO_ENABLED     TRUE                   true if local undo is enabled
```

At that point, the local UNDO tablespaces will be created when you open the PDBs.

If you want to create the UNDO tablespace yourself, you have to open the PDB, then create your UNDO tablespace, and then drop the UNDO tablespace that was created at open.

If you want to come back to shared UNDO mode, the opposite operation can be done: start upgrade, `ALTER DATABASE LOCAL UNDO OFF`, and then drop the UNDO tablespaces in PDBs because they are no longer used.

PDB$SEED

If you changed to local UNDO and you want to have the same behavior as though the database was created in local UNDO from the get-go, you have to create an UNDO tablespace in the PDB$SEED. Then new PDBs created from SEED will have it as a template.

For that, you need to open the SEED read/write:

```
SQL> alter pluggable database PDB$SEED open read write force;
SQL> alter session set container=PDB$SEED;
SQL> create undo tablespace LOCALUNDO datafile size 100M autoextend on next 100M;
SQL> alter pluggable database PDB$SEED close;
SQL> alter pluggable database PDB$SEED open read only;
```

NOTE
No error results when you open the PDB$SEED read/write because customization of PDB$SEED is allowed when you are in local UNDO for the goal of UNDO tablespace creation. If you try to open the seed in read/write mode when you are in shared UNDO, you get an error (ORA-65017: seed pluggable database may not be dropped or altered). Only sessions with "_oracle_script"=true can open the PDB$SEED when in shared UNDO mode.

When using OMF, the UNDO tablespace of PDB$SEED is automatically created, based on the CDB$ROOT tablespace attributes.

Shared or Local UNDO?

We see no reason to use shared UNDO mode in 12.2, and our recommendation is to set `LOCAL UNDO ON`. You want multitenant for PDB isolation and easy operations, so you probably want local UNDO.

Note that even in local UNDO, some UNDO records can be generated in the CDB$ROOT if they are done by internal transactions that switched temporarily to CDB$ROOT.

PDB Point-in-Time Recovery in 12.2

We have explained the complex operations that have to be done when recovering a PDB at a different time than the CDB. The reason was to get the UNDO records necessary to clean the transactions that were not completed at the point-in-time we restore to. Now let's see what is different in 12.2.

PDBPITR in Shared UNDO Mode

If you are in shared UNDO mode, the `LOCAL UNDO OFF` state, you are in exactly the same situation you were in with 12.1. The UNDO for all transactions is stored in the CDB$ROOT tablespace and shared by all PDBs. As a consequence, we cannot recover it to another point-in-time there; we need an auxiliary instance for this, along with a place for it.

When a fast recovery area (FRA) is defined, you can run RECOVER PLUGGABLE DATABASE without the AUXILIARY DESTINATION and the auxiliary instance will be created in the FRA. While it runs, you can see those files listed as AUXILIARY DATAFILE COPY in V$RECOVERY_AREA_USAGE:

```
FILE_TYPE                PCT_SPACE_USED PCT_SPACE_RECLAIMABLE NUMBER_OF_FILES
------------------------ -------------- --------------------- ---------------
CONTROL FILE                        .3                     0               1
REDO LOG                           2.5                     0               3
ARCHIVED LOG                      3.37                     0              12
BACKUP PIECE                     36.81                     0               3
IMAGE COPY                           0                     0               0
FLASHBACK LOG                     5.21                     0               7
FOREIGN ARCHIVED LOG                 0                     0               0
AUXILIARY DATAFILE COPY          17.42                     0               3
```

If no FRA is defined and you try the same operation, you will get the following error:

```
RMAN-00571: ===========================================================
RMAN-00569: =============== ERROR MESSAGE STACK FOLLOWS ===============
RMAN-00571: ===========================================================
RMAN-03002: failure of recover command at 02/08/2016 21:44:59
RMAN-05107: AUXILIARY DESTINATION option is not specified
```

Without an FRA, you need to specify a location as per the following:

```
recover pluggable database PDB
until restore point PIT auxiliary destination='/var/tmp';
```

So you have a choice: put it in FRA or choose a destination.

PDBPITR in Local UNDO Mode

With the introduction of local UNDO mode in 12.2, you have all required UNDO in the local UNDO tablespace that is restored in place, so there is no need for an auxiliary instance, and the PDB PITR is simpler and faster.

You run the same command, RECOVER PLUGGABLE DATABASE, without specifying an auxiliary location since the auxiliary instance is no longer needed. The best practice is to put the RESTORE and RECOVER commands in a RUN block with a SET UNTIL:

```
run {
  set until restore point 'T0' ;
  restore pluggable database PDB;
  recover pluggable database PDB;
  alter pluggable database PDB open resetlogs;
}
```

The point-in-time can be specified with a restore point as above, a timestamp, an SCN, or a log sequence and thread number. This is no different from the database PITR you know from versions prior to multitenant. A restore point here is used only to associate a convenient name to an SCN and can be created at CDB or PDB level, but we will discuss that later when we describe other functionalities of restore points.

Flashback PDB

When you want to revert a database to a recent point-in-time, you can use a smart alternative that does not require restoring any datafiles. Flashback PDB was one of the most important features missing in 12.1, but it is now possible in 12.2, enabled by the addition of local UNDO. Be aware that flashback requires additional logging. Conventional recovery starts from a previous state of the datafiles and uses the REDO stream to roll them forward. In contrast, Flashback Database begins from the current state of the datafiles and applies flashback logs to bring them back to a previous state.

Flashback Logging

By default, a database does not generate the flashback logs, which means that you cannot run Flashback Database operations. There are two ways to generate a flashback log: set FLASHBACK ON and guaranteed restore point.

FLASHBACK ON

You can set FLASHBACK ON even when the database is opened. It is performed at the CDB level:

```
SQL> alter database flashback on;
Database altered.
```

From this time on, the database will store flashback logs in the FRA:

```
SQL> select file_type,percent_space_used,number_of_files
     from v$recovery_area_usage;

FILE_TYPE                  PERCENT_SPACE_USED NUMBER_OF_FILES
-------------------------- ------------------ ---------------
CONTROL FILE                                0               0
REDO LOG                                    0               0
ARCHIVED LOG                              .91               1
BACKUP PIECE                            90.35               6
IMAGE COPY                                  0               0
FLASHBACK LOG                            2.08               2
FOREIGN ARCHIVED LOG                        0               0
AUXILIARY DATAFILE COPY                     0               0
```

Flashback logging has a very small overhead by itself, but there are some side effects on sessions that format new blocks, such as direct-path inserts or any UNDO generation. Usually there is no need to read those blocks before writing them, because they are new. However, with FLASHBACK ON, these sessions have to read the blocks in order to write the previous image to the flashback logs. So with FLASHBACK ON, you may see more reads from disks (`physical reads for flashback new`) in session statistics.

You don't want to keep the flashback logs forever, because Flashback Database is best used to go to a recent point-in-time only. Going weeks or months prior is more efficient with PITR. So when you set the database in FLASHBACK ON mode you also define a flashback log retention period:

```
SQL> show parameter flashback
NAME                                 TYPE        VALUE
------------------------------------ ----------- ------------------------------
db_flashback_retention_target        integer     1440
```

This value is in minutes and the default is 1440, which translates to 24 hours. Note that this is a target only, so in the case of space pressure, the database will give priority to generating the ARCHIVELOG rather than guaranteeing the flashback retention.

Even if the flashback logs contain all the information to bring datafiles back to a past image, it still requires REDO to bring them to a consistent point-in-time, so enabling FLASHBACK ON can be done only on an ARCHIVELOG mode database.

Guaranteed Restore Point

With FLASHBACK ON, you can flashback to any point-in-time in the past that fits within the retention period. That point-in-time is defined by timestamp, an SCN, or a restore point. Even when you are not in flashback mode, you can enable the possibility to flashback to a restore point when you declare that restore point with `guarantee flashback database`:

```
SQL> create restore point BEFORE_RELEASE guarantee flashback database;
Restore point created.
```

Besides the V$RESTORE_POINT view, the easiest way to list these restore points is from RMAN:

```
RMAN> list restore point all;
using target database control file instead of recovery catalog
SCN                RSP Time  Type       Time      Name
---------------- --------- ---------- --------- --------------
4702377                               31-JAN-16 END_OF_MONTH
4770509                    GUARANTEED 13-FEB-16 BEFORE_RELEASE
```

A guaranteed restore point ensures that you can flashback to that specific point. The flashback logs and archived logs required for that point are kept in the FRA, but only a minimal set specifically for that point-in-time alone.

For example, here we've deleted all backups and will try to delete all archived logs:

```
RMAN> delete archivelog all;
using target database control file instead of recovery catalog
allocated channel: ORA_DISK_1
channel ORA_DISK_1: SID=18 device type=DISK
RMAN-08139: warning: archived redo log not deleted, needed for guaranteed
restore point
archived log file name=/u02/fast_recovery_area/CDB/CDB/archivelog/2016_02_13/
o1_mf_1_133_cczbo99h_.arc thread=1 sequence=133
```

And you can see that the ARCHIVELOG sequence that covers a guaranteed restore point is protected, because it is needed to make the datafiles consistent in case of flashback to that point. We also keep the flashback logs that contain the image of all blocks that have changed since that restore point:

```
SQL> select file_type,percent_space_used,number_of_files from
v$recovery_area_usage;

FILE_TYPE                PERCENT_SPACE_USED NUMBER_OF_FILES
------------------------ ------------------ ---------------
CONTROL FILE                            .6               1
REDO LOG                                 5               3
ARCHIVED LOG                            .8               1
BACKUP PIECE                             0               0
IMAGE COPY                               0               0
FLASHBACK LOG                        12.08               8
FOREIGN ARCHIVED LOG                     0               0
```

This means that you don't want to keep old guaranteed restore points for too long, because you can't get rid of the flashback log generated since your oldest restore point.

If you want to keep a snapshot of the database for a long time and go back to it frequently, our recommendation is to drop and re-create the snapshot once you have flashed back to it. It's logically the same snapshot, and earlier flashback logs can be reclaimed.

In multitenant, flashback logging is done at the CDB level, but starting from 12.2 you can flashback individual PDBs as an alternative to PITR.

Flashback with Local UNDO

When your CDB runs with `LOCAL UNDO ON`, you can flashback a PDB alone without any side effects on the other PDBs, in the same way that you can do a PITR in place. Of course, this is possible if you have FLASHBACK ON and the point-in-time is within the flashback log retention target, but it is also possible with FLASHBACK OFF if you have a guaranteed restore point. This is achievable because

- flashback logs have all previous images of blocks that have changed
- UNDO tablespace is flashed back to the same point-in-time and then can be used to clean the transactions that were ongoing at that point-in-time

Flashback in Shared UNDO

When your CDB runs with LOCAL UNDO OFF, the UNDO cannot be flashed back in the UNDO tablespace because it's shared at CDB level. You are in exactly the same place as with PITR and the solution is the same: an auxiliary instance. You can add the AUXILIARY DESTINATION to the FLASHBACK PLUGGABLE DATABASE clause, or it will be created, implicitly, in the FRA.

Restore Points at the CDB and PDB Levels

You can create restore points at the CDB level, and then use them to flashback PDBs. In addition, it is also possible to create a restore point at the PDB level.

Here is an example in which we create a restore point at the CDB level:

```
SQL> show con_name
CON_NAME
------------------------------
CDB$ROOT

SQL> create restore point END_OF_MONTH;
Restore point created.
```

And here's one at the PDB level, with guaranteed Flashback Database:

```
SQL> alter session set container=PDB1;
Session altered.
SQL> create restore point BEFORE_RELEASE guarantee flashback database;
Restore point created.
```

While still in the same PDB, PDB1, we can see and use both these restore points:

```
SQL> select scn, name, con_id, pdb_restore_point, guarantee_flashback_
database,  clean_pdb_restore_point from v$restore_point;
       SCN NAME                      CON_ID PDB GUARANTEE CLEAN_PDB
---------- -------------------   ---------- --- --------- ---------
   1514402 BEFORE_RELEASE                 4 YES YES       NO
   1514393 END_OF_MONTH                   0 NO  NO        NO
```

But when we use the same query from another PDB, we can't see the restore points defined under PDB1. We can see only the restore points defined under the root container:

```
SQL> select scn, name, con_id, pdb_restore_point, guarantee_flashback_
database, clean_pdb_restore_point from v$restore_point;
       SCN NAME                  CON_ID PDB GUARANTEE CLEAN_PDB
---------- ---------------- ---------- --- --------- ---------
   1514393 END_OF_MONTH              0 NO  NO        NO
```

NOTE

In multitenant, CON_ID=0 displays information that is at the CDB level and not related to any specific container, neither CDB$ROOT nor any PDB.

We can also create restore points with the same name in different containers. In the following we are still in PDB2 (CON_ID=5):

```
SQL> show con_id
CON_NAME
------------------------------
5
SQL> create restore point BEFORE_RELEASE;
Restore point created.
SQL> create restore point END_OF_MONTH;
Restore point created.
SQL> select scn, name, con_id, pdb_restore_point, guarantee_flashback_
database, clean_pdb_restore_point from v$restore_point;
       SCN NAME                  CON_ID PDB GUARANTEE CLEAN_PDB
---------- ---------------- ---------- --- --------- ---------
   1514393 END_OF_MONTH              0 NO  NO        NO
   1514410 BEFORE_RELEASE            5 YES NO        NO
   1514415 END_OF_MONTH              5 YES NO        NO
```

Those restore points have the same name. However, the CON_ID and PDB_RESTORE_POINT columns let you know which one is at the PDB level.

Here is the result when running the same query from CDB$ROOT:

```
       SCN NAME                  CON_ID PDB GUARANTEE CLEAN_PDB
---------- ---------------- ---------- --- --------- ---------
   1514402 BEFORE_RELEASE            4 YES YES       NO
   1514393 END_OF_MONTH              0 NO  NO        NO
   1514410 BEFORE_RELEASE            5 YES NO        NO
   1514415 END_OF_MONTH              5 YES NO        NO
```

For those of you who would like to see this information listed in RMAN, unfortunately, at the time of writing, this functionality is missing, but we have filed an enhancement request for it:

```
RMAN> list restore point all;
using target database control file instead of recovery catalog
SCN              RSP Time  Type        Time       Name
---------------- --------- ----------- ---------- ----
1514393                                14-FEB-16  END_OF_MONTH
1514402                    GUARANTEED  14-FEB-16  BEFORE_RELEASE
1514410                                14-FEB-16  BEFORE_RELEASE
1514415                                14-FEB-16  END_OF_MONTH
```

Another piece of information lacking in RMAN is the CLEAN_PDB_RESTORE_POINT. It is another addition in 12.2, and we will get to this shortly.

PDB Level and Flashback Logging

Related to this topic, you should be aware of an important point. Using our example, with FLASHBACK OFF and a guaranteed restore point only at the PDB level for PDB1 (CON_ID=4), it seems that flashback logging is actually enabled for all CDB datafiles.

From the CDB$ROOT, we check the flashback mode:

```
SQL> select con_id,flashback_on from v$database;
    CON_ID FLASHBACK_ON
---------- ------------------
         0 RESTORE POINT ONLY
```

As expected, this is what we have when flashback logging is off, but we have a guaranteed restore point.

So let's connect to PDB2 and check that we see no guaranteed restore points from there:

```
SQL> connect demo/demo@//localhost/PDB2
Connected.
SQL> select scn, name, con_id, pdb_restore_point, guarantee_flashback_
database, clean_pdb_restore_point from v$restore_point;
       SCN NAME               CON_ID PDB GUARANTEE CLEAN_PDB
---------- ---------------- -------- --- --------- ---------
   1514393 END_OF_MONTH            0 NO  NO        NO
   1514410 BEFORE_RELEASE          5 YES NO        NO
   1514415 END_OF_MONTH            5 YES NO        NO
```

Then insert 1000 rows into an existing table:

```
SQL> insert into DEMO select lpad('x',4000,'x') from dual connect by level<=1000;
1000 rows created.
```

Now we check the session's statistics related to flashback:

```
SQL> select name,value from v$mystat join v$statname using(statistic#)
where name like '%flashback%' and value>0;
NAME                                          VALUE
-----------------------------------------    ----------
physical reads for flashback new               1008
```

This output reveals that these blocks have to be written into the flashback logs—proof that flashback logging occurs for changes in all containers, as long as one container has a guaranteed restore point.

In the current version, 12.2, you can enable flashback logging only at the CDB level, but the error message when trying it at the PDB level gives the impression that flashback logging will be a possibility at the PDB level in the future:

```
SQL> alter session set container=PDB;
Session altered.
SQL> alter database flashback on;
alter database flashback on
*
ERROR at line 1:
ORA-03001: unimplemented feature
```

Clean Restore Point

We have seen that in a shared undo CDB, the flashback PDB needs an auxiliary instance to restore the undo tablespace to clean ongoing transactions. This makes the flashback less efficient, in both time and required space. The preferable solution is to run in local UNDO mode.

However, even when in shared UNDO mode, you don't need to restore the UNDO when you know that you have no ongoing transactions at all. If you want to create a restore point in production before applying a patch or an application release, or in a test before a run of regression tests, you can close the database. And when it's closed cleanly, there are no outgoing transactions. In this scenario, we can create a clean restore point that can be used to flashback efficiently, even in shared UNDO mode.

The following example affects a database with shared UNDO, created without a LOCAL UNDO clause:

```
SQL> select * from database_properties where property_name like '%UNDO%';
no rows selected
```

As you have seen before, no property for LOCAL_UNDO_ENABLED means that it is false. We connect to PDB1, which is currently opened, and try to create a clean restore point:

```
SQL> alter session set container=PDB1;
Session altered.
SQL> show pdbs
    CON_ID CON_NAME                       OPEN MODE  RESTRICTED
    ---------- ------------------------------ ---------- ----------
         4 PDB1                           READ WRITE NO
SQL> create clean restore point REGTEST1;
create clean restore point REGTEST1
*
ERROR at line 1:
ORA-65025: Pluggable database is not closed on all instances.
```

But to be sure it's a clean restore point, we need to close the PDB:

```
SQL> alter pluggable database PDB1 close;
Pluggable database altered.
SQL> create clean restore point REGTEST1 guarantee flashback database;
Restore point created.
```

Note that we have created a guaranteed restore point here because we do not have FLASHBACK ON, and we want to be able to flashback to it.

At this point, we can open back the PDB. Any blocks written to the datafiles will have their previous image written to flashback logs, so you can quickly flashback to the initial state, without the need of an auxiliary instance thanks to the clean restore point:

```
SQL> alter pluggable database PDB1 close;
Pluggable database altered.
SQL> flashback pluggable database PDB1 to restore point REGTEST1;
Flashback complete.
SQL> alter pluggable database PDB1 open resetlogs;
Pluggable database altered.
```

The concept of a clean restore point applies to shared UNDO mode only. It makes no sense in local UNDO mode, and if you try to use the same syntax, you will get the following error:

```
ORA-39891: Clean PDB restore point cannot be created when CDB is in
local undo mode.
```

Resetlogs

This chapter is all about bringing a PDB to a point-in-time in the past. When you do that on a CDB or a non-CDB, you have to OPEN RESETLOGS. This operation resets the REDO stream because it is interrupted: the REDO that was generated before the recovery or the flashback cannot be used on that new incarnation of the database. When you open a non-CDB or a CDB with resetlogs, the online redo logs are re-created and the old ones are discarded.

The REDO stream is at the CDB level, so the "resetlogs" term may be misleading when dealing with a PDB. The redo logs are not re-created, and in this case, they just continue to log all changes for all modifications that occur in the instance. But it's the same idea: mark the REDO stream so that the REDO from that point on is known to protect a new incarnation of the PDB.

In the following example, we flashback PDB1 and try to open it without the resetlogs clause:

```
SQL> flashback pluggable database PDB1 to restore point REGTEST1;
Flashback complete.
SQL> alter pluggable database PDB1 open;
alter pluggable database PDB1 open
*
ERROR at line 1:
ORA-01113: file 11 needs media recovery
ORA-01110: data file 11:
'/u02/oradata/CDB/2BBE9EBBB1B57588E053754EA8C075FE/datafile/o1_mf_sysaux_cd1cr7y
g_.dbf'
```

The message is not explicit here, because we have two possibilities with the current state of the datafiles: we can choose to revert our flashback and apply recovery to bring it up to the latest state, or we can open it in that state, because this is what we wanted to do with the flashback operation:

```
SQL> alter pluggable database PDB1 open resetlogs;
Pluggable database altered.
```

Each PDB's open resetlogs operation creates a new incarnation of the PDB, which is a subset of the CDB incarnation. You can list the history of all incarnations by querying the V$PDB_INCARNATION view. Here is an example, where we have flashed back the PDB to the same restore point several times:

```
SQL> select db_incarnation#, pdb_incarnation#, status,incarnation_time from
v$pdb_incarnation;
```

```
DB_INCARNATION# PDB_INCARNATION# STATUS   INCARNATION_TIME BEGIN_RE END_RESE
--------------- ---------------- -------  ---------------- -------- --------
...
              1               22 ORPHAN                    20:21:17 20:21:17
              1               23 ORPHAN                    20:21:21 20:21:21
              1               24 ORPHAN                    20:21:24 20:21:24
              1               25 ORPHAN                    20:21:27 20:21:28
              1               26 ORPHAN                    20:21:31 20:21:31
              1               27 ORPHAN                    20:21:34 20:21:35
              1               28 ORPHAN                    20:21:38 20:21:38
              1               29 ORPHAN                    20:21:42 20:21:42
              1               30 ORPHAN                    20:21:45 20:21:45
              1               31 ORPHAN                    20:21:49 20:21:49
              1               32 ORPHAN                    20:21:52 20:21:52
```

This is a massive advantage of the multitenant architecture: you don't need to restart the instance when you flashback a PDB. This makes the flashback operation very fast—in fact, just a few seconds. It can be used for test databases where, for example, a number of tests must run on the same data. This is much faster than reimporting from a dump file, and it's even faster than reattaching a transportable tablespace.

Flashback and PITR

This chapter covers two ways to bring a PDB back to a previous state. They have some common effects, but are used for different situations.

When Do You Need PITR or Flashback?

Taking a production database back to a point in the past is rare, because you will lose all transactions that have happened since that point. If you encounter a logical or physical corruption, Flashback Database is considered only on those occasions where the corruption is database-wide and occurred in the last few seconds. But in other cases, you can benefit a lot from restore points and flashback. For example, before any maintenance operation, such as an application release or database upgrade, you can take a guaranteed restore point, and if anything goes wrong, your fallback scenario takes only few minutes to enact. And because you flashback before reopening the service, you don't lose any transactions. Just don't forget to drop the restore point when maintenance is completed and validated.

The benefit of flashback shows up every day in test environments, especially in continuous integration environments. If you have several runs of tests that need the same data set, without flashback, rerunning all DDL and DML simply takes too long, and a dump import is also probably not quick enough. A solution is potentially found in the transportable tablespace functionality, but even that takes too long to import all metadata. Flashback is the best solution to revert back to a previous state, but before multitenant this required an instance restart. In multitenant, the flashback PDB takes only a few seconds, so it can be run hundreds of times during a batch of nonregression tests.

> **TIP**
> *A PDB administrator can flashback a PDB as long as the admin has the SYSDBA privilege granted on that PDB. There's no need for a common user for that. So it's possible to give that right to a trusted application DBA so that he or she can interact with this PDB only.*

Impact on the Standby Database

We will detail the Data Guard configuration in multitenant in Chapter 11, but you already know that the REDO is at CDB level, and that what you do in a primary database, especially when changing the structure or in case of `OPEN RESETLOGS`, can have consequences on the physical standby.

Changing UNDO Mode

When changing from shared UNDO to local UNDO, you have to startup upgrade. If you are using real-time query (Active Data Guard), you need to stop it while the primary is in startup upgrade: the REDO from upgrade mode cannot be applied when a physical standby is open read-only. The second point is that new UNDO tablespaces will be created, so be sure that `StandbyFileManagement = 'AUTO'`.

Flashback or PITR on Primary

After a PDBPITR or a flashback PDB, you have to open the PDB with `RESETLOGS`. The managed recovery process (MRP) on the physical standby stops when it encounters the `RESETLOGS` marker because the datafiles are at the same state as the primary before the flashback, and current REDO cannot be applied on the previous incarnation. Here is what you can see in the alert.log:

```
2016-02-19T22:31:38.142324+01:00
(4):Recovery of pluggable database PDB1 aborted due to pluggable database open
resetlog marker.
(4):To continue recovery, restore all data files for this PDB to checkpoint SCN lower
than 4345934, or timestamp before , and restart recovery
MRP0: Background Media Recovery terminated with error 39874
2016-02-19T22:31:38.143019+01:00
Errors in file /u01/app/oracle/diag/rdbms/nzprod/USPROD/trace/USPROD_pr00_8201.trc:
ORA-39874: Pluggable Database PDB1 recovery halted
ORA-39873: Restore all data files to a checkpoint SCN lower than 4345934.
Managed Standby Recovery not using Real Time Apply
Recovery interrupted!
```

```
Recovery stopped due to failure in applying recovery marker (opcode 17.46).
Datafiles are recovered to a consistent state at change 4347096 but controlfile could
be ahead of datafiles.
```

The message is clear: You must do a PITR on the physical standby as well, to the same point-in-time. If the physical standby is in `FLASHBACK ON` mode, it's easy. Stop `APPLY`, flashback to the SCN given in the alert.log, and restart `APPLY`:

```
DGMGRL> edit database nzprod set state=apply-off;
SQL> flashback pluggable database PDB1 to scn 4345934;
DGMGRL> edit database nzprod set state=apply-on;
```

An alternative if you are not in flashback mode is to recover from service, which is a 12c feature:

```
DGMGRL> edit database nzprod set state=apply-off;
RMAN> restore pluggable database PDB1 from service 'usprod_dgmgrl';
DGMGRL> edit database nzprod set state=apply-on;
```

Disable Recovery on Standby

In multitenant, you don't want the standby to stop the `APPLY`, because one PDB has been flashed back. So instead of waiting for the message shown previously, you should disable recovery for that PDB before the `OPEN RESETLOGS` on the primary. In the standby database, you suspend APPLY just for the time it takes to disable recovery. Here are the commands from the Data Guard command line interface (DGMGRL) and SQL*Plus:

```
DGMGRL> edit database nzprod set state=apply-off;
SQL> alter pluggable database pdb1 close;
SQL> alter session set container=PDB1;
SQL> alter pluggable database PDB1 disable recovery;
DGMGRL> edit database nzprod set state=apply-on;
```

Then recovery occurs for the CDB except for this PDB. You can flashback or point-in-time restore the PDB1 on the primary and open it with resetlogs. Then re-enable its synchronization on standby:

```
DGMGRL> edit database nzprod set state=apply-off;
RMAN> recover database;
SQL> alter session set container=PDB1;
SQL> alter pluggable database PDB1 enable recovery;
SQL> alter pluggable database PDB1 open;
DGMGRL> edit database nzprod set state=apply-on;
```

From there, the PDB1 is synchronized again with the primary.

Auxiliary Instance Cleanup

When an auxiliary instance is created automatically, it is supposed to be cleaned up at the end of the operation. But our recommendation, after lots of testing, is to check that nothing is left over, especially when something has failed in the process. Check AUXILIARY DATAFILE COPY in V$RECOVERY_AREA_USAGE that no unreclaimable file is left over. It's also a good idea to have a look at FLASHBACK LOG to be sure that you removed the unnecessary guaranteed restore points.

You may see other traces from the auxiliary instance that remain, such as in the DIAG directory. Here is ours after a few PITRs in shared UNDO:

```
adrci> show alert
Choose the home from which to view the alert log:
1: diag/rdbms/uced_pitr_pdb_cdb/uCEd
2: diag/rdbms/cobc_pitr_pdb_cdb/CoBc
3: diag/rdbms/kqwu_pitr_pdb_cdb/kqwu
4: diag/rdbms/dwkf_pitr_pdb_cdb/dwkf
5: diag/rdbms/zcdx_pitr_pdb_cdb/zCDx
6: diag/rdbms/ccfq_pitr_pdb_cdb/ccFq
7: diag/rdbms/azfb_pitr_pdb_cdb/azFB
...
```

With this in mind, if you have automated PITR in shared UNDO, you should adapt your housekeeping scripts to clean up appropriately.

Summary

The PITR and flashback features that were missing in 12.1 have been implemented in 12.2, thanks to the introduction of local UNDO mode. On production databases, it provides a safety net for your application releases or maintenance operations, giving you an instantaneous fallback plan. But it's in development environments that the feature will bring more agility. How often do you have to refresh environments, restore the previous state of a test database, or revert a change made by a test that touched more data than required? PITR and flashback, plus the moving and cloning features we will cover in the next chapter, truly make multitenant the agile environment for modern development.

CHAPTER 9

Moving Data

There are probably very few (likely no) Oracle administrators charged with the care of a solitary database who don't need to share data among other databases. Equally implausible is an administrator who doesn't need to upgrade or move a database to a different platform at some point. In most situations, at one point or another, the administrator is required to move data at the physical level—that is, the admin will be required to move the datafiles or entire databases from one place to another.

Multitenant architecture brings new scenarios and challenges into play that must be addressed by the DBA, because it is the DBA's job to manage the database at this level. This includes new features such as the ability to move complete pluggable databases (PDBs), along with extensions to existing features, and it presents new opportunities regarding how to approach some core DBA tasks.

The multitenancy architecture encompasses multiple PDBs. The first feature we will explore is disassociating a PDB from the container database (CDB)—that is, moving the physical files, and then making the PDB part of another CDB. This *unplugging/plugging in* ability with a PDB basically involves a database move.

We also want to be able to copy a database—and even better, we want to let Oracle perform the file copy for us. Database *cloning* extends past a simple local machine copy, because in Oracle Database 12c we can clone from a remote database or harness storage features to make "cheap" copies. One facet of this feature is that the source can be an Oracle Database 12c non-CDB, thus enabling a simple way of converting a non-CDB into a PDB.

Oracle Database 12c also introduces many new data movement features that are not PDB-specific, and one of the most interesting is the ability to move databases between previously incompatible platforms.

And last, but not least, we can move PDBs to and from the cloud.

Grappling with PDB File Locations

Moving all the PDB files involves, of course, altering the file locations. The easiest approach is to work with Oracle Managed Files (OMF) and let Oracle generate the file paths and names, using the CDB name and PDB GUID—for example, /u01/app/oracle/data/SRC/29E63B5BE26B3ABEE053050011ACA3F3/datafile/o1_mf_system_cb3gffcj_.dbf. In other words, you can specify the `DB_CREATE_FILE_DEST` initialization parameter and let Oracle take care of this for you.

However, if you want to manage the locations yourself, you can use the `FILE_NAME_CONVERT` parameter to map the files to new locations in the `create pluggable database` statements.

If the datafiles for the target database are already in place, you can specify `NOCOPY`, so that Oracle uses the files already present. And if the new location is different than the source location, you can use the `SOURCE_FILE_NAME_CONVERT` clause to map the files to the new location.

The examples in this chapter show how these various options are used.

Plugging In and Unplugging

As you know, a PDB is an independent subset of a CDB. As such, it enjoys a kind of independence, which you have already learned about in the chapters on management and security. Therefore, it makes sense to be able to move data from a single PDB, or indeed the whole PDB, from one database to another.

Moving an entire non-CDB (or the CDB as whole) has always been possible with Oracle. You simply move the datafiles to a different place; set up the configuration files for networking; set up the password file, init.ora, and so on; and then start the database from the new location. The Recovery Manager (RMAN) `duplicate` command further simplifies this process, but we won't go into detail on this here. However, you should review Chapter 11, where we explain how to create a standby database, because the two processes are similar.

With multitenancy, moving databases has become easier, and the expectation is that these moves will now occur more frequently as a result. First of all, you don't need to move the entire CDB, which means that much of the tedious configuration work disappears. There is no need to handle relocating the password file, init.ora, /etc/oratab, for example, and this makes the move simpler, and thus a potentially viable option in many more scenarios.

Second, PDBs contain significantly less Oracle internal data dictionary information. So, as discussed in Chapter 4, you can create a new CDB with a new patch version, and then move the PDBs to this new CDB. From there, you can patch the PDB, which is actually much faster, because there is less dictionary data to update.

Furthermore, multitenancy is often thought of as being synonymous with consolidation, which means having many databases in a CDB. This can inevitably lead to situations in which the number of PDBs outgrows the server capacity. The easy solution now is to move some of the PDBs someplace else.

NOTE
Unlike other cloning options, the plug-in operation does not need a source database up and running; only its datafiles and an XML parameter file must be available. This opens up new scenarios for provisioning, such as making the files available on various media or for download.

Unplug and Plug In a PDB

Let's start with the simplest scenario—unplugging a PDB and then plugging it into a different CDB, as depicted in the following diagram. Note that the PDB must be closed during this operation.

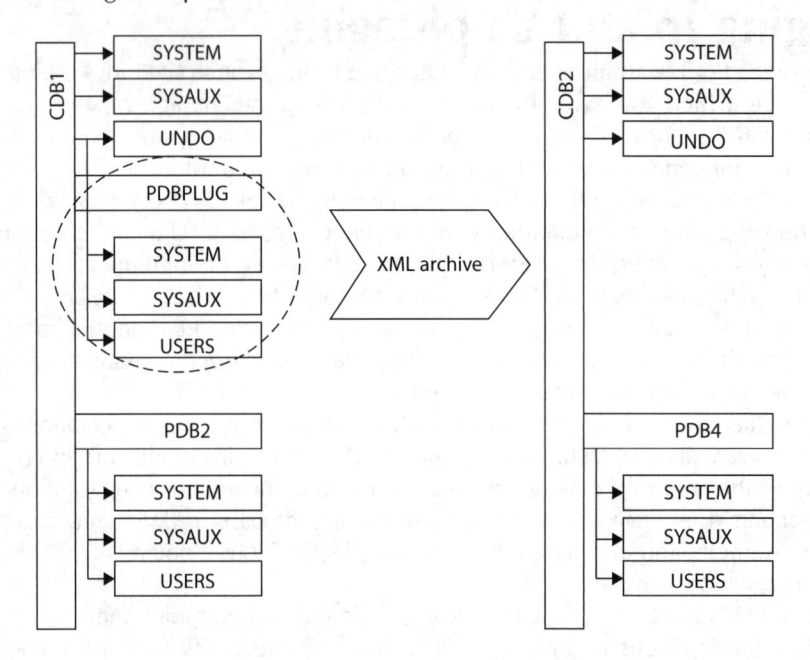

```
SQL> alter pluggable database PDBPLUG close;

Pluggable database altered.

SQL> alter pluggable database PDBPLUG unplug into '/home/oracle/
pdbplug.xml';

Pluggable database altered.
```

After this command has completed, the unplugged database (PDB) consists of its datafiles, which are still in place as they were, along with a new XML file that describes the database (version, DBID), tablespaces, datafiles, installed options, and database parameters set at the PDB level.

Now we copy the files to the target database location. A simple `scp` to the target server will do:

```
$ mkdir /u01/app/oracle/data/CDBTRG/PDBPLUG
$ scp oracle@source:/u01/app/oracle/data/CDBSRC/PDBPLUG/* /u01/app/
oracle/data/CDBTRG/PDBPLUG
```

The third step is to plug in the database. Note that the files will probably be in a different location than they were on the source, as recorded in the XML parameter file, so remapping may be required.

```
SQL> create pluggable database PDBPLUG using '/home/oracle/pdbplug.xml'
source_file_name_convert=('/u01/app/oracle/data/CDBSRC/PDBPLUG','/u01/
app/oracle/data/CDBTRG/PDBPLUG') nocopy tempfile reuse;

Pluggable database created.

SQL> alter pluggable database PDBPLUG open;

Pluggable database altered.
```

An Unplugged Database Stays in the Source

Even after we unplug a PDB and produce the related XML file, the PDB continues to be part of the source database, as shown in v$pdbs and dba_pdbs:

```
SQL> select pdb_id, pdb_name, status from dba_pdbs order by 1;

    PDB_ID PDB_NAME                       STATUS
---------- ------------------------------ ---------
         2 PDB$SEED                       NORMAL
         3 PDBPLUG                        UNPLUGGED
```

This also means that the PDB is still part of any RMAN backups, as you can see in the following:

```
RMAN> backup database;
…
channel ORA_DISK_1: starting full datafile backup set
channel ORA_DISK_1: specifying datafile(s) in backup set
input datafile file number=00013 name=/u01/app/oracle/data/CDBSRC/PDBPLUG/sysaux01.dbf
input datafile file number=00012 name=/u01/app/oracle/data/CDBSRC/PDBPLUG/system01.dbf
channel ORA_DISK_1: starting piece 1 at 09-JAN-16
channel ORA_DISK_1: finished piece 1 at 09-JAN-16
piece handle=/u01/app/oracle/data/FRA/CDBSRC/28F00F4199F504BFE053030011A
C9CBD/backupset/2016_01_09/o1_mf_nnndf_TAG20160109T235506_c937nd7c_.bkp
tag=TAG20160109T235506 comment=NONE
channel ORA_DISK_1: backup set complete, elapsed time: 00:01:05
…
```

This ensures that the PDB's data is still protected, even before we plug it into the target database and begin backing it up there. It also means that all the original datafiles are still in place, and we have ample time to copy them to the desired location for the plug-in. However, there is little else that can be done with this unplugged PDB for now:

```
SQL> alter pluggable database PDBPLUG open;
alter pluggable database PDBPLUG open
```

```
*
ERROR at line 1:
ORA-65086: cannot open/close the pluggable database
```

Once the PDB is plugged in and backed up in its new location, we can drop the PDB from the original source CDB to clean up:

```
SQL> drop pluggable database PDBPLUG;

Pluggable database dropped.
```

> **NOTE**
> *The default setting is KEEP DATAFILES. This prevents us from accidentally dropping the data files before we copy or move them to the target location.*

What Exactly Is in the XML File?

It's worth reviewing the XML file that describes the unplugged PDB. In doing so, we can see exactly what information is retained when we move the PDBs from one CDB to another, and it also shows what Oracle can actually check when considering whether the PDB is compatible to be plugged in (as we will discuss in the next section).

The following are some parameters for a PDB named PDBXML:

```
<pdbname>PDBXML</pdbname>
<cid>4</cid>
<byteorder>1</byteorder>
<vsn>203424000</vsn>
<vsns>
   <vsnnum>12.2.0.1.0</vsnnum>
   <cdbcompt>12.2.0.0.0</cdbcompt>
   <pdbcompt>12.2.0.0.0</pdbcompt>
   <vsnlibnum>0.0.0.0.24</vsnlibnum>
   <vsnsql>24</vsnsql>
   <vsnbsv>8.0.0.0.0</vsnbsv>
</vsns>
<dbid>2150329683</dbid>
<ncdb2pdb>0</ncdb2pdb>
<cdbid>1348575968</cdbid>
<guid>2A8090EFCD800637E053030011ACB487</guid>
```

In this section we see various version and compatibility-level listings. The vsn refers to the version (203424000 is 0xC200100 in hex, which is an internal representation for 12.2.0.1.0—convert the number digit-by-digit to decimal, 0xC is 12). This ensures that the versions match or, if required, whether an upgrade is needed upon plug-in. Note also the byte order; 1 is little endian.

We also see the different PDB IDs: `cid` (CON_ID), DBID, `cdbid` (CON_UID), and `guid`. This is also not a non-CDB (hence `ncdb2pdb` is 0), but later in this chapter we will discuss the details for converting such a database.

For each tablespace, we see the following section:

```
<tablespace>
  <name>SYSTEM</name>
  <type>0</type>
  <tsn>0</tsn>
  <status>1</status>
  <issft>0</issft>
  <isnft>0</isnft>
  <encts>0</encts>
  <bmunitsize>8</bmunitsize>
  <file>
    <path>/u01/app/oracle/data/CDBSRC/PDBXML/system01.dbf</path>
    <afn>12</afn>
    <rfn>1</rfn>
    <createscnbas>3081073</createscnbas>
    <createscnwrp>0</createscnwrp>
    <status>1</status>
    <fileblocks>34560</fileblocks>
    <blocksize>8192</blocksize>
    <vsn>203423744</vsn>
    <fdbid>2150329683</fdbid>
    <fcpsb>3083026</fcpsb>
    <fcpsw>0</fcpsw>
    <frlsb>2716779</frlsb>
    <frlsw>0</frlsw>
    <frlt>902125218</frlt>
    <autoext>1</autoext>
    <maxsize>4194302</maxsize>
    <incsize>1280</incsize>
  </file>
</tablespace>
```

This covers name, type (temporary tablespace has 1), encryption, list of files—file name, absolute file number, relative file number, create SCN, size in blocks, block size, version, DBID, checkpoint SCN, and autoextend settings.

```
<csid>873</csid>
<ncsid>2000</ncsid>
<options>
  <option>APS=12.2.0.1.0</option>
```

```
    <option>CATALOG=12.2.0.1.0</option>
...
    <option>XML=12.2.0.1.0</option>
    <option>XOQ=12.2.0.1.0</option>
  </options>
```

The `csid` is the database character set (873 is AL32UTF8), and `ncsid` is the national character set (2000 is AL16UTF16; we can verify this with SQL function `NLS_CHARSET_ID`). The remainder lists all the installed options and their various versions:

```
<dv>0</dv>
<APEX>5.0.3.00.02:1</APEX>
<parameters>
  <parameter>processes=300</parameter>
  <parameter>memory_target=0</parameter>
  <parameter>db_block_size=8192</parameter>
  <parameter>db_2k_cache_size=16777216</parameter>
  <parameter>compatible='12.2.0'</parameter>
  <parameter>open_cursors=300</parameter>
  <parameter>pga_aggregate_target=209715200</parameter>
  <parameter>enable_pluggable_database=TRUE</parameter>
</parameters>
<sqlpatches/>
<tzvers>
  <tzver>primary version:25</tzver>
  <tzver>secondary version:0</tzver>
</tzvers>
<walletkey>0</walletkey>
<services/>
<opatches/>
```

This penultimate section specifies the following:

- Whether Data Vault is enabled
- The APEX version
- Parameters set at the PDB level
- Installed SQL patches
- Versions of time zone file
- Wallet
- Defined services
- Patches installed by OPatch

```
      <awr>
        <loadprofile>CPU used by this session=55.038961</loadprofile>
        <loadprofile>DB time=62.853896</loadprofile>
        <loadprofile>db block changes=1944.274084</loadprofile>
        <loadprofile>execute count=1517.727127</loadprofile>
        <loadprofile>logons cumulative=0.036344</loadprofile>
...
        <loadprofile>user rollbacks=0.024011</loadprofile>
      </awr>
      <hardvsnchk>0</hardvsnchk>
      <localundo>0</localundo>
```

Finally, the XML file includes AWR load profile information, and whether local undo has been enabled.

Check Compatibility for Plug-In

In the examples so far we have taken a few shortcuts, ignoring the fact that Oracle imposes some limitations on PDBs with respect to installed options, character sets, and versions. You can either read in detail the limitations or, perhaps more effectively, ask Oracle to perform these checks, using the supplied DBMS_PDB package.

Get the XML Describing the Database

First, we need to get the XML file that describes the unplugged database. If we have unplugged the PDB, then we already have it on hand and can skip to the next step.

However, we can ask Oracle to generate the XML file even if we haven't yet actually unplugged the PDB. Although this requires an extra step, it is definitely better to have this information ahead of time, knowing the results of the compatibility check well before we perform the unplug. This will give us ample time to rectify the issues or come up with an alternate solution—such as creating a new target CDB—and all this can occur well before we incur any downtime on the database.

```
-- NB: unlike unplugging a PDB, in this case the database must be
opened (or read only)
SQL> alter pluggable database PDBPLUG open;

Pluggable database altered.
SQL> BEGIN
  DBMS_PDB.DESCRIBE(
    pdb_descr_file => '/home/oracle/pdbplug.xml',
    pdb_name       => 'PDBPLUG');
END;
/

PL/SQL procedure successfully completed.
```

Run the Compatibility Check

Running the compatibility check is simple and is achieved by executing one PL/SQL function in the target database root or application root:

```
SET SERVEROUTPUT ON
DECLARE
  compatible CONSTANT VARCHAR2(3):=
    CASE DBMS_PDB.CHECK_PLUG_COMPATIBILITY(
          pdb_descr_file => '/home/oracle/pdbplug.xml',
          pdb_name       => 'PLUGDB')
    WHEN TRUE THEN 'YES'
    ELSE 'NO'
END;
BEGIN
  DBMS_OUTPUT.PUT_LINE(compatible);
END;
/
YES

PL/SQL procedure successfully completed.
```

Of course, if the answer is NO, we want more detail, and this is readily available in the PDB_PLUG_IN_VIOLATIONS view. The view can contain data even if the answer is YES, so it is a good idea to review this regardless of the answer.

> **NOTE**
> *If you are plugging in databases as part of an upgrade, the compatibility check will return NO, because the versions are different. This is to be expected, and you can still plug in that database, although you won't be able to open it until you have first finished the upgrade. This is covered in more detail in Chapter 4.*

Read the Requirements

The list of compatibility requirements is changing with each version, so it is advisable always to review the list for the particular version in use. In short, however, there are four main requirements:

- **Platform**   The databases need to be of the same endianness.
- **Options**   The databases must have the same options installed (partitioning, data mining, and so on).

- **Versions** The source PDB must be the same version as the target CDB before the PDB can be opened. However, it is possible to plug in a PDB of an older version and upgrade it, and then it can be opened.

- **Character sets** The character sets must match. Version 12.2 eases this condition: if the CDB uses AL32UTF8, the PDB can use any character set.

Plug In a PDB as Clone

To this point we have been thinking of the plug-in/unplug process as a move operation, with a single PDB at the start and end, even if the PDB at the end runs somewhere else. Sometimes, however, we need to create a copy of the PDB. Although the other options described in the upcoming "Cloning" section are usually used for this, it is possible to use pluggable functionality to create a copy, too. The only principal difference is the number of copies that will reside in the environment, and, as with non-CDB databases, every copy needs to be uniquely identifiable; otherwise, we end up with collisions when `DBID`, `GUID`, or `CON_UID` is used. Note that the RMAN catalog mandates that `DBID` be unique, and a single database won't allow multiple identical PDBs, either. Fortunately, the solution is easier than the description of the problem itself: just add the `AS CLONE` clause when you're performing the plug-in operation.

Let's start with a simple PDB, created at the source database:

```
SQL> alter session set container = PDBCLONE;

Session altered.
SQL> select pdb_name, dbid, con_uid, guid from dba_pdbs;
PDB_NAME        DBID       CON_UID GUID
---------- ---------- ---------- --------------------------------
PDBCLONE   1307782881 1307782881 28F3AE16F69E151AE053030011ACF9A3
```

Now let's unplug it:

```
SQL> alter pluggable database close;

Pluggable database altered.

SQL> alter session set container=cdb$root;

Session altered.

SQL> alter pluggable database PDBCLONE unplug into '/home/oracle/pdbclone.xml';

Pluggable database altered.
```

Now plug it into the target database. This will be a move operation, so it will keep its existing IDs.

```
SQL> create pluggable database PDBCLONE using '/home/oracle/pdbclone.
xml' FILE_NAME_CONVERT=('/u01/app/oracle/data/CDBSRC/PDBCLONE', '/u01/app/
oracle/data/CDBTRG/PDBCLONE');
```

The PDB has been created:

```
SQL> select pdb_name, dbid, con_uid, guid from dba_pdbs where PDB_NAME like 'CLONE%';
PDB_NAME         DBID       CON_UID    GUID
----------       ---------- ---------- --------------------------------
PDBCLONE         1307782881 304242047  28F3AE16F69E151AE053030011ACF9A3
```

You can see that Oracle changed the CON_UID, but the DBID and GUID values are still the same.

As mentioned, Oracle won't allow the same database to be plugged in again:

```
SQL> create pluggable database PDBCLONE2 using '/home/oracle/pdbclone.xml' FILE_
NAME_CONVERT=('/u01/app/oracle/data/CDBSRC/PDBCLONE', '/u01/app/oracle/data/CDBTRG/
CLONE2PDB')
*
ERROR at line 1:
ORA-65122: Pluggable database GUID conflicts with the GUID of an existing container.
```

The AS CLONE prompts Oracle to generate new identifiers, thus allowing us to have multiple copies of the same source PDB in the CDB:

```
SQL> create pluggable database PDBCLONE2 as clone using '/home/oracle/pdbclone.xml'
file_name_convert=('/u01/app/oracle/data/CDBSRC/PDBCLONE', '/u01/app/oracle/data/
CDBTRG/CLONE2PDB');

Pluggable database created.
SQL> select pdb_name, dbid, con_uid, guid from dba_pdbs where pdb_name like 'CLONE%';

PDB_NAME   DBID       CON_UID    GUID
---------- ---------- ---------- --------------------------------
PDBCLONE   1307782881 304242047  28F3AE16F69E151AE053030011ACF9A3
PDBCLONE2  2901289706 2901289706 28F3F521825118DAE053030011AC0A65
```

PDB Archive File

Starting with Oracle Database version 12.2, the plug-in/unplug operations can also work with PDB archive files. A PDB archive is a compressed file containing the XML parameter file and its data files, as well as any other necessary auxiliary files (wallet). This is really just a convenience option, because it's easier to copy one compressed file than multiple files.

The basic syntax is identical to that used to unplug to XML file, with the only difference being the specified extension of the target file:

```
SQL> alter pluggable database PDBCLONE unplug into '/home/oracle/pdbclone.pdb';

Pluggable database altered.
```

And if we look at the output file more closely, we can see that it's just a plain ZIP file:

```
$ unzip -t pdbclone.pdb
Archive:  pdbclone.pdb
    testing: system01.dbf             OK
    testing: sysaux01.dbf             OK
    testing: soe.dbf                  OK
    testing: users.dbf                OK
    testing: /home/oracle/pdbclone.xml   OK
No errors detected in compressed data of pdbclone.pdb.
```

Note that the XML file inside the archive still refers to the same paths for the PDB on the source, so it's the same result that we would get from unplugging into XML; however, these paths are ignored. Instead, Oracle unpacks all the datafiles to the directory where the PDB archive is located. This is only a temporary location, Oracle then moves the files to the proper place. `NOCOPY` is not a valid option here.

```
create pluggable database PDBPLUG using '/home/oracle/pdbclone.pdb' nocopy;

ORA-65314: cannot use NOCOPY when plugging in a PDB using an archive file

create pluggable database PDBPLUG2 as clone using '/home/oracle/pdbclone.pdb'
file_name_convert=('/home/oracle','/u01/app/oracle/data/TRG/PDBPLUG2');

Pluggable database created.
```

Cloning

In contrast to unplugging operations, cloning does not go through the intermediate step of working with a staged set of files (datafiles and XML file or a PDB archive). Instead it, more directly, reads the files of a running CDB and copies them to a new PDB. This copy can either be local—inside a single CDB—or remote—to a different database, copying the datafiles over a database link.

A clone operation always assigns a new GUID and UID, and there is no concept of moving, as in plug-in/unplug. The relocate feature is no exception to this, assigning new IDs in the process.

Cloning a Local PDB

The easiest use case is a clone inside a single CDB—a *local clone*, in which no other CDB is involved. The following diagram illustrates this operation:

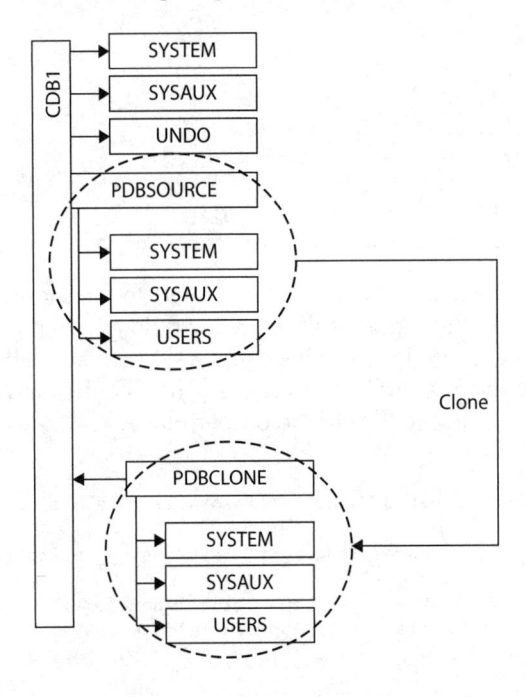

With Active Data Guard, the standby database will also do the same copy. Therefore, no manual intervention on the standby side is needed; this is unlike in virtually all other cases described in this chapter.

Although a local clone is the simplest use case, there are still multiple options to consider. Let's start with the most basic one:

```
create pluggable database PDBCLONE from PDBSOURCE;

Pluggable database created.
```

In Oracle Database 12.1, the source PDB must be open read-only (there are even bugs when Oracle doesn't check the open mode; clone in read/write mode then fails with various internal errors). From Oracle Database 12.2 on, the source PDB can be open read/write, provided that the CDB is in ARCHIVELOG mode and has local UNDO enabled. Either way, we must be logged in as a common user in the CDB root or in the application root.

After the clone finishes, we must open the database in read/write mode, because Oracle won't allow any other operation on it until the database has been opened at least once:

```
SQL> alter pluggable database PDBCLONE open;

Pluggable database altered.
```

Snapshot Copy

Given that a clone is a one-to-one copy of the source PDB, you might wonder whether the underlying file system can help in performing such copies more efficiently. After all, snapshot and copy-on-write functionality are, nowadays, widely used and proven storage features.

The answer is a "limited yes." If the database is on a supported file system, or Oracle Direct NFS is in use, a clone can be created as follows:

```
create pluggable database PDBCLONE from PDBSOURCE snapshot copy;

Pluggable database created.
```

This is one of the features that we expect will evolve rapidly, changing with every patch set, so it's advisable that you regularly review the latest status in the Oracle documentation and in My Oracle Support note 1597027.1.

Generally, Oracle favors and promotes ASM Clustered File System (ACFS) and Direct NFS. In the former, the file system provides read/write snapshots, which means that a source PDB can be open and written to. By contrast, the Direct NFS approach mandates a read-only source PDB, but on the other hand it supports many more file systems, essentially needing only sparse file support for the target files. In both cases, the source PDB cannot be unplugged or dropped.

The specification as to which snapshot technology to use is regulated by the CLONEDB initialization parameter; TRUE implies use of Direct NFS clones. Also note that Direct NFS might require setting up credentials in the keystore; refer to the documentation for more information and specific syntax.

Cloning a Remote PDB

The remote clone process extends the local clone concept, with the differentiator being that the source and target database are distinct, and the communication between the two happens over a database link, as shown in the following diagram:

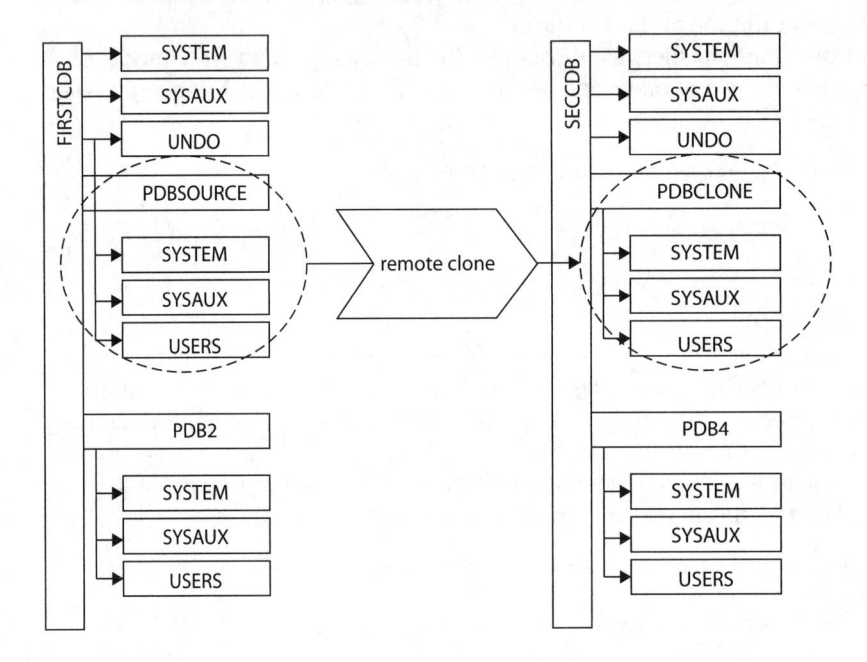

You must be logged in as a common user, either in the CDB root or in an application root. In addition, a database link must be available, because this link will be used to transfer all the metadata and datafiles. This link should be able to connect either to the target CDB or to the PDB.

With plug-in/unplug operations, the database must be compatible, as described previously in this chapter. In a local clone, these conditions are trivial to fulfill, but in a remote clone we must check them. We can use the same steps you used with the DBMS_PDB package, as outlined in the section "Run the Compatibility Check," earlier in the chapter.

As with a local clone, if we want to keep the source PDB open read/write, we need to use version 12.2+, with ARCHIVELOG mode and local UNDO enabled.

In case of a remote clone, it's sufficient if just one of the sides involved in the clone has local UNDO and ARCHIVELOG mode.

```
SQL> create pluggable database PDBCLONE from PDBSOURCE@firstcdb;

Pluggable database created.
```

Splitting the PDB

In all the clone operations, we can specify the USER_TABLESPACES clause. This is a list of all the tablespaces that we want actually cloned; Oracle will add the necessary system tablespaces, but all other tablespaces will be omitted.

In respect to this, two use cases come to mind: First, we may want to provide our developers a subset of the production database, omitting some archival data and keeping the overall size of the clones smaller. Or, second, we may want to split a large, monolith PDB into more manageable, smaller PDBs. A good example of this would be if the source PDB was created by importing a non-CDB database that consolidated multiple applications, each in its own schemas and tablespaces.

```
create pluggable database PDBCLONE from PDBSOURCE user_tablespaces =
('APPTBS1','APPTBS2');

Pluggable database created.
```

Nodata Clone

A *nodata clone* is a special type of clone. It does not contain any user data, and all the tables listed in user tablespaces are imported empty, thus effectively creating a metadata-only copy. This being the case, its value is for specific use cases only.

This function is possible only from 12.1.0.2. Furthermore, it cannot be used in conjunction with index-organized tables, table clusters, or Advanced Queuing tables, additionally constraining its usefulness.

```
create pluggable database PDBCLONE from PDBSOURCE no data;

Pluggable database created.
```

With this function, the new database has the same tablespaces as the source; however, the datafiles are not copied, but instead are created empty. The size of the datafiles matches those on the source, and in the case of datafiles set to autoextend, the new files are created with the initial size.

Refreshable Copy

A *hot clone*, or a clone from a read/write source PDB, works by recovering all the changes that occur during the copy itself, by use of the ARCHIVELOGs and UNDO data.

Extending on this idea, Oracle can also use this data to recover the clone repeatedly, regularly bringing it up-to-date with the source PDB. This type of clone in Oracle Database 12.2 is a *refreshable copy*, and it can be refreshed automatically (EVERY *nn* MINUTES) or manually on demand.

Note, however, that the PDB must be closed for the refresh to occur, both in on-demand and automatic modes. The PDB cannot ever be open read/write, as any local change would prevent Oracle from applying undo from the source. Thus this is the only case where a newly cloned PDB is not first opened read/write in order to be usable.

```
SQL> create pluggable database PDBREFR from PDBSOURCE@firstcdb refresh mode manual;
Pluggable database created.

SQL> alter pluggable database PDBREFR open read only;

Pluggable database altered.
```

As an example, let's request a manual refresh. Again, note that this must be done from within the PDB and, as mentioned, the PDB must be closed:

```
SQL> alter session set container=PDBREFR;

Session altered.

SQL> alter pluggable database PDBREFR refresh;
alter pluggable database PDBREFR refresh
*
ERROR at line 1:
ORA-65025: Pluggable database PDBREFR is not closed on all instances.

SQL> alter pluggable database close;

Pluggable database altered.

SQL> alter pluggable database PDBREFR refresh;

Pluggable database altered.
```

A manual refresh is possible for PDBs configured for both manual and automatic refresh.

A PDB configured for refresh has the status REFRESHING in the CDB_PDBS view.

Relocate

A common use case in database administration is the move of a database, not just a plain copy. To this end, version 12.2 introduces the relocate feature, which makes this explicit. Working in conjunction with the hot-cloning method introduced in the same version, this allows much shorter downtime, instead of doing a clone and then dropping the source.

When we issue the RELOCATE statement, the source database is still open, so it needs to be open read/write and requires local UNDO and ARCHIVELOGs, as expected. The first stage of this process is to clone the PDB while the users are still connected to the source:

```
SQL> create pluggable database PDBRELO from PDBSOURCE@sourcecdb
relocate;

Pluggable database created.
```

After this, the old PDB remains open and read/write, and it can still be accessed and used. At this point, the new PDB is mounted and has the status of RELOCATING:

```
SQL> select pdb_id, pdb_name, status from cdb_pdbs where pdb_name = 'PDBSOURCE';
-- source
PDB_ID     PDB_NAME    STATUS
---------- ----------  ----------
         3 PDBSOURCE   NORMAL
-- target
SQL> select pdb_id, pdb_name, status from cdb_pdbs where pdb_name = 'PDBRELO';

PDB_ID     PDB_NAME    STATUS
---------- ----------  ----------
         6 PDBRELO     RELOCATING
```

It's the opening of the new, relocated PDB that finishes the relocation and drops the old database.

```
SQL> alter pluggable database PDBRELO open;

Pluggable database altered.
```

Note that this feature requires more privileges on the source side than all the other options—namely, that the user that the database link connects to needs the sysoper and create pluggable database privileges.

```
SQL> create user c##reluser identified by oracle;

User created.

SQL> grant sysoper, create pluggable database, create session to c##reluser
container=all;

Grant succeeded.
```

> **NOTE**
> *We can also keep the existing PDB around (in RELOCATED state), to redirect the connections, if the listeners can't do it for us. This is enabled by specifying AVAILABILITY MAX in the CREATE PLUGGABLE DATABASE ... RELOCATE command, and in this case, it's up to us to drop the source PDB, when it's no longer needed.*

Proxy PDB

Sometimes, with PDBs moving around, it can be difficult for you to keep track of all the various PDBs and updating clients to connect to the correct location for each. Perhaps even more critically, features such as container map and queries using the `CONTAINERS()` clause (both described in more detail in Chapter 12) require all the participating PDBs to be in the same container database.

To address this, Oracle Database 12.2 brings to the table the concept of a *proxy PDB*. These PDBs act as a façade, redirecting all requests to the referenced underlying PDB location via an internal database link. So any user commands executed while connected to the proxy PDB affect the remote PDB, not the proxy itself, with these exceptions: `ALTER PLUGGABLE DATABASE` and `ALTER DATABASE` statements.

A proxy database has the IS_VIEW_PDB column set to YES in the CDB_PDBS view, so this is a way of identifying one:

```
SQL> create pluggable database PDBPX as proxy from PDBSOURCE@cdbtrg;

Pluggable database created.
SQL> alter pluggable database PDBPX open;

Pluggable database altered.
SQL> select pdb_id, pdb_name, IS_VIEW_PDB from cdb_pdbs where pdb_name='PDBPX';

    PDB_ID PDB_NAME   IS_VIEW_PDB
---------- ---------- -----------
         4 PDBPX      YES
```

Note that a proxy PDB actually clones the SYSTEM, SYSAUX, and temporary tablespaces of its referent, so it's not a completely empty shell.

A proxy requires a database link to be defined, and this is one that connects to the target CDB root or the PDB. Although a proxy can point back to the same source database, a database link is always required. This database link is used only during the setup, as the proxy PDB actually creates a new internal database link for passing the user requests. However, this internal database link is not a simple copy of the link that was manually created; instead, Oracle generates this using the host name of the target CDB and port 1521. Note that it is possible to specify the PORT and HOST if these defaults do not match your environment.

```
SQL> create pluggable database PDBPX as proxy from PDBSOURCE@cdbtrg
PORT=1522 HOST='trghost';

Pluggable database created.
```

Application Container Considerations

An application container, introduced in Oracle Database 12.2, does not significantly extend cloning functionality. At this stage, only individual PDBs—not the whole application—can be unplugged/plugged in and cloned, and an application root can be unplugged only when empty.

> **NOTE**
> *The location of a new PDB, created with clone or plug-in, is determined by the current container used when executing the* `create pluggable database` *command, and this can be run in the CDB root or in an application root.*

Converting Non-CDB Database

As a special case, Oracle allows a database that does not use the multitenant architecture to be plugged in. Such an operation is more of a migration path from the legacy architecture to the new container-based one, not merely a move of data.

For this feature to work, both the source non-CDB and the target CDB versions must be 12.1.0.2 or later. The endian must also match, as the datafiles cannot be converted this way and, as usual, the installed options must also cohere.

There are multiple ways to approach this procedure using PDB operations. The non-CDB can be plugged in, or it can be cloned. Both options are shown in the following illustration.

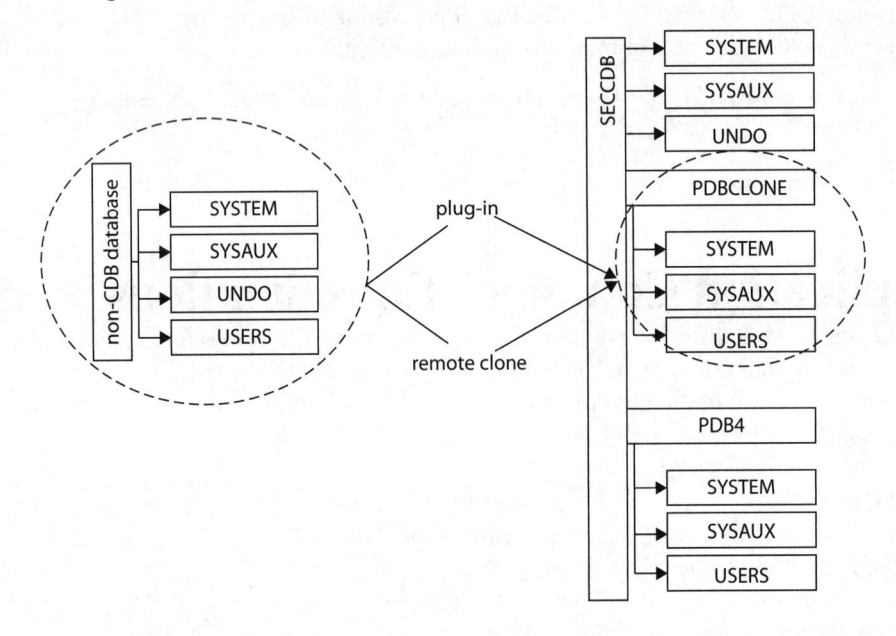

Plug In a Non-CDB

For a non-CDB plug-in, we need to run the compatibility check, and the source database must be open or open read-only. Also, as usual, we should back it up before we attempt the plug-in, in case anything goes wrong.

We create the XML file describing an unplugged database:

```
BEGIN
  DBMS_PDB.DESCRIBE(
    pdb_descr_file => '/home/oracle/noncdb.xml');
END;
/

PL/SQL procedure successfully completed.
```

Next, we can check for any issues or violations, running a simple script in the target CDB:

```
SET SERVEROUTPUT ON
DECLARE
  compatible CONSTANT VARCHAR2(3) :=
```

```
      CASE DBMS_PDB.CHECK_PLUG_COMPATIBILITY(
            pdb_descr_file => '/home/oracle/noncdb.xml',
            pdb_name       => 'NONCDBPDB')
    WHEN TRUE THEN 'YES'
    ELSE 'NO'
END;
BEGIN
  DBMS_OUTPUT.PUT_LINE(compatible);
END;
/
YES

select message, action from PDB_PLUG_IN_VIOLATIONS where name='NONCDBPDB';
MESSAGE                                         ACTION
----------------------------------------------  ----------------------------------
PDB plugged in is a non-CDB, requires           Run noncdb_to_pdb.sql.
noncdb_to_pdb.sql be run.
CDB parameter memory_target mismatch:           Please check the parameter in the
Previous 764M Current 0                         current CDB
```

In this output, the first message is obvious and expected, because we are going to plug in a non-CDB. However, the second message is an example of a parameter mismatch. Some of the parameters can be set at the CDB level only, so upon plugging in the PDB, the value of the CDB will override it. It is therefore up to us to determine whether we set the CDB parameter to match the original non-CDB one or not. This is the same issue we face when putting multiple different PDBs into the same CDB, as many parameters are global across all PDBs.

When we are satisfied with these settings, we are ready to perform the actual plug-in operation.

The XML parameter file must be created from a read-only non-CDB in order for the SCNs to be consistent. Thus, if it was generated from a read/write database, we'd set that non-CDB to read-only and create the XML file again. Following on from there, we can shut down the source database, because it won't be needed anymore. Note, however, that after the plug-in completes, we could continue to use this non-CDB source database, because unlike an unplug of a PDB, it is not marked for drop.

Then we can plug in the database:

```
SQL> create pluggable database NONCDBPDB using '/home/oracle/noncdb.xml'
file_name_convert=('/u01/app/oracle/data/NONCDB','/u01/app/oracle/data/
CDBSRC/NONCDBPDB');

Pluggable database created.
```

Alternatively, we can plug it in, keeping the files in place. In that case, we should be aware of the TEMP file trap that may be encountered in many scenarios:

unless we specify `TEMPFILE REUSE`, Oracle will try to create new tempfile(s) and fail when it finds the file already exists:

```
SQL> create pluggable database NONCDBPDB using '/home/oracle/noncdb.xml' nocopy;
create pluggable database NONCDBPDB using '/home/oracle/noncdb.xml' nocopy
*
ERROR at line 1:
ORA-27038: created file already exists
ORA-01119: error in creating database file '/u01/app/oracle/data/NONCDB/temp01.dbf'

SQL> create pluggable database NONCDBPDB using '/home/oracle/noncdb.xml' nocopy
tempfile reuse;

Pluggable database created.
```

As indicated in our earlier violation check, we need to run the conversion script, noncdb_to_pdb.sql, at this point. This step is mandatory. Although we might be able to open the database without it, we would face various issues later, such as having a corrupted dictionary, and similar. In version 12.1, it's not even possible to rerun the script if it fails, because that also corrupts the dictionary. For more on this, refer to My Oracle Support note 2039530.1.

In our tests, the longest running section of this script was in fact utl_recomp, which compiles all invalid objects.

```
SQL> alter session set container=NONCDBPDB;

Session altered.

SQL> @$ORACLE_HOME/rdbms/admin/noncdb_to_pdb.sql
...a lot of output omitted...
```

Now we can open the new PDB and begin to use it:

```
SQL> alter pluggable database open;

Pluggable database altered.
```

Cloning a Non-CDB

Another approach for non-CDB conversion is to use cloning. The difference between this and the previous approach is the same as those with unplug/plug-in versus cloning methods for PDBs. This means that a clone requires fewer steps, can be done remotely, and does not require the physical copying and transmission of files.

> **NOTE**
> *The clone of a non-CDB is always remote; the source database is different from the target.*

In the following command, we specify the special NON$CDB name for the PDB:

```
SQL> create database link OLDDB connect to system identified by oracle using 'OLDDB';

Database link created.

SQL> create pluggable database OLDDBPDB from NON$CDB@OLDDB file_name_convert=('/u01/
app/oracle/data/OLDDB','/u01/app/oracle/data/CDBSRC/OLDDBPDB');

Pluggable database created.
```

Once these commands are completed, we need to run the noncdb_to_pdb.sql script, and then we can open the database:

```
SQL> alter session set container=olddbpdb;

Session altered.

SQL> @$ORACLE_HOME/rdbms/admin/noncdb_to_pdb.sql
...a lot of output omitted...

SQL> alter pluggable database open;

Pluggable database altered.
```

Moving PDBs to the Cloud

Another use case of PDB operations is to move the database to the cloud—or back from cloud to on-premise. In essence, this does not differ from moving the PDB around our on-premise servers. The cloud (Oracle or other) database is just another Oracle database and all the operations described in this chapter are valid there as well, whether using the command line or Enterprise Manager.

Thus, for the move, we can use ordinary unplug and plug-in, remote clone, or the full range of options, such as relocate or proxy PDB. For some of the basic scenarios, note that Enterprise Manager Cloud Control has a wizard we can use, shown in Figure 9-1.

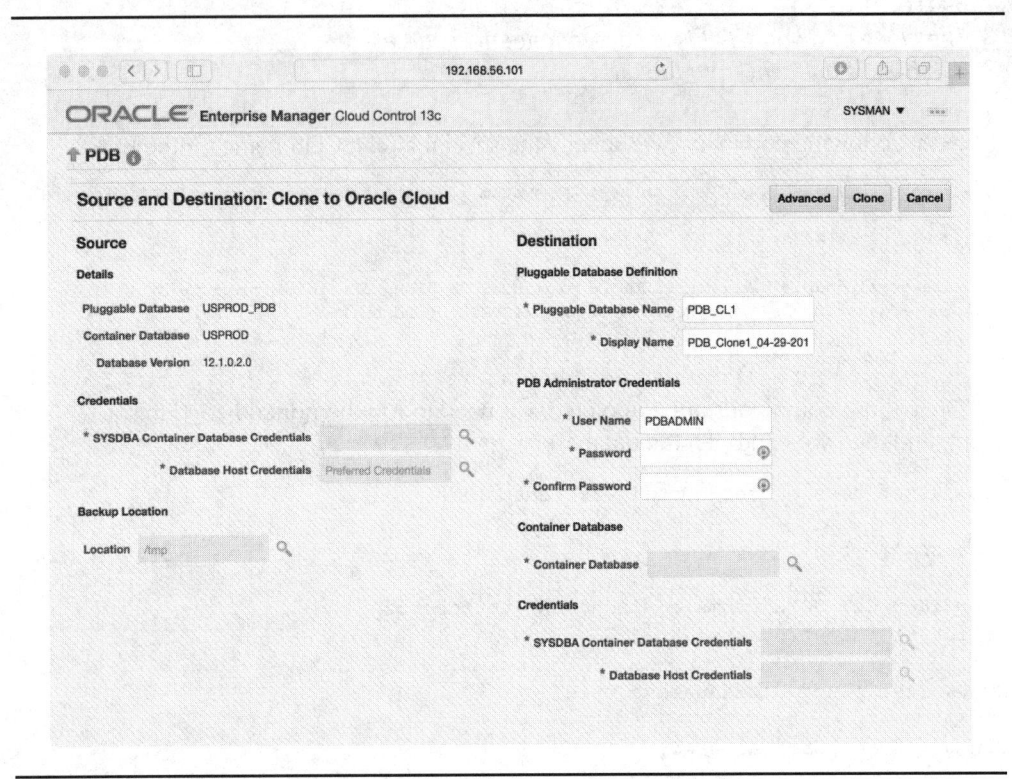

FIGURE 9-1. *Clone to Oracle Cloud in Oracle Enterprise Manager*

Triggers on PDB Operations

Like CDBs, PDBs support database event triggers, including opening and closing the database, server error, logon/logoff, and so on. The only trigger that is CDB-only is AFTER DB_ROLE_CHANGE, as switching primary/standby can occur on CDB only (we discuss Data Guard in detail in Chapter 11).

A new trigger introduced in 12c is the BEFORE SET CONTAINER or AFTER SET CONTAINER, fired when a session changes the current container using ALTER SESSION SET CONTAINER. The use of this trigger is very similar to a logon/logoff trigger, especially for connection pools and the like, where one session switches between containers; the single logon/logoff trigger is not enough to cover different requirements for the various PDBs.

Finally, and perhaps most importantly in the context of this chapter, as they apply to the types of operations described herein, two new trigger types were added that work at the PDB level only: AFTER CLONE and BEFORE UNPLUG.

As the name suggests, the `AFTER CLONE` trigger fires at the new database, after it is cloned. If the trigger fails, the new database is left in an UNUSABLE state and the only operation permitted is to drop it.

The `BEFORE UNPLUG` trigger fires when the unplug operation starts. If the trigger fails, the operation does not happen, so no XML file is created and the PDB remains part of the CDB.

In both cases, when the trigger succeeds, it is deleted.

There are several use cases for triggers—for example, if we want to delete any stored passwords and keys to external systems and drop database links before we unplug the database and distribute it. Another use case would be to employ it to mask data after we have cloned a PDB to a test environment.

Full Transportable Export/Import

The transportable database feature is a logical step-up from the trusted and proven transportable tablespace feature, first introduced way back in *8i*.

Transportable tablespace functionality was originally introduced to move just one or a few tablespaces, such as from an OLTP system to a data warehouse. But over the years, its usage developed to moving large amounts of data, such as all of the user datafiles during a migration or upgrade.

Additionally, transportable tablespace was also enhanced to handle cross-endian data movement, although one gap still existed, in that it could not move non-table objects such as views or PL/SQL.

The new transportable database feature now addresses this. It handles user tablespaces like transportable tablespace always did and, in addition, it can also export the other objects as a Data Pump export would do, in a single step. And being based on the proven foundation, it includes cross-endian conversion possibilities.

Like transportable tablespaces, the transported tablespaces must be read-only during the import process. RMAN allows a workaround for this for transportable tablespaces, in that it can create an auxiliary instance and run the export there, but this is not available for full transportable export.

This full transportable export feature has been available since version 11.2.0.3.

The multitenant twist on this feature is that the result can be imported into an existing CDB. In other words, it can be used to plug in a non-CDB into a CDB. The advantage of this, as opposed to the simpler way described earlier, is the cross-endian support. It also does not automatically copy the files, so if the conversion happens on the same machine, we do not need to copy the datafiles at all, speeding up the conversion and saving disk space.

Another scenario is plugging in a PDB that would otherwise not meet the requirements: so we can move a database cross-endian, or get around an unmatched list of installed features. (Of course, the target database needs to have installed any features the new PDB and its users and applications will use.)

Unlike the simple and standard plug-in, full transportable import requires that an already existing (empty) database be created first. The import process then imports only user data.

Note also that only one PDB is exported at a time; and when we specify a connection to the CDB, only the CDB user data is exported, not the PDB's.

As an example, let's export a non-CDB database and import it into a fresh new PDB.

First, all of the user tablespaces must be made read-only. However, the database itself must be read/write, as Data Pump creates a job table in the SYS schema:

```
SQL> alter tablespace example read only;

Tablespace altered.

SQL> alter tablespace users read only;

Tablespace altered.
```

Then we run the Data Pump export, creating a directory beforehand, if necessary. Because this exports all the object definitions, it does take some time, although this is minimal in comparison to a data export:

```
expdp system/oracle@noncdb full=y dumpfile=noncdb.dmp directory=dp
transportable=always  logfile=noncdb.log
Starting "SYSTEM"."SYS_EXPORT_FULL_01":  system/********@noncdb full=y
dumpfile=noncdb.dmp directory=dp transportable=always logfile=noncdb.log
Processing object type DATABASE_EXPORT/PRE_SYSTEM_IMPCALLOUT/MARKER
Processing object type DATABASE_EXPORT/PRE_INSTANCE_IMPCALLOUT/MARKER
...a lot of output omitted...
. . exported "WMSYS"."WM$EXP_MAP"                         7.718 KB       3 rows
Master table "SYSTEM"."SYS_EXPORT_FULL_01" successfully loaded/unloaded
******************************************************************************
Dump file set for SYSTEM.SYS_EXPORT_FULL_01 is:
   /home/oracle/dp/noncdb.dmp
******************************************************************************
Datafiles required for transportable tablespace EXAMPLE:
   /u01/app/oracle/data/SRC/example01.dbf
Datafiles required for transportable tablespace USERS:
   /u01/app/oracle/data/SRC/users01.dbf
Job "SYSTEM"."SYS_EXPORT_FULL_01" successfully completed at Fri Jan 22 03:01:35
2016 elapsed 0 00:09:38
```

As you can see, the export conveniently prints the list of necessary files—the dump file and all the datafiles—at the footer of the screen output and the log.

Now we create a new PDB:

```
SQL> create pluggable database PDBIMPORT admin user ads identified by
oracle file_name_convert=('/u01/app/oracle/data/CDBSRC/pdbseed','/u01/
app/oracle/data/CDBSRC/PDBIMPORT);
```

```
Pluggable database created.

SQL> alter session set container=PDBIMPORT;

Session altered.

SQL> alter database open;

Database altered.

SQL> create directory dp as '/home/oracle/dp';

Directory created.
SQL> grant read, write on directory dp to public;

Grant succeeded.
```

The next step is to copy the files to the destination directories and change the endian using RMAN if necessary:

```
RMAN> convert datafile '/tmp/example01.dbf', '/tmp/users01.dbf'
   from platform 'Linux x86 64-bit'
   db_file_name_convert '/tmp', '/u01/app/oracle/data/TRG/PDBIMPORT';
```

Now we import the dump:

```
$ impdp system/oracle@PDBIMPORT dumpfile=noncdb.dmp directory=dp transport_
datafiles=/u01/app/oracle/data/TRG/PDBIMPORT/example01.dbf,/u01/app/oracle/data/
TRG/PDBIMPORT/users01.dbf logfile=noncdb.log
Master table "SYSTEM"."SYS_IMPORT_TRANSPORTABLE_01" successfully loaded/unloaded
Starting "SYSTEM"."SYS_IMPORT_TRANSPORTABLE_01":  system/********@PDBIMPORT
dumpfile=noncdb.dmp directory=dp transport_datafiles=/u01/app/oracle/data/
TRG/PDBIMPORT/example01.dbf,/u01/app/oracle/data/TRG/PDBIMPORT/users01.dbf
logfile=noncdb.log
Processing object type DATABASE_EXPORT/PRE_SYSTEM_IMPCALLOUT/MARKER
Processing object type DATABASE_EXPORT/PRE_INSTANCE_IMPCALLOUT/MARKER
...a lot of output omitted...
Processing object type DATABASE_EXPORT/AUDIT_UNIFIED/AUDIT_POLICY_ENABLE
Processing object type DATABASE_EXPORT/POST_SYSTEM_IMPCALLOUT/MARKER
Job "SYSTEM"."SYS_IMPORT_TRANSPORTABLE_01" completed at Fri Jan 22 04:59:56 2016
elapsed 0 00:11:02
```

Transportable Tablespaces

Not much has been altered with this functionality since 11*g*. The transportable tablespace feature is still present in multitenant and can be used to move data from one database to another, but it's more complicated than unplug/plug-in and limited when compared to a full transportable export, although it still has its use cases.

One notable unique feature is the ability to use RMAN to obtain the datafiles without setting them to read-only, thanks to using an auxiliary instance. In 12c, RMAN has been further enhanced with the addition of syntax to specify a tablespace in a particular PDB:

```
RMAN> transport tablespace PDBCOPY:users tablespace destination '/home/oracle/tts';
```

See Chapter 12 for more examples of how transportable databases can be used.

Summary

In this chapter we covered one of the most interesting topics which the multitenant feature has given rise to: separation of the PDBs and their movement from a CDB to another one. As we have seen, there are a multitude of options, with many ways leading to Rome, and each has its own pros and cons.

As you gain more real-world experience with multitenant, you'll find this functionality more and more useful for solving problems in ways not possible before. This creative leverage comes with real-world experience, lots of experimentation and testing, and a fresh mind when approaching problems.

PART IV

Advanced Multitenant

CHAPTER 10

Oracle Database Resource Manager

Up until now we have focused on creating and configuring a multitenant database environment, including key aspects of the day-to-day administration tasks. In this part of the book we move toward some of the more advanced configuration options. We will begin with a look at Oracle Database Resource Manager, before moving on to disaster recovery (DR) implementations using Oracle Data Guard, followed by a focus on the movement and sharing of data in the final two chapters.

In this chapter, the focus is Resource Manager, which may be familiar territory for some, albeit with new considerations to factor in with Oracle 12*c*. One of the key advantages of multitenant is consolidation, but it also introduces new questions in relation to Resource Manager, such as these:

- How do you manage resources such as CPU, memory, and I/O available to your database?

- Can resource management be micromanaged in a way, enabling distribution of resources to pluggable databases (PDBs) depending on priorities or even time schedules?

- What about resource allocations inside a PDB itself?

- Can resources be managed at a more fine-grained level in a PDB?

In this chapter, we will address these questions and show how you can easily get started with Resource Manager in a multitenant database environment.

Resource Manager Basics

We have already spoken about some of the key advantages of multitenant, such as the ability to consolidate many databases easily into one, as well as the flexibility to provision new databases quickly. In conjunction with these advantages, one core area of the database functionality needs consideration, and that is database resource allocation. Imagine having a server with an abundance of resources such as CPU, memory, and fast storage, such that you would expect everything to be well-equipped for general operational purposes, only to realize later that one of the PDBs consumes virtually all of these resources during busy periods. The flow-on effect is that other PDBs are starved of resources during these times, with the end result being non-optimal performance and disgruntled end users.

By default, operating systems will attempt to distribute resources as requested and do not prioritize among different processes, because they are not aware of which processes should have higher priorities than others. There are some exceptions, but these operating systems require manual configuration or the use of additional software to effect resource allocation and prioritization in some shape or form.

Oracle Resource Manager, which resides within the database itself, has full access to all the runtime information and performance statistics. All the information that describes what is happening inside the database is available, and if Resource Manager is configured correctly, the database can draw upon this information to make decisions on resource distribution; we can ensure, then, that if one area of the database is busy, other PDBs are not starved of resources.

In using Resource Manager in a multitenant environment, the following options are available to you:

- Distribute resources among PDBs based on their priority, ensuring that PDBs requiring higher priority and more resources have the appropriate amount of resources allocated

- Limiting CPU usage of PDBs

- Limiting number of parallel execution servers of PDBs

- Limiting memory usage of PDBs, including ensuring that the minimum memory requirements of a PDB are met

- Limiting resource usage within a PDB for particular sessions

- Limiting PDB I/O generation

Key Resource Manager Terminologies

Before diving into the details of Resource Manager, let's review some key terminology.

Resource consumer group

Resource Manager will allocate resources to resource consumer groups, not to individual sessions or processes. Resource consumer groups can be thought of as sessions, grouped together, based on specific resource usage requirements. Sessions are mapped to a consumer group based on rules configured by the DBA and can be switched between different groups automatically or manually.

Resource plan directive

Resource plan directives are used to associate resource consumer groups with particular resource plans and to specify how resources are to be allocated to the associated resource consumer group. A plan directive in a current active resource plan may be associated with only one consumer group.

Resource plan

The resource plan is the top-level container for the directives. It is the resource plan itself that is activated, which then enables the underlying resource plan directives

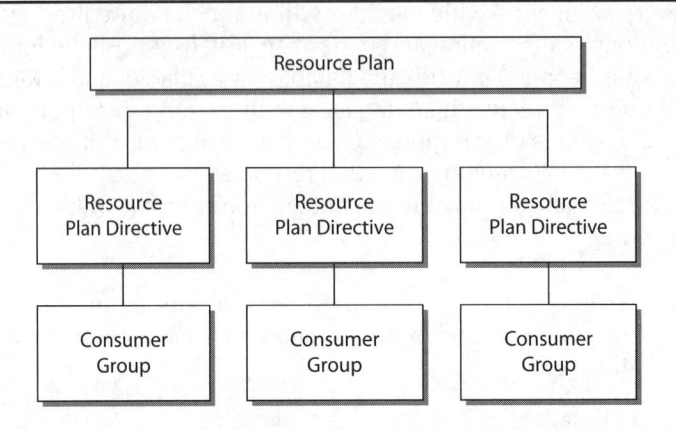

FIGURE 10-1. *A basic Resource Manager plan, directives, and consumer groups*

that specify how resources are allocated to the individual consumer groups. There can be only one active resource plan at any time in the database, but you can create many different resource plans and switch between them as needed. This can be done via the scheduler or manually using the ALTER SYSTEM commands.

This hierarchy of components is depicted in Figure 10-1.

CDB resource plan
Think of this as the master or top-level plan created at the container database (CDB) level, which specifies how resources (via the use of resource plan directives) are allocated among PDBs within the CDB. A CDB resource plan can have many directives, but each directive in an active plan may reference only one PDB or PDB profile. Note also that two directives cannot both reference the same PDB or PDB profile.

PDB resource plan
A PDB resource plan is the next step in terms of granularity, taking the resources allocated by the CDB resource plan (to specific PDBs) and determining how these resources are then distributed within the PDB among its configured consumer groups.

Figure 10-2 provides a high-level representation of the relationship between a CDB resource plan and PDB resource plans. It also indicates the plan directives and consumer groups, which will be discussed in more detail in the next section.

Subplan
A resource plan directive may reference another resource plan instead of a resource consumer group, and this "stacked" component, or *subplan*, provides additional flexibility to outwork fine-grained resource management as required.

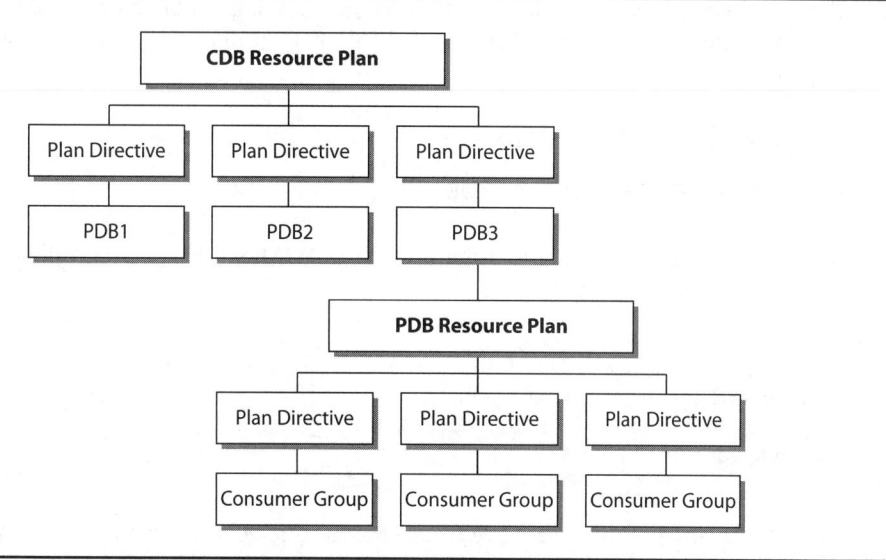

FIGURE 10-2. *A CDB and PDB resource plan relationship*

Shares
Resources on a system can be allocated proportionately using *shares*. For example, a CDB containing four PDBs can allocate one share to each of three PDBs and allocate two shares for the remaining PDB, denoting it has higher priority.

PDB profiles
When working with large numbers of PDBs, you can also make use of PDB profiles, which determine the share of system resources allocated to the PDBs to which the profile applies. This includes CPU, memory, and total parallel execution server allocations.

Resource Manager Requirements
Before Resource Manager can be used in a CDB, the CDB must have at least one PDB. Resource Manager is configured via the DBMS_RESOURCE_MANAGER package, and the system privilege ADMINISTER_RESOURCE_MANAGER is required to administer it. The ADMINISTER_RESOURCE_MANAGER system privilege is granted by default to the DBA role with the ADMIN option.

This system privilege cannot be granted via regular SQL grant or revoke statements, but must be done via the DBMS_RESOURCE_MANAGER_PRIVS package using the following two procedures:

- `GRANT_SYSTEM_PRIVILEGE`
- `REVOKE_SYSTEM_PRIVILEGE`

So, for example, if you want to grant user C##XADMIN this system privilege, you would run the following command:

```
BEGIN
    dbms_resource_manager_privs.grant_system_privilege (
      grantee_name => 'C##XADMIN',
      privilege_name => 'ADMINISTER_RESOURCE_MANAGER',
      admin_option=> FALSE);
END;
```

In this example, the parameter `PRIVILEGE_NAME` is specified even though this is not strictly required, because the default value is ADMINISTER_RESOURCE_MANAGER.

Resource Manager is configured and managed via the DBMS_RESOURCE_MANAGER package, but to allow users to switch consumer groups, they must be granted a specific system privilege using procedures available in the DBMS_RESOURCE_MANAGER_PRIVS package:

- `GRANT_SWITCH_CONSUMER_GROUP`
- `REVOKE_SWITCH_CONSUMER_GROUP`

Resource Manager Levels

Resource management in a CDB can quickly ramp up in complexity when compared to managing a non-CDB. In a CDB, you have to take into account multiple PDBs that may have differing workloads, and competition for resources both within a PDB, as well as at the CDB level. When running Resource Manager in a multitenant environment, resources can be managed at two levels:

- **CDB level** You can manage resources within the CDB, catering for the different PDB workloads and specifying how resources are distributed among them. PDBs may have different priorities, and resultant use limits can be imposed to distribute the total resources available to the CDB accordingly. In most cases in which a CDB contains multiple PDBs, it would be reasonable to assume that some PDBs will have a higher priority than others. Resource Manager at a CDB level helps to enforce and manage these priorities and limitations.

- **PDB level**   Drilling down, we can manage workloads and resource usage within a given PDB. For example, let's assume from a high-level point of view that 50 percent of the CDB resources are allocated to PDB1. Within PDB1, this 50 percent portion of the total CDB resources can then be further divided up and portioned out between the different consumer groups.

In the following sections, we will focus on CDB and PDB resource plans in more detail, with examples of how these can be configured.

The CDB Resource Plan

A CDB resource plan is the top-level resource plan, configured for the CDB itself. It directs the management of resources within the CDB, catering to different PDB workloads and resource distribution between the PDBs. When running a CDB with multiple PDBs, it is very likely that you will have to allocate more resources to a specific PDB or PDB group. Or you may need to distribute the system and CDB resources evenly to ensure that all PDBs get sufficient resources, and that no PDBs are being starved of resources. In either case, the CDB resource plan is used to map such allocations appropriately.

Resource Allocation and Utilization Limits

Using Resource Manager, you can prioritize resource usage among PDBs with *share values*. The higher the share value allocated, the higher the priority, which means there is a greater likelihood of obtaining resources when resource contention is encountered. In the same way that resource share values are implemented for individual PDBs, PDB profiles can be applied to a set of PDBs. Figure 10-3 illustrates the basic concept of using shares. In this example, we have a CDB resource plan with two resource plan directives specified, with a total of four shares; one share is assigned

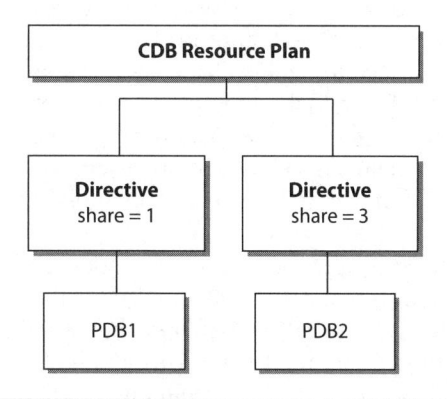

FIGURE 10-3.   *Using shares in a CDB resource plan directive*

to PDB1 and three shares to PDB2. In the event of resource contention, PDB1 will be guaranteed at least one quarter of the resources available, and PDB2 will get three quarters.

> **NOTE**
> *If there is no current resource contention, either PDB1 or PDB2 can have a larger share of the resources than what they have been assigned in the plan directive.*

In addition to using shares as a method of prioritizing resources, you can also set utilization limits for PDBs and PDB profiles, which are specified as a percentage. If not specified, the value is 100, which indicates that the associated PDB or PDBs included in a PDB profile can potentially use 100 percent of the CPU resources available in a CDB. The utilization limits can be specified for CPU, memory, and parallel execution servers. The following parameters can be set in a resource plan directive with respect to CPU and parallel execution servers:

- `utilization_limit`
- `parallel_server_limit`

The `utilization_limit` parameter differs from using shares, because it is specific to how much of the CPU resource may be used. For example, if the `utilization_limit` for a particular PDB is specified as 100, it indicates that the PDB may use up to 100 percent of the system CPU resources. If the value is set to 50, it indicates that the PDB, if the system is under load, can use up to 50 percent of the CPU resource. Shares are used to indicate which PDBs have higher priority with regard to all resources, not just CPU resource. Specifying a combination of options, such as shares, `utilization_limit`, and `parallel_server_limit`, provides you with more fine-grained control over how system resources are distributed.

In addition to `utilization_limit` and `parallel_server_limit`, two new memory limits are introduced in Oracle Database 12c Release 2. Their values are expressed as percentages in relation to the Program Global Area (PGA), buffer cache, and shared pool sizes. Even though these two parameters may be set, remember that shares are also considered to maintain the fairness of resource allocation. The following two parameters can be specified with regard to memory limits:

- **`memory_min`**   The `memory_min` limit takes a default value of 0 if not set explicitly. The goal is that each PDB should be allocated at least this minimum if requested, for the PGA, buffer cache, and the shared pool. If a PDB has reached the minimum, it will be prioritized for releasing memory if needed. If it has not yet reached its minimum, it will be preferred when requesting memory.

- **`memory_limit`** The `memory_limit` default value is 100. This is a hard limit on the maximum memory a PDB can consume. If a PDB reaches the maximum, it can allocate only memory that it has released itself, while other PDBs that have not yet reached their limit (maximum) may allocate memory that was freed from any PDB.

Figure 10-4 shows a high-level overview of how resource utilization limits can be specified as part of the resource plan directives. In the example, PDB2 does not have any utilization limits imposed (limits are specified as 100), but PDB1 limitations are specified up to only 40 percent of resources (CPU, parallel execution servers, and memory).

Memory- and I/O-related parameters can also be set at the PDB level. For more information, see the section "Manage PDB Memory and I/O via Initialization Parameters" later in the chapter.

But what happens to PDBs that are not specified in any of the created resource plan directives? The answer brings us to our next topic: default directives.

Default and Autotask Directives

Up to this point, we have discussed CDB resource plans and the resource plan directives that have been applied to specific PDBs. But what if you create a new PDB, plug a new PDB into the CDB, or have already configured PDBs that were not explicitly defined when creating directives? Default resource plan directives are used for such scenarios, and they will have one share assigned and resource limit parameters set to default values. Alternatively, you can generate new directives for freshly created PDBs or adjust the default PDB directives if you prefer.

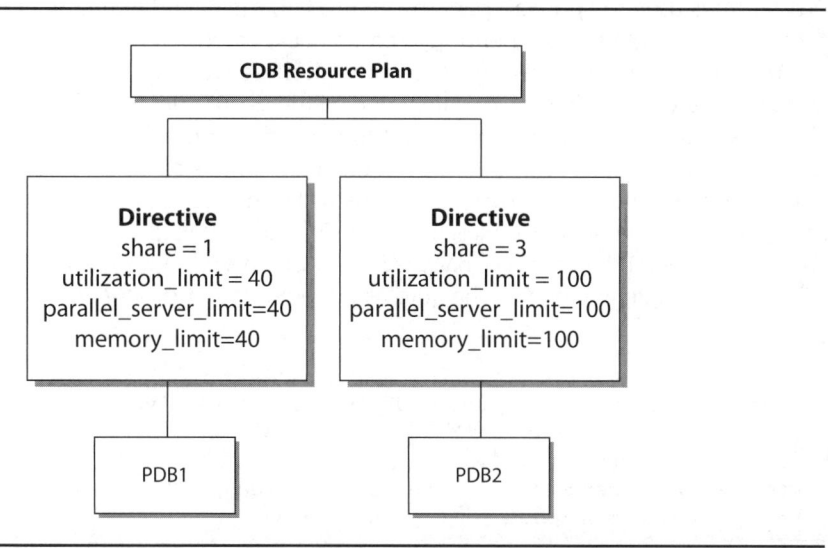

FIGURE 10-4. *High-level CDB resource plan directives with utilization limits*

> **NOTE**
> *The directive for a PDB will be retained if the PDB is unplugged from a CDB. If a directive is no longer needed, you will need to drop the directive manually.*

Should it be required, you can adjust the default directive using a procedure inside the DMBS_RESOURCE_MANAGER package called UPDATE_CDB_DEFAULT_DIRECTIVE. The following code block illustrates how the default directive may be updated:

```
BEGIN
    dbms_resource_manager.create_pending_area();
    dbms_resource_manager.update_cdb_default_directive(
          plan => 'CDB_RPLAN'
        , new_shares => 2
        , new_utilization_limit => 50);
    dbms_resource_manager.validate_pending_area();
    dbms_resource_manager.submit_pending_area();
END;
```

From this code block, we can see that the default directive for PDBs was updated to two shares and a new utilization limit of 50 percent was specified.

Notice in the preceding code block that a pending area is created and validated before being submitted. The pending area is a staging area where a resource plan is created, updated, or deleted, without affecting currently running applications. After changes are made to a pending area, it is validated using the VALIDATE_PENDING_AREA procedure. Once the pending area is validated, the SUBMIT_PENDING_AREA procedure is used to apply all pending changes to the data dictionary. Once the submission is complete, the pending area will be cleared.

The second default directive, the autotask directive, applies to automatic maintenance tasks during the maintenance windows. The default allocation is no shares (actually, –1), which means that the automated maintenance tasks gets 20 percent of the system resources. The utilization limit is set to 90 percent and the parallel server limit is set to 100 percent. As with the default directive for PDBs, you may also update the autotask directive, by using the UPDATE_CDB_AUTOTASK_DIRECTIVE procedure in the DBMS_RESOURCE_MANAGER package. In the following example, we update the autotask directive's share value to 2:

```
BEGIN
    dbms_resource_manager.create_pending_area();
    dbms_resource_manager.update_cdb_autotask_directive(
          plan => 'CDB_RPLAN'
        , new_shares => 2);
    dbms_resource_manager.validate_pending_area();
    dbms_resource_manager.submit_pending_area();
END;
```

Creating a CDB Resource Plan

Now that you understand CDB resource plans and their elements, we can launch into a few examples to show you how to create these plans. There are multiple ways to achieve this, but the most common method is to use SQL commands via SQL*Plus and execute the required DBMS_RESOURCE_MANAGER procedures. It is also possible to perform some of these tasks via Enterprise Manager Cloud Control, Enterprise Manager Database Express, or Oracle SQL Developer. In this section, we will show you how to outwork these tasks using SQL*Plus and the DBMS_RESOURCE_MANAGER package.

Example: Creating a CDB Resource Plan for Individual PDBs

Before jumping into the commands, we first need to plan out what we want to implement. A simple way of doing this is to create a table with all the allocation options listed, or perhaps even a basic flow diagram. In the first example, we will make use of the former to illustrate the CDB resource plan, which will focus specifically on individual PDBs, without the use of PDB profiles.

In this example, we will create a CDB resource plan and directives based on the information listed in the following table. This example also includes the Default and Autotask directives, and they will be modified from the default values to those specified in the table.

PDB/Directive Name	Shares	Utilization Limit	Parallel Server Limit	Memory Minimum	Memory Limit
PDB1	1	70	50	20	40
PDB2	4	100	100	50	80
Default	1	90	50		100
Autotask	2	80	80		100

The goal of this example is to show the commands needed to execute the CDB resource plan, as per the values in the table. The steps follow:

1. Create the pending area:

    ```
    dbms_resource_manager.create_pending_area();
    ```

2. Create the resource plan:

    ```
    dbms_resource_manager.create_cdb_plan(
          plan =>'CDB_RPLAN'
          ,comment => 'DEMO CDB Resource Plan');
    ```

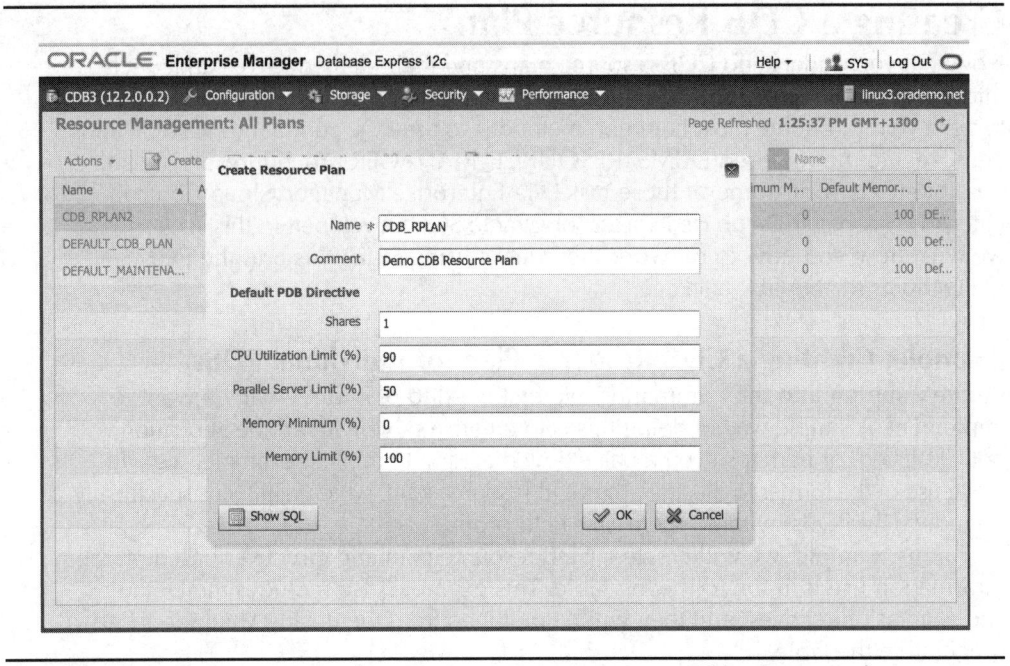

FIGURE 10-5. *Using EM Database Express 12.2 to create a CDB resource plan*

At this stage, even though we are going to perform the rest of the configuration using SQL commands, it is also possible to do this via a graphical interface. For example, Figure 10-5 illustrates how this can be done using EM Database Express 12.2 when the CDB resource plan is created. (Note also that the default directive can be updated at the CDB resource plan creation time.)

Now, returning to our command line example, the following steps will be performed using SQL commands.

3. Create two plan directives for PDB1 and PDB2:

```
dbms_resource_manager.create_cdb_plan_directive(plan => 'CDB_RPLAN'
    , comment => 'PDB1 Plan Directive'
    , pluggable_database => 'PDB1'
    , shares => 1
    , utilization_limit => 70
    , parallel_server_limit => 50
    , memory_min => 20
    , memory_limit => 40);
dbms_resource_manager.create_cdb_plan_directive(plan => 'CDB_RPLAN'
    , comment => 'PDB2 Plan Directive'
```

```
              , pluggable_database => 'PDB2'
              , shares => 4
              , utilization_limit => 100
              , parallel_server_limit => 100
              , memory_min => 50
              , memory_limit => 80);
```

4. Update the default PDB directive:

```
       dbms_resource_manager.update_cdb_default_directive(
           plan => 'CDB_RPLAN'
         , new_shares => 2
         , new_utilization_limit => 90
         , new_parallel_server_limit => 50);
```

5. Update the default autotask directive:

```
       dbms_resource_manager.update_cdb_autotask_directive(
           plan => 'CDB_RPLAN'
         , new_shares => 2
         , new_utilization_limit => 80
         , new_parallel_server_limit => 80);
```

6. Validate the pending area:

```
       dbms_resource_manager.validate_pending_area();
```

7. Submit the pending area:

```
       dbms_resource_manager.submit_pending_area();
```

At this stage, the CDB resource plan and its directives have been created, but we must keep in mind that it has not yet been enabled. We can review the CDB resource plan directives by listing the information in DBA_CDB_RSRC_PLAN_DIRECTIVES, as shown in Figure 10-6.

8. Enable the CDB resource plan:

   Now that we have created a CDB resource plan called CDB_RPLAN, we can enable it for use. This is achieved by executing the following command:

```
       SQL> alter system set resource_manager_plan = CDB_RPLAN;
```

Reviewing the database alert log and initialization parameters, we can see that the change has taken effect. When reviewing EM Cloud Control, as shown in Figure 10-7, the CDB resource plan displays with the status of Active. (Note that EM Cloud Control 13c [13.1] does not show the memory limit parameters.)

NOTE
As mentioned, it is also possible to configure the Resource Manager from Oracle SQL Developer.

```
SQL> col pluggable_database    heading "Pluggable Database|Directive" for a25
SQL> col directive_type        heading "Directive|Type" for a20
SQL> col shares                heading "Shares" for 99999
SQL> col utilization_limit     heading "Util|Lmit" for 99999
SQL> col parallel_server_limit heading "Par|Limit" for 99999
SQL> col memory_min            heading "Memory|Min" for 99999
SQL> col memory_limit          heading "Memory|Limit" for 99999
SQL> select pluggable_database
  2  , directive_type
  3  , shares
  4  , utilization_limit
  5  , parallel_server_limit
  6  , memory_min
  7  , memory_limit
  8  from dba_cdb_rsrc_plan_directives
  9  where plan='CDB_RPLAN';

Pluggable Database         Directive                      Util   Par Memory Memory
Directive                  Type                  Shares   Lmit Limit   Min  Limit
-------------------------- -------------------- ------- ------ ----- ------ ------
ORA$DEFAULT_PDB_DIRECTIVE  DEFAULT_DIRECTIVE          2     90    50
ORA$AUTOTASK               AUTOTASK                   2     80    80
PDB1                       PDB                        1     70    50     20     40
PDB2                       PDB                        4    100   100     50     80

SQL>
```

FIGURE 10-6. *Review CDB resource plan directives*

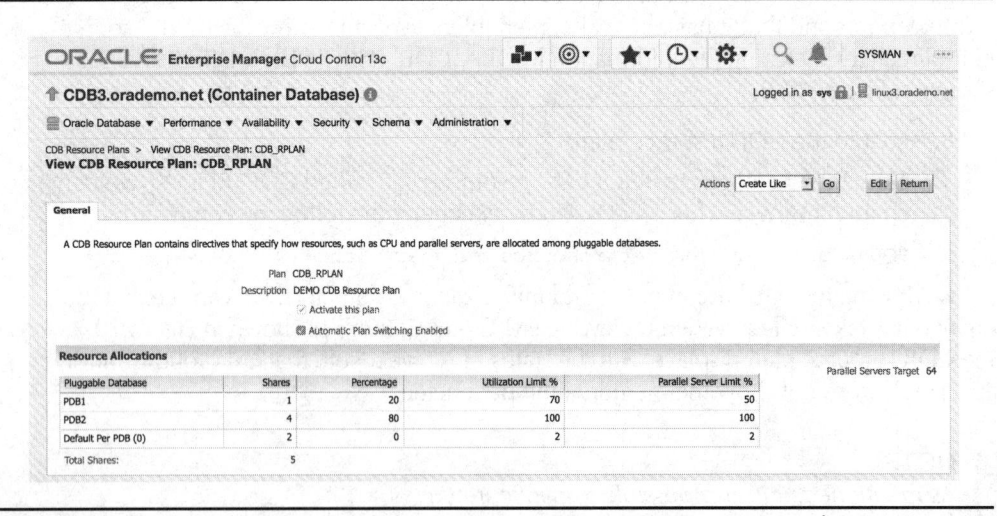

FIGURE 10-7. *EM Cloud Control showing current active CDB resource plan*

In the preceding example, the different commands to be executed were listed as discrete steps. However, instead of running each of these individually, you can group them together in one code block and execute it as a single unit. The following code block shows this, grouping all the commands described in steps 1–7; once executed, you will have created the CDB resource plan, ready to be activated when needed.

```
BEGIN
  dbms_resource_manager.create_pending_area();
  dbms_resource_manager.create_cdb_plan(
        plan =>'CDB_RPLAN'
      , comment => 'DEMO CDB Resource Plan');
  dbms_resource_manager.create_cdb_plan_directive(plan => 'CDB_RPLAN'
      , comment => 'PDB1 Plan Directive'
      , pluggable_database => 'PDB1'
      , shares => 1
      , utilization_limit => 70
      , parallel_server_limit => 50
      , memory_min => 20
      , memory_limit => 40);
  dbms_resource_manager.create_cdb_plan_directive(plan => 'CDB_RPLAN'
      , comment => 'PDB2 Plan Directive'
      , pluggable_database => 'PDB2'
      , shares => 4
      , utilization_limit => 100
      , parallel_server_limit => 100
      , memory_min => 50
      , memory_limit => 80);
  dbms_resource_manager.update_cdb_default_directive(
        plan => 'CDB_RPLAN'
      , new_shares => 2
      , new_utilization_limit => 90
      , new_parallel_server_limit => 50);
  dbms_resource_manager.update_cdb_autotask_directive(
        plan => 'CDB_RPLAN'
      , new_shares => 2
      , new_utilization_limit => 80
      , new_parallel_server_limit => 80);
  dbms_resource_manager.validate_pending_area();
  dbms_resource_manager.submit_pending_area();
END;
```

Modifying a CDB Resource Plan

The CDB resource plan can be updated using the following DBMS_RESOURCE_MANAGER procedures:

- UPDATE_CDB_PLAN
- UPDATE_CDB_PLAN_DIRECTIVE

> **NOTE**
> *The `UPDATE_CDB_PLAN` enables the update only of the comments associated with the plan.*

Updating a plan directive is similar to creating a new one, in that you have to specify PLAN and PLUGGABLE_DATABASE (directive) values to indicate which directive you would like to update. To modify the shares, comments, or limits, your parameters are all prefixed with NEW. As such, there is no need to specify the old and new values—only the new need to be specified. For example, to update the directive for PDB1 in the previously created CDB resource plan (CDB_RPLAN) and increase the `utilization_limit` from 70 to 80 percent, we can execute the following:

```
BEGIN
   dbms_resource_manager.create_pending_area();
   dbms_resource_manager.update_cdb_plan_directive(
         plan => 'CDB_RPLAN'
       , pluggable_database => 'PDB1'
       , new_utilization_limit => 80);
   dbms_resource_manager.validate_pending_area();
   dbms_resource_manager.submit_pending_area();
END;
```

Executing this update will take effect immediately, even on an active plan. It is also possible to add CDB resource plan directives at any time for a PDB using the `CREATE_CDB_PLAN_DIRECTIVE` procedure.

Enabling or Removing a CDB Resource Plan

It is possible to have more than one CDB resource plan in a container database, but only one can be active at any given point in time. The following commands can be used to enable or, when no longer required, remove a CDB resource plan.

Enable a CDB Resource Plan   To enable a CDB resource plan, use the following:

```
SQL> alter system set resource_manager_plan = CDB_RPLAN;
```

Or set `resource_manager_plan` to an empty value to disable it:

```
SQL> alter system set resource_manager_plan = '';
```

It is also possible to enable the CDB resource plan using a scheduler window, because it is commonplace for the resource usage profile of an environment to differ between day and night. The following example demonstrates how to enable a resource plan based on a scheduler window. The CDB resource plan name in this instance is DAYTIME_RPLAN:

```
BEGIN
  dbms_scheduler.create_window (
          window_name => 'DAYTIME_WINDOW',
          resource_plan => 'DAYTIME_RPLAN',
          start_date => '28-MAR-15 7:30:00AM',
          repeat_interval => 'freq=daily',
          duration => interval '12' hour);
END;
```

Remove a CDB Resource Plan   To remove a CDB resource plan, use the following:

```
BEGIN
    dbms_resource_manager.create_pending_area();
    dbms_resource_manager.DELETE_CDB_PLAN('CDB_RPLAN');
    dbms_resource_manager.submit_pending_area();
END;
```

Removing a CDB Resource Plan Directive

When performing plug-in/unplug operations on PDBs, you may encounter a requirement to remove CDB resource plan directives, although in some cases you will want to keep directives, particularly when you know you are going to plug in the PDB again. To remove a directive, the DELETE_CDB_PLAN_DIRECTIVE procedure can be used. Following is a basic example of this, in which we remove the CDB resource plan directive for the PDB1 database:

```
BEGIN
    dbms_resource_manager.create_pending_area();
    dbms_resource_manager.DELETE_CDB_PLAN_DIRECTIVE(
        plan => 'CDB_RPLAN'
        pluggable_database => 'PDB1');
    dbms_resource_manager.submit_pending_area();
END;
```

Creating a CDB Resource Plan Using PDB Profiles

We've covered how to create CDB resource plans and directives associated with individual PDBs, but what if you have a group of PDBs?

The steps to create a CDB resource plan using PDB profiles are very similar to those that we have already detailed. In short, this method is appropriate when you want to set specific directives for a resource plan that applies to a number of PDBs—in this case, you can think of the PDBs as being grouped together. One key step is required when following this method: you have to set the PDB initialization parameter DB_PERFORMANCE_PROFILE, which requires you to close and reopen the PDB once it has been set. The following commands illustrate how this can be done:

```
SQL> connect / as sysdba
SQL> alter session set container=PDB1;
SQL> alter system set db_performance_profile='IMPORTANT_PDBS' scope=spfile;
SQL> alter pluggable database close;
SQL> alter pluggable database open;
SQL> show parameter db_performance_profile
```

You can create a CDB resource plan using a PDB profile using the CREATE_CDB_PROFILE_DIRECTIVE procedure of the DBMS_RESOURCE_MANAGER package. The principles are the same as in the earlier example, but instead of specifying the PLUGGABLE_DATABASES parameter, you specify the PROFILE. Working from the earlier example, instead of using the individual PDB1 and PDB2 when the directives are created, we create two profiles: IMPORTANT_PDBS and LOWPRIORITY_PDBS. Note that in this example, the default and autotask directives are left as-is, using the default values, although you may update them if required.

```
BEGIN
   dbms_resource_manager.create_pending_area();
   dbms_resource_manager.create_cdb_plan(
         plan =>'CDB_RPLAN2'
        ,comment => 'DEMO CDB Resource Plan using PDB Profiles');
   dbms_resource_manager.create_cdb_profile_directive(
         plan => 'CDB_RPLAN2'
       , comment => 'Low Priority PDBs Directive'
       , profile => 'LOWPRIORITY_PDBS'
       , shares => 1
       , utilization_limit => 70
       , parallel_server_limit => 50
       , memory_min => 20
       , memory_limit => 40);
   dbms_resource_manager.create_cdb_profile_directive(
         plan => 'CDB_RPLAN2'
       , comment => 'High Priority PDBs Directive'
       , profile => 'IMPORTANT_PDBS'
       , shares => 4
       , utilization_limit => 100
       , parallel_server_limit => 100
       , memory_min => 50
       , memory_limit => 80);
   dbms_resource_manager.validate_pending_area();
   dbms_resource_manager.submit_pending_area();
END;
```

Once the CDB resource plan using PDB profiles has been created, you can review the directive details by selecting from DBA_CDB_RSRC_PLAN_DIRECTIVES. The following SQL query can be used for this purpose; make sure you include the `pluggable_database` and `profile` columns:

```
SQL> select plan, pluggable_database, profile, directive_type, shares,
       utilization_limit, parallel_server_limit, memory_min, memory_limit
     from dba_cdb_rsrc_plan_directives
     where plan='CDB_RPLAN2';
```

Removing a CDB Resource Plan Directive for a PDB Profile   The same procedure, DELETE_CDB_PLAN_DIRECTIVE, is used to remove a directive for a specific PDB or a PDB profile. But instead of specifying the `pluggable_database` parameter, the `profile` parameter should be used, with the profile name being the assigned value. In this example we remove the LOWPRIORITY_PDBS directive:

```
BEGIN
    dbms_resource_manager.create_pending_area();
    dbms_resource_manager.DELETE_CDB_PLAN_DIRECTIVE(
        plan => 'CDB_RPLAN'
        profile => 'LOWPRIORITY_PDBS');
    dbms_resource_manager.submit_pending_area();
END;
```

The PDB Resource Plan

When a CDB resource plan allocates resources to a PDB, the PDB resource plan then goes one step further and distributes them based on its own directives. Using this method gives you a more fine-grained level of resource management control and flexibility.

Creating a PDB resource plan is similar to the method used for Resource Manager with non-CDB configurations. The DBMS_RESOURCE_MANAGER package is invoked for this purpose, and a requirement for the following high-level steps to be performed:

- Creation of consumer groups (using CREATE_CONSUMER_GROUP)
- Setting the consumer group mapping (using SET_CONSUMER_GROUP_MAPPING)
- Creation of a PDB resource plan (using CREATE_PLAN)
- Creation of a PDB resource plan directives (using CREATE_PLAN_DIRECTIVE)

> **NOTE**
> *When performing these tasks, you must be connected to the PDB for which you are creating the PDB resource plan. To be clear, a PDB resource plan will manage the workload and resource allocations within a single PDB only.*

You should be aware of a number of PDB resource plan restrictions, including these:

- It cannot contain subplans.
- It can include a maximum of eight consumer groups.
- It cannot have a multiple-level scheduling policy.

In the next section, we will show you the steps to create a PDB resource plan. The concepts are the same as for non-CDB environments, but for more detail on consumer groups, plan directives, and mappings refer to the Oracle Database 12c documentation.

Creating a PDB Resource Plan

To bring it all together, we'll now work through how we can create a PDB resource plan. Extending the CDB resource plan, CDB_RPLAN, created earlier, in this example we will focus on a PDB called PDB2 and create a basic PDB resource plan called PDB_RPLAN. A high-level view of this configuration is shown in Figure 10-8.

We can now map out the guaranteed and estimated resource allocations:

- For consumer group GROUP_A:
  - Will be guaranteed 16 percent of the total resources: (4/5 shares) 80% × (1/5 shares) 20%
  - Limited to 20 percent of the total resources: (80% × 20%)
- For consumer group GROUP_B:
  - Will be guaranteed 48 percent of the total resources: (4/5 shares) 80% × (3/5 shares) 60%
  - Limited to 80 percent of the total resources: (80% × 100%)
- For consumer group OTHER (OTHER_GROUPS):
  - Will be guaranteed 16 percent of the total resources: (4/5 shares) 80% × (1/5 shares) 20%
  - Limited to 32 percent of the total resources: (80% × 40%)

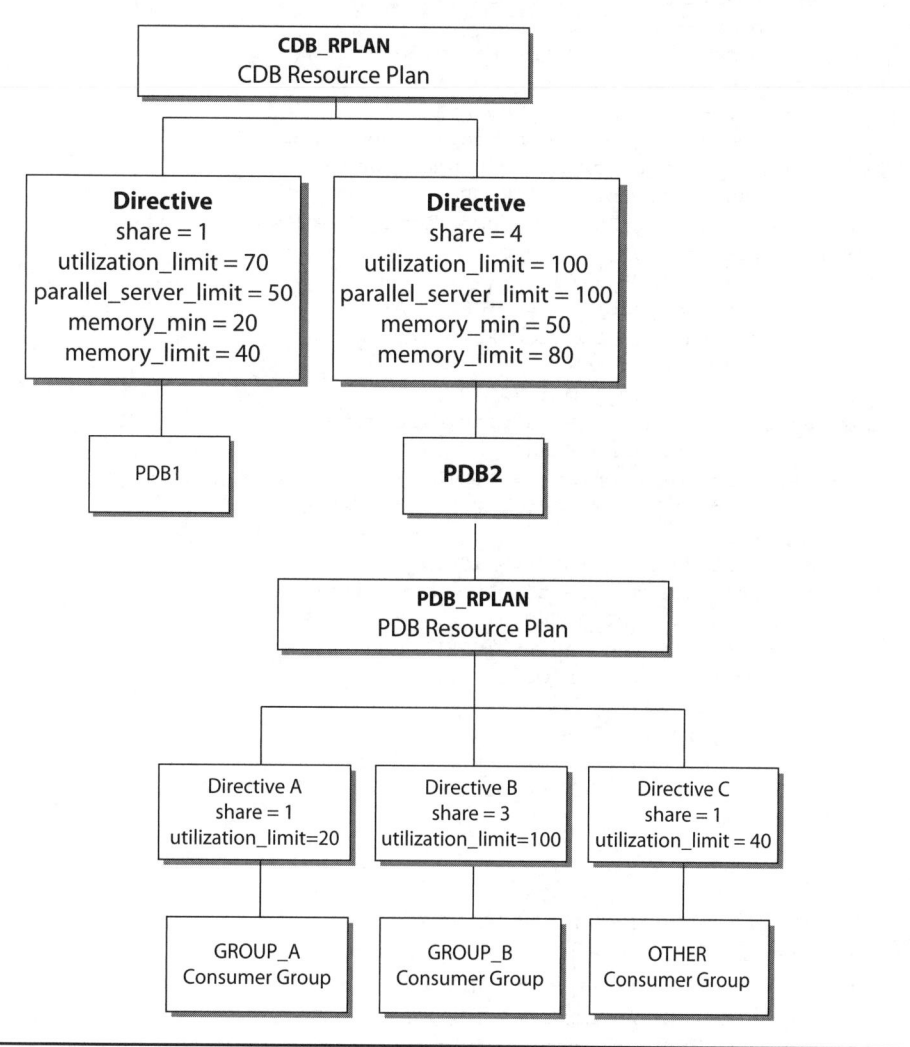

```
                    ┌─────────────────────────┐
                    │      CDB_RPLAN          │
                    │   CDB Resource Plan     │
                    └─────────────────────────┘
                      │                    │
         ┌────────────────────────┐  ┌────────────────────────────┐
         │      Directive         │  │      Directive             │
         │     share = 1          │  │     share = 4              │
         │ utilization_limit = 70 │  │ utilization_limit = 100    │
         │ parallel_server_limit  │  │ parallel_server_limit =100 │
         │        = 50            │  │                            │
         │ memory_min = 20        │  │ memory_min = 50            │
         │ memory_limit = 40      │  │ memory_limit = 80          │
         └────────────────────────┘  └────────────────────────────┘
                     │                        │
                  ┌──────┐                 ┌──────┐
                  │ PDB1 │                 │ PDB2 │
                  └──────┘                 └──────┘
                                              │
                              ┌─────────────────────────┐
                              │      PDB_RPLAN          │
                              │   PDB Resource Plan     │
                              └─────────────────────────┘
                                      │
         ┌──────────────┬──────────────┬──────────────┐
  ┌──────────────┐  ┌──────────────┐  ┌──────────────┐
  │ Directive A  │  │ Directive B  │  │ Directive C  │
  │  share = 1   │  │  share = 3   │  │  share = 1   │
  │utilization_  │  │utilization_  │  │utilization_  │
  │ limit=20     │  │ limit=100    │  │ limit = 40   │
  └──────────────┘  └──────────────┘  └──────────────┘
         │                 │                 │
  ┌──────────────┐  ┌──────────────┐  ┌──────────────┐
  │   GROUP_A    │  │   GROUP_B    │  │    OTHER     │
  │Consumer Group│  │Consumer Group│  │Consumer Group│
  └──────────────┘  └──────────────┘  └──────────────┘
```

FIGURE 10-8. *Resource Manager: CDB and PDB resource plan overview*

The code example that follows documents how this PDB resource plan can be created. Note that it does not show how users are assigned to the consumer groups; that is achieved with the DBMS_RESOURCE_MANAGER_PRIVS package, and specifically the GRANT_SWITCH_CONSUMER_GROUP procedure.

```
BEGIN
  dbms_resource_manager.clear_pending_area();
  dbms_resource_manager.create_pending_area();
```

```
  dbms_resource_manager.create_plan(
           plan =>'PDB_RPLAN'
         , comment => 'DEMO PDB Resource Plan');
  dbms_resource_manager.create_consumer_group(
           consumer_group =>   'GROUP_A'
         , comment => 'Demo Consumer Group A - Low Priority');
  dbms_resource_manager.create_consumer_group(
           consumer_group =>   'GROUP_B'
         , comment => 'Demo Consumer Group B - High Priority');
  dbms_resource_manager.create_plan_directive(
           plan => 'PDB_RPLAN'
         , group_or_subplan => 'GROUP_A'
         , comment => 'For Low Priority Users'
         , shares => 1
         , utilization_limit => 70);
  dbms_resource_manager.create_plan_directive(
           plan => 'PDB_RPLAN'
         , group_or_subplan => 'GROUP_B'
         , comment => 'For High Priority Users'
         , shares => 3
         , utilization_limit => 100);
  dbms_resource_manager.create_plan_directive(
           plan => 'PDB_RPLAN'
         , group_or_subplan => 'OTHER_GROUPS'
         , comment => 'For Other Users'
         , shares => 1
         , utilization_limit => 40);
  dbms_resource_manager.validate_pending_area();
  dbms_resource_manager.submit_pending_area();
END;
```

> **NOTE**
> *If a non-CDB is plugged into a CDB as a PDB, it will function the same as before, as long as there are no subplans, all resource allocations are at one level (level 1), and the consumer groups total does not exceed eight. If there are any violations, or any of these three mentioned restrictions exist, the plan will be converted and its status will be updated to LEGACY. It is recommended that converted plans with the status of LEGACY be reviewed thoroughly, because they may behave differently than expected.*

Enable or Disable a PDB Resource Plan

To enable or disable a PDB resource plan, you update the initialization parameter RESOURCE_MANAGER_PLAN for the specified PDB. This can be done by executing the `alter system` command while the current container is set to the PDB whose plan you want to update (enable or disable). As with the CDB resource plan, to disable the PDB resource plan, you set the RESOURCE_MANAGER_PLAN parameter to an empty value. To enable or disable the PDB resource plan—PDB_RPLAN for PDB1 in the following example—you use the following commands:

```
SQL> connect / as sysdba
SQL> alter session set container=PDB1;
SQL> alter system set RESOURCE_MANAGER_PLAN='PDB_RPLAN';
```

Use this to disable the plan:

```
SQL> alter system set RESOURCE_MANAGER_PLAN='';
```

Removing a PDB Resource Plan

To remove a PDB resource plan, use the DELETE_PLAN procedure in the DBMS_RESOURCE_MANAGER package. So, to remove the PDB resource plan created in the preceding example, PDB_RPLAN, execute the following from PDB1:

```
BEGIN
    dbms_resource_manager.create_pending_area();
    dbms_resource_manager.DELETE_PLAN('PDB_RPLAN');
    dbms_resource_manager.submit_pending_area();
END;
```

Manage PDB Memory and I/O via Initialization Parameters

You might have noticed that in Oracle Database 12c, Automatic Shared Memory Management (ASMM) is preferred over the use of Automatic Memory Management (AMM). There are a number of reasons for this, which are beyond the scope of this book, but it is recommended that you review the method you are using. If you are unfamiliar with HugePages, consult Oracle Support Note 361468.1. This functionality can have a significant impact on an environment and may assist in more effective memory management and usage.

As mentioned earlier in the chapter, one of the new features introduced in Oracle Database 12c Release 2 is the option to specify memory limits as part of the CDB resource plan directives. The two parameters mentioned previously are MEMORY_MIN and MEMORY_LIMIT, but it does not stop there; you can also control memory allocations for PDBs by using initialization parameters.

PDB Memory Allocations

You can set a number of initialization parameters at the PDB level, including some specifically related to memory. Do take caution when setting these values, however, because you need to ensure that you have sufficient memory allocated for the CDB and the rest of the PDBs contained within it. The following parameters can be configured:

- **DB_CACHE_SIZE**   Minimum guaranteed buffer cache for the PDB.

- **SHARED_POOL_SIZE**   Minimum shared pool size for the PDB. If not set at the PDB level, there is no limit to the amount of shared pool it can use (though it is limited to the CDB's shared pool size).

- **PGA_AGGREGATE_TARGET**   Maximum PGA size for the PDB.

- **SGA_MIN_SIZE**   Minimum SGA size for the PDB. This new parameter introduced in 12.2 applies to PDBs only. If this is set on a CDB level it will be ignored for the CDB but will be inherited by all PDBs in the CDB. It is not recommended to set the total sum of SGA_MIN_SIZE for all PDBs higher than 50 percent of the CDB SGA size.

- **SGA_TARGET**   Maximum SGA size for the PDB.

These parameters can be set for a specific PDB by having that PDB set as the current container, prior to running the following ALTER SYSTEM commands:

```
SQL> connect / as sysdba
SQL> alter session set container=PDB1;
SQL> alter system set SGA_MIN_SIZE=1G scope=both;
```

Limit PDB I/O

I/O can also be limited for PDBs in a similar way to how memory is controlled—at the PDB level using initialization parameters. There are two key parameters to be aware of. Both have a value of 0 by default, which actually disables any I/O limits being imposed on the PDB, and they are specific to PDBs, meaning they cannot be set in a CDB:

- **MAX_IOPS**   Specifies a limit of I/O operations per second in the PDB

- **MAX_MBPS**   Limits the megabytes per second operations in a PDB

> **NOTE**
> *The memory and I/O limit parameters can be set using the `ALTER SYSTEM` command while connected to a PDB as the current container.*

Instance Caging

Resource Manager can be configured only for one instance on a server, because it is not aware of what other instances on the same machine are doing. To overcome this limitation, *instance caging* was introduced in Oracle Database 11*g* (11.2). Prior to Oracle Database 12*c*, when multiple databases (non-CDB) were consolidated onto one server, instance caging was used to manage and distribute CPU resources among database instances. However, with the introduction of multitenant, consolidation can be taken a step further, in that these non-CDBs can be converted to PDBs. This opens the possibility of administering CPU resource allocation inside the database instance using Resource Manager.

Instance caging, together with Resource Manager, is an effective way to manage multiple database instances on a single server.

Instance Caging to Resource Manager

As mentioned earlier in the chapter, prior to 12*c*, instance caging could be used when consolidating non-CDB environments. With multitenant, this can be further enhanced by converting the non-CDBs to PDBs and making use of Resource Manager to distribute the resource between the PDBs. In this example, we will show you how this can be done.

In the next example, two non-CDB databases are located on the same server. They are CRMDEV and CRMREP. These databases use instance caging, where `CPU_COUNT` is set to 3 on the CRMREP reporting database and 1 on the CRMDEV development. The two databases are converted from non-CDB to PDBs (see Chapter 9 for more detail on how to convert a non-CDB to a PDB) in a new container database called CDB3. In this example, we will distribute the resource as shown in the following table. Notice that the default directive is also listed for completeness: the default SHARE is 1 and the `UTILIZATION_LIMIT` is 100.

PDB	SHARE	UTILIZATION_LIMIT
CRMDEV	1	25
CRMREP	3	75
DEFAULT	1	100

We use a total of four shares, and we distribute this in the same way that the `CPU_COUNT` was distributed. Using the `UTILIZATION_LIMIT` is not strictly necessary (it enforces a hard limit). Figure 10-9 shows the resource plan to be implemented.

```
                    CRM_RPLAN
                  CDB Resource Plan
```

```
   Directive              Directive           Default Directive
   share = 1              share = 3              share = 1
utilization_limit = 25  utilization_limit = 75  utilization_limit = 100
```

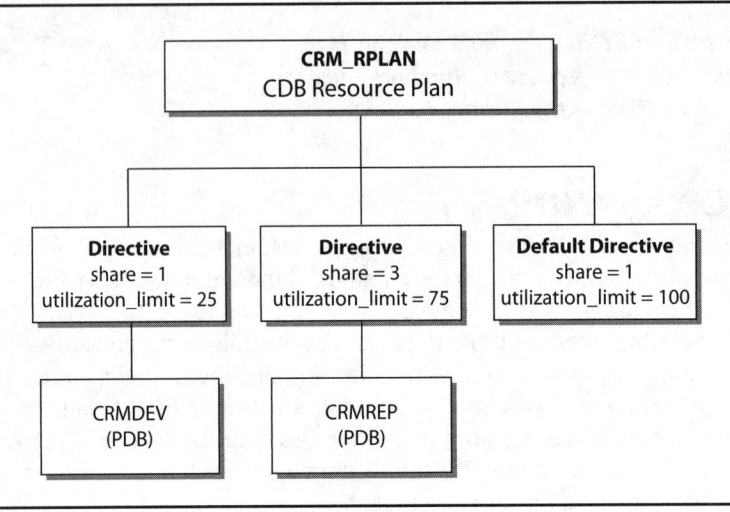

```
     CRMDEV                 CRMREP
     (PDB)                  (PDB)
```

FIGURE 10-9. *Non-CDB instance caging to CDB resource plan*

The following code example can be used to create a resource plan called CRM_RPLAN for container database CDB3 running two PDBs. The code block is executed while connected to the CDB$ROOT:

```
BEGIN
   dbms_resource_manager.create_pending_area;
   dbms_resource_manager.create_cdb_plan(plan =>'CRM_RPLAN');
   dbms_resource_manager.create_cdb_plan_directive(plan => 'CRM_RPLAN'
       , comment => 'CRMDEV Plan Directive'
       , pluggable_database => 'CRMDEV'
       , shares => 1
       , utilization_limit => 25);
   dbms_resource_manager.create_cdb_plan_directive(plan => 'CRM_RPLAN'
       , comment => 'CRMREP Plan Directive'
       , pluggable_database => 'CRMREP'
       , shares => 3
       , utilization_limit => 75);
   dbms_resource_manager.submit_pending_area;
END;
```

Monitoring Resource Manager

Monitoring Resource Manager can be challenging. Luckily, there are a number of ways to extract information with regard to how resources are used and distributed in the database. The following options are available to help you in this area:

- Oracle Enterprise Manager – Database Express 12c (EM Database Express 12c)
- Oracle Enterprise Manager Cloud Control (EM Cloud Control)

- Oracle SQL Developer
- SQL commands via SQL*Plus

Yes, SQL commands via SQL*Plus is included. At the end of the day, the other tools are running SQL statements to extract the required information required and then display it in a nicely formatted manner. Running SQL scripts might be a bit daunting for some, but once you build up a number of monitoring scripts to review your implementation of Resource Manager, you will find it is a quick and easy way to get an overview of the current status.

Viewing the Resource Plan and Plan Directives

The fastest ways to get information about the CDB resource plan and plan directives are to use the following views while connected to the CDB$ROOT:

- `DBA_CDB_RSRC_PLANS`
- `DBA_CDB_RSRC_PLAN_DIRECTIVES`

It is possible to view the information from EM Cloud Control or even EM Database Express, as shown in Figure 10-10, for example.

Monitoring PDBs Managed by Resource Manager

For monitoring, nothing beats a good graphical representation of statistics. Using EM Cloud Control or EM Database Express is highly recommended. Figure 10-11 is a

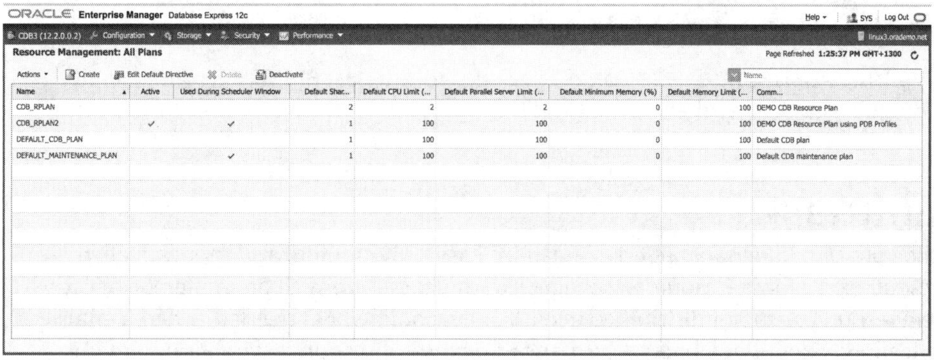

FIGURE 10-10. *Monitoring using Oracle EM Database Express*

286 Oracle Database 12c Release 2 Multitenant

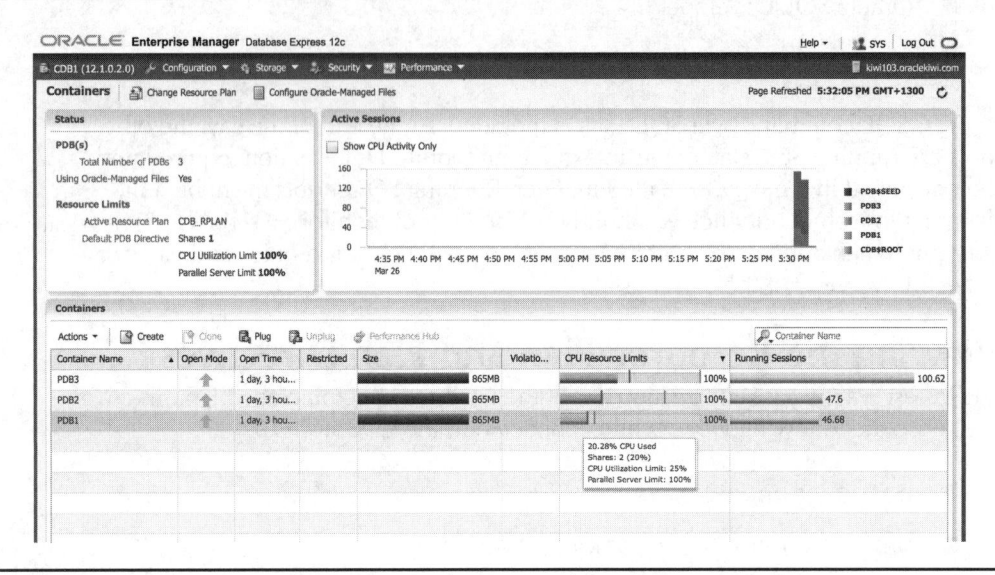

FIGURE 10-11. *Monitoring using Oracle EM Database Express 12.1*

perfect example of how EM Database Express can be used to get an overview of resource usage quickly.

It is also possible to make use of the dynamic performance views to monitor the results of a Resource Manager implementation. The following views can be used:

V$RSRCPDBMETRIC   Current statistics for the last minute are shown per PDB. One record is displayed per PDB, including one row for the CDB$ROOT. Note that this view is available only from Oracle Database 12c Release 2.

V$RSRCPDBMETRIC_HISTORY   Statistics for the last 60 minutes are displayed per PDB (including the CDB$ROOT).

Summary

At the core of multitenant are consolidation, easy provisioning, and more effective use of resources. Without Resource Manager, we might end up with an implementation where resources are not distributed evenly or available where needed, where certain applications experience bad performance because of resource starvation. It might sound easy, but careful planning and ongoing monitoring is highly recommended. Workloads change, and it is the job of the DBA to ensure Resource Manager is configured and updated when and as needed. It is recommended to start with a less complex configuration, monitor it over a period of time, and adjust it as needed. Having multiple resource plans on a CDB and PDB level is acceptable, and with the use of scheduled windows, you can enable and disable these plans as required.

This brings us to other interesting subjects: Data Guard, the sharing of data between PDBs, and then, last but not least, moving of data using logical replication. These might seem unrelated to resource management, but if you look a bit closer, you will realize that a standby database can be used to offload certain application operations, especially when Active Data Guard is in play. The end result may free up valuable resources on your primary system and help you get more value out of your disaster recovery site.

CHAPTER 11

Data Guard

An old adage says that a DBA can get many things wrong but must never fail in one single competency: database recovery. It holds that if there is a way to restore the database to the time before the error happened, then any error is potentially reversible. This saying was coined many years ago, and the boom in overall database sizes and increased dependence of modern organizations on databases as foundational to their business operations have made it all the more true!

Over time, one additional requirement has emerged—we need *fast* database recovery. Restoring a multi-terabyte database from tapes is not something the business wants to wait for. This does not mean, however, that the good-old tape backup is a relic of a bygone era; in fact, it is still a necessary part of a sound backup plan, and we covered it in detail in Chapter 7. It just happens to be the last line of defense, reserved for massive natural disasters. In the milieu of day-to-day operations, littered with faulty disks, human errors, server crashes, and building fires, we need a faster way to recover.

Since 8*i*, Oracle Database has supported the standby database functionality; improved and enhanced through the versions, it eventually evolved into the Data Guard feature. Conceptually speaking, however, a physical standby database is merely an exact copy of the production, or primary, database. This copy, or standby, is kept constantly in recovery mode, applying archived redo from the primary, in the same way that a media recovery would happen.

This basic level of functionality was introduced in Oracle Database 8*i*, and if the database is not running on Enterprise Edition, this is all that is available. It is a proven and solid foundation but lacks facilities such as automatic redo transfer and adequate monitoring. Fortunately, third-party tools are available to help automate this process and manage these environments, such as Dbvisit Standby.

With an Oracle Database Enterprise Edition, the full Data Guard functionality is available, which includes, at the very least, automatic redo transfer, the ability to apply online redo as it is shipped, the availability of the Data Guard broker and Data Guard command line interface (DGMGRL), and the administration options included in Cloud Control and Enterprise Manager Express. In this chapter, we will cover the Enterprise Edition functionality; after all, only EE supports the multitenant option.

Data Guard supports multitenant databases, and most of the management is identical to that of a non-container database (non-CDB). In this chapter, we walk through a simple setup of a physical standby database and will then look at some of the differences that multitenant brings.

Active Data Guard Option

With the standard physical standby functionality, the standby database runs in recovery mode and is unavailable for any end user operations. However, the Active Data Guard option enables the database to be opened read-only while the recovery occurs, simultaneously, in the background, enabling users to utilize the hardware and licenses dedicated to the standby database to support various loads such as reporting or local caches.

CAUTION
There is no direct initialization parameter or setting that we can use to enable or disable Active Data Guard. It is always available to be used, irrespective of whether the server is licensed for it or not, and the Oracle Database is overly "enthusiastic" about enabling this option. So it falls to us, the DBA, as our responsibility to mitigate against enabling it unintentionally and never open the database when redo apply is active; this includes not starting the database with `startup`, *but always with* `startup mount` *instead. We might well be wise to go the extra mile and create an automated task to verify that the database is not opened with redo apply active.*
We can, however, consider using the undocumented (and thus unsupported parameter) `_query_on_physical=no` *to prevent from using the Active Data Guard option. Our hope is that Oracle will eventually make the parameter documented and supported.*

All of this is true for any Oracle 11g or 12c database, whether multitenant is in use or not. We'll see later in this chapter the impact of Active Data Guard on multitenant when we discuss the various scenarios for creating, copying, and moving pluggable databases (PDBs) and how they affect the standby.

Creating a Physical Standby

As mentioned, a standby database is essentially an identical binary copy of the source database, with some configuration differences and perhaps only a subset of the source data. As such, it's essentially a backup, so using backups and backup tools to create it is an obvious choice. From the command line, this means Recovery

Manager (RMAN), and in terms of GUI options, it means Oracle's Cloud Control, which, incidentally, also uses RMAN in the background.

Over the course of the database versions, this process has been streamlined and enhanced, and nowadays very few steps are necessary. Oracle can help us generate the required configuration files, and it can create the standby both from an existing backup and from a running database.

After the standby is created, the next steps are to set up the Data Guard configuration, set the desired level of protection, and monitor the configuration. Again, both command line (DGMGRL) and Cloud Control options are available for this purpose.

In this chapter, we go through a basic scenario, focusing on differences brought by the multitenant database.

Duplicate with RMAN

As creating a standby database is a fundamental step in a Data Guard setup, it is obviously described in depth in the *Data Guard Concepts and Administration* part of the Oracle Database documentation. However, for whatever reason, for a long time this information has been split between two locations: one regular chapter that describes the process in quite vague terms, and an appendix (Appendix E) detailing the RMAN-focused steps. In both places, Data Guard Broker is not mentioned, but it is covered in another book in the Oracle Database documentation, *Data Guard Broker*. This is quite unfortunate, because the easiest way to create a nicely working Data Guard configuration is to combine these three pieces. Multitenant brings yet another element and an additional set of documentation to consider, but we hope this chapter will serve to orient the reader.

> **NOTE**
> *For the examples listed in this chapter, the current database is called USPROD and the standby is NZPROD. The source database is already in ARCHIVELOG mode, force logging is set, and* `STANDBY_FILE_MANAGEMENT` *is set to AUTO. The servers are two distinct machines, and the databases will be placed in the same locations on both of them.*

Set Up Static Network Services

The first step is to configure static service definitions for both the primary and standby container databases. There is a single purpose in this: to enable the Data Guard console to start the database instances, as necessary, during switchover and failover operations.

We edit the listener.ora on the servers and add the static service definition. Note the addition of _DGMGRL to the database unique name, so it becomes, for example, USPROD_DGMGRL and NZPROD_DGMGRL.

```
SID_LIST_LISTENER=(SID_LIST=(SID_DESC=(SID_NAME=sid_name) (GLOBAL_
DBNAME=db_unique_name_DGMGRL.db_domain)
(ORACLE_HOME=oracle_home)))
```

Although not strictly necessary, but beneficial for administration purposes, we also add an entry to /etc/oratab for the databases to be created:

```
NZPROD:/u01/app/oracle/product/12.2/dbhome_1:N
```

Back Up the Source Database

If we want to create the standby database from backup, we must first back up the database or ensure that a recent backup is available. Note that the backup itself must be accessible from the standby server. How this is done depends on the environment, and often the tape library will actually do this for us, or we can mount the disks/SAN volumes manually as necessary.

The last option is, of course, to copy the backup files to the target server. Although this option often doesn't make much sense in a production environment, because we can use duplication from an active primary directly, it's a good idea during testing and learning; any failures and retries during the process will, therefore, not force the transfer of the entire database again and again over the network.

Set Up the Network

During the setup and management of the configuration, the Data Guard Broker establishes a connection to the primary and standby databases. We therefore need to set up USPROD and NZPROD connection strings in the tnsnames.ora on both servers. Also, when we do the initial duplication using RMAN, it needs to connect to the not-yet-created NZPROD database, so a connection to a statically defined service is required. And because we might need such connections in the future, again for either of these possibilities, we add connection strings for USPROD_DGMGRL and NZPROD_DGMGRL services to tnsnames.ora, too, on both nodes.

Copy Password File and Create a Temporary Parameter File

The standby needs an exact copy of the primary password file, so we need to be aware that a newly created file will not work, even if the SYS password is identical. Note also that the name is based on DB_UNIQUE_NAME; thus, the new name of this file is orapwNZPROD.

For a backup-based process, we manually copy the password file from the primary to the standby server. Although an active database–based duplication process will perform this copy automatically, it still needs a password file present to log in in the first place, so we still must provide it.

Next we need to create a temporary parameter file for NZPROD. The duplication will copy over the correct primary (binary) SPFILE, but for now, we just need the minimum of parameters to start up an instance. The only required entry is the DB_NAME:

```
DB_NAME=USPROD
```

We could also add DB_DOMAIN if applicable for our environment. If we are creating the standby on the same server as the primary—not a good use case for a production database, but perhaps convenient for testing—we need to specify DB_UNIQUE_NAME. This ensures that the new instance name does not clash with the source, before RMAN has the chance to set DB_UNIQUE_NAME in the SPFILE.

There are, in fact, two paths we can take with respect to generating the SPFILE for the new database. The first is to create the PFILE from the source database SPFILE (using the `CREATE PFILE` command) and then manually change the file as necessary. The second is to have RMAN create a copy of the SPFILE automatically, specifying the necessary changes in the duplicate command.

The first option is more manual and time-consuming; however, during the process we actually read the parameter file and have a chance to review the settings. We can also use the parameter file to start the instance before the duplication, and thus any incorrect paths or options are brought to our attention immediately and can be amended.

On the other hand, we can let RMAN do the magic for us, but it is very possible that some parameter will turn round and bite us, so to speak, during the duplication process. This means that we will have to clean up any files already created and restart the duplication.

One such example is `LOCAL_LISTENER`; this parameter might be set to a value other than the `LISTENER` default, and in that case, we must either create such a listener on the target and update tnsnames.ora as well, or adjust this to the correct value in the RMAN duplicate command.

Also note that the target database will want some directories to be precreated for the instance startup and for the duplication to succeed. Usually this is the audit file directory, and, for non-OMF installations, also the paths to the datafiles and online REDO:

```
mkdir -p /u01/app/oracle/admin/USPROD/adump
mkdir -p /u01/app/oracle/data/USPROD
mkdir -p /u01/app/oracle/data/FRA/USPROD/
mkdir /u01/app/oracle/data/USPROD/pdbseed
mkdir /u01/app/oracle/data/USPROD/PDB1
```

> **NOTE**
> *In a multitenant database, the datafiles are scattered among multiple subdirectories, and we have to create all of them on the target.*

Run the Duplicate Process

Let's run the duplication now. As mentioned, we are not changing the file locations, so there is no need to specify DB_FILE_NAME_CONVERT and PARAMETER_VALUE_CONVERT values, but we do have to specify NOFILENAMECHECK.

```
rman target=sys/oracle@usprod_dgmgrl
auxiliary=sys/oracle@nzprod_dgmgrl
connected to target database: USPROD (DBID=3345163260)
connected to auxiliary database: USPROD (not mounted)
RMAN> DUPLICATE TARGET DATABASE
      FOR STANDBY
      FROM ACTIVE DATABASE
      DORECOVER
      SPFILE
      SET "db_unique_name"="NZPROD"
      NOFILENAMECHECK;
```

This example uses the active database–based duplication functionality, in which RMAN essentially performs an image COPY of the database datafiles. Since the release of Oracle 12c, we can request that RMAN take a backup of the source database during the DUPLICATE command and make use of these backups.

And, of course, the least sophisticated means of getting started is simply to use backups available to RMAN and created earlier. The major advantage here is minimal impact on the primary database, because the new database's files are created from the backups. As for syntax, we simply omit the FROM ACTIVE DATABASE clause.

Choosing a Subset of the Source Database

Ever since the standby database feature was made available, there has been an option to have only a subset of the source database protected by the standby. The idea is very simple: we can offline any file we don't want to have at the target and the recovery will ignore this.

> **NOTE**
> *Subsetting is a feature used for specific use cases only. With a regular standby, we want to protect the primary from disasters, which implies that we want a full copy in this secondary location. However, sometimes a PDB may only be temporary (similar to a nologging table in a data load process), or perhaps we are just using snapshot standby for testing, so we don't need all of the PDBs for the tests. In such cases, the subsetting option makes good sense.*

Oracle Database 12*c* Multitenant provides a new syntax that achieves similar results to tablespace offline, but with a superior usage. First of all, the new syntax works at the PDB level, and, second, it has dedicated syntax for recovering from such subsetting, should we later decide we actually want the PDBs.

Unfortunately, one major aspect remains unchanged: although RMAN has the `[SKIP] TABLESPACE` clause (and now with 12*c* it also has a `[SKIP] PLUGGABLE DATABASE`, too) these are not valid for `DUPLICATE FOR STANDBY`, though they are valid for the other `DUPLICATE` option that creates an independent database copy. According to Oracle (MOS note 1174944.1), this is an intentional limitation, because "a physical standby must match the primary."

In other words, Oracle forces us to create the standby as a full copy, and only then can we remove the unnecessary pieces:

```
SQL> alter pluggable database PDB3 disable recovery;

Pluggable database altered.
```

Following this command, the PDB is still known to the target database, but its recovery flag is set to disabled, meaning that no redo is applied.

```
SQL> select con_id, name, open_mode, recovery_status from v$pdbs;

CON_ID NAME             OPEN_MODE   RECOVERY
------ ---------------- ----------  --------
     2 PDB$SEED         MOUNTED     ENABLED
     3 PDB1             MOUNTED     ENABLED
     4 PDB2             MOUNTED     ENABLED
     5 PDB3             MOUNTED     DISABLED
     6 PDB4             MOUNTED     ENABLED
```

Thanks to all this metadata still present at the standby, it's easy to add the database back again. Later in this chapter, in the section "Enabling the PDB Recovery," you'll learn more about this.

Start Data Guard Broker Processes and Set Up the Configuration

Let's now quickly go over the steps necessary to finish the standby creation. The first step in properly establishing a Data Guard environment is to configure the database to run the DMON processes that act as background agents for the Data Guard configuration. To do so, on each of the databases, we set the parameter as a common user:

```
alter system set dg_broker_start=TRUE;

System altered.
```

Now with the brokers running, we can actually create a configuration specifying the primary and the standby databases.

As a rule, when using DGMGRL, we always connect using a connection string, never locally. Although most operations work fine with a local connection (that is, by relying on ORACLE_SID of the CDB), switchovers and failovers don't. Note also that DGMGRL converts all identifiers to lowercase by default, but we can use double quotes to retain case. However, we would then have to double-quote them in all other places, as well.

```
dgmgrl sys/oracle@USPROD
DGMRGL> create configuration USNZ as
primary database is USPROD
connect identifier is USPROD;

Configuration "usnz" created with primary database "usprod"

DGMGRL> show configuration
Configuration - usnz

  Protection Mode: MaxPerformance
  Databases:
    usprod - Primary database

Fast-Start Failover: DISABLED

Configuration Status:
DISABLED
```

Next we add the standby database:

```
DGMGRL> add database NZPROD as
connect identifier is NZPROD;

Database "nzprod" added

DGMGRL> show configuration
Configuration - usnz
```

```
   Protection Mode: MaxPerformance
   Databases:
     usprod - Primary database
     nzprod  - Physical standby database

Fast-Start Failover: DISABLED

Configuration Status:
DISABLED
```

Now comes the moment of truth: enabling the configuration. In this process, Oracle sets the log shipping parameters and a few others, so this step is anything but trivial and can fail for many different reasons. In such cases, the error description is usually helpful, and we can also use the oerr utility or look it up in the Error Messages documentation book.

```
DGMGRL> enable configuration;

Enabled.

DGMGRL> show configuration

Configuration - usnz

  Protection Mode: MaxPerformance
  Members:
  usprod - Primary database
    Warning: ORA-16789: standby redo logs configured incorrectly

    nzprod - Physical standby database
      Warning: ORA-16809: multiple warnings detected for the member

Fast-Start Failover: DISABLED

Configuration Status:
WARNING   (status updated 8 seconds ago)
```

Here we can see that NZPROD has more than one warning, so let's review the list by using `show database`:

```
DGMGRL> show database NZPROD

Database - nzprod

  Role:                PHYSICAL STANDBY
  Intended State:      APPLY-ON
  Transport Lag:       0 seconds (computed 49 seconds ago)
  Apply Lag:           (unknown)
  Average Apply Rate:  (unknown)
  Real Time Query:     OFF
```

```
  Instance(s):
    NZPROD

  Database Warning(s):
    ORA-16854: apply lag could not be determined
    ORA-16857: member disconnected from redo source for longer than
specified threshold
    ORA-16789: standby redo logs configured incorrectly

Database Status:
WARNING
```

To remove the ORA-16854 and ORA-16857 warnings, we can simply issue a log switch on the primary to force a redo log to be shipped. This will update the lag and satisfy Data Guard, and, of course, once we create the standby redo logs in the next section, the changes will be applied in real time.

```
SQL> alter system switch logfile;

System altered.

DGMGRL> show configuration

Configuration - usnz

  Protection Mode: MaxPerformance
  Members:
  usprod - Primary database
    Warning: ORA-16789: standby redo logs configured incorrectly

    nzprod - Physical standby database
      Warning: ORA-16789: standby redo logs configured incorrectly

Fast-Start Failover: DISABLED

Configuration Status:
WARNING   (status updated 8 seconds ago)
```

Verify the Configuration and Fill In the Missing Pieces

The next step is to fill in the missing pieces—enabling flashback and adding standby redo logs. We can do this immediately, but let's have a look at a new diagnostic command first, which outlines the steps we need to perform.

In Oracle 12c, the VALIDATE DATABASE command has been introduced in DGMGRL. Upon execution of the command, Oracle checks various settings, along with the status of the database, and prints a comprehensive summary. It's useful during an initial setup, to remind us of steps we still have to do, as well as during the course of normal processing.

```
DGMGRL> validate database USPROD

  Database Role:      Primary database

  Ready for Switchover:  Yes

  Flashback Database Status:
    usprod:  Off

DGMGRL> validate database NZPROD

  Database Role:      Physical standby database
  Primary Database:   usprod

  Ready for Switchover:  No
  Ready for Failover:    Yes (Primary Running)

  Flashback Database Status:
    usprod:  Off
    nzprod:  Off

  ...

  Log Files Cleared:
    usprod Standby Redo Log Files:   Cleared
    nzprod Online Redo Log Files:    Cleared
    nzprod Standby Redo Log Files:   Not Available

  Current Log File Groups Configuration:
    Thread #  Online Redo Log Groups  Standby Redo Log Groups  Status
              (usprod)                (nzprod)
    1         3                       0
  Insufficient SRLs
    Warning: standby redo logs not configured for thread 1 on nzprod

  Future Log File Groups Configuration:
    Thread #  Online Redo Log Groups  Standby Redo Log Groups  Status
              (nzprod)                (usprod)
    1         3                       0
  Insufficient SRLs
    Warning: standby redo logs not configured for thread 1 on usprod
```

There is still room for improvement of the VALIDATE command, and perhaps this will come in future versions; nevertheless, it's a good tool. From its output, we can see it complains about standby redo logs and Flashback Database not being enabled.

So let's now create the standby redo logs. The steps are simple: use the same size as for the redo logs and create one more than the number of online redo log groups.

```
SQL> select distinct bytes from v$log;

    BYTES
----------
 52428800
```

On the primary, add the standby logfiles and enable flashback. The naïve approach is to add the standby redo logs with the minimal syntax required on both source and target:

```
SQL> alter database add standby logfile size 52428800; -- four times
```

Unfortunately, in using the simple syntax for adding standby redo, the logs were created but unassigned to any thread. This is not such an issue for the standby itself, because the logs will be assigned to threads as required; however, the VALIDATE command ignores such unassigned redo logs and complains that there are insufficient logs for the thread(s).

The SQL command for creating the standby redo logs enables us to specify the actual thread to assign. Using this, the assignment is preset at the time of standby log creation, fulfilling the VALIDATE command criteria and, at the same time, preventing any possible surprises should the autoallocation go awry.

Thus, if we had specified the threads explicitly, as follows,

```
SQL> alter database add standby logfile thread 1 group 4 size 52428800;
SQL> alter database add standby logfile thread 1 group 5 size 52428800;
SQL> alter database add standby logfile thread 1 group 6 size 52428800;
SQL> alter database add standby logfile thread 1 group 7 size 52428800;
```

the VALIDATE command would be satisfied with the standby redo log allocation:

```
Current Log File Groups Configuration:
  Thread #   Online Redo Log Groups   Standby Redo Log Groups Status
             (usprod)                 (nzprod)
     1          3                        4
Sufficient SRLs

Future Log File Groups Configuration:
  Thread #   Online Redo Log Groups   Standby Redo Log Groups Status
             (nzprod)                 (usprod)
     1          3                        4
Sufficient SRLs
```

We should also enable Flashback Database (see Chapter 8), so we don't need to rebuild the entire previous primary database on a failover.

Finally, we can verify the validity of the configuration with the following command, although we may need to wait a minute or so for the broker configuration to be updated:

```
DGMGRL> show configuration

Configuration - usnz

  Protection Mode: MaxPerformance
  Members:
  usprod - Primary database
    nzprod - Physical standby database

Fast-Start Failover: DISABLED

Configuration Status:
SUCCESS   (status updated 2 seconds ago)
```

We can also use a new option for the SHOW CONFIGURATION command to understand what the configuration would look like if we were to switch the database roles:

```
DGMGRL> show configuration when primary is nzprod

Configuration when nzprod is primary - usnz

Members:
  nzprod - Primary database
    usprod - Physical standby database
```

Test the Configuration

The last, and perhaps most important, step is to verify that the standby database can be used in case of a disaster or to facilitate a planned maintenance window.

NOTE
You should always start your experimentation with and learning of this functionality on a test database. Disaster recovery is a business-critical function and you need to become very familiar with all the tasks it entails, and the administration of these environments, before you depend on it for the protection of a production database.

A basic test simply consists of doing a switchover back and forth. This verifies that the redo logs are being shipped and applied, and that DGMGRL can actually connect to the databases even if they are down, using the _DGMGRL static connection strings we created earlier.

If this is a nonproduction database, we can perform the test immediately; if it's a production database, we should schedule a maintenance window to run the test. This is important as a core foundation of a thorough, planned backup, recovery, and DR strategy is to verify periodically that backups can be restored, and that applications and databases can be switched over and successfully run, from the backup data center.

In our example, we want to verify in both directions, keeping the primary in its original location once concluded, so we perform two switchovers:

```
DGMGRL> switchover to nzprod;
Performing switchover NOW, please wait...
Operation requires a connection to database "nzprod"
Connecting ...
Connected to "NZPROD"
Connected as SYSDBA.
New primary database "nzprod" is opening...
Operation requires start up of instance "USPROD" on database "usprod"
Starting instance "USPROD"...
ORACLE instance started.
Database mounted.
Connected to "USPROD"
Switchover succeeded, new primary is "nzprod"

DGMGRL> switchover to usprod;
Performing switchover NOW, please wait...
Operation requires a connection to database "usprod"
Connecting ...
Connected to "USPROD"
Connected as SYSDBA.
New primary database "usprod" is opening...
Operation requires start up of instance "NZPROD" on database "nzprod"
Starting instance "NZPROD"...
ORACLE instance started.
Database mounted.
Connected to "NZPROD"
Switchover succeeded, new primary is "usprod"
```

TIP
To deepen your knowledge and familiarity with Data Guard, we recommend doing more tests, although most of them are likely to be limited to test databases. Give special attention to the multitenant scenarios described in this chapter, which are also new to us and quite often require manual intervention.

Further Configuration

Now it's time to review additional settings available in Data Guard. We might want to change the protection mode, set up an observer, and configure fast start failover. Or perhaps we want to change the RMAN retention policy to account for the standby when considering archive logs eligible for deletion. These are but a few of the many useful options available to explore. However, these are beyond the scope of this book, so we recommend again reviewing the Data Guard documentation for this material.

Create a Standby with Cloud Control

Creation of the standby using RMAN is a well-tested and proven process, but Enterprise Manager Cloud Control also has powerful capabilities, including a nice step-by-step wizard. We can get to the wizard by choosing the Availability menu (see Figure 11-1), in which both MAA Advisor and Add Standby Database options have links to the wizard.

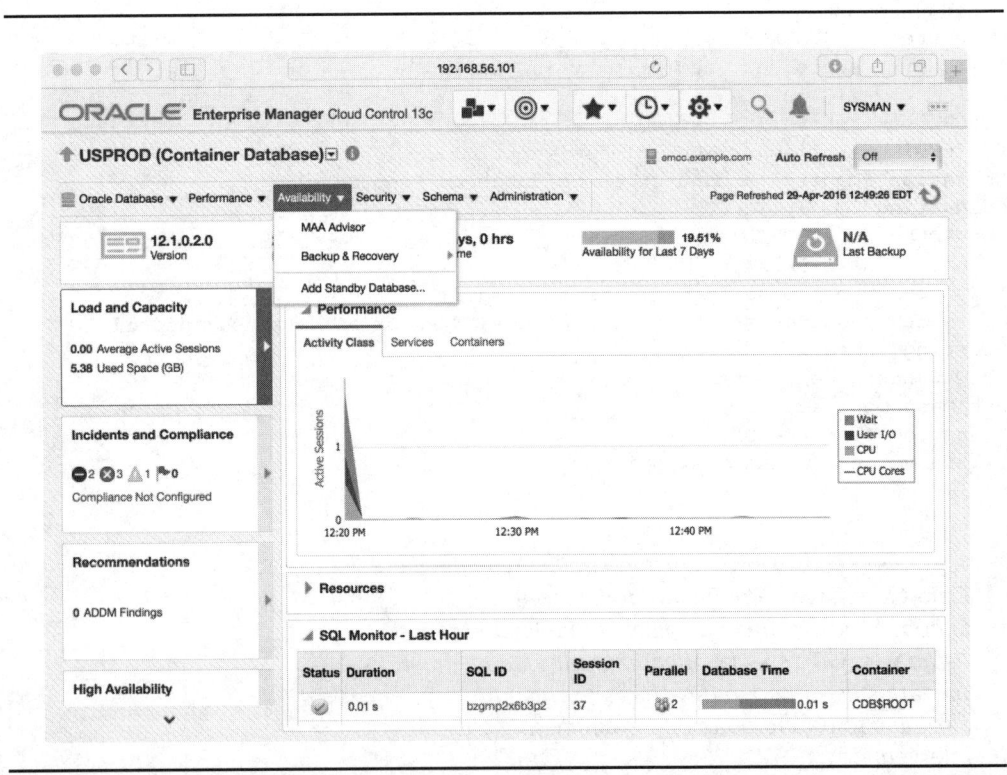

FIGURE 11-1. *The database home page*

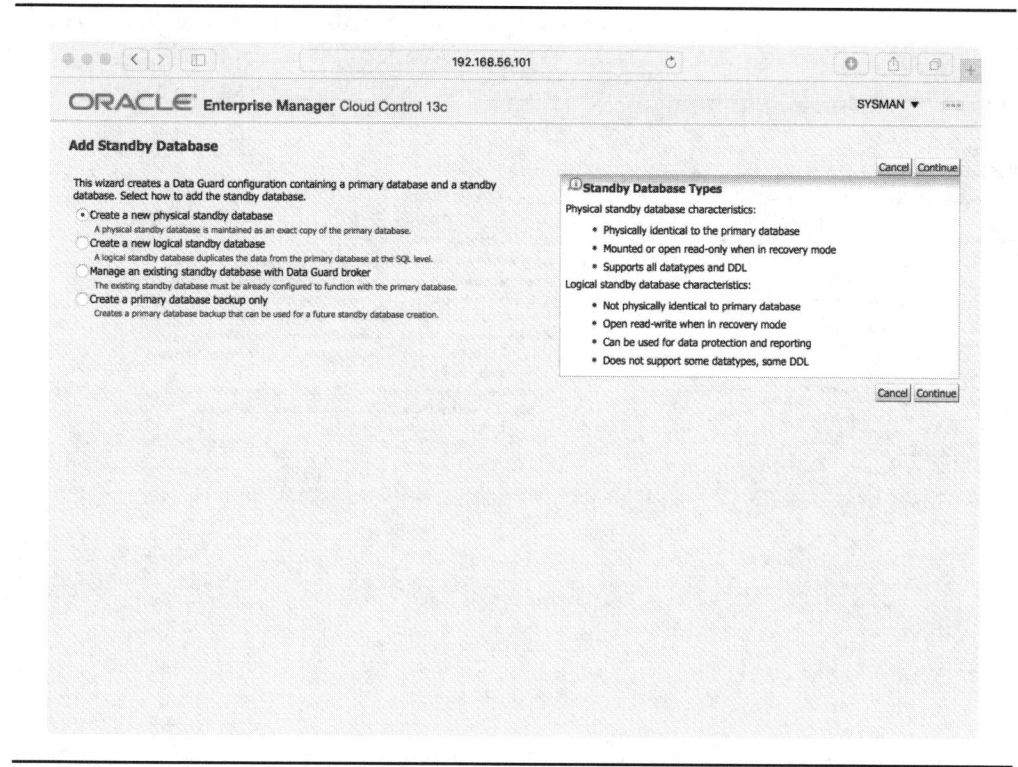

FIGURE 11-2. *The Add Standby Database wizard start page*

The wizard covers both physical and logical standbys. It can also register an existing standby—for example, one that we created manually using the steps we outlined earlier, as shown in Figure 11-2.

A general grievance with Cloud Control is the time it takes EM developers to catch up with the features that the database itself offers. One such example is shown

306 Oracle Database 12c Release 2 Multitenant

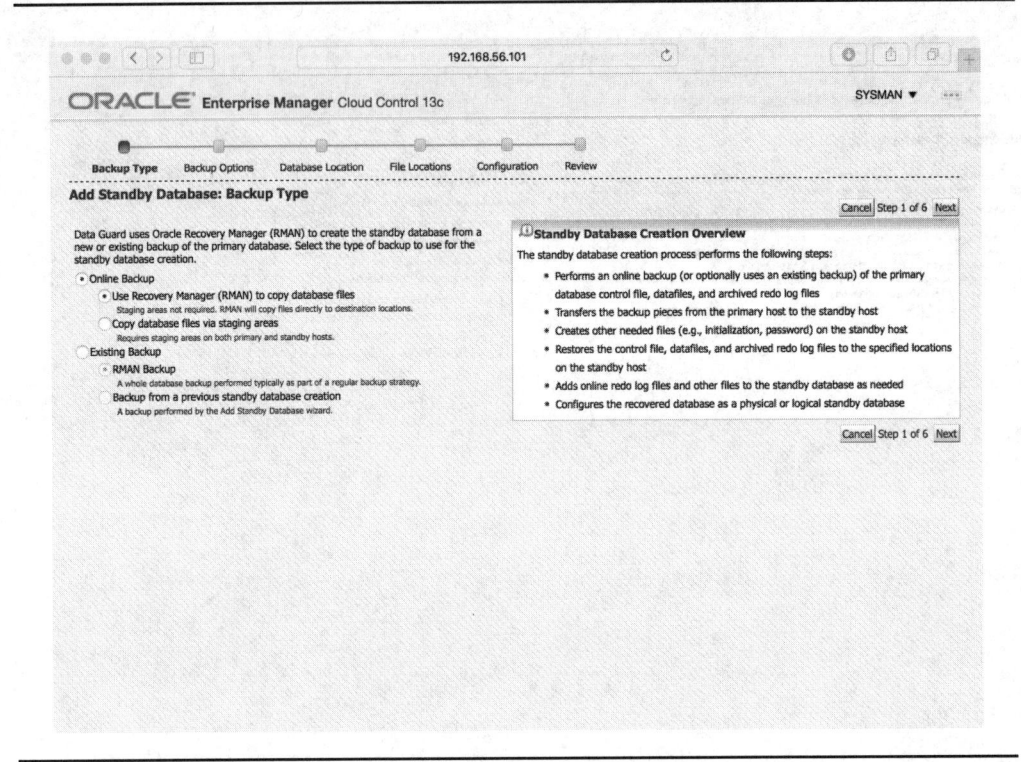

FIGURE 11-3. *Selecting a backup type page*

in Figure 11-3, where there is no option for using backup set for the duplication from an active database.

Figure 11-4 shows various options for the backup, and as we have selected active database duplication, there is really not much to configure. A nice touch is that EM will create the standby redo logs for us.

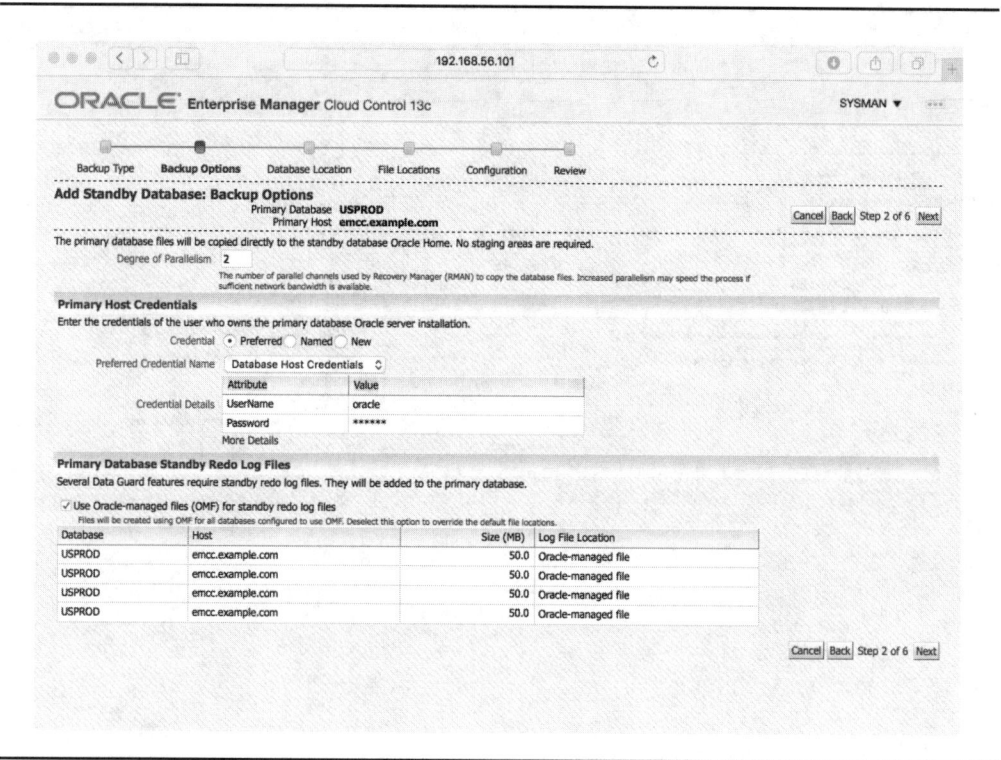

FIGURE 11-4. *Selecting backup options*

In the end (Figure 11-5), a job is created that performs the actual work of creating the standby database and setting up the Data Guard configuration, including the broker. Note that both EM and DGMGRL use the same DG Broker configuration, so it is possible to monitor and manage the configuration using either tool.

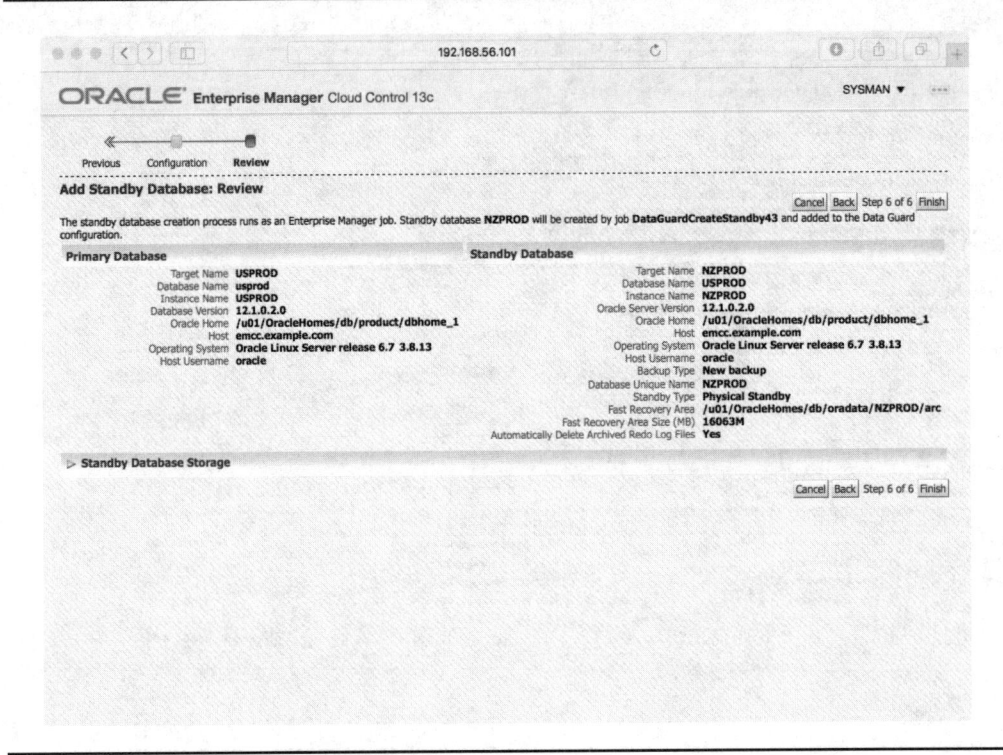

FIGURE 11-5. *Reviewing the job*

After the standby is created, the Availability menu contains new options. The Data Guard Administration page shown in Figure 11-6 displays a overview of the configuration status.

Managing a Physical Standby in a Multitenant Environment

At the basic level, a container database is still a single database, and physical standby works at the whole CDB level. That means that all the components we were used to managing in a non-CDB environment still apply and are done at the root level.

To begin with, this means that both DGMGRL and Cloud Control need to connect to the root container and issue all the commands there. This also includes parameters and options such as protection mode, standby redo logs, transport mode, real-time apply, read-only open mode, observer, and observer thresholds—and many others. It is a similar case with monitoring; the new Oracle Database 12c

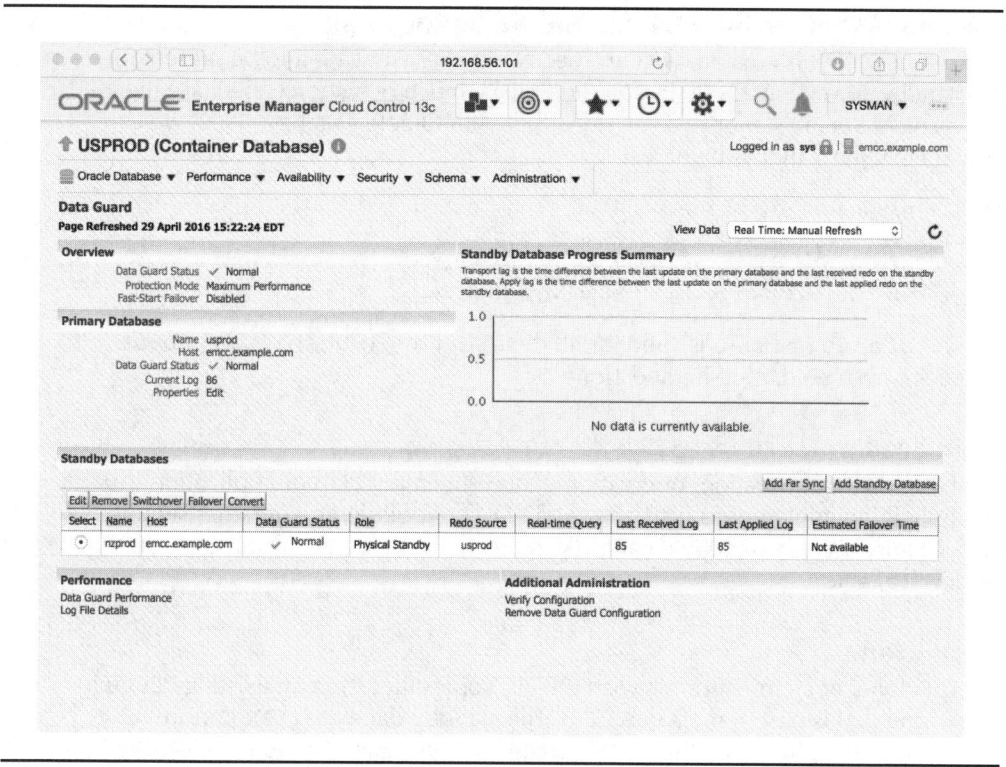

FIGURE 11-6. *The Data Guard status page*

`VALIDATE` command works at the root level, and the lag is displayed for the CDB as whole.

However, the creation, movement, and disposal of PDBs does inject new elements, and issues, into the world of the standby database. New PDBs, and related tablespaces and datafiles, should "appear" on the standby side—but how does this happen, and how can they get there?

Creating a New PDB on the Source

There are multiple ways in which we can create a new PDB on the source, including from scratch, as well as by using the different clone options discussed in Chapter 9.

Note that in all the examples, we use the (thoroughly recommended) parameter, `STANDBY_FILE_MANAGEMENT=AUTO`. Setting this to `MANUAL` would introduce extra steps in the resolutions, meaning that we would first need to set the desired names for all the files involved, and that can get tedious.

Deciding Whether the PDB Should Be on the Standby

When a new PDB is created, we can specify whether we want it to be present on the standby. In version 12.1.0.2, you didn't have much of a choice, because the PDB was available on all standbys or on none, but with Oracle Database 12.2, we can now specify the standbys by name.

```
create pluggable database pdb7 as clone using
'/home/oracle/pdbunplug.xml' standbys=none;
create pluggable database pdb7 as clone using
'/home/oracle/pdbunplug.xml' standbys=(NZPROD);
```

This `standbys` clause is valid for all the `create pluggable database` varieties—from seed, plug-in, and clone.

From Seed

The basic database creation, or creation of a fresh, empty PDB or application in an application container, is from the seed PDB or application container seed PDB. In this case, the standby database will create the PDB, too, as it has the seed readily available.

Local Clone

A local clone, or a clone from the same PDB, copies files from an existing PDB into a new one that is part of the same CDB. The standby databases can perform a similar operation; however, this feature requires Active Data Guard to be enabled at the time.

If Active Data Guard is not in use, the standby will stop applying the redo and wait for a resolution:

```
ALTER DATABASE RECOVER MANAGED STANDBY DATABASE
*
ERROR at line 1:
ORA-00283: recovery session canceled due to errors
ORA-01274: cannot add data file that was originally created as
'/u01/oracle/data/USPROD/PDB5/system01.dbf'
```

At this time, we have to decide whether or not to include the database in the standby. If not, we can simply issue the following:

```
alter pluggable database PDB5 disable recovery;

Pluggable database altered.
```

Of course, if we don't want to have the PDB at the standby, its easier to specify that directly in the statement creating the PDB, as shown in the previous section. However, if we decide that we want to include the PDB, we need to provide the missing files. Provided that we still have available a consistent version of the files (the clone was from a closed PDB and the PDB is still closed), it is sufficient to copy them to the expected path and restart the recovery (that is, `alter database recover managed standby database disconnect from session`). For other cases, see the section "Enabling the PDB Recovery" later in this chapter.

Note that if working with a clone from a closed PDB, and the filenames on standby are known in advance (for example, they don't use OMF, which includes GUID, which is unknown before the clone happens), then the easiest way is to copy the files beforehand. Doing so means that the redo apply won't even have to stop.

Remote Clone

The remote clone option is, in fact, very similar to a local one. In this case, Active Data Guard does not have access to the source files and thus it cannot perform the copy automatically. All the other options are valid here, though, including both skipping the PDB as well as providing the files to the standby.

Plug-in

For a plug-in operation, we have the files on hand before the operation, so it is easy to copy them to the standby and place them in the correct location. If we plug in a PDB archive, we must unpack the files manually on the standby. The documentation gives the impression that making such a copy beforehand is always enough.

Although this operation works for basic scenarios, in real life, we may encounter additional complexity, including various situations in which the datafiles are modified during the plug-in, such as when the database is plugged in as a clone. In such cases, the standby will reject the files, meaning that we will have to copy the files again from the source, after the plug-in has occurred.

Proxy, Relocate

All the other clone operations are variations of the basic cloning option and must be treated as such—that is, copy the files after the operation is done, or use RMAN to add the PDB back.

Removing PDB from Source

Obviously, sometimes we want to get rid of a PDB, too. As removing does not need any new datafiles to be created, it is generally an easier task to do on with a standby database in place.

And let's look at how a rename happens, too.

Drop

The `DROP PLUGGABLE DATABASE` command affects all configured standby databases, meaning that the specified PDB will be dropped from all of them.

For this command to succeed, the PDB must be closed on all standbys. This obviously applies only to Active Data Guard configurations, as otherwise none of the PDBs can be open. If they are not closed, the redo apply stops and must be restarted again after the PDB is closed before proceeding.

Unplug
An unplug operation on a primary is also honored by all standbys. On the standbys, there is no XML or PDB archive created; instead, the PDB is simply marked as UNPLUGGED. As with the drop operation, the PDB must be closed on all the standbys for this to succeed.

Rename
A rename of PDB is, again, honored by all standbys. The operation requires the source to be in open restricted mode and closed on the standbys.

Changing the Subset
We can also change the list of included PDBs later on the fly. Let's see how to handle these scenarios.

Remove an Existing PDB
The standby database must be open in order to be modified. Furthermore, the actual statement must be run with the selected PDB:

```
SQL> alter database recover managed standby database cancel;

Database altered.

SQL> alter session set container=pdb1;

Session altered.

SQL> alter pluggable database pdb1 disable recovery;

Pluggable database altered.

SQL> alter session set container=cdb$root;

Session altered.

SQL> alter database recover managed standby database disconnect from session;

Database altered.
```

In this example, the alert log confirms that the datafiles have just been taken offline:

```
Warning: Datafile 12 (/u01/app/oracle/data/USPROD/PDB1/system01.dbf) is
offline during full database recovery and will not be recovered
```

After this, no redo is applied to the PDB, and the PDB is no longer usable.

The pre-12c method would be to alter the datafiles offline. This is, of course, more cumbersome and does not set the recovery column of v$pdbs. However, it's the only option in version 12.1.0.1, and more importantly, it's still a valid way to remove only selected tablespaces from the standby.

Once these commands have been run, we can delete the physical files because they are no longer needed if the removal is a permanent one.

Enabling the PDB Recovery

There are multiple reasons why we might want to have a PDB made available again on the standby—the most important being in those instances where the database never made it to the standby in the first place, such as during remote cloning. Other cases include various testing scenarios, human errors, and many others that only the real-world experience of a DBA will reveal.

If the files are still present on the standby, we can try enabling the recovery:

```
alter pluggable database PDB5 enable recovery;

Pluggable database altered.
```

Oracle will attempt to recover the database using the redo available on the standby. Note that this command requires redo apply to be stopped and might also necessitate a restart of the standby to mount mode. If this fails or the files are not available, we can use RMAN to restore the files to the standby.

First of all, we need to determine whether Oracle knows where the missing files should be located. In some cases, such as with the STANDBYS clause, Oracle generates a name such as UNNAMED00178. In others, it carries over the name from the source, modifying it according to DB_FILE_NAME_CONVERT settings if those are configured. These new names are listed in the alert.log as well in v$datafile.

```
File #22 added to control file as 'UNNAMED00022'. Originally created as:
'/ u01/oracle/data/NZPROD/PDB6/system01.dbf'
because the pluggable database was created with nostandby or the tablespace belonging
to the pluggable database is offline.
```

Or

```
ORA-01565: error in identifying file '/u01/oracle/data/NZPROD/PDB7/system01.dbf'
ORA-27037: unable to obtain file status
Linux-x86_64 Error: 2: No such file or directory
```

For the next step, we must decide whether we want RMAN to access the primary to retrieve the datafiles, or whether we want to use backups. In the latter case, these must be accessible from the standby. Recovery catalog, or simply the `catalog` command in RMAN, can be a great help here.

If the database knows the target filenames and we are happy with these, we can issue the `restore` command:

```
restore pluggable database PDB7;
```

Or copy from the primary:

```
restore pluggable database PDB7 from service USPROD;
```

If we want new filenames, we have to detail them. Note also that we can specify NEW to let the standby generate OMF filenames, as an alternative:

```
run {
set newname for datafile 22 to
'/u01/oracle/data/NZPROD/PDB7/system.dbf';
set newname for datafile 23 to
'/u01/oracle/data/NZPROD/PDB7/sysaux.dbf';
restore pluggable database PDB7;
}
```

This second example uses OMF:

```
run {
set newname for pluggable database PDB7 to new;
restore pluggable database PDB7;
}
```

Now we can enable the recovery and restart the redo apply.

```
alter pluggable database PDB7 enable recovery;

Pluggable database altered.

alter database recover managed standby database disconnect from session.

Database altered.
```

Cloud Control

Unfortunately, PDB management in EM has no provision for standby databases. It does not offer to specify the STANDBYS clause and is not helpful in the resolution of any issues.

The Data Guard administration page shown in Figure 11-7 displays the status after a clone, and we now have to resolve the situation manually, with little or no help from EM.

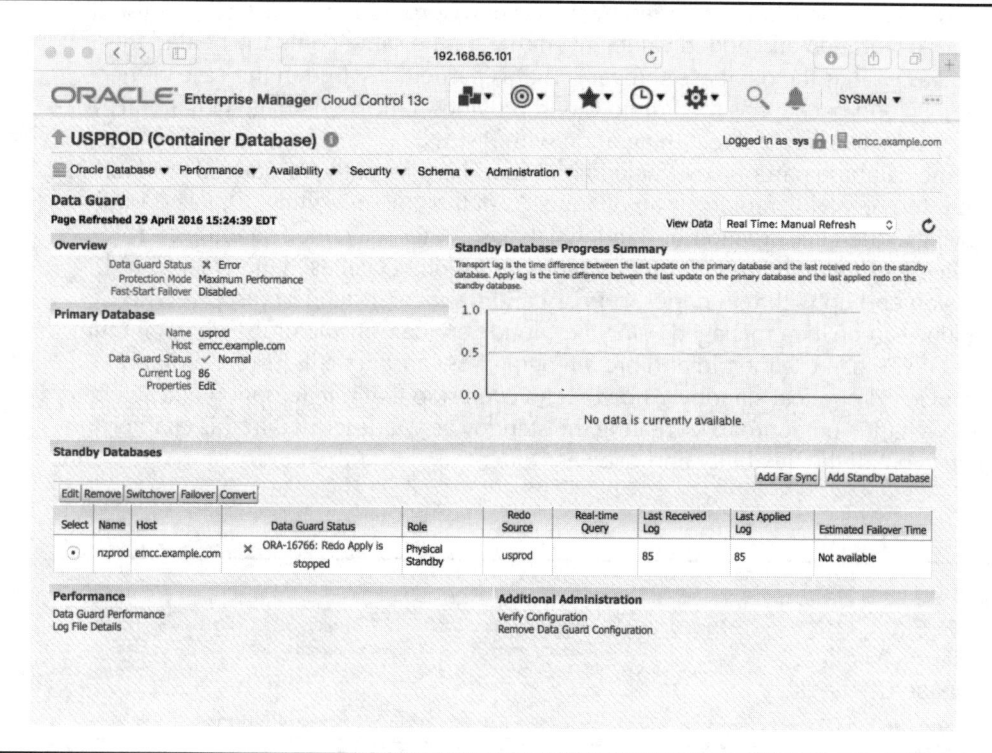

FIGURE 11-7. *Standby redo apply failure after clone operation*

Standby in the Cloud

As with RMAN backups, the cloud provides a cost-effective option for disaster recovery. The reasons for using it for this purpose are even more compelling than those for its use for primary production databases.

Two main points stand out: First, it's much cheaper and easier to run a standby in the cloud than to build a whole new data center—a backup site in case of a disaster—that might not ever be fully used. Second, the cloud usage charges are determined by allocated capacity, and a standby database, which only applies redo changes, needs much less processing power than the primary database. At the same time, if a switch to the cloud backup database is required, cloud technology means that it is easy to scale up the capacity as required.

Numerous cloud provider options are available, and many can run an Oracle database. After all, it's just an application running on a commodity operating system, usually Windows or Linux on Intel.

Oracle Public Cloud provided by the Oracle Corporation, however, promises tighter integration and added value, given that it's the same company behind this cloud as well as the database software. That is particularly true in the case of the RMAN cloud backup, as the Public Cloud provides a media management library for the cloud backup and direct integration with RMAN.

The database part of the Oracle Public Cloud is a recently introduced product and is thus evolving rapidly as an offering. As of the time of writing, Oracle started proving a one-click creation of standby database. After selecting Database as a Service (as shown in Figure 11-8), just select "Standby Database with Data Guard" and you end up with two nodes, primary and standby, instead of just one. The standby can be then managed using the Cloud Service Console or the dbaascli utility.

Or you can use the old and proven dgmgrl because it's still just an ordinary Data Guard physical standby. And you can even skip that magic option and select a more hands-on approach, creating the standby as we described in this chapter, giving you all the flexibility and choices.

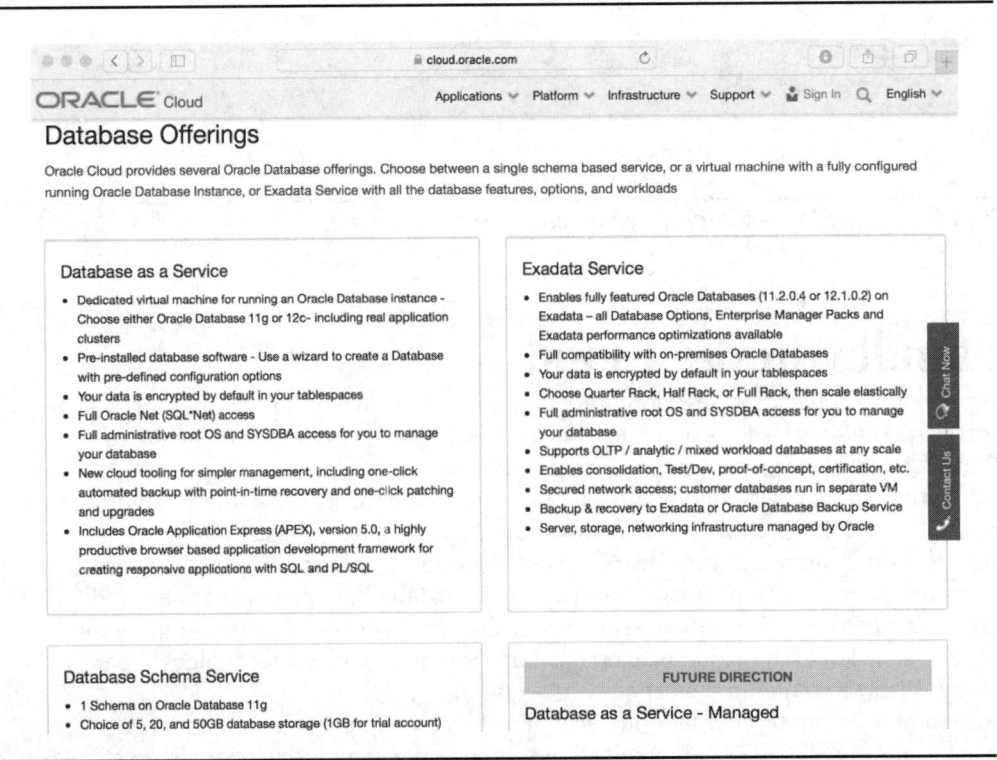

FIGURE 11-8. *The list of Database Offerings for Oracle Cloud*

You should be aware that the cloud virtual machine comes with a license included in the price. For multitenant, we need to select at least the High Performance Service, and for Active Data Guard, only the Extreme Performance Service fits the requirement (this is true both for manually created standby and for the automatically provisioned, too).

If we already back up our on-premise database to the cloud, we can use these backups to create the standby. Again, the steps are identical to those within a local environment: install the Oracle Database Cloud Backup Module using opc_install. jar, and then instruct RMAN to use the library:

```
$ mkdir -p /u01/app/oracle/OPC/wallet
$ mkdir -p /u01/app/oracle/OPC/lib
$ export ORACLE_SID=CLSBY
$ export ORACLE_HOME=/u01/app/oracle/product/12.1.0/dbhome_1
$ java -jar opc_install.jar -serviceName <defined service name>
-identityDomain <backup service domain> -opcId '<user@company.com>' -opcPass
'<OPC password>' -walletDir /u01/app/oracle/OPC/wallet -libDir
/u01/app/oracle/OPC/lib
Oracle Database Cloud Backup Module Install Tool, build 2015-05-12
Oracle Database Cloud Backup Module credentials are valid.
Oracle Database Cloud Backup Module wallet created in directory
/u01/app/oracle/OPC/wallet.
Oracle Database Cloud Backup Module initialization file
/u01/app/oracle/product/12.1.0/dbhome_1/dbs/opcCLSBY.ora created.
Downloading Oracle Database Cloud Backup Module Software Library from file
opc_linux64.zip.
Downloaded 23169388 bytes in 20 seconds.
Download complete.
```

In RMAN, set `SBT_LIBRARY` to use this module, either in the run block, before there is a control file available,

```
run {
   allocate channel dev1 device type sbt
   parms='SBT_LIBRARY=/u01/app/oracle/OPC/lib/libopc.so';
   restore spfile TO '/tmp/spfile.ora' from autobackup;
}
```

or permanently in the control file:

```
RMAN> CONFIGURE CHANNEL DEVICE TYPE 'SBT_TAPE' PARMS 'SBT_LIBRARY=/
u01/app/oracle/OPC/lib/libopc.so, ENV=(OPC_PFILE=/u01/app/oracle/
product/12.1.0/dbhome_1/dbs/opcCLSBY.ora)';
```

Again, the process is exactly the same when using RMAN on-premise, backing up/restoring from the cloud. The notable difference is that, in this case, the data remains in the cloud, so the restore is not limited by the bandwidth of our Internet connection.

In summary, there is very little multitenant-specific functionality in terms of cloud disaster recovery. We must carefully select the machine type to have the multitenant option included in the license, and from there the further handling of PDBs is similar to that for an on-premise standby database.

Summary

In this chapter, we covered one of the less glamorous, yet very important, features of Oracle Database and the cornerstone of the Maximum Availability Architecture: Data Guard.

You've seen that it is not difficult to create a standby database, although working with one effectively requires experience that comes from trying things over and over. We emphasized that the Oracle documentation related to this is strewn across multiple locations. On the other hand, disaster recovery is such a critical topic that digging, experimentation, and practice are beneficial in the long run.

To conclude, multitenant itself does not change how a standby database works; however, in enabling cloning and plug-in/unplug operations, such features have the potential for major impact, and many of them break that "setup standby once and then forget it" attitude we may have once held.

CHAPTER 12

Sharing Data Across PDBs

Is a multitenant database one database, or is it many? This is a question that runs like a silver thread throughout this entire book, and, as you have seen so far, the answer is, "it depends." For some operations, we need to think of multitenant as a single database; for others, we have to think at the pluggable database (PDB) level and treat each PDB independently.

In this chapter, we investigate how to access the data stored in one PDB from data stored in another PDB, and we will show that, again, we can address the problem from both of the angles described. Furthermore, we will discuss how Oracle introduces a completely new point of view.

At a very basic level, on one hand, we can completely ignore all the new multitenant features, treat all PDBs as completely separate databases, and, as ordinary users, log into a PDB and create a database link to another database, regardless of whether this is part of the same container database (CDB) or not. Or we can tunnel through the wall constructed by Oracle between the PDBs, asking for data from another PDB directly, although this can get very complex and elaborate, as you will see. Let's take a look at the various options in detail.

Database Links

A database link is a tried-and-tested feature, proven over time, that has been with us since Oracle Database 5.1. That's 30 years! This is a proven solution, one that DBAs and users are familiar with, and it is congruent with the Oracle message that nothing changes for users when the multitenant architecture is adopted.

Of course, there are some limitations on what type of operations are possible over a database link, but even those are being addressed. For example, Oracle Database 12.2 fills in one long-standing gap, which is support for large object (LOB)–based datatypes.

In addition to the familiarity of this functionality, there is one more major advantage, and this is the opacity of the link to the user. The user does not need to know where the target PDB actually resides. So when a DBA moves the PDB to a new CDB, only the resolution of the connection string has to change, by editing tnsnames.ora, for example. Again, a database link behaves in the same way as it always did, multitenant or not.

In a non-CDB, database links can be split into two basic categories: a remote database link connecting to an external database, and a so-called "loopback" database link connecting to the same database. We can think of the loopback link as an aberrant case, but there are times when it has its place—for example, when two applications are consolidated to the same database, and a database link is required between them for use by the applications. Oracle Database recognizes this special case and introduces some optimizations, such as having only one single transaction on the database shared by both ends of the link. And Oracle Database 12c promises even more performance optimizations, as Oracle expects more links pointing back to the same (container) database.

Multitenant also brings a new distinction to database links, in conjunction with the remote/loopback connection, so that a database link can now connect either to the root container or to a PDB. Note that there is no way to change the current container of the remote end of a database link, because there is no `alter session set container` for it.

Because of this, a root container database link is useful for administration only. As you saw in Chapter 9, remote clones can use such a link, and we don't have to create a new one for every single PDB we want to clone. But for accessing data in PDBs, we need to create links connecting directly to the desired PDBs. Although some of the techniques described later in this chapter make user data visible even in the root container, in some cases a CDB link may make sense to access data, too.

As you can see in Figure 12-1, Enterprise Manager offers all the usual options to create a database link. There is no special option to specify whether the target is a PDB or a CDB, because this is implied by the Net Service Name.

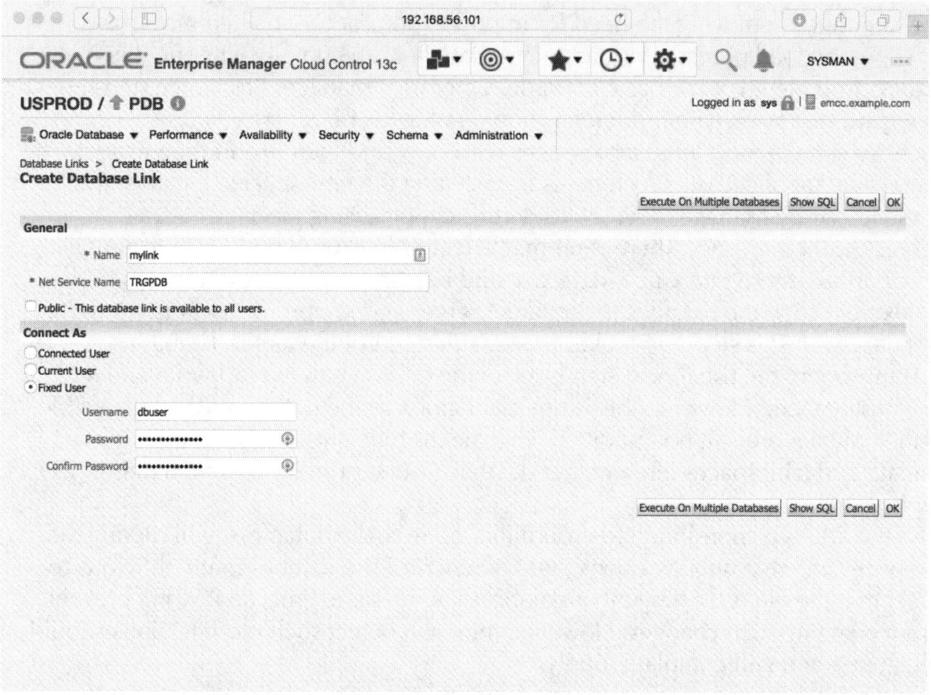

FIGURE 12-1. *Creating a database link in Enterprise Manager Cloud Control*

Sharing Common Read-Only Data

A special case of data sharing is sharing of the same read-only data by multiple databases. For example, if we want to provide multiple development databases and include large historical data—data that is only queried and no longer modified—it would be ineffective to copy such data multiple times, both in terms of the time taken to perform this operation and in respect to the storage consumed. In a sense, this is a poor man's solution to making database cloning less storage demanding.

> **NOTE**
> *Some of the options described here will also work with read/write data, although the options' usefulness shines in cases when the data is seldom modified.*

Transportable Tablespaces

In 8*i*, Oracle introduced the transportable tablespaces feature. Its prominent use case is to copy data from a production online transaction-processing database into a data warehouse, removing the need for import/export, or for an alternative data extraction and load process. Instead, entire datafiles are copied, with only the metadata imported. For the basic scenario, Enterprise Manager has a nice step-by-step wizard that starts with the screen shown in Figure 12-2.

First, we make the source tablespaces read-only and then export the metadata. If our users and applications preclude us from setting the tablespaces to read-only, we can use Recovery Manager (RMAN) to do this export (using the TRANSPORT TABLESPACE command). There is no magic technology used by RMAN; it simply does a partial restore into a new database and runs the export there.

Next, we copy the datafiles to the target server and import the metadata into the target database. This step also makes the datafiles part of the target database.

At this point, the usual next step is to set the tablespaces to read/write and let users modify them. However, this is not mandatory, as the data is already accessible and the datafiles are still not modified. This means that we can also import the same metadata and tablespaces into another database—one or many more databases, as we wish.

It's the DBA's responsibility to ensure that none of the databases will modify the tablespaces and that nobody opens them read/write. The databases are oblivious to the fact that the file is used by other databases at the same time, so it won't prevent us from enacting such changes. However, they will detect such modifications should they happen and will complain loudly.

Of course, because the files are not modified at all, it isn't necessary for us to copy them from the source database, and even the source database itself can be one

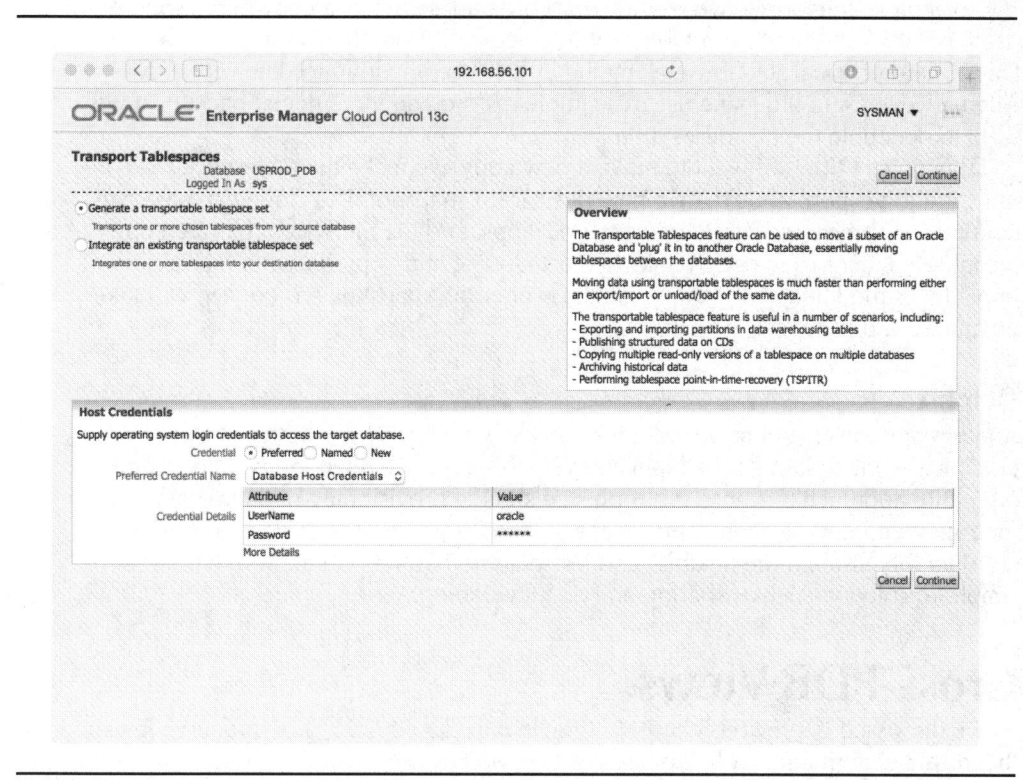

FIGURE 12-2. *Transportable tablespaces in Enterprise Manager Cloud Control*

of the sharing databases. Whether we want to do this depends a lot on our use case and environment. Such sharing is not appropriate on a production database, which is probably on separate storage and should not bear the penalty of I/O generated by test and development, but in other cases it might be a very useful option.

Storage Snapshots and Copy on Write

A simple extension of the same idea is to leverage storage to provide copies of the tablespaces. This enables us to have multiple copies of the same tablespace, but as of different points in time, or even read/write copies. Of course, this is then more of a "copy-provisioning" option than sharing, but it still has its use cases. After all, when using such tablespaces to provision read-only copies of a production database for testing, having the copy as of multiple points in time is a very beneficial facility.

So when and where might we find use for tablespace copies? In some cases, a test has to be done with multiple copies of the data, while in others we can just build new test environments as we go and update data over time.

To achieve the former, we would create a database that is a copy of the source database and run the transportable tablespace export from there. This copy can be a Data Guard physical standby, making the task of keeping it up-to-date very easy. Alternatively, we could make use of a simple restore and incremental backups if we want to decouple the databases more.

Then, every time we want to make a new copy, we make the tablespace read-only, run the export, and create a new file system snapshot. The clone database can continue to receive redo or incremental backups, and the file system has the copy of the tablespace for us to use. Thanks to the snapshot and copy-on-write facilities, only blocks modified by the clone database after the snapshot was created will take up any extra disk space.

Delphix

Another option is Delphix (www.delphix.com), which provides both fast and cheap cloning as well as storage de-duplication. In this case, we might do well to rethink our entire approach, because this tool excels in the provisioning of entire databases for testing and development. This means that the building of such databases is considerably faster, more flexible, and less painful than we can achieve with a simplistic solution such as sharing one or a few tablespaces.

Cross-PDB Views

As we discussed in previous chapters, Oracle introduced CDB_% dictionary views that display information collected from all open PDBs. In version 12.1.0.1, Oracle used a trick with an internal function called CDB$VIEW to achieve this. This was not documented, and some scenarios caused internal Oracle errors instead of proper results or appropriate error messages.

Fortunately, that version is now a relic of the past, and as of version 12.1.0.2, Oracle Database switched to using the CONTAINERS() clause, which is properly documented and supported.

Delving into this a little deeper, here's the definition of CDB_USERS in Oracle Database 12.1.0.2:

```
SELECT "USERNAME", "USER_ID", "PASSWORD", "ACCOUNT_STATUS", "LOCK_DATE",
"EXPIRY_DATE", "DEFAULT_TABLESPACE", "TEMPORARY_TABLESPACE", "CREATED",
"PROFILE", "INITIAL_RSRC_CONSUMER_GROUP", "EXTERNAL_NAME", "PASSWORD_
VERSIONS", "EDITIONS_ENABLED", "AUTHENTICATION_TYPE", "PROXY_ONLY_
CONNECT", "COMMON", "LAST_LOGIN", "ORACLE_MAINTAINED", "CON_ID" FROM
CONTAINERS("SYS"."DBA_USERS")
```

In other words, the DBA_USERS view is wrapped in the CONTAINERS() clause and references one new column created by this clause, con_id, obviously referencing the container ID of the PDB.

The `CONTAINERS()` clause causes Oracle to execute the same query on each of the open PDBs, but skipping PDB$SEED. It is valid to query such a view even from a PDB, but in that case only data for the current PDB is returned.

Let's have a look at the same view in Oracle Database 12.2.0.1:

```
SELECT k."USERNAME", k."USER_ID", k."PASSWORD", k."ACCOUNT_STATUS",
k."LOCK_DATE", k."EXPIRY_DATE", k."DEFAULT_TABLESPACE", k."TEMPORARY_
TABLESPACE", k."LOCAL_TEMP_TABLESPACE", k."CREATED", k."PROFILE",
k."INITIAL_RSRC_CONSUMER_GROUP", k."EXTERNAL_NAME", k."PASSWORD_VERSIONS",
k."EDITIONS_ENABLED", k."AUTHENTICATION_TYPE", k."PROXY_ONLY_CONNECT",
k."COMMON", k."LAST_LOGIN", k."ORACLE_MAINTAINED", k."INHERITED",
k."DEFAULT_COLLATION", k."IMPLICIT", k."CON_ID", k.CON$NAME, k.CDB$NAME
FROM CONTAINERS("SYS"."DBA_USERS") k
```

You can see that Oracle started using a table alias (k) in the query. For this particular view, it also added three new columns. What interests us here, in particular, are the two new columns generated by the `CONTAINERS()` clause: CON$NAME and CDB$NAME.

The first is the name of the PDB where the records come from, essentially translating the `con_id` into the PDB name. The second new column is the name of the CDB itself, and you will see later in this chapter when this might be useful.

We already noted that querying from the PDB will show us data from the PDB only, while querying from CDB$ROOT gives us data from all the PDBs except the seed. If we run the query from an application container root, we get data from the application root and all its application PDBs, except the application seed.

Simple User Tables

Because the `CONTAINERS()` clause is documented and supported, Oracle allows us to query our own user tables as well as build views on top of them, aggregating data from multiple PDBs.

Simple Status Query

Let's start with a simple example query, supposing that we want to monitor multiple PDBs. For this, we will assume that each has a user table called ERRORLOG, and we want to query for all error messages inserted there. We are interested in only the single table, and we want to query across all the PDBs.

First of all, we need a common user to query the data, as a local user would always see data from its PDB only:

```
SQL> create user c##errorquery identified by oracle;

User created.

SQL> grant create session, create view to c##errorquery container=current;
```

```
Grant succeeded.

SQL> grant set container, create table, unlimited tablespace to
c##errorquery container=all;

Grant succeeded.
```

The ERORRLOG table must be present in all of the PDBs (actually, only in those PDBs we want to query, as you'll see later) and in the root, too, and the Data Definition Language (DDL) of all these copies must match. Because the table must also be in the root, we have to create it under a common user schema, or we can create it under local users in the PDBs and let the common user have views or synonyms. In these examples, we don't use application containers, so the common user is created in CDB$ROOT; this mandates that the user's name is prefixed by the COMMON_USER_PREFIX, which defaults to c##.

We run this create DDL in the CDB, then in all the PDBs:

```
SQL> create table c##errorquery.errorlog (i number primary key, message
varchar2(4000), when date);

Table created.

SQL> alter session set container=PDB1;

Session altered.

SQL> create table c##errorquery.errorlog (i number primary key, message
varchar2(4000), when date);
…etc…
```

As simple test data, let's insert one row in each of the PDBs:

```
SQL> insert into  c##errorquery.errorlog values (0, 'root', sysdate);

1 row created.

SQL>  commit;

Commit complete.

SQL> alter session set container=PDB1;

Session altered.

SQL>  insert into  c##errorquery.errorlog values (1, 'PDB1', sysdate);

1 row created.

SQL>  commit;

Commit complete.
```

Now we can query the data:

```
SQL> select * from containers(errorlog);

 I MESSAGE          WHEN        CON_ID
-- ---------------  ---------   ------
 0 root             13-FEB-16        1
 1 PDB1             13-FEB-16        3
```

As noted, the DDL must match. If, for example, we generate a new PDB and create the table differently, like this (same would happen if the table is not there at all):

```
SQL> create table c##errorquery.errorlog (i number primary key, message
varchar2(4000));

Table created.
SQL> insert into table c##errorquery.errorlog values (2, 'PDB2');

1 row created.

SQL> commit;

Commit complete.
```

Oracle silently ignores this table:

```
SQL> select * from containers(errorlog);

 I MESSAGE          WHEN        CON_ID
-- ---------------  ---------   ------
 0 root             13-FEB-16        1
 1 PDB1             13-FEB-16        3
```

However, there is some leeway for allowed differences. Oracle takes the metadata from the table in the root, so if the PDB tables have extra columns, that's fine, because they will be ignored.

So, let's fix the missing column and add one more:

```
SQL> alter table errorlog  add (when date, who char);

Table altered.
```

Now the query from the root works again—ignoring the extra column:

```
SQL> select * from containers(errorlog);

 I MESSAGE          WHEN        CON_ID
-- ---------------  ---------   ------
 0 root             13-FEB-16        1
 1 PDB1             13-FEB-16        3
 2 PDB2                              4
```

Querying Only Some of the PDBs

Oracle runs the query only in the containers where it makes sense to do so. So if we specify a condition such as con_id, to choose only some of the PDBs, Oracle will look in these PDBs only:

```
SQL> select i, message, when, con_id, con$name, cdb$name
from containers(errorlog) where con_id in (1,3);

 I MESSAGE          WHEN       CON_ID CON$NAME    CDB$NAME
-- --------------- ---------- ------- ----------  ----------
 0 root            13-FEB-16        1 CDB$ROOT    CDBSRC
 1 PDB1            13-FEB-16        3 PDB1        CDBSRC
```

And we can use CON$NAME, too:

```
SQL> select i, message, when, con_id, con$name, cdb$name
from containers(errorlog) where CON$NAME='PDB1';

 I MESSAGE          WHEN       CON_ID
-- --------------- ---------- ------
 1 PDB1            13-FEB-16       3
```

For another, more sophisticated, approach to this problem, see the "Container Map" section later in this chapter.

Query Hint

In some cases, we might want or need to add a hint to a query that uses the CONTAINERS() clause. But if we put it in the usual syntax, it will apply only to the last aggregation step, not to the queries that are run in each of the PDBs.

Fortunately, Oracle introduced a way for us to "push down" such hints into the queries. The CONTAINERS(DEFAULT_PDB_HINT='...') syntax specifies these hints:

```
SQL> select /*+CONTAINERS(DEFAULT_PDB_HINT='FULL')*/ *
from containers(c##errorquery.errorlog) where con_id in (1,3);
```

Querying the Data from a PDB

As already noted, accessing the CONTAINERS() query from within a PDB gives us data only for that particular PDB.

In the previous examples, we had a logging table, and the query collected errors from all the PDBs. So what if one of the PDBs is a monitoring application that actually needs to access and process all these error logs?

Well, the solution is trivial: we can just create a database link pointing to the common user in the CDB, and query the data over the database link. We can't put the `CONTAINERS()` clause around a remote object, but we can work around this simply by creating a view.

```
SQL> create view errorlog_v as select * from containers(errorlog);

View created.

SQL> alter session set container = 'PDB1';

Session altered.

SQL> create database link common connect to c##errorquery identified by
oracle using 'CDBSRC';

Database link created.

SQL> select * from errorlog_v@common;
```

Consolidated Data

One of the use cases of multitenant that really fits its features and advantages, and perhaps the one that Oracle had in mind when designing this feature, is consolidation of instances of the same application. Imagine a service provider that sells an SaaS application to its customers and needs multiple copies of the same application running on the same hardware. Or perhaps a company IT department provides the same application for multiple branches or franchisees; the application is the same and the users need data separation, but the head office wants to access the data from all of the PDBs at the same time to run various reports. These types of companies can benefit from consolidated access to their data.

In the pre-multitenant world, we could either do schema consolidation and put all the users into the same database if the application supported such an approach, or we could build one consolidated staging/data warehouse and load the necessary data into it, and then run reports from there. However, as you have seen in the previous section, multitenant enables us to access all the PDBs at the same time and thus build queries that run consolidated reports on the data directly (although with imposed limitations such as having the same table names and structure). The approach described in the previous section can achieve this, but it could be a bit cumbersome should we do it for more than a handful of tables.

Oracle Database 12.2 unleashes a number of features that make this consolidation a much more prominent citizen of the database ecosystem. Oracle promotes application containers as one of the key pieces of the solution for these scenarios, although many of the features don't actually require them. Still, if we find that working with consolidated PDB data is an important piece in our application, it might be a good time to dig deeper into the application containers and consider whether building the application using them would be a good fit.

Linking Tables Across Containers

You have already seen in Chapter 1 how Oracle links the dictionary objects between the CDB and the PDBs using metadata and object links. Oracle now enables us to do the same with our objects and data—well, kind of.

This implies storing data in the root container, and Oracle is strict here in that it does not want us to enter into the bad practice of creating user objects in the CDB root. It thus mandates that we create an application container instead and store the data in its container root.

So let's create an application container with a couple of application PDBs in it, with a common user. In this simple example, we won't create an application seed in the application container.

```
SQL> create pluggable database appcont as application container admin user ac
identified by oracle;

Pluggable database created.

SQL> alter session set container=appcont;

Session altered.

SQL> alter pluggable database open;

Pluggable database altered.

SQL> create pluggable database ACPDB1 admin user ap1 identified by oracle;

Pluggable database created.

SQL> alter pluggable database acpdb1 open;

Pluggable database altered.

SQL> create pluggable database ACPDB2 admin user ap2 identified by oracle;

Pluggable database created.

SQL> alter pluggable database acpdb2 open;

Pluggable database altered.
```

Chapter 12: Sharing Data Across PDBs **331**

```
SQL> create pluggable database ACPDB3 admin user ap3  identified by oracle;

Pluggable database created.

SQL> alter pluggable database acpdb3 open;

Pluggable database altered.

SQL> alter session set container=appcont;

Session altered.

SQL> create user shareapp identified by oracle container=all;

User created.

SQL> grant create table, create session to shareapp container=all;

Grant succeeded.
```

Metadata-Linked Objects   As the application common user in the application container root, we can now create a metadata-linked table. The table definition, or metadata, is in the container root; the actual data segments are private to each application PDB. The following illustration shows such arrangement of data:

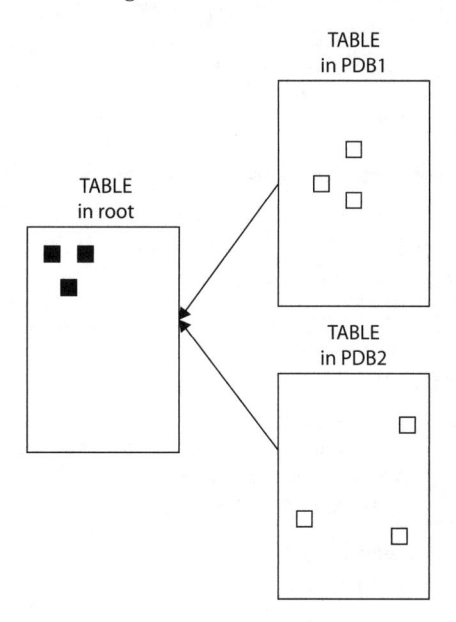

Note that we are modifying the application root, and Oracle requires us to mark any such modifications as "application install," to be able to replay the changes in the containers.

```
SQL> alter pluggable database application appcont begin install '1';

Pluggable database altered.

SQL> create table mlink sharing=metadata  (i number, message varchar2(20));

Table created.

SQL> insert into mlink values (1, 'global, install');

1 row created.

SQL> commit;

Commit complete.

SQL> alter pluggable database application appcont end install;

Pluggable database altered.

SQL> insert into mlink values (2, 'global, postinstall');

1 row created.

SQL> commit;

Commit complete.

SQL> update mlink set message='modified global' where i=1;

1 row updated.

SQL> commit;

Commit complete.

SQL> select rowid, i, message from mlink;

ROWID                      I MESSAGE
------------------ ---------- --------------------
AAAS8FAABAAAIWxAAA         1 modified global
AAAS8FAABAAAIWxAAB         2 global, postinstall

SQL> alter session set container=acpdb1;

Session altered.

SQL> alter pluggable database application appcont sync;

Pluggable database altered.
```

```
SQL> select rowid, i, message from mlink;

ROWID                     I MESSAGE
------------------       --- --------------------
AAAS8DAABAAAIWhAAA        1 global, install
```

As you can see, any objects and data created during the application install are synchronized to the PDB from the application root. However, no changes done after the install are reflected, and the `rowid` shows that these are really distinct rows; the sync does a one-time copy, and from then on the rows are not linked in any way.

However, there *is* some value to these oversimplified nonlinked tables. Oracle knows which containers have this particular version installed and thus contain the table; it does not complain that some of the containers don't have the table present yet, and we don't need to limit the query manually on `con_id`.

```
SQL> select * from containers(mlink);

         I MESSAGE                  CON_ID
---------- --------------------    -------
         1 modified global              6
         2 global, postinstall          6
         1 global, install              7
```

Extended Data Metadata-Linked Objects   A special flavor of metadata-linked objects is an *extended data object*. In this case, the data is stored in both the application root (common data, visible by all PDBs) and in the application PDBs (data private to each of the PDBs), as shown in the following illustration:

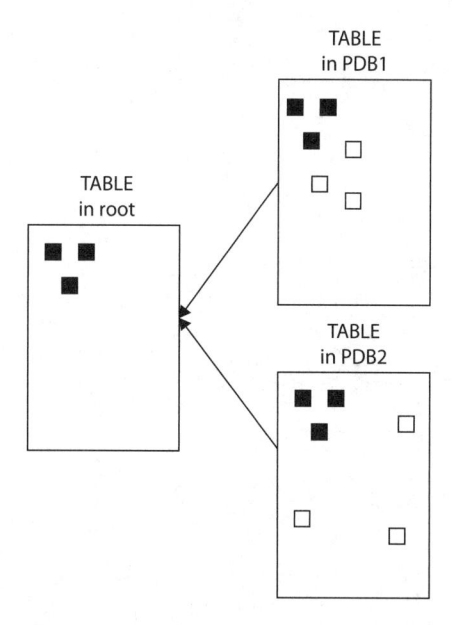

The steps are similar to those in the previous example, with the notable inclusion of the EXTENDED DATA clause in the DDL.

In this example, the application is already installed, thanks to the example we ran in the previous section, and we now add a new table there in a patch:

```
SQL> alter pluggable database application appcont begin patch 1 minimum version '1';

Pluggable database altered.

SQL> create table edlink sharing=extended data
(i number, message varchar2(20));

Table created.

SQL> insert into edlink values (1, 'global, install');

1 row created.

SQL> commit;

Commit complete.

SQL> alter pluggable database application appcont end patch;

Pluggable database altered.

SQL> insert into edlink values (2, 'global, postinstall');

1 row created.

SQL> commit;

Commit complete.

SQL> update edlink set message='modified global' where i=1;

1 row updated.

SQL> commit;

Commit complete.

SQL> select rowid, i, message from edlink;

ROWID                      I MESSAGE
------------------ ---------- --------------------
AAAS8RAABAAAIXxAAA          1 modified global
AAAS8RAABAAAIXxAAB          2 global, postinstall

SQL> alter session set container=acpdb1;
```

```
Session altered.

SQL> alter pluggable database application appcont sync;

Pluggable database altered.

SQL> select i, message from edlink;

         I MESSAGE
---------- --------------------
         1 modified global
         2 global, postinstall
```

We observe that the application PDB sees current values of objects in the root, including any changes done out of the application action. (Note that we can't use ROWID in the query in a PDB, however, because it will fail with an ORA error.) And it can also add new records, private to the application PDB:

```
SQL> insert into edlink values (3, 'from PDB');

1 row created.

SQL> commit;

Commit complete.

SQL> select  i, message from edlink;

         I MESSAGE
---------- --------------------
         1 modified global
         2 global, postinstall
         3 from PDB
```

However, we cannot modify records inherited from the root; an update command does not see these rows, even if a select query at the same time does.

```
SQL> update edlink set message='new' where i=1;

0 rows updated.
```

Although the root can, of course, modify the row:

```
SQL>  alter session set container=appcont;

Session altered.

SQL> update edlink set message='new' where i=1;
```

```
1 row updated.

SQL> commit;

Commit complete.

SQL> select con_id, i, message from containers(edlink);

    CON_ID          I MESSAGE
---------- ---------- --------------------
         6          1 new
         6          2 global, postinstall
         7          1 new
         7          2 global, postinstall
         7          3 from PDB
```

One caveat, as you have seen, is that each PDB shows its own copy of the common rows, and the parallel slaves executing a CONTAINERS() query across the PDBs do not remove these duplicates.

Data-Linked Objects An object-linked object exists in one place only: in the application container root. We are not allowed to modify the data the PDBs.

As the next illustration reveals, this is really common data shared by all PDBs, modified only during maintenance:

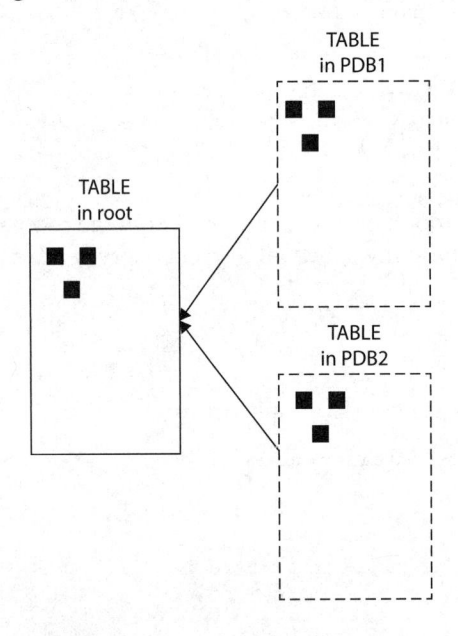

Or, looking at it from a completely different point of view, this could be considered read-only data shared by all PDBs—very similar to that which was achieved with transportable tablespaces.

```
SQL> alter session set container=appcont;

Session altered.

SQL> alter pluggable database application appcont begin patch 2 minimum version '1';

Pluggable database altered.

SQL> create table dlink sharing=data (i number, message varchar2(20));

Table created.

SQL> insert  into dlink values (1, 'global, install');

1 row created.

SQL> commit;

Commit complete.

SQL> alter pluggable database application appcont end patch;

Pluggable database altered.

SQL>  select rowid, i, message from dlink;

ROWID                I MESSAGE
------------------ --- --------------------
AAAS8KAABAAAIXJAAA   1 global, install
```

The root container can modify these contents even if not in the special application patch or upgrade mode:

```
SQL> insert into dlink values (2, 'global, postinstall');

1 row created.

SQL> commit;

Commit complete.
```

Now let's switch to the application PDB:

```
SQL> alter session set container=acpdb1;

Session altered.
```

```
SQL> alter pluggable database application appcont sync;

Pluggable database altered.

SQL>  select i, message from dlink;

   I MESSAGE
 --- -------------------------------------
   1 global, install 2 global, postinstall

SQL> insert into dlink values (3, 'from PDB');

insert into dlink values (3, 'from PDB')
            *
ERROR at line 1:
ORA-65097: DML into a data link table is outside an application action
```

The application PDB cannot modify the table. There is really only one copy of the data, the PDBs can access it read-only, seeing all changes done in the CDB.

A minor limitation is that it is not possible to query rowid of the table while in a PDB - such query fails with ORA-02031: no ROWID for fixed tables or for external-organized tables.

Cross-PDB DML

In Oracle Database 12.2, and not limited to application containers, we can actually issue DML on a table wrapped in the CONTAINERS() clause. In other words, we can change data in multiple PDBs with a single operation, from a single transaction.

```
SQL>  update containers(nolink) set message='u'||message;

4 rows updated.
```

We can even specify the con_id to limit the execution to selected PDBs.

```
SQL> update containers(nolink) set message='u'||message
where con_id in (3,4);

2 rows updated.
```

Oracle introduces a new setting that we can use to specify which PDBs should be affected by this DML. This way, we don't have to specify the con_id condition in each DML, which means we don't have to modify the scripts every time we want to run it on a different set of PDBs.

To get the current setting, we can look at DATABASE_PROPERTIES:

```
SQL> select property_value from database_properties
where property_name='CONTAINERS_DEFAULT_TARGET';
```

And we can change the values with this:

```
alter [pluggable] database containers default target = ...
```

The `pluggable` keyword is to be used when we issue the statement in the application root (which is a kind of PDB itself), although we omit the keyword if we execute it in CDB$ROOT. As for the target specification, we can use <a list of PDBs>, ALL, ALL EXCEPT <a list of PDBs>, or NONE.

Note that the default is NONE, which, contrary to its name, actually contains all (application) containers, except the seed and root.

Containers Default

If we find that we are using the CONTAINERS() clause heavily, we might realize it's too much work, and too error-prone, to add the clause dutifully to every reference for the tables we want to query this way. Or perhaps we want to reuse existing code and queries and want to minimize the changes needed to update the code to use the clause. Fortunately, Oracle had introduced a new table setting, which, if enabled, will result in every query and DML on that table or view being automatically wrapped in the CONTAINERS() clause.

```
SQL>  alter table c##errorquery.errorlog ENABLE CONTAINERS_DEFAULT;

Table altered.
```

The setting can be easily checked in the data dictionary:

```
SQL> select CONTAINERS_DEFAULT from user_tables where table_name='ERRORLOG';

CON
---
YES
```

Container Map

When we have multiple PDBs with the same tables but different data (such as data for different customers or branches) and we run queries on this data, all these PDBs are interrogated, unless we specify `con_id` in the `where` condition.

In a sense, this is a partitioning schema; data for a single customer or branch resides in a single PDB only—it doesn't overlap—and if we search for a single branch, only one PDB will contain data for it, as shown in the illustration:

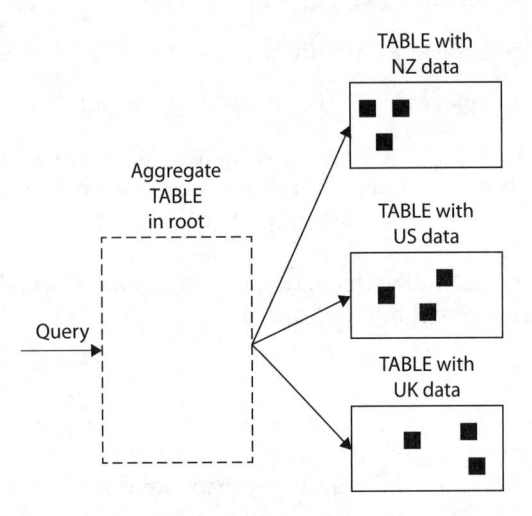

Therefore, it stands to reason that Oracle should have a method for selectively pruning these queries, like it does with ordinary partitions. Indeed, Oracle now enables us to declare the mapping, such that the optimizer then knows how to respond accordingly. This is called a *container map*. In it we create a dummy table with no data, which describes just the partitioning schema, with the requirement that the names of the partitions must match the names of the PDBs.

So let's create an example table in the CDB$ROOT and a few PDBs:

```
SQL> create table dwhdata(region varchar2(2), value number, descr varchar2(20));

Table created.

SQL> alter session set container=PDB1;

Session altered.

SQL> create table dwhdata(region varchar2(2), value number, descr varchar2(20));

Table created.

SQL> insert into dwhdata values ('NZ', 1, 'one NZ');

1 row created.
```

```
SQL> commit;

Commit complete.

SQL> alter session set container=PDB2;

Session altered.

SQL> create table dwhdata(region varchar2(2), value number, descr varchar2(20));

Table created.

SQL> insert into dwhdata values ('US', 1, 'one US');

1 row created.

SQL> commit;

Commit complete.

SQL>  alter session set container=PDB3;

Session altered.

SQL>  create table dwhdata(region varchar2(2), value number, descr varchar2(20));

Table created.

SQL> insert into dwhdata values ('UK', 1, 'one UK');

1 row created.

SQL> commit;

Commit complete.
```

We can now check that there is a row in each of the containers:

```
SQL> alter session set container=cdb$root;

Session altered.

SQL> select * from containers(dwhdata)

RE     VALUE DESCR                CON_ID
-- ---------- -------------------- ------
US         1 one US                    3
UK         1 one UK                    4
CZ         1 one CZ                    5
```

Now let's create the container map and set it. Note that the container map is global for the root or application container root.

```
SQL> create table partrule
  (region varchar2(2))
   partition by list(region)
     (partition PDB1 values ('US'),
      partition PDB2 values('UK'),
      partition PDB3 values ('CZ'));

Table created.

SQL> alter database set container_map='c##errorquery.partrule';

Database altered.
```

The last step is to enable the table(s) to declare that they should be handled in this special way:

```
SQL> alter table errorlog enable container_map;

Table altered.
```

In this example, we used a list-partitioning schema, but Oracle also allows `RANGE` and `HASH`. The inclusion of a `HASH` schema points to the idea that dividing a large application database into PDBs may be done to split the amount of data and user load, with no further attempt to determine the allocation based on any human-defined condition; `HASH` would simply split the data into PDBs of more or less the same size.

Location Independence

We have seen in Chapter 9 that it's easy to copy and move PDBs from one CDB to another. Usually we just update the Transparent Network Substrate (TNS) connection string after the move to a different server, and the clients will connect to the new location. We mentioned that Oracle can also create a proxy PDB, and you might wonder whether a proxy PDB is really such a big deal. The answer, once we begin working with consolidation queries, is a resolute yes.

The `CONTAINERS()` clause can work on one CDB only; it cannot reference remote PDBs, and there is no syntax to specify such PDBs or database links. However, there is one notable exception: proxy PDB. From the view of the queries, a proxy PDB is a pluggable database like any other, sitting locally on the CDB. The queries are not aware that their requests are actually passed on further, to a remote PDB. In other words, the `CONTAINERS()` clause will gather data from both regular, local PDBs as well as from proxy PDBs.

If we add the fact that the limit of PDBs in a single CDB has been raised to 4096, we can now run queries across many, many PDBs, even if having so many PDBs on a single machine would be practically untenable because of resource requirements.

Cross-Database Replication

Another option for data sharing is to look at solutions that work across databases. They also usually allow the target to be the same database as source (have it loop back), or at least a different PDB than the source. We discuss this in further detail in Chapter 13.

Summary

We have discovered that the gamut of the options for data sharing is vast. We can stay entrenched in current thinking and use proven features, such as database links or transportable tablespaces, or we can begin to rethink our approach completely and build our applications on application containers, shared objects, and container maps.

Oracle DBAs are typically conservative, so whether these ideas gain significant traction within this community (let alone among users in general) is yet to be seen apart from a few obvious types for whom these features of multitenant specifically appeal, such as cloud and SaaS providers.

CHAPTER 13

Logical Replication

A database, as the name implies, is a place to store data, but as DBAs, we are often most interested in the physical properties and implementation of the database. For example, we may want to create a backup of the database, create a standby database, or maintain a specific file of an unplugged, pluggable database (PDB). We know that if we understand these mechanisms well, when required, we can create a one-to-one copy of the database or restore the database to the exact same state as before—bit-for-bit. This is a *physical copy*, as the physical structure of the database is maintained. If we then keep this copy in sync with the source by continuously recovering the archive logs, for example, we call it a *physical replication*.

Developers—and their applications—tend to view the database as tables, rows, and columns, and should they want the data to appear somewhere else, they copy these structures, and their contents, again. They are not concerned with datafiles or archive logs, and as long as they see the same data reproduced, they are happy. This is often referred to as a *logical copy*, as only the logical structures, or data, are retained in the process. A *logical replication*, then, keeps such a target in sync with the source via a mechanism such as SQL statement replay.

Physical replication is more robust, because if our source and targets are identical at the bit level, bit-for-bit, then we can be 100-percent sure that the data is also identical. It follows then that in this context we also don't need to be nervous about different character sets, length semantics, or cross-version feature support—or putting the data into a non-Oracle database.

The other approach, logical replication, offers a higher degree of flexibility, however, and there are far fewer limitations as to where we can put the data. We are interested in the changes made to the "source" data, and so long as we get an initial copy of this data, followed by all subsequent changes, we will have an identical copy at the target.

We can identify three major use cases in which the benefits of this method outweigh the disadvantages of its complexity:

- *We can enable databases with mismatched versions to be paired up.* In this way, we can keep a copy of the database in another location, running on a different version and/or platform. A common use case for this is migration, which enables us to perform near-zero-time downtime upgrades or migrations. We create a copy in a new database, keep it in sync, and then switch users over to this new database.

- *We can copy the data to a different database.* This database might be Oracle or some other RDBMS flavor, as required by the application, and the data may be complete or perhaps just a subset. This approach is commonly used to offload reporting from a source database to a secondary, less critical, one or from Oracle to a database such as MySQL, thereby saving on Oracle

Database licensing costs. We can also develop distributed applications based on such replication configurations, giving each location its own copy of the data, which is then synchronized with all the others.

- *Once we work at the data level, we are not limited to keeping the data as-is.* For example, we can treat the changes as a stream of events—in other words, see it as a continuous flow of changes made to the tables. This can in turn feed stream-oriented processing flows, using frameworks such as Apache Kafka, Apache NiFi, or Apache Samza, or it can simply be written to data stores, such as Hadoop, where it can be duly processed by custom logic. This opens an additional dimension of data for analysis: evolution over time. Analysts are often interested in how data has changed chronologically. For example, they want to see how a customer has added and removed items from a shopping cart before completing her purchase. So even if a database retains only details of the final order—the final state—the flow of changes leading up to that point is useful as it depicts how the shopping cart contents changed during the checkout process, which can give insight into customer behavior and the website's effectiveness.

NOTE
Active Data Guard also targets the simple report offloading use case; it is, however, limited to read-only queries and cannot, for example, add indexes, materialized views, or summary tables. It is also limited to an Oracle Database Enterprise Edition as a target. On the other hand, it retains the simpler and more robust physical replication 100-percent copy method.

These use cases for logical replication are not exclusive to multitenant, nor are they in fact even Oracle-specific. However, multitenant is a major architectural change and not all logical replication features and products support it.

Oracle LogMiner

Oracle LogMiner is not a replication solution per se; instead, it extracts changes from the redo logs and displays them in the v$logmnr_contents view.

Other replication products (unless they implement a trigger-based approach) work on the same basis, collecting all the changes as they happen in the redo stream. So it is interesting to play with LogMiner and observe how database changes show up there, because it allows us to see and understand the various challenges and requirements facing the logical replication products. For example, changes are recorded row-by-row, meaning that a large update changing 1000 rows shows as 1000 separate update statements, each affecting exactly one row.

A number of third-party products actually make use of LogMiner, through the exposed PL/SQL API and v$ view. This works fine for basic operations, but it easily breaks for more complicated operations such as those dealing with large objects (LOBs).

Other products implement their own version of the log miner, completely independent of the Oracle code. These are much harder to implement than using LogMiner, but they enable more flexibility, are not limited only to the information that Oracle makes available in the v$ view, and are more efficient since they avoid calls to the database. The older "classic" version of the GoldenGate extract falls in this category.

Yet another approach is to use triggers, although this technique is less favored, because it increases load on the source database and does not scale well in terms of performance. From an administration point of view, it is also harder to maintain when DDL changes happen.

Obsolete Features

The list of logical replication features and functionality provided by Oracle is surprisingly long, although this has been extensively pruned since the introduction of Oracle Database 12c. For the sake of completeness, let's quickly review features provided for logical replication in Oracle Database 11g, which were not updated to support PDBs.

Oracle CDC

Oracle Change Data Capture, or CDC, was a trigger- or redo log–based logical replication mechanism that was introduced in Oracle Database 9i. It provided a list of all changes, in the form of an event/log table stored in the database itself. But, as was already announced with the earlier Oracle Database 11gR2 release, Oracle CDC is no longer included in future versions and has been omitted from 12c.

A number of third-party tools used Oracle CDC in the past as a quick way to support Oracle as a source in logical replication, especially those sorts of applications for which the Oracle Database was not the primary database of interest.

Oracle Streams

Oracle Streams, introduced in Oracle 9iR2, is a redo log–based replication mechanism, which means that it reads the changes recorded in redo logs, instead of relying on changes captured by triggers defined on the table, thus putting no additional load on the database as a result. It then sends the source database changes, which have been harvested, downstream to a different Oracle Database.

Although still available in 12c, Streams is now deprecated. However, unlike Oracle CDC, which never gained significant popularity, Streams was adopted by many DBAs and organizations, and thus Oracle has been slower to retire this option.

Nevertheless, Oracle Streams doesn't support any of the new features introduced in Oracle Database 12c, which means that PDBs are not supported by it and never will be.

Oracle Advanced Replication

Another casualty of the Oracle Database 12c "lay offs" was Advanced Replication, which is a replication method based on updateable materialized views. This feature was formally deprecated in Oracle Database 12.1.

Oracle GoldenGate

It is clear that Oracle regards Oracle GoldenGate as the future of its replication offering. This is the product that is intended to solve all our requirements for logical replication, and that's why Oracle Streams, Oracle CDC, and Advanced Replication are no longer available.

It is true that Oracle GoldenGate is a superior product in many respects, because it is more robust, scales better, and supports databases in addition to Oracle, as both source and targets. On the other hand, it is expensive, whereas Streams and CDC were included for free with the Enterprise Edition. It also lacks support for some Oracle features, but this has rapidly improved since it was re-engineered to use elements of the Streams code for redo extraction.

Last but not least, it was created by a company that was later acquired by Oracle, so the user interface is very different from what we were used to with Streams and CDC. As a product, it is not particularly easy to learn or use, although the new GoldenGate Management Studio GUI is a huge step forward.

Multitenant Support in Oracle GoldenGate

In GoldenGate, only the new, integrated extract supports multitenant databases. The source extract process is defined at the CDB level and connects to the database as a common user. It can extract data for one or multiple PDBs.

On the target side, each replicat process connects to a single PDB. So if we replicate multiple PDBs on the source, we have to use multiple replicat processes on the target.

Let's set up a simple replication for a multitenant database and examine the differences that multitenant brings.

Topology in the Example

In this example configuration, the source database has multiple PDBs, but we are interested only in PDB1 and PDB2. On the target database, we have prepared PDBT1 and PDBT2 to hold the data, although there is, of course, no need to have all the PDBs in the same target database, since each has its own replicat process.

```
SQL> select name, con_id, pdb from v$services where pdb in ('PDB1','PDB2');

NAME                CON_ID PDB
------------------- ------ ------------------------------
pdb1                     4 PDB1
pdb2                     5 PDB2
```

On PDB1 we will replicate tables from the HR sample schema to PDBT1; on PDB2 we will replicate the SCOTT schema to PDBT2:

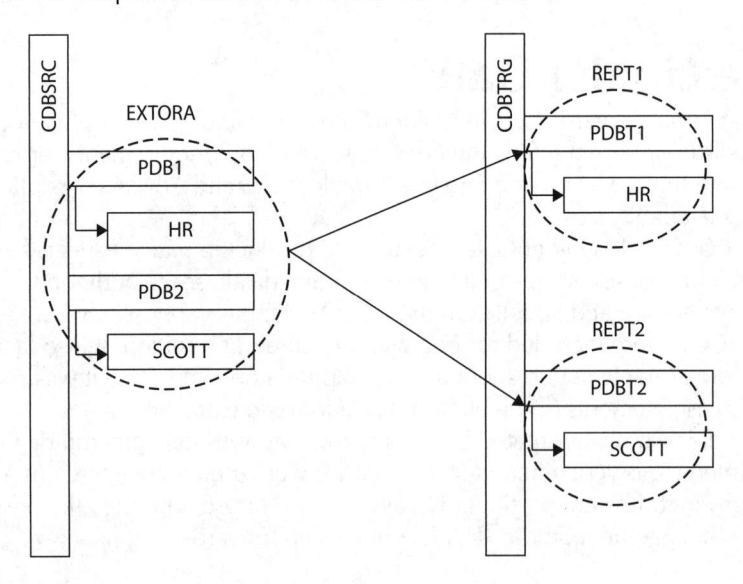

Source Database Setup

First of all, we have to tell the database that it's OK to use features that require a GoldenGate license, which assumes that we have actually purchased this license. A parameter, `enable_goldengate_replication`, was added in 11.2.0.4, and GoldenGate checks that this is set, or otherwise errors out, refusing to register the extract. The parameter also enables functionality such as disabling triggers on the target during replication.

> **NOTE**
> *In 11.2.0.3 and earlier, these features were free to use (included in the database license), before Oracle decided to disallow other third-party tools from using them, by virtue of requiring a GoldenGate license to enable them.*

Run this SQL as a common user:

```
SQL> alter system set enable_goldengate_replication=true;

System altered.
```

Every Oracle GoldenGate replication needs a connection to the source database—that is, to the CDB, to be more precise. For this we must grant a couple of additional privileges:

```
SQL> create user C##GGADMIN identified by ggadmin;

User created.

SQL> exec dbms_goldengate_auth.grant_admin_privilege('C##GGADMIN', container=>'ALL');

PL/SQL procedure successfully completed.

SQL> grant dba to c##ggadmin container=all;

Grant succeeded.
```

Every logical replication also needs to have basic supplemental logging enabled, because a row can be chained or migrated—that is, the database can store a row in multiple pieces. Minimal supplemental logging adds information that allows LogMiner, or the logical replication tools, to stitch these pieces together, and this is set at the PDB level:

```
SQL> alter session set container=PDB1;

Session altered.

SQL> alter pluggable database add supplemental log data;

Pluggable database altered.

SQL> alter session set container=PDB2;

Session altered.

SQL> alter pluggable database add supplemental log data;

Pluggable database altered.
```

Table Supplemental Logging

Logical replication also needs supplemental logging on primary keys enabled to ensure that primary key information is *always* written to the redo log. This is necessary for every logical replication tool, because Oracle writes only changed values to redo, by default. That is OK for recovery or physical standbys, as they identify rows by rowid (data block and row position in the block), but logical replication does not preserve rowids and thus needs a primary key, or similar, to uniquely identify the row affected.

In our example, we want to replicate an entire schema, so we use `SCHEMATRANDATA` to set it for all tables in the schema—it would be `TRANDATA` if we wanted to set it for a table only. We do this through the GoldenGate Software Command Interface (GGSCI), the command interface between users and Oracle GoldenGate functional components.

```
[oracle@source ogg]$ ./ggsci

Oracle GoldenGate Command Interpreter for Oracle
Version 12.2.0.1.1 OGGCORE_12.2.0.1.0_PLATFORMS_151211.1401_FBO
Linux, x64, 64bit (optimized), Oracle 12c on Dec 12 2015 02:56:48
Operating system character set identified as US-ASCII.

Copyright (C) 1995, 2015, Oracle and/or its affiliates. All rights reserved.

GGSCI (source) 1> dblogin userid hr@PDB1, password hr
Successfully logged into database PDB1.

GGSCI (source as hr@CDBSRC/PDB1) 2> add schematrandata PDB1.hr

2016-04-04 17:51:16  INFO    OGG-01788  SCHEMATRANDATA has been added on schema hr.

2016-04-04 17:51:16  INFO    OGG-01976  SCHEMATRANDATA for scheduling columns has been added on schema hr.

GGSCI (source as hr@CDBSRC/PDB1) 3> dblogin userid scott@PDB2, password tiger
Successfully logged into database PDB2.

GGSCI (source as scott@CDBSRC/PDB2) 4> add schematrandata pdb2.scott

2016-04-04 17:52:37  INFO    OGG-01788  SCHEMATRANDATA has been added on schema scott.

2016-04-04 17:52:37  INFO    OGG-01976  SCHEMATRANDATA for scheduling columns has been added on schema scott.
```

Configure and Start Manager

The next step is simple: let GGSCI create all necessary directories and start the manager processes.

First, the directories:

```
GGSCI (source) 2> create subdirs

Creating subdirectories under current directory /home/oracle/ogg
Parameter files                /home/oracle/ogg/dirprm: created
Report files                   /home/oracle/ogg/dirrpt: created
Checkpoint files               /home/oracle/ogg/dirchk: created
Process status files           /home/oracle/ogg/dirpcs: created
SQL script files               /home/oracle/ogg/dirsql: created
Database definitions files     /home/oracle/ogg/dirdef: created
Extract data files             /home/oracle/ogg/dirdat: created
Temporary files                /home/oracle/ogg/dirtmp: created
Credential store files         /home/oracle/ogg/dircrd: created
Masterkey wallet files         /home/oracle/ogg/dirwlt: created
Dump files                     /home/oracle/ogg/dirdmp: created
```

Next, we configure the manager parameter file:

```
GGSCI (source) 3> edit params mgr
```

Then, in the editor, we simply enter the following:

```
PORT 7809
```

Back in GGSCI, we can now start the manager:

```
GGSCI (source) 4> start manager
```

And we also need to repeat these steps for the target server.

Extract Configuration File

Now we configure the extract process to read from the source database redo:

```
GGSCI (source) 5> edit params extora
```

In our example, we will specify only the basic settings:

```
EXTRACT EXTORA
USERID c##ggadmin@CDBSRC, PASSWORD ggadmin
RMTHOST localhost, MGRPORT 7809
RMTTRAIL ./dirdat/rt

DDL INCLUDE MAPPED
LOGALLSUPCOLS
UPDATERECORDFORMAT COMPACT

TABLE pdb1.hr.*;
TABLE pdb2.scott.*;
```

Because this is not a GoldenGate handbook, we have simply referred to the original product documentation for explanation on the settings as well as the steps to encrypt the password. However, notice the second and the last two lines, where you can see that the extract process connects to the container database (CDB) as a common user. In addition, we specify the tables to be replicated in a single configuration file, specifying the names with three parts—PDB, schema, and table.

Now let's register the extract process just defined and configure the remote trail:

```
GGSCI (source) 1> dblogin userid c##ggadmin@CDBSRC, password ggadmin
Successfully logged into database CDB$ROOT.

GGSCI (source as c##ggadmin@CDBSRC/CDB$ROOT) 2> register extract extora database
container (PDB1,PDB2);

2016-04-04 18:05:11  INFO    OGG-02003  Extract EXTORA successfully registered with
database at SCN 1894436.

GGSCI (source as c##ggadmin@CDBSRC) 3> add extract extora, integrated tranlog, begin now
EXTRACT (Integrated) added.


GGSCI (source as c##ggadmin@CDBSRC) 4> add rmttrail ./dirdat/rt, extract extora,
megabytes 100

RMTTRAIL added.
```

Set Up the Target Database

Let's now move on to the target database. Unlike the extract, a replicat process connects to one specific target PDB. We have two PDBs replicated, so we have to create users in both of these databases. First of all, we must enable the "magic parameter" as we did for the source database, as follows:

```
SQL> alter system set enable_goldengate_replication=true;

System altered.

SQL> alter session set container=PDBT1;

Session altered.

SQL> create user repuser identified by rep_pass container=current;

User created.

SQL> grant dba to repuser;

Grant succeeded.

SQL> exec dbms_goldengate_auth.grant_admin_privilege('REPUSER',container=>'PDBT1');

PL/SQL procedure successfully completed.
```

```
SQL> alter session set container=PDBT2;

Session altered.

SQL> create user repuser identified by rep_pass container=current;

User created.

SQL> grant dba to repuser;

Grant succeeded.

SQL> exec dbms_goldengate_auth.grant_admin_privilege('REPUSER',container=>'PDBT2');

PL/SQL procedure successfully completed.
```

Configure Parameter Files for Replicat Processes

Now let's configure two replicat processes—one for each PDB:

```
GGSCI (target) 1> edit params rept1
REPLICAT REPT1
ASSUMETARGETDEFS
DISCARDFILE ./dirrpt/repora1.dsc, PURGE, MEGABYTES 100
DDL INCLUDE MAPPED
DBOPTIONS INTEGRATEDPARAMS(parallelism 6)
USERID repuser@pdbt1, PASSWORD rep_pass
MAP pdb1.hr.*, TARGET pdbt1.hr.*;
```

And here's the second one:

```
GGSCI (target) 2> edit params rept2
REPLICAT REPT2
ASSUMETARGETDEFS
DISCARDFILE ./dirrpt/repora2.dsc, PURGE, MEGABYTES 100
DDL INCLUDE MAPPED
DBOPTIONS INTEGRATEDPARAMS(parallelism 6)
USERID repuser@pdbt2, PASSWORD rep_pass
MAP pdb2.scott.*, TARGET pdbt2.scott.*;
```

Now we can register the replicat processes:

```
GGSCI (target) 3> add replicat rept1, integrated, exttrail ./dirdat/rt
REPLICAT (Integrated) added.

GGSCI (target) 4> add replicat rept2, integrated, exttrail./dirdat/rt
REPLICAT (Integrated) added.
```

Initial Extract

As with every replication, we must provision the source data to the target to create a baseline, so they match as of a specific starting point. Let's set this starting point to the current database system change number (SCN):

```
SQL> SELECT current_scn from v$database;

CURRENT_SCN
-----------
    1939272
```

We use GoldenGate's initial extract for the provisioning, which means we ask GoldenGate to load the initial data as a set of inserts, obtained by a select into the source database.

> **NOTE**
> *We have manually created empty tables at the target databases prior to this—for example, using metadata only Data Pump import.*

```
GGSCI (source) 1> edit params initext1
```

Let's use two extracts, as an example to demonstrate that we are not limited to a single extract in a CDB:

```
EXTRACT INITEXT1
USERID c##ggadmin@cdbsrc, PASSWORD ggadmin
RMTHOST localhost, MGRPORT 7809
RMTTASK REPLICAT, GROUP INITREP1
TABLE pdb1.hr.*, SQLPREDICATE 'AS OF SCN 1939272';
```

And similarly, for the second extract:

```
GGSCI (source) 2> edit params initext2
```

We use the SCN in the predicate for the tables, effectively turning this into a flashback query:

```
EXTRACT INITEXT2
USERID c##ggadmin@cdbsrc, PASSWORD ggadmin
RMTHOST localhost, MGRPORT 7809
RMTTASK REPLICAT, GROUP INITREP2
TABLE pdb2.scott.*, SQLPREDICATE 'AS OF SCN 1939272';
```

NOTE
The TABLE clause can also accept a VIEW. This does not matter for regular extract processing, although a VIEW generates no redo, so no changes will ever be captured. However, for an initial extract, in which data is queried using a select, the data would be extracted, and replicat would fail, because it can't insert into that VIEW. If it could, we would otherwise end up with primary key violations or duplicate data in the underlying table.

Let's configure the replicat processes now:

```
GGSCI (target) 1> edit params initrep1
```

There is nothing special about the configuration in this file:

```
REPLICAT INITREP1
ASSUMETARGETDEFS
DISCARDFILE ./dirrpt/init1.dsc, APPEND
USERID repuser@PDBT1, PASSWORD rep_pass
MAP pdb1.hr.*, TARGET pdbt1.hr.*;
```

Again, the second file differs from the first only in the replicat and filenames, as well as login and tables:

```
GGSCI (target) 2> edit params initrep2
REPLICAT INITREP2
ASSUMETARGETDEFS
DISCARDFILE ./dirrpt/init2.dsc, APPEND
USERID repuser@PDBT2, PASSWORD rep_pass
MAP pdb2.scott.*, TARGET pdbt2.scott.*;
```

Finally, we can register the processes:

```
GGSCI (source) 1> add extract initext1, sourceistable
EXTRACT added.

GGSCI (source) 2> add extract initext2, sourceistable
EXTRACT added.
```

And then also on the target:

```
GGSCI (target) 1> add replicat initrep1, specialrun
REPLICAT added.

GGSCI (target) 2> add replicat initrep2, specialrun
REPLICAT added.
```

Run the Initial Extract
Now we run the provisioning load:

```
GGSCI (source) 1> start extract initext1

Sending START request to MANAGER ...
EXTRACT INITEXT1 starting


GGSCI (source) 2> start extract initext2

Sending START request to MANAGER ...
EXTRACT INITEXT2 starting
```

We verify that both ran successfully, and through to completion:

```
GGSCI (5212e334b10e) 71> info extract initext1

EXTRACT     INITEXT1    Last Started 2016-04-04 19:20   Status STOPPED
Checkpoint Lag          Not Available
Log Read Checkpoint     Table PDB1.HR.REGIONS
                        2016-04-04 19:20:55  Record 4
Task                    SOURCEISTABLE
```

In the detailed report, which is too long to list here, we verify there were no errors:

```
GGSCI (5212e334b10e) 72> view report initext1
...
```

Obviously, we need to perform the same check for the three other processes.

Start Extract and Replicats
Now, with the data loaded, we are at the place where can start the replication. Note, however, that we could actually start the extract much sooner, because only the replicats have to wait for all the data to be loaded:

```
GGSCI (source) 1> start extract extora

Sending START request to MANAGER ...
EXTRACT EXTORA starting


GGSCI (5212e334b10e) 110> info extract extora

EXTRACT     EXTORA      Last Started 2016-04-04 19:34   Status RUNNING
Checkpoint Lag          00:00:10 (updated 00:00:03 ago)
Process ID              31008
Log Read Checkpoint     Oracle Integrated Redo Logs
                        2016-04-04 19:34:26
                        SCN 0.1951977 (1951977)
```

We then start the replicats:

```
GGSCI (target) 1> start replicat rept1, aftercsn 1939272;

Sending START request to MANAGER ...
REPLICAT REPT1 starting

GGSCI (target) 2> start replicat rept2, aftercsn 1939272;

Sending START request to MANAGER ...
REPLICAT REPT2 starting
```

Finally, we check that the processes are up and running correctly:

```
GGSCI (target) 3> info replicat rept1

REPLICAT    REPT1      Last Started 2016-04-04 19:29    Status RUNNING
INTEGRATED
Checkpoint Lag         00:00:00 (updated 00:00:09 ago)
Process ID             30825
Log Read Checkpoint    File ./dirdat/rt000000000
                       2016-04-04 19:29:55.118374   RBA 0

GGSCI (target) 4> info replicat rept2

REPLICAT    REPT2      Last Started 2016-04-04 19:30    Status RUNNING
INTEGRATED
Checkpoint Lag         00:00:00 (updated 00:00:00 ago)
Process ID             30911
Log Read Checkpoint    File ./dirdat/rt000000000
                       2016-04-04 19:30:45.269029   RBA 0
```

Big Data Adapters

Oracle GoldenGate now supports various Big Data or event streaming targets, and these adapters are available for Hadoop HDFS, HBase, Hive, Flume, Kafka, and Spark. Collectively, this is marketed as Oracle GoldenGate for Big Data. A complete example would span many pages, so let's succinctly summarize how to use these Big Data adapters.

On the source side, nothing really changes, and we still have to define an extract process to get the data. For the target side, there is still a replicat process, but it needs to be pointed to a Java class and parameter file.

The easiest way is to start with the example for Kafka (Apache Kafka is fast, scalable, and durable publish-subscribe messaging, rethought as a distributed commit log, and distributed by design) provided in AdapterExamples/big-data/kafka directory in the Big Data adapters installation. We won't go into detail on Kafka here; we recommend that you visit the Apache Kafka project web page for more details, documentation, and use cases. Here, we set up a very basic example.

We can use the example replicat definition right away, just changing the tables to be included in the replication:

```
REPLICAT rkafka
-- Trail file for this example is located in "AdapterExamples/trail" directory
-- Command to add REPLICAT
-- add replicat rkafka, exttrail AdapterExamples/trail/tr
TARGETDB LIBFILE libggjava.so SET property=dirprm/kafka.props
REPORTCOUNT EVERY 1 MINUTES, RATE
GROUPTRANSOPS 10000MAP PDB1.hr.*, TARGET PDB1.hr.*;
```

The kafka.props file referenced here is where all the Kafka-specific settings are stored. Again, we can start off with the supplied example, although we will want to change at least the topic (stream of events describing changes on a table; in this example we put all source tables to a single event stream) and schema topic (event stream where replicat puts Avro schemas for the replicated tables) names, and possibly expand the classpath to include Avro libraries (if we go with the Avro format, as set in the example file):

```
gg.handlerlist=kafkahandler
gg.handler.kafkahandler.type=kafka
gg.handler.kafkahandler.KafkaProducerConfigFile=custom_kafka_producer.properties
gg.handler.kafkahandler.TopicName=oggtopic
gg.handler.kafkahandler.format=avro_op
gg.handler.kafkahandler.SchemaTopicName=mySchemaTopic
gg.handler.kafkahandler.BlockingSend =false
gg.handler.kafkahandler.includeTokens=false

gg.handler.kafkahandler.mode =tx
#gg.handler.kafkahandler.maxGroupSize =100, 1Mb
#gg.handler.kafkahandler.minGroupSize =50, 500Kb


goldengate.userexit.timestamp=utc
goldengate.userexit.writers=javawriter
javawriter.stats.display=TRUE
javawriter.stats.full=TRUE

gg.log=log4j
gg.log.level=INFO

gg.report.time=30sec

gg.classpath=dirprm/:/var/lib/kafka/libs/*:

javawriter.bootoptions=-Xmx512m -Xms32m -Djava.class.path=ggjava/ggjava.jar
```

This configuration in turn references one more configuration file: the description of the Kafka server we want to connect to. The only reference we need to change in this custom_kafka_producer.properties file is the first line—bootstrap servers (Kafka servers that provide information on the Kafka cluster configuration; in the simple case of a standalone server, just specify this server):

```
bootstrap.servers=host:port
acks=1
compression.type=gzip
reconnect.backoff.ms=1000

value.serializer=org.apache.kafka.common.serialization.ByteArraySerializer
key.serializer=org.apache.kafka.common.serialization.ByteArraySerializer
# 100KB per partition
batch.size=102400
linger.ms=10000
```

As discussed earlier, it is a simple process to register the replicat, as follows:

```
GGSCI (target) 1> add replicat rkafka, exttrail dirdat/or, begin now
REPLICAT added.
```

There is much more to be configured and set up for various use cases; see Oracle Golden Gate for Big Data documentation.

Oracle XStream

As we mentioned previously, Oracle GoldenGate now uses the *integrated extract*. This code, which sits in the Oracle executable itself, is based on LogMiner and Oracle Streams original code, further developed to satisfy the needs of Oracle GoldenGate and to accommodate all the new features.

However, since the Oracle GoldenGate extract and the Oracle Database executables are separate processes, Oracle had to introduce an API to enable them to talk to each other.

Oracle decided to make this API public and called it XStream. This API consists of PL/SQL packages and v$ views for management. For the actual processing of changes, there are Oracle Call Interface functions for C, along with a Java API. Logically, the API is split in two: one for data coming out of the database ("extract" in GoldenGate, XStream Out) and one for data coming into the database ("replicat" in GoldenGate, XStream In).

Oracle also decided that since all the code for GoldenGate for Oracle source databases is contained within XStream, we need an Oracle GoldenGate license to use it. This relegates the use of XStream to special use cases that GoldenGate does not directly support, meaning that it is anything but a "limited, but free" solution like the original Streams offering was.

> **NOTE**
> *The XStream API is indeed an API, meaning it's intended for application programmers, not for database administrators. You need to write a C or Java program to make use of it.*

Logical Standby

In Chapter 11, we covered Oracle Data Guard physical standby, ignoring at that time the fact that there is also another type available: the often forgotten logical standby.

Conceptually, this is similar to Streams or GoldenGate, in that redo is mined for changes, and these changes are then applied to the target using SQL statements. This implies similar limitations to those for Streams and GoldenGate, including limited datatype support and no duplicate rows in tables. Unlike Streams, however, logical standby is not deprecated, and unlike GoldenGate, it does not require any additional licensing. In reality, though, even logical standby is destined to be replaced by GoldenGate—with one notable use case exception, as you will see.

One special aspect of a logical standby to be aware of is that it is instantiated from a physical standby—that is, its setup begins with the same steps used for a physical standby, including the selection of PDBs to include in the standby, and the same steps also apply for including PDBs created later. In having been generated from a physical standby, it is always built at the CDB level and starts out with all PDBs, with one notable exception: application containers are skipped. Generally, we can't convert a logical standby back to a physical one, because the two are no longer one-to-one copies of each other. However, in the special case of an upgrade (see the next section), it is indeed possible.

This instantiation from a physical standby is both a curse and a blessing. On the positive side of the ledger, it is very easy to do it right and to be 100-percent sure that all the source data is initially copied correctly to the target. On the other hand, though, it imposes the same restrictions that a physical standby does: it requires the same Oracle versions (when the logical standby is created) and platform compatibility.

Use in Upgrade

The unique feature of a logical standby, and the use case that has become its point of difference, is its function in a rolling upgrade. In this scenario, a logical standby is automatically converted from a physical standby. Oracle is then upgraded on this logical standby and it becomes the new primary, and then the other database in the configuration is upgraded. This makes the upgrade much simpler than it would have been with GoldenGate—we don't need to rebuild any database after the upgrade is completed, because logical standby can convert back to physical standby in this case.

Oracle Database 12.1 introduced the DBMS_ROLLING package that, along with Active Data Guard, enables automation of such an upgrade process and can be especially beneficial if there are multiple standby databases in the configuration.

As for a multitenant database, not much is different, although in this special case, application containers are supported. Note, however, that an upgrade of an application container cannot happen at the same time a rolling upgrade is performed, and vice versa.

To ensure that there is no data loss during this process, all PDBs must be plugged in and opened when the transient logical standby becomes the new primary.

Other Third-Party Options

As mentioned, other companies provide alternatives to Oracle GoldenGate. In general, they lag behind Oracle GoldenGate in terms of features and performance, but they provide competitive alternatives by majoring on ease-of-use and price.

Dbvisit Replicate

Dbvisit Replicate, not to be confused with Dbvisit Standby (which is similar to physical standby), is a logical replication tool that uses its own implementation of a redo parsing engine. Only Oracle Database as source is supported.

PDBs are supported. The mine process connects to a single PDB at the source and replicates this sole PDB. Replication of multiple or all PDBs at the same time using a single replication is not supported as of the time of writing.

Although not as feature-rich as Oracle GoldenGate, Dbvisit Replicate's strength lies in its ease-of-use. As a point of comparison, the example we went through earlier to configure GoldenGate requires significantly less manual work. In fact, most of the steps are performed automatically by a single script that the Replicate Setup Wizard creates, after asking a handful of simple questions about your databases and the tables/schemas you want replicated. Unfortunately, there is no GUI available at this point in time.

Replicate also supports Event Streaming mode, producing a stream of changes, similar to the output Oracle CDC produced. Using this functionality, or published APIs, it supports for example Apache Kafka and Apache NiFi targets.

Dell SharePlex

Dell SharePlex, known as Quest SharePlex before Dell acquired Quest Software, is another alternative to Oracle GoldenGate. Again, it is more cost-effective than GoldenGate, but it also supports only the Oracle Database as a source.

Since late 2014, SharePlex has supported PDBs, and each of the PDBs requires its own configuration and capture process.

The configuration is text-based, but the SharePlex Manager does offer a basic GUI for configuration and monitoring.

Summary

We have only briefly touched on the merits of logical replication. To be fair, it is a topic that warrants a book in its own right, and indeed, there are already multiple books on Oracle GoldenGate alone. With the advent of Big Data and event streaming, these tools are even more important to consider in our environments.

Oracle Multitenant is the direction that the Oracle Database is going in, so all logical replication tools need to support it. Unfortunately, this has become a stumbling block for many of the features we were familiar with prior to 12c, and the Oracle-recommended replacement is an expensive one.

Index

A

AaaS (Application as a Service), Oracle Database 12c, 5
ACFS (ASM Clustered File System), 241
Active Data Guard
    automating upgrades, 363
    changing UNDO mode, 223
    cloning local PDB, 240
    enabling read-only database in recovery, 291
    physical replication 100-percent copy, 347
    simple report offloading, 347
Add Standby Database wizard, Cloud Control, 304–305
administer key management
    creating keystore, 160–161
    creating master key, 162–163
    opening keystore in TDE, 162
ADMINISTER_RESOURCE_MANAGER system privilege, 263
administration. *See also* DBA (database administrator)
    creating CDB using DBCA GUI, 39
    multitenant. *See* day-to-day management
    root container database link only for, 321
Advanced Configuration, creating CDB with DBCA GUI, 41–42
AFTER CLONE trigger, 252–253
AFTER DB_ROLE_CHANGE trigger, CDB-only, 252
AFTER LOGON ON PLUGGABLE DATABASE, 26
AFTER SET CONTAINER ON PLUGGABLE DATABASE, 26
AFTER SET CONTAINER trigger, 26, 252
alert logs, 121–122, 184
ALL option, ALTER LOCKDOWN PROFILE, 156
ALTER DATABASE, modifying PDB, 98
ALTER LOCKDOWN PROFILE, 155–156
ALTER PLUGGABLE DATABASE CLOSE, 93–94, 96
ALTER PLUGGABLE DATABASE OPEN, 93–94, 96
ALTER PLUGGABLE DATABASE SAVE STATE, 95, 96
ALTER SESSION SET CONTAINER trigger, 23, 26, 252
ALTER SESSION SET CURRENT_SCHEMA, 23
ALTER SYSTEM
    changing parameters in SPFILE, 113
    disabling with lockdown profiles, 156–157
    limiting PDB I/O parameter, 283
    PDB memory allocation, 282
    PDB SPFILE equivalent, 114
    single-tenant security lockdown, 75–76
ALTER SYSTEM KILL SESSION, thread processes, 125
ALTER SYSTEM RESET, removing persistent setting for parameter, 116
ALTER SYSTEM SET
    administer key management replacing, 161

365

ALTER SYSTEM SET (*cont.*)
    CDB SPFILE, 114
    lockdown profile, 157
ALTER USER
    administering temporary tablespaces, 92
    authorizing container access, 151
Amazon Web Services (AWS), back up to cloud, 195
AMM (Automatic Memory Management), 281
APEX (Oracle Application Express), 30–31, 107
application containers
    considerations, 247
    linking tables across, 330–338
    prefix for, 80–83, 151
application metadata
    separating system metadata from, 18–19
    vs. system metadata, 13–14
application servers, Oracle Database 11*g*, 5
APPLICATION_USER_PREFIX, application containers, 151
APPOWNER, proxy users, 154
archive files, plug-in/unplug PDB, 238–239
archive log list, hot backups, 172
archive logs
    backup schedule for, 183
    in full CDB backups, 176
    full CDB recovery with, 185
    hot backups generating, 171–172
    PDB backup restrictions, 183
ARCHIVELOG mode
    cloning local PDB, 241–242
    cloning remote PDB, 242
    enabling FLASHBACK ON, 214
    flashback logging, 215
    hot backups, 171–172
    hot cloning remote PDB, 241–242
    modifying entire CDB, 90
arguments, creating PDB with catcon.pl, 68–69
AS APPLICATION CONTAINER clause
    application containers, 80
    CREATE PLUGGABLE DATABASE with, 57
    linking tables across containers, 330

AS CLONE clause
    CREATE PLUGGABLE DATABASE with, 57
    deciding if PDB should be on standby, 310
    plugin PDB as clone, 237–238
ASM (Automatic Storage Management)
    creating CDB using DBCA GUI, 39
    creating CDB using OMF, 44–45
    Oracle Managed Files used with, 37
    recommended for database files, 36
ASM Clustered File System (ACFS), 241
ASMM (Automatic Shared Memory Management), 281
atomicity of transactions, PITR of UNDO tablespace, 200
auditing of log in, as proxy user, 153–154
Automatic Memory Management (AMM), 281
Automatic Shared Memory Management (ASMM), 281
Automatic Workload Repository (AWR), collecting statistics, 31–32
autotask directive, CDB resource plan, 268, 270–273
auxiliary instance
    PDBPITR in local UNDO mode, 212
    point-in-time recovery, 205–206
    restore/recover PDB with RMAN, 202–205
availability
    multitenant option, 80
    single-tenant consolidation, 76
Availability menu, creating standby in Cloud Control, 304–308
AWR (Automatic Workload Repository), collecting statistics, 31–32
AWS (Amazon Web Services), back up to cloud, 195

B

backup
    of archive logs, 183
    block corruption check, 193–194
    CDB recovery and, 175–180
    before CDB upgrade, 103–104
    to cloud, 195–196
    Cloud Control for, 194–195

Index   367

creating physical standby for, 291–292
hot vs. cold, 170–172
overview of, 170
PDB, 175–176, 180–183
and recovery. *See* recovery
RMAN backup redundancy, 174
RMAN default configuration, 173–174
RMAN optimization, 189–193
of source to standby with RMAN, 293
SYSBACKUP for, 174–175
`backup database` commands, 173–174, 181
`BACKUP OPTIMIZATION ON`, consolidating single-tenant CDB, 77
`BEFORE SET CONTAINER` trigger, 26, 252
`BEFORE UNPLUG` trigger, 252–253
Big Data adapters, 359–361
`BIGFILE/SMALLFILE` datafile, 92, 98
block change tracking, RMAN, 191–192
block corruption checks, 193–194
BPU (Bundle Patch Update), 112

C

case-insensitivity, common user prefix, 151
case-sensitivity, `DB_UNIQUE_NAME` clause, 118
`catalog` command, PDB recovery on standby, 313
catalog options, creating CDB in SQL*Plus, 53
catcon.pl script
    creating CDB in SQL*Plus, 50–51
    creating PDB, 67–69
    pre-upgrade check for CDB, 102
    recompiling invalid objects for CDB, 55
    running preupgrade script, 104–105
catctl.pl utility, upgrades, 105–106
catoctk.sql script, creating CDB, 53
catproc.sql script, creating CDB, 53
catupgrd.sql, upgrading CDB, 105–107
CDB backup and recovery
    full backups, 176–178
    overview of, 175–176
    partial backups, 178–179
    reporting using RMAN, 179–180
    restore and recovery, 184–187

CDB (container database)
    avoid putting all databases in same, 79–80
    cloning local PDB, 240–241
    connecting to containers, 23–26
    creating common users for admin, 140–141
    dictionary views, 26–27
    dropping, 90
    files common to all containers, 27–30
    holding multiple pluggable databases, 14–16
    identifying containers, 20–23
    managing, 89–92
    managing physical standby, 308–314
    managing resources in Resource Manager, 264
    modifying entire, 90–91
    as multitenant database, 14
    multitenant dictionaries and, 16–20
    PDB level parameters vs., 113–118
    recovery scenarios, 183–187
    removing running database, 47
    Resource Manager requirements, 263
    single-tenant, 74–79
    startup and shutdown, 90–91
    unplugging PDB/plugging into different, 230–231
    upgrades. *See* upgrades, CDB
CDB, creating
    Oracle Managed Files and, 36–37
    overview of, 36
    using `CREATE DATABASE` or DBCA, 90
    using DBCA CLI, 42–44
    using DBCA GUI, 37–42
    using one PDB (FS and non-OMF), 46–47
    using SQL*Plus, 47–55
    using two PDBs (ASM and OMF), 44–45
CDB resource plan, Resource Manager
    creating, 269–273
    creating with PDB profiles, 275–277
    default and autotask directives, 267–268
    defined, 262
    enabling/removing, 274–275
    managing, 273–274

CDB resource plan, Resource Manager (*cont.*)
    overview of, 265
    removing directive for, 275
    removing directive for PDB
        profile, 277
    resource allocation and utilization
        limits, 265–267
    viewing, 285
CDB SPFILE, 114
CDB_PDB_HISTORY view, 97
CDB$ROOT
    block change tracking, 191
    changing UNDO mode, 211
    common users, local users and, 140
    complete recovery of, 185–186
    connecting to CDB via, 89–90
    creating CDB, 54, 90
    creating common users, 144–146
    creating database with local
        UNDO, 208
    data links, 20
    Data Recovery Advisor run
        only from, 193
    dictionary views from, 17–18, 26–27
    full CDB backup of, 176–177
    full PDB backup of, 180–181
    granting common privileges,
        147–148
    identifying containers, 22–23
    metadata links, 18–19
    modifying entire CDB, 90–91
    modifying root container, 92
    multitenant dictionaries and, 16–17
    overview of, 15–16
    partial backup details, 179–180
    partial PDB backup from, 182
    recompiling invalid objects, 55
    recovering from lost datafile, 186
    recovering from lost tablespace, 186
    recovering PDB nonsystem
        datafile, 188
    recovering PDB system datafile, 188
    recovering PDB tablespace,
        188–189
    recovering PDB until time, 203–204
    in Resource Manager, 284–285
    restore points at CDB/PDB levels,
        216–218
    restricting access to container data,
        151–153
    results of querying from, 325, 328
    specifying `DATABASE` for
        backups, 175
    UNDO for all transactions in, 211
CDB_views, common users, 151
CDC (Change Data Capture), 348
changed blocks, incremental backups,
    189–191
CLI (command-line interface)
    creating CDB with DBCA, 42–44
    creating PDB with DBCA, 65–66
`CLONEDB` initialization parameter,
    snapshots, 241
cloning
    copying database by, 228
    with Delphix, 324
    non-CDB, 250–251
    to Oracle Cloud in OEM, 251–252
    overview of, 239–240
    plug in a PDB as, 237–238
    remote. *See* remote clone
    with TDE, 164–165
close state, PDBs, 93–94
cloud
    backup options for, 195–196
    consolidating PDBs, 14–15
    moving PDBs to, 251–252
    Oracle Database 12c, 5
    running standby in, 315–318
Cloud Control
    backup options, 194–195
    creating CDB resource plan, 271–273
    creating database link, 321
    creating PDB, 66–67
    creating physical standby, 29s
    creating standby, 304–308
    monitoring PDBs managed by
        Resource Manager, 285
    monitoring Resource Manager, 284
    opening/closing PDBs, 95–96
    setting up TDE, 161
    transportable tablespaces, 322–323
Cloud Services, back up to Oracle, 195–196
cluster database, opening PDB in, 96
Codd's rules, 11
cold (consistent) backups, 170–172, 185
columns, TDE encrypting all table, 163–164
command-line interface (CLI)
    creating CDB with DBCA, 42–44
    creating PDB with DBCA, 65–66

commands, pluggable databases accepting all, 15
COMMENT clause, for permanently changed parameters, 115
common roles, creating, 153
common users
    avoid mixing local users in same namespace as, 144
    conflict resolution between local and, 148–150
    connecting through local proxy user to, 153–154
    creating with CONTAINER=ALL option, 144–146
    granting common privileges to, 147–148
    granting local privileges to, 146–147
    keeping conflict resolution clear and simple, 150–151
    querying V$ views for information, 151
    restricting access to container data, 151–153
    stored in every single PDB, 140–141
COMMON_USER_PREFIX
    for all common user names, 144–145
    keeping clear and simple, 151
compatibility checks
    cloning remote PDB, 242
    converting non-CDB by plugging in, 248–250
    running, 236
compatibility, plug-in, 235–237
COMPATIBLE parameter
    multisection incremental backups, 192–193
    upgrade CDB with catupgrd.sql, 105
compressed backup set output, full CDB backups, 176–177
CON_DBID, identifying pluggable database, 31
configuration file, extract process in GoldenGate, 353–354
conflict resolution, 148–151
CON_ID, identifying containers, 20–22, 31
CONNECT role, creating new PDB from PDB$SEED, 59
connection
    to application containers, 81
    basics of traditional database, 120–121
    to CDB, via root container, 89–90
    to containers, 23–26
    default services and PDB, 125–129
connection brokers. multithreaded networking, 124
CONNECTION_BROKERS database parameter, 124
consistent (cold) backups, 170–172, 185
consolidated data
    container map, 339–342
    containers default, 339
    cross-PDB DML, 338–339
    linking tables across containers, 330–338
    location independence, 342–343
    sharing data across PDBs, 329–330
consolidated servers, 5
consolidation
    data/metadata at CDB level, 30–33
    files common to all CDBs, 27–30
    history of database use, 5
    managing multiple databases with one instance, 10
    with multitenant option, 14–15, 83, 123–124
    pros and cons of, 11
    road to multitenant architecture, 5–6
    schema. See schema consolidation
    server, 9–10
    single-tenant CDBs, 76–77
    single-tenant vs. multitenant options, 83
    summary of strategies for, 10–11
    table, 9
consumer groups
    creating PDB resource plan, 277–280
    mapping, 277
container map, sharing data across PDBs, 339–342
CONTAINER=ALL clause
    changing parameter for all PDBs, 116–117
    CREATE USER/CREATE ROLE option, 142
    creating master key, 163
    opening keystore in TDE, 162
CONTAINER=CURRENT clause, 142, 146–147
CONTAINER_DATA, restricting common user access to, 151–153

containers
- application, 80–83
- CDB$ROOT. *See* CDB$ROOT
- choosing, 88–89
- connecting to, 23–26
- dictionary views from, 26–27
- identifying, 20–23
- linking tables across, 330–338
- multitenant, 14
- Oracle database vs. lightweight, 6
- PDB$SEED, 16
- separating system/application metadata, 13–14
- setting trigger, 26

`CONTAINERS()` clause
- cross-PDB DML, 338–339
- cross-PDB views, 324–325
- default value in grant statement, 148
- `ENABLE CONTAINERS_DEFAULT` vs., 339
- gathering data from local/proxy PDBs, 342–343
- querying own user tables, 325–329

containers default, sharing data across PDBs, 339

control files
- common to all containers in CDB, 27–28
- in full CDB backups, 176
- modifying entire CDB, 90

CON_UID, identifying containers, 21–23
`CONVERTING` status, non-CDBs, 21
`COPIES` clause, RMAN backup redundancy, 174

copy
- database. *See* cloning
- database to different database with logical replication, 346–347
- password file for standby with RMAN, 293–295

copy on write, sharing data across PDBs, 323–324
CPU (Critical Patch Update), 112
CPU usage of PDBs, Resource Manager limiting, 261
Create A Database option, DBCA GUI, 38–39
Create As Container Database option, DBCA GUI, 40–41
`CREATE_CDB_PROFILE_DIRECTIVE`, 276
`CREATE DATABASE`
- creating CDB, 51–52
- in local UNDO mode, 207–208
- managing CDB, 90

`CREATE PFILE`, 115, 294
`CREATE PLUGGABLE DATABASE`
- connecting to containers, 23
- creating new PDB from PDB$SEED, 56–59
- creating PDB in SQL*PLUS, 55
- locating new PDB created with clone/plug-in, 247
- relocating database, 246

`CREATE ROLE`, 142
`CREATE SESSION`, privileges, 147–148
`CREATE USER`
- as common user with `CONTAINER=ALL`, 144–146
- as local user with `CONTAINER=CURRENT`, 142–143
- overview of, 142

`CREATE_CDB_PLAN_DIRECTIVE`, 274
`CREATE_CONSUMER_GROUP`, 277, 280
`CREATE_FILE_DEST`, 159
`CREATE_PLAN`, 277, 280
`CREATE_PLAN_DIRECTIVE`, 277, 280
credentials, Direct NFS, 241
Critical Patch Update (CPU), 112
cross-database replication, data sharing with, 343
cross-PDB DML, 338–339
cross-PDB views
- consolidated data, 329–330
- container map, 339–342
- containers default, 339
- cross-PDB DML, 338–339
- linking tables across containers, 330–338
- location independence, 342–343
- overview of, 324–325
- simple user tables, 325–329

cumulative incremental backups, RMAN, 189–191
cursor sharing, schema consolidation, 8–9
cursors, connecting to containers, 24–26

D

DAS (direct attached disks), Oracle Database 8*i* and 9*i*, 4–5
data
    analysis, with logical replication, 347
    consolidating at CDB level, 30–33
    moving. *See* moving data
    in multitenant containers, 14
    sharing. *See* sharing data across PDBs
    storing metadata with, 11–12
Data Definition Language (DDL), 8, 326–327
data dictionary table, user/role definitions, 141
Data Guard
    Active Data Guard, 291
    Cloud Control, 314–315
    creating physical standby, 291–292
    creating physical standby in multitenantt, 308–314
    creating standby with Cloud Control, 304–308
    duplicating standby with RMAN, 292–304
    overview of, 290
    standby in cloud, 315–318
Data Guard Broker
    configure network setup for standby, 293
    Data Guard configuration and, 292
    start processes/finish configuration, 297–299
data-linked objects, linking tables across containers, 336–338
data links (object links), 18–19, 80
Data Manipulation Language (DML), 89
Data Pump, 75, 254–255
Data Recovery Advisor, 193
data security
    `CONTAINER_DATA`, 151–153
    `CREATE_FILE_DEST`, 159
    creating roles, 153
    encryption. *See* TDE (Transparent Data Encryption)
    lockdown profiles, 155–158
    `PATH_PREFIX`, 158
    PDB isolation, 158–159
    proxy users, 153–155

data table, application containers, 81
database administrator. *See* DBA (database administrator)
Database as a Service (DBaaS), 5, 79
Database Configuration Assistant. *See* DBCA (Database Configuration Assistant)
Database Express 12.2
    creating CDB resource plan, 270–273
    monitoring PDBs managed by Resource Manager, 285–286
    monitoring Resource Manager, 284
`DATABASE` key word, CDB and PDB backups, 175
database links, 8, 320–321
database offerings, Oracle Public Cloud, 316
database time zone, 92, 98
Database Upgrade Assistant. *See* DBUA (Database Upgrade Assistant)
`DATABASE_PROPERTIES`, cross-PDB DML, 339
databases, creating
    container. *See* CDB (container database)
    overview of, 36
    pluggable. *See* PDBs, creating
datafiles
    for all containers in CDB, 30
    CDB administrator restricting, 159
    creating standby with RMAN, 294–295
    enabling PDB recovery on standby, 313
    in full CDB backups, 176
    nodata clones and, 243
    partial PDB backup of, 181–182
    recovering from CDB$ROOT, 186
    recovering PDB nonsystem, 188
    recovering PDB system, 187–188
    remove existing PDB from standby, 312–313
    restoring PDB to previous state, 200
    restoring/recovering PDB, 202–204
    setting transportable tablespaces to read-only, 322
day-to-day management
    CDBs, 89–92
    choosing container, 88–89
    overview of, 88

day-to-day management (cont.)
    patching, 112–113
    patching and upgrades, 100–101
    PDBs. See PDBs, managing
    plug-in, 111–112
    upgrading CDB, 101–111
    using CDB-level vs. PDB-level parameters. See parameters, CDB-level vs. PDB-level
DBA (database administrator)
    lockdown profiles, 155–159
    management tasks. See day-to-day management
    as proxy user, 153–155
    separation of roles, 155
DBaaS (Database as a Service), 5, 79
DBA_CDB_RSRC_PLAN_DIRECTIVES, CDB resource plan, 277
DBA_CONTAINER_DATA dictionary view, 152
DBA_ENCRYPTED_COLUMNS, TDE-encrypted columns, 164
DBA_HIST views, AWR, 31
DBA_OBJECTS, Oracle-maintained objects, 13
DBA_PDBS dictionary view, PDBs/their status, 21–22
DBA_PDB_SAVED_STATES view, opening/closing PDBs, 96
DBA_ROLES, Oracle-maintained objects, 13
DBA_SOURCE view, 16–18
DBA_USERS view, 13, 324–325
+DBBACKUP disk group, full CDB backup, 177
DBCA CLI, creating CDB, 42–44
dbca command, creating CDB, 38
DBCA (Database Configuration Assistant)
    creating CDB, 90
    creating CDB using DBCA CLI, 42–44
    creating CDB using DBCA GUI, 37–42
    creating database in local UNDO, 207
    creating PDB, 65–66
DBCA GUI, creating CDB, 37–42
DB_CACHE_SIZE parameter, PDB memory allocation, 282
DB_FILE_NAME_CONVERT settings, PDB recovery on standby, 313
DBID, identifying containers, 22–23, 31

DBMS_SQL.PARSE, SQL on multiple PDBs, 98
dbms_preup package, pre-upgrade check for CDB, 102
DBMS_RESOURCE_MANAGER package
    adjusting default directive, 268
    creating CDB resource plan, 269, 276
    modifying CDB resource plan, 273–274
    removing PDB resource plan, 281
    Resource Manager configuration/management, 263
    updating autotask directive, 268
DBMS_RESOURCE_MANAGER_PRIVS package, 264
DBMS_ROLLING package, automatic upgrades, 363
DBMS_SERVICE package, creating services, 133–134
DB_PERFORMANCE_PROFILE, CDB resource plan, 275–276
DBUA (Database Upgrade Assistant)
    automating database backup, 104
    automating upgrade process, 103
    overview of, 110–111
DB_UNIQUE_NAME clause, primary vs. standby databases, 117–118
Dbvisit Replicate, logical replication tool, 363
DDL (Data Definition Language), 8, 326–327
dedicated listener, creating for PDB, 134–137
default directives, CDB resource plan, 267–268, 270–273
DELETE_PLAN, PDB resource plan, 281
deleting (removing)
    CDB resource plan, 275
    CDB resource plan directive, 275, 277
    PDB resource plan, 281
Dell SharePlex, 363
Delphix, cloning/storage de-duplication with, 324
describe file, PDB SPFILE equivalent, 115
dictionaries
    multitenant, 16–20, 72
    system. See system dictionary

Index

dictionary tables, 16
dictionary views
    from containers, 26–27
    of dictionary objects, 19
    listing all PDBs and their status, 21–22
    overview of, 17–18
    querying metadata with, 11
    stored in CDB$ROOT, 16
differential incremental backups, RMAN, 189–190
direct attached disks (DAS), Oracle Database 8*i* and 9*i*, 4–5
Direct NFS, Oracle favoring/promoting, 241
directories
    configuring/starting manager in GoldenGate, 353
    creating standby with RMAN, 294
    schema consolidation and, 8
`DISABLE` clause, `ALTER LOCKDOWN PROFILE`, 156
disable database options, with lockdown profiles, 155–156
disaster recovery. *See* Data Guard
DML (Data Manipulation Language)
    cross-PDB DML, 338–339
    limiting to current container, 89
drop operations
    `DROP DATABASE`, 90
    `DROP PLUGGABLE DATABASE`, 90, 99–100, 311–312
`DUPLICATE` command, create standby with RMAN, 295
duplication, RMAN backup redundancy, 174

E

`ENABLE` clause, `ALTER LOCKDOWN PROFILE`, 156
`ENABLE CONTAINERS_DEFAULT`, 339
`ENABLE PLUGGABLE DATABASE`
    creating CDB in SQL*Plus, 48–52
    creating database in local UNDO, 207–208
    defining multitenant architecture, 72
`enable_goldengate_replication`, source database setup, 350–351
`ENCRYPT` keyword, TDE, 163–164

encryption. *See* TDE (Transparent Data Encryption)
Enterprise Edition, single-tenant in, 77–79
Enterprise Manager
    Cloud Control. *See* Cloud Control
    Database Express 12.2. *See* Database Express 12.2
    opening/closing PDBs, 95–96
error messages
    Data Guard broker and, 298–299
    documentation book for, 298
    query user tables for, 325–327
Event Streaming mode, Dbvisit Replicate, 363
event triggers, on PDB operations, 252–253
expire all unused accounts, creating CDB, 54
export, full transportable, 253–255
extended data metadata-linked objects, 333–336
extract process, GoldenGate
    BigData support, 359–361
    initial extract, 356–357
    multitenant support, 353–354
    running initial extract, 358
    starting, 358–359

F

fallback scenario, planning before upgrades, 104
Fast Recovery Area (FRA), 39, 104, 212
features
    disabling with lockdown profiles, 158
    not compatible in multitenant, 73–74
file storage (FS), creating CDB without OMF, 46
`FILE_ID`, datafiles, 30
`FILE_NAME_CONVERT` clause, creating new PDB from PDB$SEED, 58–59
files, CDB container
    control files, 27–28
    datafiles, 30
    overview of, 27–30
    redo logs, 29
    SPFILE, 27
    temporary tablespaces, 28–29
    UNDO tablespace, 28
files, naming database, 36–37

FILESPERSET, multisection incremental backups, 192–193
flashback database, 300–302
flashback logs
    in auxiliary instance cleanup, 225
    modifying root container, 92
    overview of, 213–215
    at PDB level, 218–219
    planning backup for CDB upgrades, 104
FLASHBACK OFF, 216, 218
FLASHBACK ON, 213–215
flashback PDB
    auxiliary instance cleanup, 225
    cleaning restore point, 219–220
    flashback logging, 213–215
    impacting standby database, 223–224
    with local UNDO, 215–216
    overview of, 213
    PITR vs., 221–222
    resetlogs, 221–222
    restore points at CDB/PDB levels, 216–219
    in shared UNDO, 216
    single-tenant in Enterprise Edition, 77–78
FORCE LOGGING mode, modifying PDB, 99
FORMAT option, full CDB backups, 176–177
FRA (Fast Recovery Area), 39, 104, 212
FS (file storage), creating CDB without OMF, 46
full CDB backups, 176–178
full CDB recovery, 185
full PDB backups, 180–181
full transportable export/import, 253–255
FULL=Y, IMPDP options, 12

G

-generateScripts, database, 48
GGSCI (GoldenGate Software Command Interface), 352–353
global database name, modifying entire CDB, 90
GoldenGate
    configure and start manager, 352–353
    configure parameter files for replicat, 355–357
    extract configuration file, 353–354
    logical replication with, 349
    multitenant support in, 349–351
    replacing Oracle Streams in multitenant, 73
    run initial extract, 358
    set up target database, 354–355
    start extract and replicat, 358–359
    supporting big data adapters, 359–361
    table supplemental logging, 352
GoldenGate Software Command Interface (GGSCI), 352–353
grant statement, privileges, 146–148
GRANT_SWITCH_CONSUMER_GROUP, Resource Manager, 264, 279–280
GRANT_SYSTEM_PRIVILEGE, Resource Manager, 264
groups, temporary tablespace, 92
guaranteed restore point, flashback logs, 214–215
GUI (graphical user interface)
    creating CDB, 37–42
    creating PDB, 65
GUID
    clone operations, 240
    identifying containers, 22

H

hard-coded users, 142
hard-coding schema name, 7–8
HASH schema, for container map, 342
history
    of database use, 4–5
    viewing PDB operation, 97
HOST, proxy DBs, 247
hot clone (refreshable copy), 244, 245–246
hot (online, inconsistent) backups, 171–172
HugePages, impact on memory management, 281

I

I/O (input/output)
    managing PDB via initialization parameters, 281–283
    Resource Manager limiting PDB, 261
    setting parameters at PDB level, 267

Index

IaaS (Infrastructure as a Service), 5
IDs (identifiers)
    `CON_ID` for containers, 20–22
    `CON_UID` and `DBID` for containers, 22–23
    `DBA_HIST` views, AWR, 31
    `FILE_ID`, datafiles, 30
image copies
    full CDB backups, 176–177
    multisection incremental backups, 192–193
    restore and recover PDBs, 187
    view full CDB backup details with `LIST`, 177
importing
    full database into new database, 12
    full transportable database, 253–255
incremental backups, RMAN
    block change tracking for, 91, 191–192
    combining with multisection backups, 192–193
    keeping image copies up to date with, 176
    for optimization, 189–191
Information Lifecycle Management, 74
Infrastructure as a Service (IaaS), 5
inheritance, conflict resolution, 149
initial extract, Golden Gate replication, 356–357, 358
initialization parameters
    creating CDB resource plan with PDB profile, 275–276
    enabling/disabling PDB resource plan, 281
    managing PDB memory and I/O, 281–283
init.ora, storing parameters in older versions in, 113
instance caging, 283–284
instance recovery, CDBs, 184
instance(s)
    AWR collecting, 31–32
    creating service with SRVCTL, 130–132
    initialization parameters controlling, 113
    multiple databases managed by one, 4, 10–11
    RMAN commands to restore/recover PDB, 203
    server consolidation and, 9–10
    in traditional database connection, 120–121
invalid objects, recompiling, 55
`ISPDB_MODIFIABLE`, 116
`ISSYS_MODIFIABLE`, 116

J

Java, preupgrade.jar file, 103
JDBC (Java Database Connectivity), connecting to containers from, 25

K

`KEEP DATAFILES`, unplugged PDB, 231
keystore, TDE, 160–163

L

levels, Resource Manager, 264–265
LGWRs (Log Writers), redo logs, 29
licenses
    cloud virtual machines requiring, 317
    creating PDB in Enterprise Edition, 78–79
    multitenant requiring, 72–73
    single-tenant not requiring, 72
    virtualization and, 10
links, public synonyms and database, 8
`LIST` command, view full backups, 177–178, 181
listener registration (LREG) background process, 121–123, 127
`listener_address` string, dedicated listener for PDB, 135
`LISTENER_NETWORKS`, dedicated listener for PDB, 135
listener.ora file
    creating dedicated listener for PDB, 135–136
    setting listener to allow threads, 124
    static network definition setup, 293
listeners
    creating PDB dedicated, 134–137
    creating service with SRVCTL, 131–132

listeners (*cont.*)
    default services/connecting to PDBs, 125–129
    Oracle Net Listener, 120–121
    registration process, 121–123
    setting to allow threads, 124
load options, creating CDB with SQL*Plus, 53
local clone
    create new PDB for standby, 310
    creating inside single PDB, 240–241
    creating new PDB, 59–60
local roles, creating, 153
local UNDO
    cloning local PDB, 241
    cloning remote PDB, 242
    flashback with, 215–216
    hot cloning remote PDB, 241–242
local UNDO, in 12.2
    changing to shared UNDO from, 223
    changing UNDO mode, 209–211
    changing UNDO tablespace, 208–209
    creating database, 207–208
    database properties, 207
    overview of, 206–207
    PDBPITR in, 212–213
    using shared or, 211
`LOCAL UNDO OFF` state, shared UNDO, 211–213, 216
`LOCAL UNDO ON` state, local UNDO, 211, 215–216
local users
    conflict resolution between common and, 148–150
    creating with `CONTAINER=CURRENT`, 142–143
    granting local privileges to, 146–147
    keeping conflict resolution clear and simple, 150–151
    namespace for, 144
    as proxy users in multitenant, 153
    stored only in single PDB, 140–141
    SYSBACKUP privilege for, 174–175
`LOCAL_LISTENER` parameter, create standby, 294
locally managed tablespaces, 12
`LOCAL_UNDO_ENABLED` property, database, 207
location independence, sharing data across PDBs, 342–343
locations, altering PDB file. *See* PDBs, moving files
lock all unused accounts, creating CDB with SQL*Plus, 54
lockdown profiles
    disable ALTER SYSTEM, 156–157
    disable database options, 155–156
    disable features, 158
    overview of, 155
    PDB isolation, 158–159
    single-tenant security and, 76
log in, auditing as proxy users, 153–155
Log Writers (LGWRs), redo logs, 29
logical replication
    defined, 346
    deprecated features, 348–349
    Oracle LogMiner and, 347–348
    with Oracle XStream, 361–363
    with other third-party options, 363
    overview of, 346–347
logical replication, Oracle GoldenGate
    configure and start manager, 352–353
    configure parameter files for replicat processes, 355–357
    extract configuration file, 353–354
    multitenant support, 349–351
    overview of, 349
    run initial extract, 358
    set up target database, 354–355
    start extract and replicats, 358–359
    supporting big data adapters, 359–361
    table supplemental logging, 352
logical standby database, 362
logs
    flashback, 213–215
    multitenant support in GoldenGate, 352
    pre-upgrade check for CDB, 102–103
    resetlogs, 221–222
    resuming CDB upgrade after failure, 108
loopback database link, non-CDBs, 320–321
LREG (listener registration) background process, 121–123, 127
`lsnrctl start listener_pdb` command, 135–136

Index 377

M

maintenance, autotask directive, 268
management. *See* day-to-day management
manager, configure GoldenGate, 352–353
mapping, container, 339–342
master key
    create and store in keystore, 162–163
    shipping when plugging in/unplugging, 164–165
    Transparent Data Encryption setup, 159–160
    verifying created keys, 163
`MAX_IOPS` parameter, limiting PDB I/O, 282
`MAX_MBPS` parameter, limiting PDB I/O, 282
`MAX_SHARED_TEMP_SIZE`, temporary tablespace quota, 28
memory
    creating CDB resource plan, 269–271
    managing PDB, 281–283
    Resource Manager limiting usage of PDBs, 261
    server consolidation and, 9–10
    setting memory limits, 266–267
    setting utilization limits for PDBs, 266–267
    virtualization and, 10
`memory_limit`
    CDB resource plan, 266–267, 270–271, 273
    CDB resource plan using PDB profiles, 276–277
    PDB resource plan, 279
`memory_min` limit
    CDB resource plan, 266, 270–271, 273
    CDB resource plan using PDB profiles, 276–277
    PDB resource plan, 279
metadata
    application container table, 81
    Codd's rules for RDBMS, 11
    consolidating at CDB level, 30–33
    links, 18–19
    in multitenant containers, 14
    in pluggable database, 72
    stored in system dictionary, 11–12
    system vs. application, 13–14
    transportable tablespaces in multitenant and, 7

metadata-linked objects, 331–336
MIGRATE state, PDBs, 93
migration, logical replication use case for, 346
`modify service`, for Oracle RAC PDB, 133
monitoring, Resource Manager, 284–286
MOUNTED state, PDBs, 93, 212
mounted state, performing cold backups with RMAN in, 171
moving data
    altering PDB file locations. *See* PDBs, moving files
    in application containers, 247
    by cloning, 239–240
    by cloning local PDB, 240–241
    by cloning remote PDB, 242–247
    converting non-CDB, 247–250
    full transportable export/import for, 253–255
    overview of, 228
    in PDBs to cloud, 251–256
    transportable tablespaces for, 255–256
    triggers on PDB operations for, 252–253
multiple channel backup, RMAN, 192
multisection incremental backup, RMAN, 192–193
multitenant administration. *See* day-to-day management
multitenant databases
    application containers, 80–83
    consolidation, 5, 83
    data movement, 75
    database links, 321
    non-CDB depreciation and, 72–73
    not an option, 72–74
    overview of, 79–80
    purchasing license for, 72
    supported in GoldenGate, 349–351
    unsupported features in, 73–74
multitenant, introduction to
    connecting to containers, 23–24
    consolidation at CDB level, 27–33
    consolidation pros and cons, 10–11
    data and metadata at CDB level, 30–33
    dictionary views from containers, 26–27
    history of database use, 4–5

multitenant, introduction to (*cont.*)
    identifying containers, 20–23
    list of containers, 21–22
    multiple databases managed by one instance, 10
    multitenant containers, 14–16
    multitenant dictionaries, 16–20
    overview of, 4
    road to multitenant, 5–6
    schema consolidation, 6–9
    server consolidation, 9–10
    system dictionary. *See* system dictionary
    system dictionary, containers, 14–16
    table consolidation, 9
    virtualization, 10
multithreaded mode
    LREG running in, 122–123
    and multitenant, 123–125
My Oracle Support (MOS), 100, 101

N

name collision, schema consolidation and, 7–8
names
    avoid hard-coding schema, 7–8
    creating CDB using DBCA GUI, 40
    identifying containers with, 20–22
    identifying objects with schema/object, 88–89
    public synonyms and schema, 8
    service, 125–129
    tablespace, 8
    using OMF for database file, 36–37
namespace
    avoid mixing common/local users in same, 144
    keeping clear and simple, 150–151
NAS (network-attached storage), 5
NEED UPGRADE status, PDBs, 21
network-attached storage (NAS), 5
networking and services
    creating dedicated listener for PDB, 134–137
    creating services, 129–134
    LREG process, 121–123
    networking, multithreaded and multitenant, 123–125
    Oracle Net, 120
    Oracle Net Listener, 120–121
    overview of, 120
    service names, 125–129
networking packages, disabling, 158
NEW status, PDBs, 21–22
NLS_DATE_FORMAT environment variable, RMAN, 173
NOARCHIVELOG mode
    backing up database in, 104
    modifying entire CDB, 90
    performing cold backups in, 171, 185
nodata clone, remote PDB, 243
NOFILENAMECHECK, RMAN, 295
NOLOGGING mode, modifying PDB, 99
NOMOUNT state
    creating CDB using SQL*Plus, 51–52
    restoring CDB using cold backup, 185
    unavailable for PDBs, 22, 93
non-CDB (non-container database)
    container database vs., 14
    converting, 247–251
    Data Recovery Advisor used in, 193
    database link categories in, 320–321
    depreciation of, 72–73
    instance caging to CDB resource plan, 283–284
    movement away from. *See* day-to-day management
    noncompatible features, 73–74
    object identification in, 88
    running APEX on, 30–31
    as system dictionary in past, 11–14
NORMAL status, PDBs, 21–22
null string, avoid setting prefix to, 144

O

object links (data links), 18–19, 80
objects
    creating CDBs by recompiling invalid, 55
    identifying in non-CDB, 88
    identifying in PDB, 88–89
    identifying Oracle-maintained, 12–13
obsolete logical replication features, 348–349
OCI (Oracle Call Interface), connecting to containers, 25

Index   379

OEM (Oracle Enterprise Manager), 144–146
oerr utility, 298
OMF (Oracle Managed Files)
    cloning PDB within same CDB, 59
    creating CDB using file storage without, 46
    creating CDE with two PDBs, 45–46
    creating new PDB from PDB$SEED, 56–58
    enabling/disabling block change tracking, 191–192
    enabling PDB recovery on standby, 314
    file naming with, 36–37
    identifying PDB in directory structure, 22
    restoring/recovering PDB with RMAN, 203–204
open normally, end of CDB upgrade, 108
OPEN RESETLOGS, 221–222
open state, PDBs, 93–94
operating systems. *See* OSs (operating systems)
OPT_PARAM hint, 113
Oracle Advanced Replication, as deprecated, 349
Oracle Application Express (APEX), 30–31, 107
Oracle Call Interface (OCI), connecting to containers, 25
Oracle Change Data Capture (CDC), as deprecated, 348
Oracle Cloud Services, back up to, 195–196
Oracle Database Resource Manager. *See* Resource Manager
Oracle Database versions, history of, 4–5
Oracle Enterprise Manager (OEM), creating local/common user, 143–146
Oracle GoldenGate. *See* GoldenGate
Oracle LogMiner, 347–348
Oracle Managed Files. *See* OMF (Oracle Managed Files)
Oracle Net, 120
Oracle Net Listener, 120–121
Oracle Net Services, 120
Oracle Public Cloud, running standby in, 315–318
Oracle Streams
    as deprecated, 348–349
    only supported in non-CDB architecture, 73
Oracle XStream, logical replication, 361–363
ORACLE_HOME directories
    patching using, 112–113
    pre-upgrade check for CDB, 101–103
    upgrade CDB with catupgrd.sql, 105–106
ORACLE_MAINTAINED column, 142
ORACLE_MAINTAINED flag, 13
ORACLE_SID, consolidating single-tenant CDBs, 76
ora_lreg_*SID*, LREG process, 121
OSs (operating systems)
    credentials in single-tenant security, 76
    database resource allocation, 260
    distributing resources with Resource Manager, 261
    limiting interaction with file system/processes, 158

P

parallel execution servers, Resource Manager, 261
parallel_server_limit, CDB resource plan, 266
parameters
    configure replicat processes, 355
    create CDB using SQL*Plus, 49–50
    create standby with RMAN, 293–295
    modifying entire CDB, 90–92
    modifying PDB, 98–99
    plugging in non-CDB, 249
    resuming CDB upgrade after failure, 108–109
    running catupgrd.sql to upgrade CDB, 105–107
parameters, CDB-level vs. PDB-level
    ALTER SYSTEM RESET, 116
    CDB SPFILE, 114
    Container=ALL, 116–117
    DB_UNIQUE_NAME, 117–118
    ISPDB_MODIFIABLE, 116
    overview of, 113–114
    PDB SPFILE equivalent, 114–115
    SCOPE=MEMORY, 116

parent cursors, consolidation of, 8–9
partial CDB backups, 178–179
partial PDB backups, 181–182
partitions, table consolidation and, 9
passwords
    create standby with RMAN, 293–295
    creating CDB using DBCA CLI, 44–45
    creating CDB using SQL*Plus, 50–51
    proxy users and, 153–155
Patch Set Update (PSU), 112
patching
    CDBs (container databases), 112–113
    overview of, 100–101
PATH_PREFIX, lockdown profile, 158
PDB level, Resource Manager, 265
PDB profiles
    CDB resource plan, 266–267, 275–276
    Resource Manager, 263
PDB SPFILE equivalent, 114–115
PDBADMIN user, creating CDB, 39, 41
PDB_DBA role, 41
PDB_LOCKDOWN parameter
    disable ALTER SYSTEM, 157
    disable database options, 156
    disable features, 158
PDB_OS_CREDENTIALS, lockdown profile, 158
PDBPITR (PDB point-in-time recovery).
    See also flashback PDB
    in local UNDO mode, 212–213
    overview of, 200–201
    restore/recover PDB with RMAN, 201–204
    in shared UNDO mode, 211–212
    summary of 12.1, 205–206
    where is the UNDO? 204–205
PDB_PLUG_IN_VIOLATIONS
    conflict resolution, 151
    running compatibility check, 236
    upgrading PDBs, 111–112
PDBs, creating
    overview of, 55–56, 92–93
    from PDB$SEED, 56–59
    using catcon.pl script, 67–69
    using Cloud Control, 66–67
    using DBCA, 65–66
    using local clone method, 59–60
    using SQL Developer, 60–64

PDBs, managing
    dropping, 99–100
    modifying, 98–99
    new, 92–93
    opening and closing, 93–96
    overview of, 92
    running SQL on multiple PDBs, 97–98
    view operation history, 97
    view state of, 97
PDBs, moving files
    altering file locations, 228–229
    application container considerations, 247
    cloning, 239–240
    cloning local PDB, 240–241
    cloning remote PDB, 242–247
    to cloud, 251–252
    converting non-CDB database, 247–251
    full transportable export/import, 253–255
    transportable tablespaces, 255–256
    triggers, 252–253
PDBs, moving files with plug-in/unplug
    application containers, 247
    check compatibility for plug-in, 235–237
    overview of, 229
    PDB archive files, 238–239
    plug in PDB as clone, 237–238
    plug in/unplug operations, 229
    plugging in non-CDB, 248–250
    unplug/plug in PDB, 230–231
    unplugged database stays in source, 231–232
    XML file contents, 232–235
PDBs (pluggable databases)
    accepting all commands, 15
    backups, 175–176, 180–183
    CDB level parameters vs., 113–118
    connecting to containers, 23–26
    creating CDB, examples, 44–47
    creating CDB resource plan, 269–273
    creating dedicated listener, 134–137
    creating in SQL*PLUS, 55
    creating on source database, 309–311
    creating services, 129–134
    creating with PDB$SEED container, 17

default services and connecting to, 125–129
dropping, 90
enabling recovery on standby, 313–314
encryption key when plugging in/unplugging, 164–165
isolation, 158–159
listing all/status of all, 21–22
managed by Resource Manager, 285–286
managing memory and I/O, 281–283
modified when modifying CDB, 90–91
one instance opening multiple, 4
querying data, 328–329
removing from source database, 311–312
removing from standby, 312–313
Resource Manager requirements, 263
resource plan, 262, 277–281
restoring and recovering, 187–189
sharing data across. See sharing data across PDBs
single-tenant in Enterprise Edition, 77–79
single-tenant in Standard Edition, 74–77
temporary tablespaces in, 28–29
understanding, 14–15
upgrading, 111–112
PDB$SEED
consolidating single-tenant CDBs, 77
create new PDB on source database, 310
created as part of CREATE DATABASE, 52
creating new PDB, 56–59
creating UNDO tablespace, 210–211
full CDB backup of, 176
opening pluggable database, 53
overview of, 16
PFILE
creating CDB using SQL*Plus, 51–52
creating SPFILE for standby with RMAN, 294
creating SPILE from, 54
recreating SPFILE from, 113
storing parameters in older versions, 113

PGA_AGGREGATE_TARGET, PDB memory allocation, 282
PHASE_TIME number, CDB upgrade after failure, 108–109
physical copy, of database, 346
physical replication, 346, 347
physical standby database, 362
PITR (point-in-time recovery). See also PDBPITR (PDB point-in-time recovery)
auxiliary instance cleanup, 225
flashback PDB. See flashback PDB
flashback vs., 222–224
impact on standby database, 223–224
local UNDO. See local UNDO, in 12.2
overview of, 200
resetlogs, 221–222
plug, and clone with TDE, 164–165
plug-in/unplug PDB
moving files. See PDBs, moving files with plug-in/unplug
for standby database, 311–312
PLUGGABLE DATABASE keywords
full CDB backup, 177–178
partial CDB backup, 178–179
PDB backup, 175
PDB backup without, 181
pluggable databases. See PDBs (pluggable databases)
pluggable keyword, cross-PDB DML, 339
PMON (Process Monitor) process, 121
point-in-time recovery. See PDBPITR (PDB point-in-time recovery)
PORT, proxy DBs, 247
pre-upgrade, CDB, 101–104
prefix
application container, 151
C##, 144–145, 151
preupgrade.jar file, CDB, 103
preupgrd.sql script
post-upgrade scripts generated by, 109
pre-upgrade check for CDB, 101–103
prechecking fast recovery area, 104
running, 104–105
privileges
cloning remote PDB, 245
conflict resolution between common/local users, 148–150
defining roles for same group of, 141
granting common, 147–148

privileges (*cont.*)
    granting local, 146–147
    keeping clear and simple, 150–151
    Resource Manager configuring, 263–264
    SYSBACKUP system, 174–175
    user, 141–142
Process Monitor (PMON) process, 121
profiles, lockdown. *See* lockdown profiles
properties
    changing UNDO mode from database, 207–209
    creating PDB, 61, 63
Provision Pluggable Databases, creating PDB, 66–67
provisioning
    running initial extract, 358
    source data to target, to create baseline, 356–357
proxy PDBs, 246–247, 342–343
proxy users, 153–155
`ps` command
    identifying LREG thread, 123
    viewing thread and process details, 125
PSU (Patch Set Update), 112
Public Cloud, standby in Oracle, 315–318
public synonyms, schema consolidation and, 8

Q

queries
    BOOTSTRAP$ table, 14
    CDB_ views, 151
    current state of all PDBs, 97
    flashback, 356
    user table, 325–329
`_query_on_physical=no`, prevent use of Active Data Guard, 291
Quest SharePlex, 363
quota, temporary tablespace, 28

R

RAC (Real Application Clusters)
    adding service for PDB, 132–133
    in Oracle Database 8i and 9i, 4
    Oracle Net Listener and, 120–121

RANGE schema, container map, 342
RDBMS, Codd's rules for, 11
read-only data
    Active Data Guard enabling, 291
    cloning local PDB, 241
    multiple databases sharing common, 322–324
    for transportable database during import process, 253
READ ONLY state, PDBs, 93
read/write mode
    cloning local PDB in 12.2, 241
    cloning remote PDB, 242
    cloning remote PDB as refreshable copy, 244–245
    opening PDB$SEED, 211
READ WRITE state, PDBs, 93
RECOVER command
    PDBPITR in local UNDO mode, 212
    syntax, 204–205
RECOVER PLUGGABLE DATABASE, PDBPITR, 212–213
recovery. *See also* Data Guard; flashback PDB; PITR (point-in-time recovery)
    backup and. *See* backup
    CDB restore and, 184–187
    with Data Recovery Advisor, 193
    DBA must never fail in, 290
    disabling on standby, 224
    enabling for PDB with standby, 313–314
    instance, 184
    overview of, 170
    PDB restore and, 187–189
    SYSBACKUP privilege for, 174–175
Recovery Manager. *See* RMAN (Recovery Manager)
redo apply, PDB recovery on standby, 313–314
redo logs
    common to all containers in CDB, 29
    create standby with Cloud Control, 306
    create standby with RMAN, 300–302
    Data Guard broker/duplicate database and, 298–299
    LogMiner extracting/displaying changes from, 347–348
    modifying entire CDB, 90
    testing standby created with RMAN, 302–303

REDO, PDB point-in-time recovery, 200
REDO stream, resetlogs, 221–222
redundancy, RMAN backup, 174
refreshable copy (hot clone), 244, 245–246
registration
    creating new PDB, 125–126
    listener, 121–123
    in traditional database connection, 120–121
`RELOCATE` statement, 96, 245–246
`RELOCATED` status, 246
`RELOCATING` status, 245
remote clone
    of non-CDB, 250–251
    plug/unplug operations in, 75
    from previous versions, 112
remote clone PDB
    create new PDB for standby, 311
    nodata, 243
    overview of, 242–243
    proxy PDB, 246–247
    refreshable copy (hot clone), 244–245
    `RELOCATE` statement, 245–246
    root container database link used by, 321
    splitting PDB, 243
    for standby database, 311
remote database link, non-CDBs, 320–321
remote file server (RFS), remote cloning from previous version, 112
`remove service`, Oracle RAC PDB, 133
rename of PDB, 312
replicat processes, BigData support in GoldenGate, 359–361
replicat processes, GoldenGate
    configure parameter files, 355
    defined, 349
    initial extract, 357
    setup target database, 354–355
    topology example, 350
replication
    data sharing with cross-database, 343
    logical. *See* logical replication
    physical vs. logical, 346–347
reports
    Automatic Workload Repository, 31–32
    CDB backup, 179–180
    PDB backup, 181, 183

`RERESHING` status, 244
resource consumer groups, Resource Manager allocating resources to, 261
Resource Manager
    basics, 260–261
    creating CDB resource plan. *See* CDB resource plan, Resource Manager
    creating PDB resource plan, 277–281
    instance caging, 283–284
    levels, 264–265
    managing PDB memory/I/O, 281–283
    monitoring, 284–286
    overview of, 260
    requirements, 263–264
    terminologies, 261–263
resource plan directives
    adding to CDB resource plan, 274
    adjusting default and autotask, 267–268
    creating CDB resource plan, 269–273
    default, 267–268
    removing CDB, 275, 277
    Resource Manager, 261
    specifying resource utilization limits, 267
    updating CDB resource plan, 273–274
    viewing CDB, 285
resource plan, Resource Manager
    creating CDB. *See* CDB resource plan, Resource Manager
    creating PDB, 277–280
    defined, 261–262
    enabling/disabling/removing PDB, 281
    viewing CDB, 285
`RESOURCE_MANAGER_PLAN` parameter, enable/disable PDB resource plan, 281
resources, prioritizing with Resource Manager. *See* Resource Manager
response file, creating CDB, 43–47
`restore` command
    enabling PDB recovery on standby, 314
    PDBPITR in local UNDO mode, 212–213
restore points
    at CDB and PDB levels, 216–219
    for CDB upgrades, 103–104

restore points (*cont.*)
    clean, 219–220
    dropping when testing upgraded application, 109
    flashback logs using guaranteed, 214–215
retention period, flashback log, 214
`REVOKE_SWITCH_CONSUMER_GROUP`, Resource Manager, 264
`REVOKE_SYSTEM_PRIVILEGE`, Resource Manager, 264
RFS (remote file server), remote cloning from previous version, 112
RMAN (Recovery Manager)
    backup optimization, 189–193
    backup redundancy, 174
    CDB and PDB backups, 175
    CDB reporting, 179–180
    cold backups, 171
    commands to restore/recover PDB, 201–204
    creating standby database. *See* standby database, creating with RMAN
    default backup, 173–174
    incremental backups, 90
    PDB backup restrictions, 183
    running standby in the cloud, 317
    setting transportable tablespaces to read-only, 322
    `TAG` option, 170
    unplugged databases part of, 231
roles
    creating with `CREATE ROLE`, 142
    lockdown profile, 155–158
    proxy user, 153–155
    schema consolidation and, 8
    understanding, 141–142
ROLES clause, creating PDBs with SQL*Plus, 41
roll-forward recovery phase, point-in time, 200–201
rollback recovery phase, point-in time, 200–201
rolling upgrades, logical standby used in, 362–363
root container database link, administration only, 321

S

SAN (storage area network), 5
`SAVE STATE` command, 95–96
scheduler window, CDB resource plan, 274–275
schema
    names, 88–89
    synonymous to user, 141
schema consolidation
    cursor sharing, 8–9
    multitenant overcoming limitation of, 23–26
    overview of, 6
    pros and cons, 11
    public synonyms and database links, 8
    roles, tablespace names, and directories, 8
    schema name collision, 7–8
    transportable tablespaces, 7
SCN (system change number), Golden Gate replication, 356–357
`SCOPE=MEMORY` clause, 116
`SCOPE=SPFILE` clause, 116–117
scp command, copying files to target database location, 230
`scriptDest`, database creation scripts, 48
security
    creating CDB using SQL*Plus, 54
    overview of, 140
    proxy users and, 153–155
    single-tenant and, 75–76
security, data
    `CONTAINER_DATA`, 151–153
    lockdown profiles, 155–158
    PDB isolation, 158–159
    roles, 153
    Transparent Data Encryption, 159–165
Security Patch Update (SPU), 112
security, user
    common grants, 147–148
    common vs. local, 140–141
    conflict resolution, 148–150
    `CONTAINER-CURRENT` clause, 142–143
    `CONTAINER=COMMON` clause, 144–146

keeping clear and simple, 150–151
local grants, 146–147
understanding, 141–142
servers
consolidation of, 9–10
Oracle Database 11g application, 5
Oracle Database 8i and 9i client, 4–5
service names, 125–129
services
creating generally, 129–130
creating with DBMS_SERVICE, 133–134
creating with SRVCTL, 130–133
updating with LREG process, 122
sessions
initialization parameters controlling behavior of, 113
user, 141
SESSIONS parameter value, PDBs vs. CDB, 91
SET CONTAINER privilege, users, 154
setasmgidwrap utility, creating CDB in SQL*Plus, 49
SET_CONSUMER_ GROUP_MAPPING, PDB resource plan, 277
SGA_MIN_SIZE parameter, PDB memory allocation, 282
SGA_TARGET parameter, PDB memory allocation, 282
sharding, and multitenant, 74
share values, CDB resource plan, 265–266
shared UNDO mode
changing, 209–210
changing to local UNDO mode from, 223
clean restore point in, 219–220
flashback in, 216
LOCAL_UNDO_ENABLED in, 207
no reason to use in 12.2, 211
PDBPITR in, 211–213
problem with, 206–207
SHARED_POOL_SIZE parameter, PDB memory allocation, 282
shares, Resource Manager, 263
sharing data across PDBs
common read-only data, 322–324
cross-database replication, 343
database links, 320–321
overview of, 320

show all, RMAN configuration, 173–174
SHOW CONFIGURATION, 302
SHOW SPPARAMETER, 114–116
shutdown, CDB, 90–91
shutdown pluggable database, PDBs, 94–95
-silent parameter, CLI
creating CDB using DBCA, 42, 44
creating CDB using DBCA CLI, 44–45
single-instance CDB, Data Recovery Advisor, 193
single-tenant configuration
defined, 72
in Enterprise Edition, 77–79
estimating length of time for CDB upgrade, 110
in Standard Edition, 75–77
upgrading CDB with needed components, 107
skip scan index optimization, table consolidation, 9
snapshot copy, cloning local PDB, 241
software keystore. *See* keystore, TDE
source database
create new PDB on, 309–311
create standby with RMAN, 293, 295–296
logical replication in sync with, 346–347
plugging in non-CDB, 248–250
setup multitenant for GoldenGate replication, 350–351
unplugged database stays in, 231–232
SOURCE$ dictionary table, multitenant dictionaries and, 16–17
SPFILE parameters
CDB, 114
common to all containers in CDB, 27
creating from PFILE, 54
creating standby with RMAN, 294
full CDB backup of, 176
PDB equivalent to, 114–115
for site vs. service, 118
storing in current versions, 113
upgrading CDB with catupgrd.sql, 105
SPU (Security Patch Update), 112
SQL
creating PDB using SQL Developer, 61–63
running on multiple PDBs, 97–98

SQL Developer
    configuring Resource Manager, 271
    creating PDB, 60–64
    monitoring Resource Manager, 285
sqlnet.ora, keystore location setup for TDE, 160
SQL*Plus
    creating CDB resource plan, 269
    monitoring Resource Manager, 285
    `startup pluggable database` and, 94–95
SQL*Plus, create CDB manually
    add default USERS tablespace, 52
    adding database to Oracle Restart, 55
    creating basic parameter file, 49–50
    creating catalog and load options, 53–54
    creating password file, 51
    creating pluggable database, 55
    creating SPFILE from PFILE, 54
    lock/expire all unused accounts, 54
    opening PDB$SEED PDB, 53
    overview of, 47–48
    prerequisite steps, 49
    recompiling all invalid objects, 55
    setting up for catcon.pl script, 50–51
    starting database instance in nomount, 51–52
    updating /etc/oratab file, 50–51
SRVCTL utility
    adding service for Oracle RAC PDB, 132–133
    creating service, 130–133
    stopping service, 129
Standard Edition, single-tenant in, 74–77
standby database
    Active Data Guard option for, 291
    in cloud, 315–318
    Cloud Control, 314–315
    create physical, 291–292
    creating with Cloud Control, 304–308
    duplicating with RMAN. *See* standby database, creating with RMAN
    evolving into Data Guard, 290
    as exact copy of primary database, 290
    impact of flashback on, 223–224
    logical, 362–363
    managing physical, in multitenant, 308–314
standby database, creating with RMAN
    back up source database, 293
    choose subset of source database, 295–296
    further configuration, 304
    overview of, 292
    password file/ temporary parameter file, 293–295
    run duplicate process, 295
    set up network, 293
    set up static network services, 292–293
    start Data Guard broker/ configuration, 297–299
    test configuration, 302–303
    verify configuration/fill in missing pieces, 299–302
`STANDBY_FILE_MANAGEMENT=AUTO` parameter, create new PDB on source database, 309–311
`standbys` clause, 309–311, 313
`START` request, multitenant support in GoldenGate, 358
startup, CDB, 90–91
`startup pluggable database` statement, opening/closing PDBs, 94
state
    modifying PDB, 61, 64
    opening/closing PDBs, 95–96
    viewing PDB, 93, 97
static connection, testing RMAN standby database, 302–303
static network definition, creating RMAN standby database, 292–293
Statspack, statistics collection, 33
status
    adding service for Oracle RAC PDB, 132–133
    listing all containers and their, 21–22
    reviewing PDB, 64
storage
    consolidation, 5
    limit, for PDBs, 98
    snapshots, 104, 323–324
storage area network (SAN), 5
`STORAGE` clause, creating new PDB from PDB$SEED, 59
strace utility, viewing LREG, 122

Index **387**

Streams
  as deprecated, 348–349
  non-CDBs supporting, 73
SUBMIT_PENDING_AREA procedure, 268
subplan, Resource Manager, 262
subsetting, create standby with RMAN, 295–296
supplemental logging, multitenant support in GoldenGate, 352
switchover, testing standby database, 302–303
synonyms
  database links and public, 8
  schema names using private, 8
SYSAUX tablespace
  cloning with proxy PDBs, 246
  restore/recover PDB with RMAN, 202–204
  storing metadata in, 11–12
  tablespace point-in-time recovery, 200
SYSBACKUP privilege
  for backup and recovery, 174–175
  in full PDB backup, 180
SYS.COL$, column metadata stored in, 13
SYSDBA privilege
  dropping PDB, 99–100
  flashback PDB, 222
SYS.TAB$, table/dictionary table metadata stored in, 13–14
system change number (SCN), Golden Gate replication, 356–357
system data, in CDB$ROOT, 72
system dictionary
  connecting to containers, 23–24
  databases storing metadata in, 11–12
  dictionary views from containers, 26–27
  identifying containers, 20–23
  list of containers, 21–22
  multitenant containers, 14–16
  multitenant dictionaries, 16–20
  previous versions of, 11–14
system metadata
  in CDB$ROOT, 72
  separating application metadata from, 18–19
  vs. application metadata, 13–14
system packages, stored in CDB$ROOT, 16
system privilege, Resource Manager, 263–264

system roles, avoid mixing with user roles, 153
SYSTEM tablespace
  CDB$ROOT container and, 16–17
  metadata stored in, 11–12
  proxy DBs cloning, 246
  restore/recover PDB with RMAN, 202–204
  in tablespace point-in-time recovery, 200

T

tables
  consolidation of, 9, 11
  creating CDB resource plan, 269
  definitions stored in dictionary, 13
  linking across containers, 330–338
  sharing data across PDBs, 325–329
  system vs. application metadata, 13–14
  TDE encrypting columns of, 163
tablespace point-in-time recovery (TSPITR), 200–201
tablespace(s)
  application containers, 81
  backing up database, 104
  CDB administrator restricting, 159
  metadata stored in, 11–12
  nodata clones and, 243
  partial CDB backup of, 178–179
  partial PDB backup of, 181–182
  recover CDB$ROOT, 186
  recover lost PDB, 188–189
  restore complete PDB, 201
  schema consolidation and, 8
  splitting PDB and, 243
  storage snapshots/copy on write, 323–324
  SYSAUX. *See* SYSAUX tablespace
  SYSTEM. *See* SYSTEM tablespace
  TDE encrypting all data in, 164
  temporary. *See* temporary tablespace
  transportable. *See* transportable tablespace
  UNDO. *See* UNDO tablespace
  USERS. *See* USERS tablespace
TAG option, RMAN, 170, 176–177

target database, multitenant support in GoldenGate, 354–355
TDE (Transparent Data Encryption)
  Cloud Control setup, 161
  creating keystore, 160–161
  creating master key, 162–163
  encrypting data, 163–164
  keystore location setup, 160
  opening keystore, 162
  overview of, 159
  plug and clone with, 164–165
  setting up, 159–160
  summary of, 165
  verifying created keys, 163
TEMP file trap, plugging in non-CDB, 249–250
TEMPFILE REUSE, plugging in non-CDB, 150
tempfiles, recovery from lost CDB, 186–187
temporary tablespace
  common to all containers in CDB, 28–29
  modifying entire CDB, 92
  modifying PDB, 98
  proxy DBs cloning, 246–247
terminologies, Resource Manager, 261–263
testing, standby database created with RMAN, 302–303
third-parties
  logical replication, 363
  LogMiner/creating own log miner, 348
thread processes, killing, 125
THREADED_EXECUTION=TRUE, configuring multithreaded option, 124
TIMESTAMP WITH LOCAL TIME ZONE, modifying root container, 92
TNS (Transparent Network Substrate) connection string, 342
tnsnames.ora file
  dedicated listener for PDBs, 137
  network setup for standby with RMAN, 293
  service names and, 127–129
topology, multitenant support in GoldenGate, 350
transactions
  opening in another container, 24
  point-in-time recovery using auxiliary instance, 205–206
  roll-forward recovery phase and, 200–201
  rollback recovery phase and, 200–201, 204
  UNDO containing information about all, 206
Transparent Data Encryption. *See* TDE (Transparent Data Encryption)
Transparent Network Substrate (TNS) connection string, 342
TRANSPORT TABLESPACE command, 322
transportable database, 253–255
transportable tablespace
  data movement with single-tenant and, 75
  limitations of, 255
  schema consolidation and, 7
  sharing common read-only data, 322–323
  transportable database vs., 253–254
  use case for, 255–256
triggers
  Oracle LogMiner vs. use of, 348
  PDB operations, 252–253
  setting container, 26
TSPITR (tablespace point-in-time recovery), 200–201

U

UID, in clone operations, 240
UNDO mode
  changing, 208–209
  defining to local in 12.2, 206–207
  impact on standby of changing, 223
  UNDO tablespace vs., 28
UNDO tablespace
  common to all containers in CDB, 28
  local UNDO in 12.2, 206–211
  modifying root container, 92
  PDBPITR in local UNDO, 212–213
  point-in-time recovery and, 200
  recover PDB to point-in-time, 204–205
  restore/recover PDB with RMAN, 202–204
unplug operation. *See* PDBs, moving files with plug-in/unplug
UNPLUGGED status, PDBs, 21–22

UNUSABLE status, PDBs, 21–22
UPDATE_CDB_ DEFAULT_DIRECTIVE, CDB resource plan directive, 268
UPDATE_CDB_PLAN, CDB resource plan, 273–274
UPDATE_CDB_PLAN_DIRECTIVE, CDB resource plan, 273–274
updates
    autotask directive in CDB resource plan, 268
    CDB resource plan directives, 273–274
    default directive in CDB resource plan, 268
upgrades
    compatibility check for, 236
    logical standby used in rolling, 362–363
    overview of, 100–101
upgrades, CDB
    backup or restore point, 103–104
    with catupgrd.sql, 105–107
    estimating length of time for, 110
    open normally, 108
    overview of, 101
    patching, 112–113
    plugging in, 111–112
    post-upgrade scripts, 109
    pre-upgrade, 101–103
    pre-upgrade script, 104–105
    test and open service, 109–110
    upgrade resume after failure, 108–109
    using Database Upgrade Assistant, 110–111
USER$ data dictionary table, user and role definitions, 141
user security
    common vs. local users, 140–141
    conflict resolution, 148–150
    creating common users, 144–146
    creating local users, 142–143
    creating users with CREATE USER, 142
    granting common privileges, 147–148
    granting local privileges, 146–147
    identifying system users, 142
    understanding, 141–142

user tables
    adding query hint, 328
    querying data from PDB, 328–329
    querying only some PDBs, 328
    simple status query on, 325–327
users
    creating roles, 153
    proxy, 153
USERS tablespace
    creating CDB using SQL*Plus, 52
    partial CDB backup of, 178–179
    partial PDB backup of, 182
    restoring/recovering PDB with RMAN, 202
USER_TABLESPACES clause, cloning remote PDB, 243
utilization limits
    autotask resource plan directives, 267–268
    creating CDB resource plan, 270–273
    setting in CDB resource plan, 266–267
    using instance caging with Resource Manager, 283–284
utilization_limit parameter, CDB resource plan, 266
utluppkg.sql script, CDB, 101
utrlp.sql script, 55

V

V$ views, 151
VALIDATE command, block corruption check, 193–194
VALIDATE DATABASE command, standby configuration, 299–300
VALIDATE_PENDING_ AREA procedure, default resource plan directive, 268
validation, default resource plan directive, 268
/var/tmp, restore/recover PDBs in RMAN, 203
V$DATABASE view, 27
v$encrypted_tablespaces, viewing, 164
versions, logical replication pairing databases with mismatched, 346

views. *See also* V$ views
    dictionary, 17–18
    PDB operation history, 97
    state of PDBs, 97
virtual machines, 5
virtualization
    Oracle Database 12c, 5
    overview of, 10
    pros and cons of consolidation, 11
v$logmnr_contents view, LogMiner, 348
V$PARAMETER view, 116
V$PDB_INCARNATION view, 221–222
V$PDBS view, 96
V$PROCESS view, 125
V$RMAN_*CONFIGURATION* view, 173–174
V$SERVICES view, 131–132
V$SESSION view, 177

W

wallet directory, specifying backup, 163

X

XML file
    contents of, 232–235
    moving PDB archive files, 238–239
    plug-in compatibility for, 235
    plugging in non-CDBs, 248–249
    unplugging/plugging in PDBs, 230–231
XStream, logical replication with, 361–363

Join the Largest Tech Community in the World

- Download the latest software, tools, and developer templates

- Get exclusive access to hands-on trainings and workshops

- Grow your professional network through the Oracle ACE Program

- Publish your technical articles – and get paid to share your expertise

Join the Oracle Technology Network
Membership is free. Visit community.oracle.com

@OracleOTN   facebook.com/OracleTechnologyNetwork

ORACLE®

Copyright © 2016, Oracle and/or its affiliates. All rights reserved. Oracle and Java are registered trademarks of Oracle and/or its affiliates.

Climb the Career Ladder

Think about it—97 percent of the Fortune 500 companies run Oracle solutions. Why wouldn't you choose Oracle certification to secure your future? With certification through Oracle, your resume gets noticed, your chances of landing your dream job improve, you become more marketable, and you earn more money. It's simple. Oracle certification helps you get hired and get paid for your skills.

93% Hiring managers who say IT certifications are beneficial and provide value to the company[1]

7% Salary growth for Oracle Certified professionals[5]

70% Believe that Oracle certification improved their earning power[2]

90% Say that Oracle certification gives them credibility when looking for a new job[2]

68% Think that certification has made them more in demand[3]

6x Increased LinkedIn profile views for people with certifications, boosting their visibility and career opportunities[4]

Take the next step
http://education.oracle.com/certification/press

[1] "Value of IT Certifications," CompTIA, October 14, 2014, [2] Oracle Certification Survey, [3] "Certification: It's a Journey Not a Destination," Certification Magazine 2015 Salary Edition, [4] "The Future Value of Certifications: Insights from LinkedIn's Data Trove," ATP 2015 Innovations in Testing, [5] Certification Magazine 2015 Annual Salary Survey Copyright © 2015, Oracle and/or its affiliates. All rights reserved. Oracle and Java are registered trademarks of Oracle and/or its affiliates. Other names may be trademarks of their respective owners.

ORACLE®

Push a Button
Move Your Java Apps to the Oracle Cloud

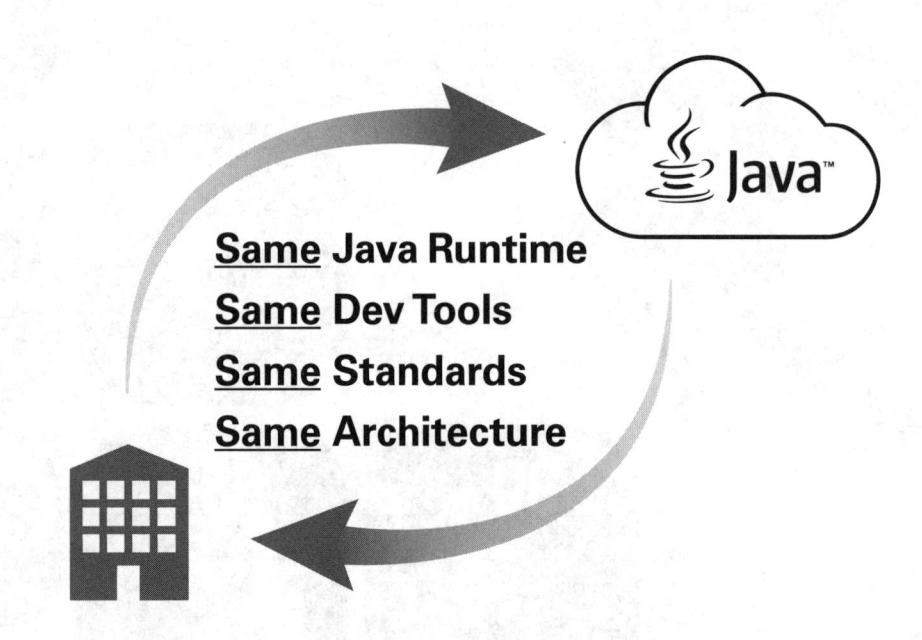

Same Java Runtime
Same Dev Tools
Same Standards
Same Architecture

... or Back to Your Data Center

ORACLE®

cloud.oracle.com/java

Copyright © 2016, Oracle and/or its affiliates. All rights reserved. Oracle and Java are registered trademarks of Oracle and/or its affiliates.

Beta Test Oracle Software

Get a first look at our newest products—and help perfect them. You must meet the following criteria:

- ✓ Licensed Oracle customer or Oracle PartnerNetwork member
- ✓ Oracle software expert
- ✓ Early adopter of Oracle products

Please apply at: pdpm.oracle.com/BPO/userprofile

ORACLE®

If your interests match upcoming activities, we'll contact you. Profiles are kept on file for 12 months.

Copyright © 2014, Oracle and/or its affiliates. All rights reserved. Oracle and Java are registered trademarks of Oracle and/or its affiliates.

Reach More than 640,000 Oracle Customers with Oracle Publishing Group

Connect with the Audience that Matters Most to Your Business

Oracle Magazine
The Largest IT Publication in the World
Circulation: 325,000
Audience: IT Managers, DBAs, Programmers, and Developers

Profit
Business Insight for Enterprise-Class Business Leaders to Help Them Build a Better Business Using Oracle Technology
Circulation: 90,000
Audience: Top Executives and Line of Business Managers

Java Magazine
The Essential Source on Java Technology, the Java Programming Language, and Java-Based Applications
Circulation: 225,00 and Growing Steady
Audience: Corporate and Independent Java Developers, Programmers, and Architects

For more information or to sign up for a FREE subscription: Scan the QR code to visit Oracle Publishing online.

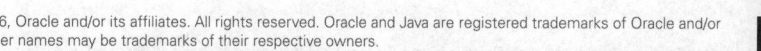